MARRIAGE TO DEATH

MARRIAGE TO DEATH

THE CONFLATION OF WEDDING AND FUNERAL RITUALS IN GREEK TRAGEDY

RUSH REHM

PRINCETON UNIVERSITY PRESS

PRINCETON, NEW JERSEY

Copyright © 1994 by Princeton University Press
Published by Princeton University Press, 41 William Street,
Princeton, New Jersey 08540
In the United Kingdom: Princeton University Press, Chichester, West Sussex
All Rights Reserved

Rehm, Rush.
  Marriage to death : the conflation of wedding and funeral rituals
in Greek tragedy / Rush Rehm.
     p.   cm.
  Includes bibliographical references and index.
  ISBN 0-691-03369-2 (CL)
  ISBN 0-691-02916-4 (PBK)
     1. Greek drama (Tragedy)—History and criticism.   2. Funeral rites
and ceremonies in literature.   3. Marriage customs and rites in
literature   4. Weddings in literature.   5. Death in literature.
I. Title.
PA3331.R39   1994
882'.0109—dc20   93-39939

This book has been composed in Trump Medieval

Princeton University Press books are printed on acid-free paper
and meet the guidelines for permanence and durability of the
Committee on Production Guidelines for Book Longevity of the
Council on Library Resources

Third printing, and first paperback printing, 1996

Printed in the United States of America by Princeton Academic Press

10 9 8 7 6 5 4 3

CONTENTS

ILLUSTRATIONS

ACKNOWLEDGMENTS

SOME PASSAGES of Chapter 7 (on Euripides' *Medea*) and Chapter 8 (on Euripides' *Supplices*) appeared in my "Medea and the Logos of the Heroic," *Eranos* 87 (1989), and *Greek Tragic Theatre*, Chapter 8 (Routledge 1992), respectively. I am grateful to the editors of *Eranos* and the publishers at Routledge for permission to include those passages here.

Initial work on this book benefited from a National Endowment for the Humanities Summer Stipend, an Emory University Research Grant, and an American Council of Learned Societies grant for recent recipients of the Ph.D. Their support allowed me to use the resources at the Beazley Archive of the Ashmolean Library, Oxford, and at the American School of Classical Studies, Athens. My thanks to Tom Carpenter, then of the Beazley Archive, and to the staff of the American School in Athens: Professor William Coulson, Director; John M. Camp, Mellon Professor of Archaeology; Bob Bridges, Secretary; and Nancy Winters, Librarian.

Subsequent work on the project took place at the Center for Hellenic Studies in Washington, D.C. My thanks to Zeph and Diana Stewart for making the year so enjoyable, and to my fellow Junior Fellows—particularly Josh Ober, Ian Morris, and Jagoda Luzzatto—for sharing their thoughts so freely with me.

I am grateful to the anonymous readers at Princeton University Press for improving the manuscript, to Press Editors Joanna Hitchcock and Lauren Osborne for supporting the project, and to Manuscript Editor Marta Steele and my graduate assistant James Loehlin for editorial help. For their ongoing support, advice, and conversation, I owe special thanks to my treasured Emory colleagues Cynthia Patterson and Bonna Wescoat, and to their Stanford counterparts Ron Davies, Mark Edwards, Charles Lyons, Marsh McCall, and Andrea Nightingale. Finally, to my co-conspirator Sissy—Va por Cuba! ¡Venceremos!

A NOTE TO THE READER

I HAVE USED GREEK when specific words or lines from literary sources make the point more strongly. However, if a word is repeated several times, or if it is a formal term associated with weddings or funerals, I give the transliterated form after the first occurrence and use transliteration thereafter. *All* passages—Greek and transliterated—are followed by an English translation, and quotations in other foreign languages are translated in the notes. The renditions are my own, unless otherwise noted, and generally tend to the literal rather than the literary.

Regarding the English spelling of Greek words, I use *k* for the Greek kappa, because the Greeks had no letter *c*. This gives us Klytemnestra for Clytemnestra, Herakles for Heracles, which should cause no problems of identification for the non-classicist. I use the Latinized version of a name when the Greek transliteration might not be recognizable (e.g., Hecuba, not Hekabē), and in proper names I have avoided the more accurate equivalents for Greek vowels, which can generate such bizarre forms as Thoukudides and Mēdeia for Thukydides and Medea. I have tried to respect original spelling in quotations.

All dates are B.C. unless otherwise noted. Abbreviations for ancient authors, texts, and scholarly journals are included in the List of Abbreviations at the beginning of the book. Generally, I follow Liddell-Scott-Jones, *A Greek-English Lexicon*, with Supplement (Oxford 1968), for Greek authors and texts, and *L'Année philologique* (founded by J. Marouzeau, Paris) and the *American Journal of Archaeology* for scholarly journals. There are minor exceptions—for example, I use *Tro.* for Euripides' *Troades* instead of *LSJ*'s *Tr.* to distinguish it from Sophokles' *Trachiniae*, also *Tr.*

The abbreviations "Ch.," "App.," and "n." refer respectively to a Chapter, an Appendix, and a note, frequently applied internally to this book. I use "cf." in the sense of "contrast," indicating a view substantially different from, or opposed to, the previous citation. The references in the notes limited to author, year, and page number are keyed to the entries in the Bibliography, where full publication information can be found.

Generally I follow the Oxford editions of the plays, especially Denniston and Page, *Agamemnon*; Lloyd-Jones and Wilson, *Sophoclis Fabulae*; and Diggle, *Euripidis Fabulae* I and II. I use Kannicht's edition of *Helen*, because Diggle's third volume of Euripides has yet to appear. These editions are supplemented by other texts, all of which are listed in the Bibliography under the editor's name.

ABBREVIATIONS

Primary Sources

A.	Aeschylus
Ag.	*Agamemnon*
Ch.	*Choephoroi*
Eu.	*Eumenides*
Pers.	*Persians*
Pr.	*Prometheus Bound*
Supp.	*Supplices*
Th.	*Seven Against Thebes*
Ael.	Aelianus
VH	*Varia Historia*
Aeschin.	Aeschines
And.	Andokides
AP	*Palatine Anthology*
Apollod.	Apollodorus
Bibl.	*Bibliotheca*
Ar.	Aristophanes
Ach.	*Acharnians*
Av.	*Aves (Birds)*
Eq.	*Equites (Knights)*
Lys.	*Lysistrata*
Nu.	*Nubes (Clouds)*
Pax	*Peace*
Pl.	*Plutos (Wealth)*
Ran.	*Ranae (Frogs)*
Thesm.	*Thesmophoriazusae*
Vesp.	*Vespae (Wasps)*
Arist.	Aristotle
EN	*Nicomachean Ethics*
Pol.	*Politics*
Rh.	*Rhetoric*
B.	Bacchylides
Clem.Al.	Clement of Alexandria
Strom.	*Stromateis*
D.	Demosthenes
D.S.	Diodorus Siculus

E.M.	*Etymologicum Magnum*
Eur.	Euripides
Alk.	*Alkestis*
Andr.	*Andromache*
Ba.	*Bacchae*
El.	*Elektra*
Hec.	*Hecuba*
Hel.	*Helen*
Herakl.	*Herakleidae*
HF	*Herakles (Furens)*
Hipp.	*Hippolytus*
Hyps.	*Hypsipyle*
IA	*Iphigenia in Aulis*
IT	*Iphigenia among the Taurians*
Kyk.	*Kyklops*
Med.	*Medea*
Or.	*Orestes*
Ph.	*Phoenissae*
Phaeth.	*Phaethon*
Rh.	*Rhesus*
Supp.	*Supplices*
Tro.	*Troades*
Eust.	Eustathius
FGrH	*Fragmente der griechischen Historiker*, ed. F. Jacoby (Berlin 1923–)
H.	Homer
Il.	*Iliad*
Od.	*Odyssey*
Harp.	Harpokration
h.Cer.	*Homeric Hymn to Ceres (Demeter)*
Hdt.	Herodotus
Hes.	Hesiod
Op.	*Opera et Dies (Works and Days)*
Sc.	*Scutum Herculis (Shield of Herakles)*
Th.	*Theogony*
Hsch.	Hesychius
I.G.	*Inscriptiones Graecae*
Is.	Isaios
LSCG	*Lois sacrées des cités grecques*, ed. F. Sokolowski (Paris 1969)
Lycurg.	Lykurgus
Lys.	Lysias

Men.	Menander
Dysk.	*Dyskolos* (*The Bad-Tempered Man*)
Mis.	*Misoumenos* (*A Hated Man*)
Pk.	*Perikeiromenē* (*The Shorn Girl*)
Sam.	*Samia* (*The Girl from Samos*)
Paus.	Pausanias
Phot.	Photius
Pi.	Pindar
O.	*Olympian Odes*
P.	*Pythian Odes*
Pl.	Plato
Cra.	*Cratylus*
Cri.	*Crito*
Grg.	*Gorgias*
Hp.Ma.	*Hippias Major*
Lg.	*Leges* (*Laws*)
Phd.	*Phaedo*
R.	*Republic*
Sym.	*Symposium*
Tht.	*Theaetetus*
Plu.	Plutarch
Mor.	*Moralia*
Per.	*Perikles*
Phoc.	*Phocion*
Sol.	*Solon*
Poll.	Pollux
P.Oxy.	*Oxyrhynchus Papyri*, ed. B. P. Grenfell and A. S. Hunt (London 1898–)
Prokl.	Proklus
Chr.	*Chrestomathia*
in Ti.	commentary on Plato's *Timaeus*
Ps.	Pseudo-
S.	Sophokles
Aj.	*Ajax*
Ant.	*Antigone*
El.	*Elektra*
OC	*Oedipus at Kolonos*
OT	*Oedipus Tyrannus*
Ph.	*Philoktetes*
Tr.	*Trachiniae*
SEG	*Supplementum Epigraphicum Graecum*, ed. J.J.E. Hondius et al. (Leiden 1923–)

Theok.	Theokritus
Thuk.	Thukydides
X.	Xenophon
Mem.	*Memorabilia*
HG	*Historia Graeca (Hellenica)*
X.Eph.	Xenophon of Ephesus
Zen.	Zenobius

SECONDARY SOURCES

AA	*Archäologischer Anzeiger*
ABull	*Art Bulletin*
ABV	Beazley 1956 (v. Bibliography)
AC	*L'Antiquité Classique*
AClass	*Acta Classica*
Add²	Carpenter 1989 (v. Bibliography)
AHB	*Ancient History Bulletin*
AION(arch)	*Annali di Istituto Universitario Orientale,*
	Sezione di Archeologia e Storia Antica
AJA	*American Journal of Archaeology*
AJP	*American Journal of Philology*
AK	*Antike Kunst*
AncS	*Ancient Society*
AncW	*Ancient World*
APA Abstracts	*American Philological Association Abstracts*
ArchCl	*Archeologia Classica*
AR	*Archaeological Reports*
ARV²	Beazley 1963 (v. Bibliography)
BA	*Bollettino d'Arte*
BCH	*Bulletin de correspondance hellénique*
BICS	*Bulletin of the Institute of Classical Studies*
BMMA	*Bulletin of the Metropolitan Museum of Art*
BSA	*Annual of the British School at Athens*
CA	*Classical Antiquity*
CC	*Catalogue des Vases Peints du Musée National*
	d'Athènes, ed. M. Collignon and L. Couve
	(Paris 1902–4).
CGita	*Cahiers des Gita* (du Groupe Interdisciplinaire du
	Théâtre Antique, Montpelier)
CJ	*Classical Journal*
C&M	*Classica et Mediaevalia*
CQ	*Classical Quarterly*

CP	Classical Philology
CPCPh	California Publications in Classical Philology
CR	Classical Review
CSCA	California Studies in Classical Antiquity
CVA	Corpus Vasorum Antiquorum (v. Bibliography)
CW	Classical World
DK	Fragmente der Vorsokratiker, ed. H. Diels and W. Kranz, 6th ed. (Berlin 1951)
G&R	Greece and Rome
GRBS	Greek, Roman and Byzantine Studies
HSCP	Harvard Studies in Classical Philology
ICS	Illinois Classical Studies
JDAI	Jahrbuch des deutschen archäologischen Instituts, Athenische Abteilung
JHS	Journal of Hellenic Studies
JÖAI	Jahreshefte des österreichischen archäologischen Instituts
LIMC	Lexicon Iconographicum Mythologiae Classicae (Zurich and Munich)
LSJ	Greek-English Lexicon (with Supplement), ed. Liddell, Scott, Jones, and McKenzie (Oxford 1968)
MAL	Memorie della Accademia dei Lincei
MDAI(A)	Mitteilungen des deutschen archäologischen Instituts, Athenische Abteilung
MH	Museum Helveticum
MonAnt	Monumenti antichi pubblicati dall'Accademia dei Lincei
MusJ	Museum Journal
NY Rev	New York Review of Books
Para	Beazley 1971 (v. Bibliography)
PCPhS	Proceedings of the Cambridge Philological Society
PMLA	Proceedings of the Modern Language Association
PP	Parola del Passato
REA	Revue des études anciennes
RevPhil	Revue de philologie
REG	Revue des études grecques
RM	Rheinisches Museum
SCO	Studi Classici e Orientali
TAPA	Transactions of the American Philological Association
TLS	Times Literary Supplement

WS	*Wiener Studien*
WüJbb	*Würzburger Jahrbücher*
YCS	*Yale Classical Studies*
ZPE	*Zeitschrift für Papyrologie und Epigraphik*

MISCELLANEOUS

fr.	fragment
fr. dub.	doubtful fragment
pl.	plate, plates
s.v.	*sub verbo* ("under the word")
v.	*vide* ("see")

MARRIAGE TO DEATH

INTRODUCTION

IN THE Smith College Museum of Art, Gustave Courbet's oil painting "The Preparation of the Bride" has been re-titled "The Preparation of the Dead Girl."[1] Radiography revealed that the body of the main figure originally was nude. Otherwise, nothing on the canvas has changed—the preparations for washing the girl's feet, readying her new garments, reading from the Bible—and yet a radically different set of responses has been sanctioned. The preliminaries of a wedding have become the first steps of a funeral.

The confusion between such apparently antithetical events holds out enormous possibilities for creative manipulation, and we find the interplay between weddings and funerals exploited time and again in art, literature, and drama. Frequently the two rites are simply juxtaposed, joining areas of human experience that—in a better world—would be kept distinct. So Hamlet condemns the enjambment of the two rituals in the Danish court:

HOR.   My lord, I came to see your father's funeral.
HAM.   . . . /I think it was to see my mother's wedding.
HOR.   Indeed, my lord, it followed hard upon.
HAM.   Thrift, thrift, Horatio! The funeral bak'd-meats
         Did coldly furnish forth the marriage tables.[2]

Hamlet views the juxtaposition as a sign of social corruption, but over the course of the play he finds himself increasingly implicated in this marriage/funeral dyad. At the burial of Ophelia, he overhears Gertrude lament that one rite has replaced the other: "I hop'd thou shouldst have been my Hamlet's wife;/ I thought thy bride-bed to have deck'd, sweet maid,/ And not have strew'd thy grave" (5.1.238–40). The juxtaposition of funeral and wedding at the outset of the play has given way to the premature burial of a potential bride. Caught in this unnatural turn of events, Hamlet himself leaps into Ophelia's grave, proclaiming his love for the dead girl. His confrontation there with her brother Laertes anticipates the duel and gathering of corpses in the final scene.

Shakespeare revels in the juxtaposition of weddings and deaths. The tragical/comical demise of Pyramus and Thisbe played before the Athenian court offers ironic commentary on the nuptials of Theseus and Hippolyta. Romeo and Juliet marry in the tomb of the Capulets, a dramatically fitting location for what will prove to be a lasting union in the grave. After killing her husband and father-in-law (the King), Richard accosts Lady Anne at the King's funeral and woos her in the presence of the corpse, achieving the unthinkable by mocking ritual propriety. Othello compares the sleeping Desdemona to the monumental alabaster of a tomb and then strangles his new bride in the bed strewn with their wedding sheets.

The Jacobean dramatists spin out the motif of a fatal marriage union with a twist toward the macabre. In Heywood's *A Woman Killed with Kindness*, Frankford speaks over the corpse of his bride: "New marry'd and new widowed! O, she's dead,/ And a cold grave must be our nuptial bed" (scene 17, 123–24). The flirtatious repartee between the Duchess and Antonio in Webster's *Duchess of Malfi* anticipates the horrific events that convert their eventual marriage into a union with death:

> ANTONIO: I'd have you first provide for a good husband.
> Give him all.
> DUCHESS: All?
> ANTONIO: Yes, your excellent self.
> DUCHESS: In a winding sheet?
> ANTONIO: In a couple. (1.2.327–28)

We find significant links between marriage and death in dramatic works ranging from Seneca's *Medea* to Middleton and Rowley's *The Changeling*, from Racine's *Phèdre* to Ibsen's *Rosmersholm* and *When We Dead Awaken*, from Schiller's *Bride of Messina* to Lorca's *Blood Wedding*. The fusion of love and death also becomes a staple of the opera. While Gessler gasps out his last breath in Rossini's *William Tell*, the sound of a wedding procession is heard in the distance. The musical climax of Donizetti's *Lucia di Lammermoor* occurs during the fatal wedding night, Odabella in Verdi's *Attila* kills the barbarian on their wedding day, and the Liebestod in Wagner's *Tristan and Isolde* celebrates the achievement of eros in—and through—the act of dying.

As with many of our artistic and cultural paradigms, the idea of a "marriage to death" receives an early, powerful instantiation in Greek tragedy. This pairing may reflect nothing more than a poetic attraction of opposites and the lure of the oxymoron. However, in some tragedies the juxtaposition proves so forceful that one ritual seems to engender the other. On occasion, weddings and funerals intermingle to such an extent that the two rites become inseparable. Characters conceive of their deaths in terms of a marriage to a loved one already dead, or as a union with Hades, where the god of the underworld takes the place of a living bride or groom.

What accounts for the mutual attraction of two such disparate events? Early in this century, the anthropologist Arnold van Gennep (and to a lesser extent Robert Hertz) offered a functional explanation —both weddings and funerals mark important rites of passage from one social and biological circumstance to another.[3] The two rituals share a tripartite structure, consisting of a separation from the old phase, transition through a liminal period, and incorporation or aggregation into the new phase.[4] The ritualized celebration (we might say "performance") of such a change signals the personal and communal significance of the event, providing a pattern of behavior for those involved that is simultaneously conventional and symbolic.[5] More recently, Victor Turner has emphasized the liminal stage in these rites de passage, giving rise to transitional qualities of "betwixt and between" that reveal the interrelationship between high and low, between in and out, on which *communitas* ("community," "fellowship") paradoxically depends. For Turner, liminality is a period and space of ambiguity ("going two ways at once") that exists within specific social and mental structures, a place of danger and vulnerability for those making the transition, but also one of freedom, providing an opportunity for disordered play that serves as "the seedbeds of cultural creativity."[6]

In *The Ego and the Id*, Sigmund Freud offers a very different explanation for the relationship between love and death, positing a primal struggle between two elemental forces in the mind, Eros and Thanatos.[7] This instinctual dualism may lie behind the artistic conflation of weddings and funerals, where one ritual merges with, or gives itself over to, the other. Freud's formulation of a basic psychological conflict finds a popular counterpart in the "tragic-romantic" conception of erotic passion as the paradoxical drive toward union and dissolution. In such a scenario, the individual's desire for the other may lead to a concomitant loss of self, and that loss writ large is death, a conversion of Eros into the death-wish. Alternatively, Georges Bataille discusses the strong link between possessive desires and death, describing how erotic love can "raise the feeling of one being for another to such a pitch that the threatened loss of the beloved . . . is felt no less keenly than the threat of death."[8] A variation is the morbidly romantic idea of a love that can live (literally) beyond the grave—Heathcliff and Catherine in *Wuthering Heights*—or, in its materialist form, a love that cannot leave the grave, with necrophilia as its end term.[9]

Such ideas about the mutual attraction of love and death are intrinsically interesting. But the primary concern of my study lies elsewhere, in the tragic theater of fifth-century Athens. How, and why, did this complex set of associations between marriage and death, between weddings and funerals, take dramatic shape in the plays of Aeschylus, Sophokles, and Euripides?

Increasingly, classicists find a fundamental ambiguity toward the marriage ceremony in tragedy, especially the sense of loss that female characters express when thinking ahead to, or back on, their weddings. Integrating poetic image with dramatic structure, Anne Lebeck offers a stimulating account of "the *telos* of marriage and the *telos* of death" in Aeschylus' *Oresteia*.[10] In a series of important articles, Richard Seaford traces wedding motifs in Greek tragedy, emphasizing that, time and again, "the negative tendency of the [wedding] ritual prevails."[11] More recently, Nicole Loraux posits a strong and weak version of what I call generally a "marriage to death," distinguishing a union *with* Hades from a marriage *in* Hades. However, she renders such distinctions—as well as those of dramatic context and the workings of individual tragedies—subordinate to her overall project, which is to demonstrate that the (male) tragic signifier countenances risk, unorthodoxy, and flirtation with difference only as a means of controlling and taming the very deviance it seems to allow.[12]

A more fruitful line of inquiry derives from the early work of Froma Zeitlin on corrupted rituals in Aeschylus' *Oresteia* and Euripides' *Elektra*, and from the more recent studies of Helene Foley on the formative role of ritual in the plays of Euripides. However, both Zeitlin and Foley tend to focus on the practice and perversion of ritual sacrifice, a topic that has generated its full share of scholarly research and speculation, leaving the conflation of wedding and funeral rituals somewhat to the side.[13] Without downplaying the remarkable fact that Greek tragedy frequently describes (and often enacts) death in terms of sacrifice, we should linger a moment over the differences between sacrificial ritual and the rituals of weddings and funerals.

Unlike the blood, entrails, and bones burnt on an altar, weddings and funerals were not offerings directed to the Olympian gods. As transitional "social" rituals, they focused directly on the human participants—the bride and groom, the recently deceased, the family paying homage to the dead, consoling and reconstituting itself after loss, or, in the inverse of that process, celebrating collectively the inclusion of a new member via marriage. To be sure, both rites called for dedicatory and propitiatory offerings to various gods, but weddings and funerals in themselves did not constitute such offerings. No priest or cult leader oversaw *any* of their varied aspects, whereas Greek public sacrifice frequently required the presence of select intermediaries to dedicate the beasts and guarantee ritual order and efficacy.[14]

In contrast to the individual and familial inducements of a wedding or funeral, the rituals of animal sacrifice demanded far less emotional investment. No personal attachment adhered to the victims, and there was no dictum requiring that one offer his or her favorite bull or pet goat. Rather, the Greeks proposed a series of objective criteria to be met for sacrifice, involving animal type, gender, color, physical wholeness, age, and purity. At large-scale public sacrifices, such as those at the City Dionysia and the Panathenaia, the ritual slaughter had less of a sacred character than many scholarly discussions indicate. An enormous number of victims were offered (some 240 at the City Dionysia in 333 B.C. alone), but, as was customary among the Greeks, only the inedible parts of the animal were dedicated to the god. The rest were cooked and distributed to the gathered throng in a city-sponsored feast. A similar practice was followed at local sacrifices and in individual households, allowing the participants to enjoy meat that was far too expensive to be consumed on less than special occasions.[15]

Clearly, weddings and funerals engaged responses significantly different in kind and degree from those of ritual sacrifice. I venture that no one at a sacrifice would have experienced anything like the immediate connection to the ritualized events felt by the bride, groom, family, and friends at a wedding or would have undergone the complex mixture of emotions felt by the family and kin at the burial of one of their own.[16] To extend this observation to the plays, when a tragic wedding gets confused with a funeral, when either ritual is perverted or twisted by the events of the play, we should attend very closely. In the theater, something of dramatic moment has been signaled, and an emotional plumb line is sounding the audience. Through language, image, and action, the play draws on memories and associated thoughts of those who celebrated their own wedding or that of a son, daughter, or relative, who shared with their kin the grief over loved ones whom they buried, or who looked ahead to a time when the marriage or funeral ritual would mark the key transition in their own lives and the lives of their families.

The conflation of weddings and funerals in tragedy sheds particularly strong light on women, recalling the oft-noted, although not fully appreciated, fact that female characters attain a prominence that could not be predicted from what we know of women's status in the fifth century.[17] Although Athenian women organized and celebrated certain festivals and oversaw a number of religious cults, the public events in which they played the most important part were weddings and funerals. Not only was her wedding viewed as the "red-letter day" for a maiden, but the mothers of the bride and groom (as well as other women in lesser roles) were integral to the ceremony. Similarly, during the preparations for burial and the funeral proper, the women of the family had important ritual offices to fulfill— bathing and adorning the corpse, performing the threnodies and other lamentations—and they took much of the responsibility for subsequent rites at the tomb. By giving prominence to weddings and funerals in their plays, the tragedians took advantage of the public opportunities that these events offered their female characters.

In the juxtaposition and confusion of the two rituals, however, Greek tragedy does more than open up the stage to women only to thrust them firmly back into their conventional roles. The conflation of weddings and funerals introduces a kind of dramatic alchemy whereby female characters become the bearers of new possibilities, not only for themselves but also for the dominant male population. As we shall see, tragic women frequently challenge the values and modes of behavior represented by male authority, and tragic men often come to new understandings through a feminizing process, whereby their pain and insight is described in terms of female experience.[18]

Of course, these "female" challenges to dominant authority were the product of male playwrights and realized in performance by male actors. The circumstances of Greek theatrical production (along with much other evidence) warn us against drawing a simple one-to-one correspondence between women on the stage and their counterparts in the fifth-century world. Assuming that the relationship between tragic females and living women was tenuous, we still must reckon with the fact that the heroines offer a surprising perspective on a male-dominated society whose basic assumptions the original audience took as the norm. Perhaps for this reason the struggles of the great mythic women—Klytemnestra, Kassandra, Iphigenia, Elektra, Deianeira, Antigone, Alkestis, Medea, Evadne, Helen, Hecuba, Andromache, Polyxena, Kreusa, Phaedra—remain among the most troubling, and most vital, legacies of the ancient theater.[19] As will emerge in the course of this study, the dramatic power and appeal of many of these heroines arises from their being engaged in, committed to, or trapped by a "marriage to death."

Marriage granted the female "outsider" a central place on the inside, opening one family to the influence of another and to contending claims of loyalty and support.[20] A funeral, on the other hand, asked women to consolidate the family in the midst of loss, effecting a transition not only for the deceased but also for the survivors. Both rituals focused on the Greek household, or οἶκος (oikos), the private world in which women played their crucial roles—providing heirs, nurturing them as they grew, sustaining the family, and guaranteeing due homage to its dead members. By pushing the concerns of female characters into the public sphere, tragedy brought into conflict the world of the *oikos* with that of the city, or πόλις (*polis*), the traditional arena for male activity. Time and again tragic heroines prove that the latter depends on the former for its survival and prosperity. Time and again a male hero comes to grief for overlooking problems in the *oikos* or for underestimating its ultimate value. When tragic weddings and funerals—rituals constitutive of the family—go awry or fail to effect their desired transitions, it is not simply the individual *oikos* that suffers.[21] The ripples spread with increasing force to shake the *polis* as well, probing the nature of its social and political underpinnings and challenging those in the theater audience to consider new, and often radically different, directions for their city.

If these observations have merit, then rituals in tragedy do not create order in the midst of chaos, as much as they represent a powerful means of measuring that chaos.[22] Marriages and deaths, weddings and funerals are shifted and confused to provide experiences of *instability*, to shake the audience out of comforting notions of order and to challenge accepted social and ideational norms. They force the spectators to see what they would rather not, what is hard to glimpse in the everyday world, glossed over by patterns of habit and custom.

It should be clear from these remarks that my interest in "marriage to death" is not, finally, thematic.[23] Rather, by using the dramatic conjunction of weddings and funerals as a fulcrum, I hope to gain new (and perhaps better) interpretive purchase on specific tragedies, and to arrive at a clearer understanding of how these plays worked on their fifth-century audiences. Grappling with questions of production and dramatic impact admits no easy or secure answers, but the process is essential if we are to learn from the tragic stage and the culture that produced it. As Adrian Poole observes, "The power of Greek tragedy to outlive the local conditions of its original production depends on the quality of the challenge which it once offered to those local conditions."[24] Identifying that challenge is a necessary step toward understanding how these plays might work for us.

To develop points of contact between the rituals in the tragedies and the "local conditions" that produced them, I begin by reviewing the actual practice of weddings and funerals in Athens (Chapter 1). Here we discover specific elements shared by both rituals which offered the playwright fertile opportunity for dramatic development and exploitation. In Chapter 2 I examine the representation of the two rites in the visual arts of the period, primarily Attic vase-painting. Invaluable for our understanding of popular notions about weddings and funerals, this visual material provided the tragedians with a traditional body of iconography to be referred to in the plays and even enacted on stage.

The heart of the study lies in Chapters 3 through 9, where I examine "marriage to death" as presented in Aeschylus' *Agamemnon*, Sophokles' *Antigone* and *Trachiniae*, and Euripides' *Alkestis*, *Medea*, *Supplices*, *Helen*, and *Troades*.[25] In the course of dealing with these plays, I also discuss passages from other tragedies that make use of similar motifs or illustrate comparable thematic patterns. In the Conclusion, I summarize the ways in which the conflation of marriage and death enriches our interpretation of tragedy in its political and social context. A series of Appendices follows, dealing with issues that would swamp the text or further burden the notes.

On the occasions when I seem to stray from "marriage to death," from weddings and funerals, I ask the reader's forbearance. My observations ultimately spring from these odd bedfellows, but they are not limited to them. It is hardly surprising that the confluence of two such opposed aspects of ritual and emotional life should serve dramatic ends beyond themselves, a fact that becomes increasingly evident in the last third of the fifth century when immediate political concerns impinged with ever greater force on the tragic stage. In analyzing specific works, however, I try to avoid the "thematizing" trap pointed out by Richard Levin, whereby plays cease to be primarily dramatizations of actions but become instead explorations of a thematic idea that the characters and actions subserve. Levin locates this critical tendency in the fact that "most thematists are much more interested in the intellectual theme they derive from a play than in its emotional effect."[26]

Leaning in the opposite direction, I attempt to link the emotional effects of marriages and deaths to *other* issues raised by the tragedies, following as far as possible the path of the play itself. Only a critical naif would think such a trail clearly marked and without its detours and dead ends. However, we can keep from heading completely in the wrong direction by recalling that tragedy was a genre whose telos was production in the theater, and by checking our observations accordingly. The fact that such considerations—from the pragmatics of staging to the ever-changing commerce between actors and audience in performance—barely surface in the discussion of ritual perversion in tragedy, is not the least of my reasons for exploring these "marriages to death."[27]

Chapter 1

FIFTH-CENTURY MARRIAGE AND FUNERAL RITES

T
O UNDERSTAND the paradox of "marriage to death" in Greek tragedy, we must familiarize ourselves with the events that constituted a fifth-century wedding and funeral. There is general agreement on the practice, if not the significance, of the two rituals, and several comprehensive studies gather the primary sources.[1] Drawing on these works, and with the help of visual material, primarily vase paintings, I propose a narrative reconstruction of a generic Athenian wedding and funeral.

A marriage was constituted by the acts of ἐγγύη (*enguē*), ἔκδοσις (*ekdosis*), and γάμος (*gamos*), although we should not think of this triad as rigidly defined steps in a clear-cut legal process.[2] We must walk a tightrope in translating the Greek words, which seem to have meant both more and less than their English equivalents. The first term, *enguē* ("pledge"), refers to what we would call the "betrothal," arranged by the κύριοι (*kurioi*, legal guardians, usually the fathers) of the prospective couple, or between the *kurios* of the bride and the groom himself if the latter had reached his majority (age 18).[3] As the bride was not a legal agent, her presence was unnecessary at the *enguē*. One of the arrangements settled there was the dowry—"the property which goes with a woman when she is married"[4]—paid by the *kurios* of the bride to the groom (or his family). If marital relations terminated in the future, this sum would accompany the woman who returned to her former *kurios* (father, male relative of her father, or her father's heir).[5] In other words, the dowry was designed to provide the wife with some protection if her husband abandoned or divorced her, because he was required by law to return the dowry or pay 18 percent annual interest on the value. Although the *enguē* could be conducted when one or both of the future couple were children, it more likely took place closer to the actual "wedding," designated by the other two terms in the triad, *ekdosis* and *gamos*.

Our information regarding the *enguē* comes primarily from fifth- and fourth-century orators and speech writers in the context of law-court cases, but we do catch glimpses of the "betrothal" in Euripides. In *Orestes*, the protagonist acts as his sister's *kurios* and promises

Elektra to Pylades (*katēnguēs'* 1079); in the bizarre reversal at the end of the play, Menelaus in turn "pledges" (*katēnguō* 1675) his daughter Hermione to be Orestes' bride. As Antigone's *kurios* in *Phoenissae*, Eteokles arranges for her wedding to Haimon (*ekhenguan* 759) by settling affairs with Kreon, who acts as Haimon's *kurios*. Otherwise, the subject does not appear in extant drama until Menander.[6] There is but one identifiable representation of the *enguē* in the art of the period—perhaps the subject failed to engage the interest of those on the market for painted pottery.[7]

The aspect of the Greek wedding that did inspire the artistic imagination (and the commemorative desires of the engaged parties) was the *ekdosis*, or "giving away" of the bride. The term implies not so much a final parting as a "loaning out" of the bride by her father or guardian to the bride's husband, for the purpose of making and keeping a household (*oikos*).[8] The duties facing the new wife included bearing children (above all providing a male heir or heirs) and raising and caring for them. She also performed ritual functions reserved for women, in particular those involving the weddings and funerals of family members. The primary purpose of marriage, then, was to re-create the *oikos* under control of the husband, to guarantee the continuity of family property (land, house, and retainers) by providing heirs, and to secure the continued religious observances owed to its dead members.[9]

The *ekdosis* is best understood not as a single moment, but rather as the process by which the bride was transferred from her parents' (or guardians') home to that of her husband. Preceding this change of domicile, a series of preparatory events took place—some with formal names and prescribed actions, others characterized by ongoing activity—most of which focused on the bride. Scenes on domestic vases, including *pyxides* (cosmetic and perfume jars) and *epinetra* (thigh guards for sewing), depict women carding, spinning, weaving, or sewing, in contexts that suggest they are readying the bridal trousseau or otherwise preparing for a wedding (figure 1a).[10] At an unspecified time on or before the wedding day, various "preliminary sacrifices," προτέλεια (*proteleia*), were offered independently by the two families "whose corporate identities were thereby reaffirmed at the moment they were to be rent by the separation of one member."[11] In some locales the bride marked her passage from childhood to maturity by dedicating a lock of hair and/or childhood toys at the shrine of the Nymphs. The horde of pottery fragments and terracotta figurines found at the shrine of Νύμφη (*Numphē*) indicates a similar practice in Athens. Offerings and sacrifices were made to other divinities—Aphrodite, Hera, Athena, the Eumenides, Ouranos and

Figure 1a. Wedding preparations (ARF pyxis, Eretria Painter). The bride-to-be is represented serially—spinning at the left, seated underneath a mirror (women bring her a box and jewelry), and assisted by a young girl and attendant on the right. Note the loutrophoros with myrtle sprigs, and the two lebetes gamikoi by the door. One depicts a wedding procession, with a groom leading his bride and a figure holding nuptial torches.

Figure 1b. Wedding procession via chariot (ARF pyxis, Marlay Painter). The groom mounts a chariot beside his veiled bride and drives off to their new home (shown at the right). Others join the procession, carrying vases, gifts, and torches. At the doorway on the left, the bride's mother bids farewell to her daughter.

Ge (the primal couple, sky and earth), the Tritopatores—but particularly to Artemis, who was associated (variously) with menstruation, virginity, and childbirth.[12]

On the wedding day, the bride and groom (separately) were given a ritual bath with water brought from the *Kallirroë* spring.[13] The special vessel used for this purpose came to be known as a λουτροφόρος (loutrophoros), although technically the word means "someone who carries the bathwater." During these various activities, the bride was assisted by a νυμφεύτρια (numpheutria), the "bride helper"—possibly her mother, or a sister or other female relative—who helped adorn her for the wedding night, a common scene on red-figure vases (figures 2, 3). At the banquet held at her family's home, the bride appeared "veiled"—a stricture that may mean that her head was covered rather than her face. Both bride and groom dressed distinctively, wearing a crown or garland, στέφανος or στεφάνη (stephanos, stephanē), and other adornments to mark the occasion.[14] The unveiling of the bride, the ἀνακαλυπτήρια (anakaluptēria), may have taken place during this feast, but more likely it followed the arrival of the couple at the marriage chamber, or θάλαμος (thalamos), in their new home.[15] Music and dancing played an important part in the festivities, and perhaps during the evening friends and family called the bride and groom "blessed" for the first time.[16] This ritual blessing, μακαρισμός (makarismos), may have been a regular feature of the ὑμέναιοι (hymenaioi), the wedding songs that were sung at the banquet and during the subsequent procession.[17]

The actual transfer of the bride—often referred to as ἐξαγωγή (exagōgē), "leading out" of the father's house, or εἰσαγωγή (eisagōgē), "leading in" to the groom's[18]—took place at night, after the bridal banquet. Unlike a Christian or Jewish ceremony, there was no formal exchange of vows, nor was the transition marked by liturgy officiated by priests or priestesses, who played no part in Greek wedding or funeral rituals. Having prepared for departure, the groom took the bride by the wrist (the gesture "hand on wrist," χεῖρα ἐπὶ καρπῶι (cheira epi karpōi), henceforth abbreviated XEK) and led her to her new home (figures 2, 3). If economic and other circumstances allowed, the journey itself could be made by horse- or mule-cart. This form of transferal was a popular motif on black-figure vases (figure 4), although almost always with the heroic substitution of a chariot for a cart (figures 1b, 5), suggesting (as often) the difference between the real event and its artistic depiction.[19] The procession included torchbearers (particularly the bride's mother) and other friends and family who played music and sang more wedding songs.[20]

The couple were met at the threshold of their new home by the

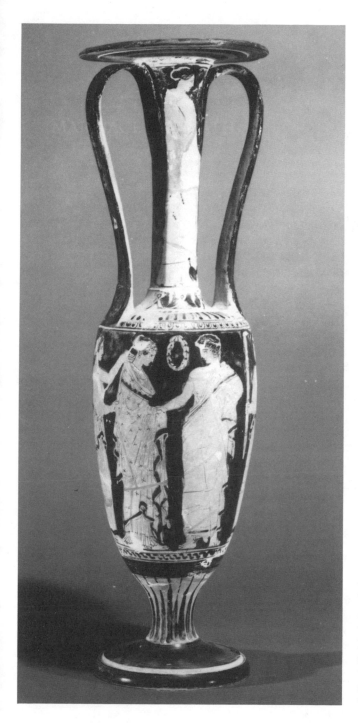

Figure 2. Wedding procession on foot (ARF loutrophoros, Painter of London 1923). With a demure glance the groom takes his bride by the wrist (the XEK gesture). Framing the couple are female attendants who adjust the bride's veil and carry the marriage torch. The wedding wreath between the pair symbolizes their new union. Because a loutrophoros was used for the nuptial bath, the vase-shape itself evokes and commemorates the wedding.

Figure 3. Wedding procession on foot (ARF pyxis, Wedding Painter). The groom leads the bride by the wrist (the XEK gesture), while a woman adjusts her cloak. In contrast to the previous illustration—where the composition conveys an almost portraitlike feeling—this scene emphasizes the transferal (ἐξαγωγή, or "leading out") of the bride. Note the extended arms of the couple, the groom's twisted body and raised foot, and the door of the bride's former home at the left.

groom's parents; and the groom's mother, holding the wedding torch, led the newlyweds inside (fig 6).[21] Bride and groom were seated near the hearth where dried fruit, nuts, sweetmeats, and/or seeds were poured over their heads in the καταχύσματα (katachusmata), a rite to guarantee the future prosperity and fertility of the union, performed not long before the couple withdrew to bed.[22] A good illustration of the preliminaries of this rite is found on the white-ground pyxis from Eretria (ARV² 899.146), in which the groom leads the veiled bride XEK toward the altar/hearth, preceded by an aulos player and the groom's mother holding two torches. On the other side of the hearth, the goddess Hestia holds a fig in her hand, symbolizing the katachusmata.[23]

As part of this rite of incorporation, the bride then ate a quince or apple, and she may have been fed wedding cake made of sesame seeds and honey.[24] Various interpretations have been offered for the eating of fruit: a sympathetic guarantee of fertility, a demonstration that the bride's livelihood now comes from her husband, a way of marking her initiation into the new oikos, an indication of the impending loss of her virginity, and (for the non-symbolists) a practical means of sexual arousal.[25] In the Hymn to Demeter, Persephone's eating of a pomegranate seed binds her to marriage with Hades in the underworld.[26] Whether the mythical account of Persephone influenced the wedding ritual or the influence went the other way is impossible to determine.

Once the couple entered their bedroom to consummate the marriage, a friend of the groom may have been stationed at the door to act as guard.[27] If not before, the bride now removed her veil in the anakaluptēria (discussed in Appendix A), a moment of revelation with similarities to the Eleusinian Mysteries where "things revealed," ἐποπτεία (epopteia), provided the climactic moment in the initiation.[28] Unveiling may have been the single act in the wedding that the bride performed by herself, signifying her formal consent (if nothing more) to the marriage.

The ritualized intimacy symbolized by the anakaluptēria led to the physical union of bride and groom in the marriage bed.[29] Although probably unpleasant for a virgin wife,[30] intercourse marked the τέλος (telos, "end" or "goal") in the transferal of the bride to her husband, and the consummated marriage was referred to as gamos, "a pairing."[31] During the night, the parties who accompanied the procession sang epithalamia, songs "outside the thalamos" (marriage chamber), a practice parodied by the satyr-chorus in Euripides' Kyklops 511–18. The men and women took the side of their respective friend within the house, celebrating with mockery, ribaldry, and possibly dancing as well.[32]

The couple were awakened in the morning by more epithalamia, and later in the day husband and wife received friends bearing gifts in a ceremony called the ἐπαυλία (epaulia).[33] Sources differ as to who gave what to whom, but several vases depict an outdoor procession of people bringing gifts, or an indoor scene (often only of women) with the seated bride receiving presents. It seems that in the evening a final wedding banquet was given by the husband's family. From this point on, the couple "lived together in marriage, συνοικεῖν/ξυνοικεῖν (sunoikein/xunoiken), the word indicating that the relationship involved "keeping and sharing an oikos." As Patterson concludes, an Athenian marriage was "a relationship between a man and woman which had the primary goal of producing children and maintaining the identity of the oikos unit (the household) within the social and political community."[34]

These collective events constituted the Greek wedding, although variations in the ceremony reflecting economic class, social background, and the pressures of war were not uncommon. At some point after his wedding, an Athenian husband offered a sacrifice and feast for phratry members, an event called the γαμηλία (gamēlia).[35] This notification of marriage may have laid the groundwork for establishing the citizenship of any future offspring, a process that became essential with the Citizenship Law of 451/50, which limited Athenian citizenship to individuals both of whose parents were Athenian.[36]

In the case of a woman whose father died leaving her no brothers, there was another possible scenario for her marriage. Called an ἐπίκληρος (epiklēros, "upon the inheritance"), this brotherless daughter could be compelled to marry the closest male relative to her deceased father in order to provide heirs and recreate the oikos. It is important to note that it was the daughter who continued the line of descent springing from her father, because her husband was chosen from the bilateral relatives, ἀγχιστεία (anchisteia), of the deceased—a group including patrilineal and matrilineal kin to the degree of children of cousins. Moreover, the man who married an epiklēros could not alienate the property he acquired from the union. The estate would pass on to the son or sons of the epiklēros, and not to those of her new husband (if, for example, he had children previously).[37] Nominally

opposite page: Figure 4. Wedding procession in cart (ABF lekythos, attributed to the Amasis Painter, ca. 560 B.C.). The bride, holding out her veil and wedding wreath, sits next to the groom on the cart as they make their way from her family's home to his. On the shoulder of the vase, a musician plays and women dance, suggesting the wedding festivities that precede the bride's departure.

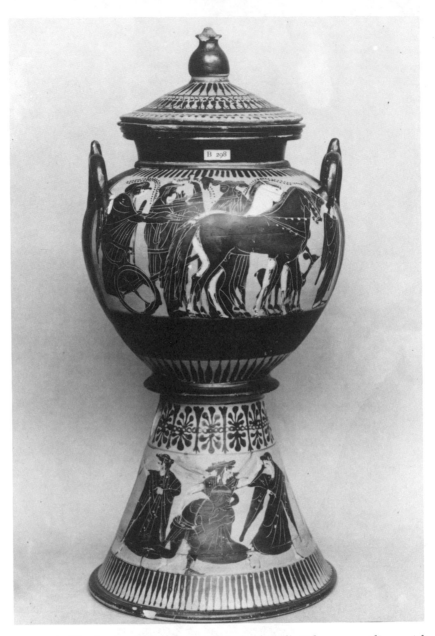

Figure 5. Chariot wedding procession; (pedestal) Peleus wrestling with Thetis (ABF lebes gamikos, 500–480 B.C.). The wedding procession is probably that of Zeus and Hera, who stand side by side in a chariot. Other gods—marked by their attributes—are in attendance: Apollo (with his lyre), Dionysus, and Artemis (trailed by a fawn). Below, the mortal Peleus wrestles with the divine Thetis, whom he later marries. The offspring of their union is the warrior Achilles, who meets his death in the Trojan War. The juxtaposition of a formal wedding and a violent abduction suggests competing or analogous ways of securing a bride (Ch. 2 pp. 36–39).

the heiress of her father's estate, she passed the inheritance on to her first son—if and when she had one—when he attained his majority.

The legal procedure that awarded an *epiklēros* as wife to a family relative was called ἐπιδικασία (*epidikasia*). By such a ruling, a previously married daughter who became *epiklēros* with the death of her father could be forced to abandon her (first) husband and (new) family and marry instead her closest male relative. The survival of her father's *oikos* took legal and social priority over that of the *oikos* of her (first) husband, who was of course free to remarry. There is evidence to suggest, however, that the original marriage would subsist if it had produced a male heir, because that son would be the grandson of the *epiklēros*'s father and, with no other heirs, would stand to inherit his grandfather's estate when he reached the age of 30.[38]

The apparent heartlessness of these arrangements was mitigated by the fact that an *epidikasia* could be avoided with a little planning. A *kurios* who lacked a male heir, for example, could procure one by adoption (usually a kinsman), thus keeping his daughter from becoming claimable as *epiklēros* when he died.[39] However, the speechwriter Isaios reports that "many men who were already married had their own wives taken away," a statement that may be exaggerated but would have lost its efficacy in a law case had it been totally false.[40] The destruction of one marriage to benefit another has tragic implications, as we shall see in *Medea*, but the subject in its "epikleric" guise became theatrically popular only later in New Comedy.

FUNERALS

One purpose of marriage was to guarantee the religious observances expected of the *oikos*, particularly the funeral rites for its deceased members.[41] To Sokrates' query about what constitutes "the beautiful," Hippias answers that it includes a man's arriving at old age "and, having buried his parents beautifully, to be buried beautifully and fittingly by his own offspring" (*Hp.Ma.* 291d–e). This attitude is echoed time and again in Greek tragedy.[42] The premium placed on burial in one's own *polis*—allowing easy access to the gravesite— indicates the commemorative function of these offices for the dead.[43] The fate of the exile was pitiful precisely because this ritual tendance was lost, as poignantly expressed by Elektra vis-à-vis her brother Orestes in Sophokles' *Elektra* (865–70, 1131–42).

We get a sense of the importance of these ongoing rites for the dead in a version of the legend of Sisyphus. As his end approaches, he cleverly arranges with his wife Merope that she *not* provide the customary rites for him upon his death.[44] The ruse works, for Hades, god of the underworld, grows so enraged at this lack of honor for the dead that he allows Sisyphus to return to the light and punish his wife for her disrespect. Reunited with Merope in the land of the living, the hero attains a second span of life. In this tale of mythic reversal, the need to ensure honor for the dead proves sufficient to conquer death itself.

The connection between wedding and funeral rites was encoded in the term κῆδος (*kēdos*), a word-group that refers both to a "relation by marriage" (*kēdē, kēdea, kēdestēs* were "in-laws") and to the "funeral ritual."[45] Perhaps the original idea of "related by marriage" implied an obligation on behalf of one's new *oikos* to participate in the family's "funeral rites," or κηδεία (*kēdeia*).[46] As they did at weddings, women played the most significant role in mourning rituals, including washing, anointing, dressing, crowning, and covering the body after adorning it with flowers.[47] Prepared in this manner, the corpse was "laid out" at the πρόθεσις (*prothesis*) on a "bed" or "couch," κλίνη (*klinē*), probably in the inner courtyard of the house. There it remained on view for two days, long enough—in an age of rudimentary medicine—to ensure that the person was really dead.

In cases of contested inheritance, the party who had possession of the body and arranged the *prothesis* had a prima facie argument for inheriting the deceased's property, because only the closest relations (*anchisteia*) tended the dead in this intimate way.[48] In several law-court speeches, Isaios works interesting variations on the topic: the fact that a party helped prepare the corpse proves that this person is related to the deceased and hence deserves the inheritance (2.36–37); the fact that a person or group did *not* tend the corpse establishes that they are not relatives and have no claim to the estate (4.19–20, 9.4); and the fact that they are not relatives (read "not Isaios' clients") proves that they should not have been allowed to perform the rites in the first place (9.32).[49]

Mourners dressed in black and cut their hair short when they paid their respects to the dead. During these visits, the women of the family sang and wailed dirges. In vase-painting and funerary plaques, women stand over the corpse at the top end of the couch, where they beat their head or breasts, lacerate their cheeks, or tear their hair (figures 7, 8), conventional activities of female mourners.[50] Some-

opposite page: Figure 6. Continuation of the scene in figure 4. A friend or relative of the newlyweds (perhaps the bride's *numpheutria*) accompanies the wedding procession with torches. The mother of the groom waits at the door of the couple's *oikos*, also holding torches to guide them inside.

Figure 7. Funeral *prothesis* (funerary plaque, ca. 510 B.C.). A male corpse is laid out on a bier, surrounded by female mourners who lament by striking their head and tearing at their hair. To the left, two men extend their right arms with palms out, a gesture of farewell to the dead that may have been reserved for males (see Ch. 7 p. 105).

times a woman cradles the head of the deceased in her hands, the same gesture used by Homer's Thetis for her doomed son Achilles (*Il.* 18.71), by Achilles himself for Patroclus (23.136–37), and by Andromache and the Trojans for the dead Hektor (24.712, 724). When present in the scene, men often raise their right hands with their palms out (figure 7) or exhibit a flexed arm with palm of the hand on or near the head, gestures repeated on vases and grave sculptures that show men in procession—either on foot or on horseback—toward the grave.

We can guess at some of the meanings that the ritual activities held for the participants. To don dark clothing similar to that of the deceased is a way of identifying with the dead, a sign of honor and respect through self-denial. As Durkheim has shown, by such means the mourners reaffirm their solidarity, defining their group by honor-

Figure 8. *Prothesis* with mourning man and woman (Attic white-ground lekythos, Sabouroff Painter). A male and female mourner dressed in black grieve over the corpse of a youth. The lekythos shape itself befits the scene, for such a container would have held the oil and perfume used to prepare the corpse for the *prothesis* depicted on the vase.

ing those who have been lost to it.[51] An interesting parallel may exist
between mourners cutting their hair and the similar action during
ritual sacrifice, when a priest cuts a lock from the animal to be killed
to demonstrate its willingness to die. By shearing their hair or by
offering a lock at the grave, the mourners may indicate their willingness to consign the dead to the other world. Alternatively, the practice may resemble laceration and other forms of self-mutilation that
were aspects of female grieving, a way to lessen emotional anguish by
converting it into actual physical pain. Here mourning takes on aspects of self-punishment, implying that death is to some extent the
mourner's fault. Or, as Burkert imagines, the physical blows of the
mourners may begin as a reflex to protect the endangered member,
but finding no external enemy save the inevitability of death, the
blows turn back on the mourners themselves.[52] In politically charged
environments, outpourings of grief at a funeral also provide the opportunity for a clan to display its might, and for the authorities to
assert theirs by limiting or denying ritual observance.[53] The latter
situation is dramatized in Aeschylus' *Oresteia* (Chapter 3), Sophokles' *Antigone* (Chapter 4), and Euripides' *Supplices* (Chapter 8).

After the *prothesis*, the corpse was removed for burial at the ἐκφορά
(*ekphora*, "carrying out") before the dawn of the third day after
death.[54] If money and terrain allowed, a mule- or horse-cart trans-
ported the corpse to its resting place, usually one of the cemetery
areas that lined the main roads outside the city gates. Dressed in
black, men led the funeral cortège and women followed behind the
bier, probably reciting the ritual lament, or θρῆνος (*thrēnos*).[55] Several
vases show musicians playing the αὐλός (*aulos*, the same reed instrument used in tragic performances), which might indicate the presence of professional dirge-singers in the procession.

Athenian burials were of two general types, cremation and inhu-
mation. The former seems to have been preferred in the archaic period and usually took place in the grave itself. In the classical period
both practices were popular, the choice between cremation and inhu-
mation a matter of personal or family preference.[56] Over time there
seems to have been a rise in secondary cremations, where the dead
were not burnt in the grave itself but on a nearby pyre. The ashes were
gathered and placed in a cinerary urn that then was buried. In a related
practice, the city introduced an annual public funeral in the Kerameikos for Athenians who died in battle. Formerly the fallen had
been buried on the battlefield, but at some point after the Persian
Wars Athens instituted the so-called πάτριος νόμος (*patrios nomos*),
or "ancestral custom." Bodies recovered in battle were cremated,
their bones or ashes were sent back to Athens for burial, a casualty list

was erected, and the occasion was marked by a full-scale ceremony including a funeral oration or ἐπιτάφιος (epitaphios).[57] Aeschylus refers to the practice in Agamemnon (Chapter 3), and Euripides brings several aspects of it to the stage in Supplices (Chapter 8).

There has been much speculation about what these changes in Athenian funerary practice meant. Were the "public/city" funerals a means by which the polis wrested from the oikos the prerogatives of burial? If so, did this mark the impersonal state invading the practices of private citizens, or did it reflect the democratic control of the citizen "mass" over an economically privileged "elite?" Was there a connection between the institution of the patrios nomos and the purported enactment of sumptuary legislation for private funerals? If so, why do we find a pan-Hellenic shift away from monumental lavishness in private funeral markers in the fifth-century? And why are the war graves so unprepossessing?[58] Were these new funerary arrangements aimed at the exclusion of women? Then why is this not reflected in private burial practice, where we find men and women buried together in family plots, with children's graves around the edges? Were state burials an abrogation of women's roles in the ritual process?[59] Or could the new civic practices indicate that the solidarity instilled by funeral rituals was being broadened from a small circle of kin to the citizenry as a whole, an appeal of special significance during times of war? In Euripides' Supplices, for example, is Theseus being "feminized" by washing the corpses of the recovered Argives, or is he representing an Athenian polis that forcibly excludes women from their traditional roles? We shall deal more fully with these questions in subsequent chapters.

Whether inhumed or cremated, the dead were buried along with gifts and offerings, many of which have come to light in excavation: various shapes of pottery (mostly decorated), stone vases, and items connected with the deceased (perhaps favored possessions), including mirrors, strigils, toys, and other personal belongings. Among pottery deposited in or at the grave, white-ground lēkythoi with appropriate funeral iconography prove to be the most popular from the 460s to around 410 B.C.[60] The presence of vases associated with weddings among the grave gifts—mainly loutrophoroi, but also lebētes gamikoi—indicate that the grave was probably that of a young man or woman who died before marriage, a subject treated in more detail in the next chapter.

As with the wedding, no priest or priestess offered formal prayers or otherwise sanctified the final moments at the gravesite, although there is evidence that a preliminary sacrifice may have preceded the burial.[61] The mourners made offerings of fruit, returning to the earth a token of its own bounty, and then they buried the body (or urn) and erected a marker. After singing a dirge or threnody and possibly performing a dance (as depicted on the great funerary amphora of the early archaic period), the funeral party offered a final pouring at the grave and departed for home. The house of the deceased was cleansed, and all who attended the funeral may have bathed as a means of purification from contact with the dead.[62] A banquet or περίδειπνον (perideipnon) followed, during which eulogies were delivered and songs may have been sung.[63] Perhaps on this occasion or earlier during the *prothesis*, the deceased would be called μακάριος (makarios), "blessed," both a euphemism and an acknowledgment that the difficulties of life were over.[64]

A formal return to the grave occurred after nine days, annual rites were celebrated, and there were other less formal visits to the tomb. Apparently these are the occasions represented on white-ground lekythoi that show visitors offering cuttings of hair, libations, wreaths, flowers, and small ceramic vessels, particularly lekythoi themselves.[65] Frequently women sit in mourning nearby, and often the grave monument is decorated with ribbons. Kurtz points out that the predominance of women on funerary white lekythoi "confirms their critical role in the tendance of the dead and the family grave. . . . [T]hese scenes depict women doing what society required—looking after the living at home and the dead at the grave."[66]

Among the various memorials erected after burial, *stēlai* were the most common in the archaic period. Beginning as roughly worked, undecorated slabs, the *stēlē* shaft later was decorated with a figure meant to represent the deceased, either painted, incised, or carved in relief, and frequently topped with sphinxes.[67] The production of such gravestones in Athens seems to have diminished greatly at the end of the sixth century, presumably the result of legislation that limited funerary extravagance, although a pan-Hellenic change in fashion also may explain the evidence.[68] From the last third of the fifth century, however, we perceive another shift, as Attic graves increasingly are adorned with stone or marble carved in high relief. The scenes often represent the deceased in generic, not portrait, style, placed within a family context. The fact that these family-group reliefs do not strive to make the dead stand out from the living may emphasize the survival and continuity of the family even after death.[69]

Sometimes the grave monument took the form of a large stone or marble loutrophoros, a monumentalizing of the ceramic loutrophoroi that mourners customarily placed in the grave or by the tomb to mark the passing of men and women who died before marriage. Having failed to establish their own families, these dead possessed graves that called to mind the nuptial bath and married life they never would experience.[70] Other iconographic parallels between grave reliefs and wedding scenes on Attic vases will be discussed in Chapter 2.

Our summary of wedding and funeral practices reveals several overlapping elements in the two rituals. A bride will offer a lock of hair before her marriage; mourners will offer the same when visiting a grave.[71] Like the bride and groom, the dead are ritually bathed, dressed, adorned, and crowned, activities in which women play a crucial role. The corpse is covered, the bride is veiled; the dead are laid out on a bed or couch, the wedding leads to the nuptial bed. Both events involve a journey at night to a new "home," often taken by horse- or mule-cart, in a procession that includes torchbearers, family, and friends, and where song and dance mark the occasion. A *makarismos* blessing is used for the "happy" couple and the "blessed" dead. The bride receives gifts in her new home, corpses receive gifts in theirs, and both rites include a final banquet. The connection between weddings and funerals is made explicit for the young who die unmarried, for their graves are crowned with large stone loutrophoroi representing the ritual vessel for nuptial bathing. The points of shared activity between weddings and funerals find literal expression on epitaphs, which seek to evoke aspects of both rituals in those who read them.[72]

The conflation of marriages and funerals on the Attic stage speaks to the signal importance of these rituals in the lives of the audience, and suggests an overriding continuity (at least during the fifth century) in the way they were conceived and understood.[73] Before turning to the exploitation of these common elements in tragedy, however, let us examine the juxtaposition and confusion of the two rituals in the visual arts, particularly vase-painting and grave reliefs.

Chapter 2

WEDDINGS AND FUNERALS

THE VISUAL RECORD

THE TRAGEDIANS incorporated images of weddings and funerals as actually practiced *and* as conventionally represented in the visual arts. Besides providing valuable evidence for ritual observance, scenes on ritually specific vase shapes—particularly loutrophoros, lebes gamikos, and (white-ground) lekythos—reveal the most popular iconography for weddings and funerals, complemented by depictions on other vases and on grave reliefs. Because landscape was rare in Greek art, and spatial markers few and allusive, a small detail could signal a full scene and context—preparations for a wedding, a nuptial procession, a visit to the tomb. Armed with this iconographic shorthand, the artist could focus his energies on representing the human image and actions, an aesthetic in tune with that of the ancient theater.[1]

RITUAL VASES, RITUAL MESSAGE

In black-figure, most wedding scenes occur on *amphorai* and *hydriai*, vessels used for holding and carrying water and wine, presumably linked to nuptial bathing and feasting. The most common marriage motifs show the gesture of unveiling (pointing to the *anakaluptēria*) and chariot processions with bride and groom.[2] As red-figure technique reached full maturity (around the middle of the fifth century), wedding scenes became far more frequent on loutrophoroi and lebetes gamikoi, where ritual function often is reflected in the painted decoration.[3] Loutrophoroi were used to bring water for the nuptial bath, and it is not surprising to find them decorated with wedding scenes. When they depict a wedding procession on foot (a red-figure motif that supplanted the chariot processions preferred on black-figure), the groom often leads his bride by the wrist (the XEK gesture discussed in Chapter 1), accompanied by torch-bearers and others carrying possessions or gifts (figure 2). Occasionally the procession to draw water for the nuptial bath is shown, including women actually bearing loutrophoroi for the bath.[4] In this popular motif of the "vessel on the vessel," the vase reveals in its decoration the occasion of its ritual use. The horde of loutrophoroi fragments found in the sanctuary of Nymphē at the foot of the Athenian Acropolis suggests that most wedding loutrophoroi in Athens were dedicated there, probably after the nuptial bath. However, a red-figure *pyxis* in Berlin shows loutrophoroi being brought to the bride as part of the *epaulia*.[5] Perhaps the bridal loutrophoros used *in* the wedding ritual could, on some occasions, become a memento *of* it.

Because of their link with weddings, loutrophoroi also served as grave offerings for those who died unmarried. Frequently the *prothesis* is depicted—on a red-figure example, a dead maiden on her *klinē* (death-bed/bier) is surrounded by women grieving over her, a poignant contrast to the attentions she would have received from the same group of women on her wedding day. An older lady (possibly her mother), hair cropped in mourning, cradles in her hands the young woman's head on which is placed a wedding coronal.[6]

The neck of these funerary vases often shows a woman in mourning, and on occasion she herself holds a loutrophoros. Perhaps we are to understand that she will dedicate the vase at the burial of the corpse depicted in the *prothesis* below. The grieving woman with loutrophoros recalls the ritual bathing that preceded the laying out of the body, the only "nuptial bath" the dead youth will ever take.[7] This is the implied scenario of a black-figure loutrophoros in Athens: depicted on the neck is a loutrophoros at the grave of the man who, on the body of the vase, is being mourned at his *prothesis*.[8]

In addition to motifs of weddings and funerals, the so-called battle-loutrophoroi often represent a cavalry battle with a tomb acting like a stage backdrop and a frieze below the main picture showing a funeral procession with mourners making the ritual gesture of farewell. It seems that these vases were placed at the tombs of unmarried men who had died in battle.[9] The iconography recalls the young man's bravery in combat, while the vase shape points to the married life he will never realize.

When Athenian families could afford the expense, and sumptuary legislation (or fashion) allowed, marble loutrophoroi might crown the graves of those who died unmarried.[10] These markers tend to follow the iconography of other grave reliefs rather than the motifs of vase painting. A seated figure—usually meant to represent the deceased, most frequently a woman—shakes the right hand of a standing figure. Although the exact meaning is uncertain, the δεξίωσις (*dexiōsis*) gesture may signal the ongoing community of the living and the dead.[11] Marble battle-loutrophoroi also were erected, usually carved in the round and often showing a warrior carrying his shield.[12]

According to Vernant, the Greeks viewed warfare and marriage as the two poles that informed (and differentiated) male and female experience, summarized by his oft-quoted statement, "Marriage is for the girl what warfare is for the boy."[13] It is true that an Athenian girl achieved adult status through marriage and childbirth, while an Athenian male became an adult when he reached his majority and assumed various civic roles, including that of soldier. However, the popularity of the loutrophoros shape for tomb markers of unmarried men suggests that wedded life in Athens provided a *telos* for males as well as for females.[14] That idea is given passionate expression in Megara's lament over her three young sons in Euripides' *Herakles*. They are doomed to die unwedded, to be washed with a mother's tears rather than the nuptial bath, forced to marry spirits of the underworld, with Hades as their father-in-law and death as their fate (*HF* 476–84). Time and again tragedy undermines the neat polarities that characterize many modern reconstructions of ancient male/female experience, suggesting that civic and domestic affairs in Athens might better be understood as a complex weave rather than as antithetical poles. This is not to imply that fifth-century Athenians had a *romantic* view of marriage, for there is never a suggestion that the deceased is denied a specific partner. Rather, grave goods and tomb markers commemorated the fact that those who died unwedded— maiden or bachelor—failed to share in a crucial part of adult life, the establishing and sustaining of an *oikos*.[15]

Unlike the specific role of the loutrophoros in ritual bathing, various functions for the lebes gamikos have been proposed—a bowl for mixing wine or preparing food for the wedding banquet, a storage vessel used during the festivities, a container for warming water (or holding water that was warmed elsewhere) for the nuptial bath, a vase for flowers, a jar for aromatic water to be sprinkled with myrtle, or simply "ein symbolisches Hochzeitsgeschenk."[16] In whatever way the vessel was used during the ritual, it seems to have been given as a wedding gift afterward, judging from the visual evidence. The painted iconography of lebetes gamikoi is almost exclusively nuptial, predominantly wedding processions in black-figure (figure 5) and scenes of gift-giving at the *epaulia* in red-figure.[17] On a mid-fourth-century lebes, one of the women walking toward the seated bride carries a lebes gamikos (with pedestal) in her arms.[18] A lebes in the Louvre depicts *two* lebetes gamikoi, one held in the lap of the seated bride, the other carried by one of the females who bring gifts.[19] Again, the representation of the vase-type on the vase itself unites iconography with function. The self-referential decoration conveys the commemorative purpose of the vessel by calling the original occasion to the viewer's mind in both the shape and the scene.

Scholars once believed that the lebes shape had nothing to do with the cult of the dead, but lebetes gamikoi have been found that depict funeral scenes.[20] Other red-figure examples with wedding scenes have been excavated in Attic graves, probably placed there (like loutrophoroi) to honor those who died unmarried.[21] Some of these vases may have been produced specifically as grave gifts, because the Athenians could see such untimely deaths "als einer Vermählung der Verstorbenen mit dem Todesgott."[22] The notion that unmarried girls made a marriage with Hades invokes the paradigm of Persephone in the *Hymn to Demeter*, discussed later in this chapter. More generally, by serving as both wedding and funeral gifts, lebetes gamikoi reflect the Athenian penchant for juxtaposing, and conflating, the two rituals.

Scenes on white lekythoi from ca. 460 to 410 B.C., on the other hand, appear to be almost exclusively funereal.[23] *Lēkythos* is the name for an oil bottle, a significant item in Attica where olive oil played a key role in the economy, diet, and personal hygiene of the populace.[24] The prominence of lekythoi in funeral contexts reflects the emphasis placed on preparing the body for the *prothesis*—the loutrophoros held water for washing the corpse and the lekythos contained oil for anointing it.[25] As noted in Chapter 1, ritual bathing and anointing the body also were steps in preparing the bride and groom for their wedding.

Kurtz believes that the majority of funeral white lekythoi present "realistic portrayals of contemporary Athenian practices."[26] Among preburial scenes, the *prothesis* appears frequently (figure 8), often with mourners stretching out their right hand to bid farewell to the dead. Visitations to the tomb are common, with scenes of decorating the monument with ribbons, of offering wreaths, fillets, and vases (often lekythoi are shown), of female mourners sitting at the tomb or pouring libations. In a related vein, Reilly identifies 109 interior scenes on white-ground and red-figure lekythoi depicting a woman attended by her female servant, featuring dressing motifs along with baskets, fillets, and containers for jewelry and perfume (e.g., figure 9). Questioning the traditional view that they illustrate preparations for a visit to the tomb, Reilly argues persuasively that these scenes show the bridal arrangements for a young woman who never lived to see her wedding day. Like funerary loutrophoroi, the vases were intended for the grave of a woman who died unmarried: "The bride on the lekythoi is always preparing for a wedding that never takes place; her

attendants busy themselves for a wedding procession that never arrives."[27]

Other comminglings of wedding and funeral motifs on white-ground lekythoi require us to consider less-frequent illustrations of the coming of death: 1) Charon arrives with his boat to ferry the dead over the river Styx (also referred to in A. *Th.* 854–60 and Eur. *Alk.* 252–57, 259–62); and 2) Hermes as ψυχοπομπός (*psychopompos*, "escort of souls") takes the deceased by the wrist (XEK) and leads her either to a waiting Charon or to her grave. As noted above, the same XEK gesture was used in Athenian weddings and frequently appears in illustrations of the ceremony.[28] On a funerary lekythos in Boston, Hermes leads a girl XEK to Charon's boat like a groom leading his bride home.[29] In a similar scene on a white-ground lekythos in Brussels, Hermes takes the woman by the hand. Her fingers remain passive, so the effect is that of the XEK gesture, in which the female "is taken hold of" by the male without reciprocating the clasp.[30] On a white lekythos in Palermo, Hermes again leads a young girl XEK to the underworld, although no Charon is present.[31]

The link between the gesture and death appears again on a hydria depicting Neoptolemus leading Polyxena to be sacrificed at the grave of Achilles.[32] A funeral lekythos found in a grave in Selinus offers a near parallel. Teukros leads Iphigenia (both names are inscribed) to an altar where she is to be sacrificed, his hand clasping Iphigenia's garment just below her upraised wrist in a gesture close to XEK.[33] These vases are of special relevance to tragedy, because there is a trace of the same ritual confusion at the sacrifice of Iphigenia in *Agamemnon* (developed in Euripides' *Iphigenia in Aulis*), as well as at the sacrifice of Polyxena in *Hecuba*.[34]

Toward the end of the fifth century, white lekythoi with figural decoration were much less common as grave offerings, perhaps because of the rise in the number of stone and marble lekythoi used as tomb markers.[35] Generally the iconography shifts to that found on grave reliefs (mainly domestic scenes that include the deceased),[36]

opposite page: Figure 9. A funerary/wedding scene (Attic white-ground lekythos, Quadrate Painter). A seated maiden (perhaps a bride-to-be) cradles a loutrophoros with one hand, while the other holds a piece of fruit (a pomegranate?). A female attendant offers her a box, and a mirror hangs on the wall. Because the lekythos shape is linked to funerals, the scene may imply that the young maiden has died unmarried. The loutrophoros in her lap evokes both the nuptial bath she will never know and the funeral bath she receives as a corpse. Similarly, the mirror on the wall—often a sign of nuptial preparations—may point to its final use as a grave-gift.

but an exception involves a variation of the XEK gesture. On a marble funerary lekythos (figure 10), the carved figure of Hermes takes Myrrhine (inscribed) by her passive hand and leads her to the underworld.[37] Without the attributes to identify the god Hermes, the same scene would be interpreted as a husband leading his bride if it were found anywhere save in a funeral context. By joining wedding and funerary iconography, the grave marker reminds the viewer that death has replaced marriage and that the "bride" has departed for a new home in Hades.

There are three other circumstances in which Hermes is shown taking a woman XEK: vase-paintings of the god leading Persephone out of the underworld,[38] the Orpheus reliefs in which Hermes leads Eurydike back to Hades (figure 11);[39] and votive reliefs dedicated to Hermes and the nymphs.[40] By employing a gesture linked to weddings, these images give Hermes *psychopompos* the look of an ersatz bridegroom. In the case of Persephone, the story itself (as told in the Homeric *Hymn to Demeter*) provides a mythic paradigm for the marriage to death, discussed in Chapter 8. Abducted by the god of the dead in his chariot, separated from her mother Demeter, fed a pomegranate seed in the underworld, Persephone literally becomes the bride of Hades. However, through Demeter's intervention, she inverts the rites of passage enacted at a wedding and a funeral. Led out of the underworld in an ἄνοδος (anodos, "journey up"), Persephone leaves her husband and is reunited with her mother. Her ascent also reverses the journey that mortal women take when Hermes leads them like a bride down to the land of the dead.

GESTURE AND ATTRIBUTE

Taking his bride by the wrist, a groom displays his power over her at the moment of their wedding. However, Sutton points out a shift from possession toward mutuality in XEK scenes of the last half of the fifth century, "emphasizing a state of union, rather than the act" (e.g., figure 2). Even in the earlier, more active scenes of a husband leading his bride XEK, "the artist takes care to alleviate any hint of harshness in the bridegroom's gesture by providing an element of strong emotional contact between the two figures. This is usually achieved in part by having the groom turn back to look at his bride" (e.g., figure 3).[41]

Sutton's conclusions help to balance the view that the XEK gesture was one of several elements of mock-abduction in the Athenian wedding ritual.[42] The memory of earlier, violent marriage practices may

Figure 10. Hermes leads a woman to the underworld (marble funerary lekythos—the "Myrrhine" lekythos—ca. 400 B.C.) The deceased Myrrhine is led to the underworld by Hermes (note the winged sandals) in his role as *psychopompos*, "escorter of souls." The XEK gesture recalls illustrations of a groom taking his bride by the wrist and leading her to her new home. The delicate carving suggests that Hermes is leading Myrrhine *past* the group on the left. They may represent the surviving kin who mourn the dead woman, gathered at the site where the marble lekythos itself would have served as the grave marker.

Figure 11. Hermes, Eurydike, and Orpheus (a three-figured relief, Roman copy of Greek original, ca. 420 B.C.). Hermes leads the veiled Eurydike away from Orpheus and back to the underworld (their names are carved above). As in the previous illustration, the god takes a mortal woman by the wrist—the very gesture used by a groom to lead his new bride home. Death is figured as a wedding, with Hermes acting as surrogate husband taking his deceased "bride" to her new "dwelling."

have survived in myth—the rape of Persephone by Hades is an obvious example—but the results of these legendary abductions are generally disastrous. The distinction between rape and marriage seems to have been crucial to Athenian culture, epitomized in the myth of the Lapiths and Centaurs. At the wedding of Perithoös and

Hippodameia, the bestial Centaurs become drunk and try to carry off the new bride, along with her bridesmaids and the female guests. After a terrible battle, the Lapiths prevail and drive the surviving Centaurs from Thessaly. The story was popular in Attic sculptural programs of the fifth century and appeared on wall-paintings as well as on red-figure vases.[43] These images clearly differentiate a marriage celebration from its disruption by rape. We might view the pairing on Attic vases of a mythological abduction with a wedding scene as a way of indicating two different and contrasted means by which a husband secured a wife (figure 5).[44]

The XEK gesture does occur in illustrations of the abduction and recovery of mythological women, particularly Helen.[45] In scenes of Paris leading Helen by the wrist, however, the wedding motif is still applicable since he brings a new bride to Troy. The gesture also may hint at the *broken* marriage of Helen and Menelaus that brings on the Greek siege and sack of the city. Menelaus' recovery of Helen from Troy constitutes a remarriage, and frequently he leads Helen by the wrist like a bride. The recovery scene can exhibit violent tendencies, for Menelaus often is depicted brandishing a weapon in his other hand, a fitting reminder that a devastating war has been fought to achieve this reunion.

A similar doubling occurs in illustrations of Agamemnon's removal of Briseis from Achilles (based on *Il.* 1.327–50). Briseis is led off XEK while Achilles remains seated, wrapped up in his cloak to signal his powerlessness and shame. The wedding gesture highlights the breach in custom, because Agamemnon tears the war bride from her "husband," against both their desires.[46] Ancient viewers of these vases familiar with the poem would recall that Achilles himself had captured Briseis by force, and the visual image suggests the cycle of contention over women that is central to the epic.

In sum, the action of a man taking a woman by the wrist evokes a cluster of meanings involving marriage, death, abduction, and recovery. Certainly in the visual arts of the fifth century, the dominant context was the wedding ritual itself, and it seems fair to assume that the XEK gesture was understood primarily as nuptial. However, we do find the gesture in scenes of Hermes leading away the dead and in illustrations of the abduction and recovery of mythological females, including the return of Persephone from the underworld. When XEK is referred to in tragic texts or enacted in performance, the playwright would seem to appeal to a similar set of associations, one of which is a marriage to death. In Euripides' *Ion* 887–96, for example, Apollo takes Kreusa "by her white wrists" (891) while she is plucking flowers in a field, and then the god rapes her in a sunless cave. The actions combine the gesture of a groom taking his bride XEK with the paradigm of Hades' rape of Persephone, a marriage to death that casts a dark shadow over a play often viewed simply as a comedy.[47]

The unveiling of a bride is another wedding motif that found its way into funeral iconography. On Attic grave stelai from the last third of the fifth century, scenes in a domestic setting predominate. Frequently they show a woman holding a mirror and adorning herself, or unveiling herself as on the night of her wedding.[48] On the stele of Ktesileos and Theano, for example, the seated woman makes the gesture of unveiling, as does the seated Hera with Zeus on the Parthenon east frieze and the standing Hera on the metope of Temple E at Selinus.[49] By alluding to a ritual aspect of the wedding, grave reliefs produce an effect similar to that of the Myrrhine lekythos (figure 10) where the dead girl is treated like a bride.

Unveiling with both its marital and funereal connotations occurs frequently in epic,[50] and it plays an important role in Aeschylus' *Agamemnon*, Sophokles' *Trachiniae* and *Elektra*, and Euripides' *Alkestis*, *Hippolytus*, and *Phoenissae*. In *Hippolytus*, for instance, Phaedra urges the Nurse to help her veil her face and hide her shame (243–46), an effort to recapture a bridelike modesty that causes the Nurse to wish that death might veil her body too (250–51). In the final scene, the Nurse's wish is granted—not for herself, but for the dying Hippolytus. The young man begs that death might "put my life to bed" (κατά τ᾽ εὐνᾶσαι/τὸν ἐμὸν βίοτον 1376–77), and in his last words he asks Theseus to "cover my face as fast as you can with the funeral shroud [lit. "robes"]" (1459).[51] The visual connection between reveiling the "violated" wife and shrouding the innocent youth underscores at the ritual level the closure so beautifully expressed in Hippolytus' forgiveness of Theseus. Played out before the female Chorus and the secondary group of Hippolytus' followers, the final scene unites formerly opposed factions in what has become "common grief for all the citizens" (1462).[52] Weddings and funerals emerge as the cornerstones of personal and social experience, highlighted by the rites associated with Hippolytus after his death, namely to receive offerings from maidens on the verge of marriage.

In addition to the gestures of XEK and veiling/unveiling, attributes of person and place can help identify painted and sculpted scenes as nuptial or funereal. Describing an early funerary lekythos, Johansen notes that "the home milieu is suggested by the mirror hanging on the wall."[53] The seated woman depicted on the vase holds a lekythos in one hand and pomegranate in the other (a traditional attribute of the dead, associated with Persephone), objects that transform this domestic scene into a funerary one.[54] On a lekythos in Oxford, the

Tymbos Painter purposefully conflates such a domestic scene with a tomb visitation. A woman sits beneath a mirror on the wall while she lifts her arms out to a grave stele that is immediately before her. Kurtz concludes that "the painter has not connected his compositions structurally or iconographically."[55] She is right in her first judgment, but comparing the scene with the lekythos described by Johansen suggests that the mirror provides the iconographical link between the two parts of the composition. This possibility is supported by the presence of a hanging mirror in what is clearly an exterior scene at the grave on an unattributed lekythos in Athens.[56] A woman bearing grave gifts approaches the tomb, but a mirror hangs in midair over the basket she holds in her arms. The mirror no longer indicates a domestic scene per se but has become part of the funerary iconography (as in figure 9). In a similar scene on another lekythos by the Tymbos Painter, the grave stele is "carved" with an image of the deceased looking at herself in a mirror.[57]

Considering the presence of mirrors on funerary lekythoi, it is not surprising to find representations of a woman with a mirror on classical grave reliefs.[58] Often in these scenes, a subsidiary figure presents a jewel box or adornments to a seated woman (presumably the deceased). Such grave reliefs recall nuptial scenes on red-figure vases where a hanging mirror establishes an interior setting, or where the mirror is held by a woman, identifying her as a bride and the situation as the preparation for a wedding or the gift-giving ceremony the morning after.[59] The attributive function of mirrors carved on funerary stelai is not unconnected with the fact that mirrors were among the presents given to the bride at the *epaulia* and also among the gifts commonly buried with the dead.[60] We shall return in Chapter 7 to the importance of mirrors in wedding and funeral iconography when discussing the transformation of a marriage celebration into its fatal opposite in *Medea*.

A variety of other objects help to identify a painted or carved scene as a wedding or a funeral: torches, carriages or carts (figures 4, 6, 1b), wedding chests, loutrophoroi, lebetes gamikoi (figures 1a, 9), other vases borne by participants, ribbons and lekythoi to be given at the grave, crowns or coronals, veils for the bride, fruit for the *katachusmata*, the quince fed to the bride or pomegranate held by the newly deceased, a marriage bed or funeral couch, the door that marks the couple's entrance into a new house or that separates the living from the dead.[61] Gestures linked with these objects can establish more clearly a wedding or a funeral context. In addition to XEK and veiling, we should add the keening gestures of women, the right-arm farewell of the men, and the *dexiōsis* shown on grave reliefs. Whether these gestures refer to the rituals as practiced *and* as conventionally represented, or to only one of the two, they were familiar to the Athenian audience and provided the dramatist with an effective repertoire of allusions to weddings and funerals that could be marked in the text or incorporated into the stage action.

From vase-paintings and grave stelai, we learn that the conflation "marriage to death" found in tragedy was no mere dramatic fiction, nor was it a vague idea existing at a historical or mythological remove from the audience. Allusions to wedding and funeral rituals referred to contemporary practice, not to a code of foreign behavior or a set of abstract visual conventions.[62] These rituals offered an efficient way for the tragedians to move mythical and heroic stories into the sphere of the fifth century, making powerful and immediate contact with the spectator. In so doing, tragedy challenged contemporary audiences with a vision of their own life writ large, rather than a version of the heroic life writ small.

Chapter 3

THE BRIDE UNVEILED

MARRIAGE TO DEATH IN AESCHYLUS' *AGAMEMNON*

MARRIAGE TO DEATH in *Agamemnon* emerges with dramatic force through the experience of four female characters—Klytemnestra and Kassandra who take the stage, and Iphigenia and Helen who do not (although they are evoked vividly in the lyric). With fatal consequences, the sisters Klytemnestra and Helen betray their respective marriages to the Atreid brothers Agamemnon and Menelaus. Iphigenia and Kassandra are cut down like animals at a sacrifice, but their deaths also take the form of a twisted wedding ceremony that leads to the bloodshed of the bride, part of the *Oresteia*'s complex weave of ritual perversion.[1]

In the parodos, the Chorus refer to Helen as the "woman/wife of many men/husbands" (πολυάνορος ἀμφὶ γυναικός 62), the reason that Trojans and Greeks fell in battle as a "first offering" (ἐν προτελείοις 65). The term means "preliminary offering or sacrifice," specifically the sacrifice before the rite (*telos*) of marriage.[2] In accordance with ritual sequence, the deaths of the Trojan and Greek warriors should precede the wedding of Paris and Helen, but Aeschylus plays with temporal and spatial logic throughout the trilogy. Here he opens the possibility that the *telos* served by these sacrifices is not simply the destructive wedding of Paris and Helen, but the larger goal or "completion" toward which the trilogy aims, which—as we shall see—confirms the importance of marriage to the *polis*.

The Chorus return to the wedding of Paris and Helen in the first stasimon, where Helen "brings to Troy a dowry of death,/ passing lightly through/ the city gates" (ἄγουσά τ' ἀντίφερνον Ἰλίωι φθορὰν/ βεβάκει ῥίμφα διὰ/ πυλᾶν 406–8). The image of bridal homecoming anticipates the appearance of the bridelike Kassandra later in the play and *her* entrance into the palace through the "gates of Hades" (Ἅιδου πύλας 1291). Kassandra arrives to meet her death, but Helen is a bride who brings death in her wake.

In the second stasimon the Chorus develop the conceit that Helen and Paris have made a marriage of death. "A spear-bride fought over by both sides" (686), Helen abandoned the "gentle curtains" (προκαλυμμάτων 691, "coverings" or "veils") of her Spartan home, hinting at the veil she wore at her wedding to Menelaus.[3] The root noun κάλυμμα (*kalumma*) is used by Kassandra for bridal veils (*Ag.* 1178), and Elektra applies the same word to the net that trapped Agamemnon and also to the coverings laid over his corpse (*Ch.* 494).[4] Employing more double language of weddings and funerals, the Chorus call Helen "a true *kēdos*" (*Ag.* 699), referring both to her relationship by marriage to the house of Priam and to the mourning rites that result from that union.[5] The "wedding hymn" (705–6, 707) turns into a funeral dirge (711, 714), and the marriage-bed becomes a "bed of death" (712). In the end, the arrival of Helen at Troy accomplishes "bitter rites of marriage" (γάμου πικρὰς τελευτάς 745), rites that reveal "the bridal-weeping Fury" (749)—the noun "Fury" ringing out as the final word of the strophe.[6]

Klytemnestra herself bears a Fury-like resemblance to her sister Helen, above all when she appears with the corpses of Agamemnon and Kassandra late in the play. The Chorus compare her double murder to the destruction wreaked by Helen (1448–61), and they speak of a "divine force" of vengeance (1468, 1482) that lives in the race. By betraying her husband, the Fury-like Helen unleashed death on the many young men at Troy; the "beyond-human" drive to vengeance in Klytemnestra leads her to "shame her marriage bed" (1626) and bring death to her own house.

The various marriage and funeral motifs come into sharpest focus in the Kassandra scene. Her entrance with Agamemnon in his cart resembles the journey a bride and groom take to their new home, a scene illustrated frequently on black-figure vases (figure 4).[7] Developing these nuptial possibilities, Agamemnon introduces Kassandra to Klytemnestra as a "stranger," ξένη (*xenē* 950), to be welcomed kindly into the palace. Being Trojan, Kassandra is literally a foreigner (*xenē*, as the Chorus call her at 1062 and 1093), but the word also defines the Greek bride, a stranger incorporated into her husband's *oikos*.[8] Klytemnestra reminds Kassandra that she will stand at the altar with the other slaves and share in the household rites (1036–38), particularly the sacrifice to be carried out at the hearth (1056–58). A ritual of incorporation welcomed the arrival both of a new slave and a new bride into the home, and the language may hint at the ritual overlap.[9] Agamemnon himself says that Kassandra must wear the "slave's yoke" (δουλίωι . . . ζυγῶι 953, repeated by the Chorus at 1071), a common metaphor for servitude. But the yoke also has marital implications—the active and middle form of ζεύγνυμι, "I yoke," was used when a man took a wife.[10] Kassandra is not simply yoked to slavery, for, as Agamemnon admits, she is his "select flower" (ἐξαίρετον/ ἄνθος 954–55), a familiar trope for a Greek bride.[11]

After remaining onstage and mute for some 250 lines, the last 31 of which focus on her *refusal* to speak to Klytemnestra, Kassandra finally breaks her silence by uttering the name of her destroyer, the god Apollo (1073). The Chorus later ask if sex with the god resulted "in the work of child-bearing" (τέχνων εἰς ἔργον 1207), a phrase that "would recall to every Athenian hearer the solemn marriage-formula."[12] Punished for denying children to Apollo (1208), Kassandra is "taken" by prophecy as she was by the god. The results are similarly fruitless, for she is cursed to make predictions that no one will believe.

Kassandra brings out the erotic source of her possession, crying out in anguish, "Such fire, it burns through me!/ Ahh! Wolf-god Apollo!" (1256–57).[13] From the the Wolf-god who violated her, Kassandra next visualizes a "two-footed lioness in bed with a wolf" (1258–59), meaning the unnatural ménage of Klytemnestra and Aegisthus in the palace. It is as if the source of Kassandra's prophetic power makes her particularly attuned to a sexual union between "different species," the egregious adultery with an enemy to which Klytemnestra has succumbed.

If Kassandra is both possessed and ruined by Apollo, she bears a similar relationship to Agamemnon, for she is bound to the enemy general who destroyed her city. Kassandra epitomizes the innocent female dominated by males, both divine (Apollo) and mortal (Agamemnon). She even must suffer death at the hands of a woman "too much like a man."[14] Powerless in a male world she can predict but cannot control, Kassandra lives out a worst-case scenario for a "bride" with Janus-like prophetic powers. Seeing both past and future of the house, she focuses on the offspring of an earlier marriage—the children of Thyestes, whom Atreus killed and fed to their own father (1096–97). By referring to these victims as "witnesses" (1095), Kassandra underlines her affinity with them, for she too bears witness (in advance) to the sacrificial murder in which she herself must play the victim.[15] Kassandra's similarity to, and sympathy for, the murdered children suggests how close her fate is to another youthful innocent, Iphigenia, who also became a creature to be sacrificed (*Ag.* 231–47).

From events in the past, Kassandra shifts to the immediate present, particularly Klytemnestra's plot to kill "the husband who shares her bed" (1108). Merging wedding vocabulary with terms for completion and fulfillment (*teleis* 1107, *telos* 1109)—the "*telos* of marriage and the *telos* of death"[16]—Kassandra locates the common ground for these rites in the bath where Klytemnestra will murder Agamemnon (1109). There is a hint of nuptial bathing in the fact that Klytemnestra is Agamemnon's "bedmate" (ξύνευνος 1116),[17] suggesting the marriage bed that he will never see again. Having arranged this fatal bath, Klytemnestra also resembles a wife dutifully (if ironically) washing her husband's corpse before burial.[18] A further link with funerary rites lies in the word for the bathtub itself, λέβης (lebēs) (1129), also used by the Chorus for the cinerary urns returned from Troy (Ag. 444), and by Orestes for the urn in which *his* ashes supposedly have been placed (Ch. 686).[19] Introduced by Kassandra, the bath becomes the place for the murder of a husband by his wife and the vessel for the ritual purification of the corpse.

Aeschylus raises the dramatic stakes by having Kassandra draw the Chorus out of dialogue meter and into her dance at the very moment she envisions Agamemnon's death. At the point of shifting from iambic trimeters into dochmiacs (1121), the Chorus exclaim that the seer's prophecy "does not make us happy" (οὔ με φαιδρύνει λόγος 1120). The phrase literally means "your story does not wash me clean," echoing Kassandra's description of Klytemnestra "washing her husband clean in the bath" (λουτροῖσι φαιδρύνασα 1109). Kassandra sweeps the Chorus up into her world both imagistically and lyrically, creating Agamemnon's murder as a conflation of ritual bathing at a wedding and a funeral.

When Kassandra first sings, the Chorus reprove her for calling on Apollo with funeral cries (1075, 1079) rather than with the paeans customarily addressed to the god as healer. A similar inversion occurs when the Herald sounds a "paean to the Furies" (645), a disturbing oxymoron for the news he brings of victory at Troy and the loss of the Greek fleet on the return home.[20] The motif of perverted song is heard again, for the hymn for Paris' and Helen's wedding turns into a funeral dirge (705–16). When Kassandra sings of "dying together" (ξυνθανουμένην 1139) with Agamemnon, the Chorus hear in her lament a "song that is not a song" (1142), "like . . . / . . . a nightingale crying out 'Itys, Itys' for a life flourishing/ with troubles" (1142–46).

Here, the Chorus refer to the myth of Procne and Philomela, a parallel story of marriage and death in which Procne's husband Tereus rapes her sister Philomela and then cuts out her tongue to keep her from accusing him.[21] When Philomela communicates the deed in her weaving, the two sisters take their revenge by killing Tereus' son by Procne, Itys. Transformed into a beautiful-songed nightingale, Procne forever laments her dead son, while the speechless Philomela is turned into a swallow, whose song struck the Greeks as garbled and unmelodic.

By alluding to the Procne myth, Aeschylus evokes the ambiguities of a song that combines lamentation, wedding, and death.[22] In his *Supplices*, the Chorus of women (facing marriage with their cousins) also compare their lament to that of Procne, the "hawk-chased nightingale" (*Supp.* 60–67).[23] The comparison is even more apt for Kassandra in *Agamemnon*,—she is raped by Apollo, forced to "marry" Agamemnon, and finally sings a lament for the destruction of her family and city as she faces her own death. Earlier in the scene, Klytemnestra likens the silent Kassandra to a swallow who sings incomprehensibly (1050–51), the Philomela character in the story. If we are right to connect Kassandra-as-swallow (Philomela) before she sings with Kassandra-as-nightingale (Procne) near the end of her lyric, then Aeschylus has the prophetess take on both female voices of the myth, eliciting our double sympathy. Like Philomela and Procne, Kassandra is the victim of a male world that makes her prophecies unintelligible to those around her and leaves her manifold grief as her most eloquent legacy.

In the last strophe, Kassandra turns to another fatal union, "the marriage, the marriage of Paris,/ destroyer of loved ones" (ἰὼ γάμοι, γάμοι Πάριδος,/ ὀλέθριοι φίλων 1156–57). She recalls the waters of the river Scamander where she grew up (1157–59), contrasting them to the waters of Kokytus and Acheron, the twin rivers of Hades, where she soon will sing her prophetic song (1160–61). Rivers of life and death form a natural contrast, but they also suggest a familiar aspect of wedding and funeral rites. An ancient Athenian source tells us that Trojan maidens bathed in the Scamander before marriage, their version of the nuptial bath.[24] By recollecting the river of her childhood, Kassandra may allude to the Trojan wedding she will never have, even as the fatal bath that awaits her will "consummate" her bridal homecoming with Agamemnon. It is fitting that the Chorus close their lyric dialogue with Kassandra on a funereal note, referring to her song of "woeful, death-dealing sufferings" (μελίζειν πάθη γοερὰ θανατοφόρα 1176).

Just as Kassandra's first utterances in lyric refer to her rape by Apollo, so her first words in dialogue meter place her visions of death firmly within a nuptial context: "No longer will my prophecies peek out/ from under veils, like a newly wedded bride" (καὶ μὴν ὁ χρησμὸς οὐκέτ᾽ ἐκ καλυμμάτων/ ἔσται δεδορκὼς νεογάμου νύμφης δίκην· 1178–79). Comparing herself (and her predictions) to a bride unveiling at the *anakaluptēria*, Kassandra makes explicit what she previously only implied. Her words "will rush toward the sunrise/ like a bright dawn wind that holds a wave/ at the point of breaking" (1180–82), the moment when the water is most transparent. Fraenkel notes that the adjective (λαμπρός) modifying "wind" signifies not only "clear" but also "uncovered," a meaning that fits the image of bridal unveiling.[25] More significantly, as Sissa demonstrates, "le rituel nuptial est, dans tous ses détails, une lutte contre le secret."²⁶ By evoking the wedding ritual, Kassandra highlights her struggle to reveal fully the secrets of the house she has been brought to as an ersatz bride.

Given the many marriage motifs in her lyric, Kassandra's simile does more than compare physical and verbal acts of disclosure. As argued in Appendix A, the *anakaluptēria* may have taken place on the wedding night in the bride's new home and then been "made public" the following morning, suggested here by Kassandra's juxtaposition of bridal unveiling with the clear light of dawn. The imagined ritual action illuminates her own complex transition from innocence to experience, for Kassandra throws off her metaphoric veils just as she later discards the robes she wears as priestess of Apollo (1269–78). With both "undressings" she acknowledges the truth of her situation, that she will enter her new home like a bride and share in rites of sacrifice that, paradoxically, will incorporate her forever into the house of Atreus.

As her revelations unfold, Kassandra draws on other aspects of weddings and funerals. She identifies a chorus (1186) who never leave the house, a band of revelers (κῶμος 1189) who "sing their hymn as they besiege the chambers" (ὑμνοῦσι δ' ὕμνον δώμασιν προσήμεναι 1191). We are encouraged to think of this band of Furies as the celebrants who accompany the wedding procession and sing outside the newlyweds' bedroom through the night.²⁷ However, the Furies' hymn does not end the morning after ("this choir never leaves the house" 1186), nor does it praise a new marriage. Rather, their song denounces the *betrayal* of a wedding, "a brother's bed and the man who trampled it" (πατοῦντι 1193), referring to Thyestes' fatal seduction of Atreus' wife Aerope.

The hymn of the house carries undertones of other "trampled" or twisted marriages—that of Paris and Helen (whose wedding hymn turns to a dirge), Aegisthus and Klytemnestra, and Agamemnon and Kassandra. The same word applied to Atreus' marriage-bed (πατοῦντι) also is used for Paris' abduction of Helen (πατοῖθ' 372), and for Klytemnestra and Aegisthus' slaying of Agamemnon (πατοῦντες 1357). Agamemnon himself tramples the red tapestries (πατῶν 957, πατησμόν 963) as he walks to his fate, and the word (πατεῖς 1298) describes Kassandra's departure when she finally enters the palace to join Agamemnon in death.

Turning her thoughts to Klytemnestra, Kassandra calls her (among other things) a "raging mother of Hades" († θύουσαν Ἅιδου μητέρ' † 1235). Critics believe that the phrase identifies Klytemnestra as mother of the dead Iphigenia, but it also may refer to the groom's mother who traditionally welcomed the newly wedded couple home

(Chapter 1, p. 17 and figure 6). Earlier Agamemnon instructed Klytemnestra to "escort inside with kindness this foreign woman" (τὴν ξένην δὲ πρευμενῶς/ τήνδ᾽ ἐσκόμιζε 950–51), supporting the view that Klytemnestra is asked, metaphorically, to shift roles from wife to mother.[28] Taplin makes the important point that the queen guards the threshold of the palace throughout the play.[29] Here, as the "mother of Hades," she metaphorically guides the young bride through the "gates of Hades" (Ἅιδου πύλας 1291), Kassandra's term for the entrance that leads to her new, and fatal, home.[30]

The conversion of wedding motifs into their funerary counterparts accelerates as the scene draws to a close. A "smell as if from a tomb" (1311) repels Kassandra from the palace and leads her to sing a funeral lament, κωκυτός (*kōkutos*), for herself and Agamemnon (1313).[31] She introduces her last speech in the play with the wish that she might sing a final dirge, θρῆνος (*thrēnos*), on her own behalf (1322–23). Having sung of other marriages to death—the "trampled bed" of the house of Atreus and the fatal union of Paris and Helen—Kassandra enters the palace like a doomed bride intoning her own funeral dirge. When Klytemnestra later celebrates over the corpses, she describes Kassandra's death in just such terms: "Here lies his [Agamemnon's] lover,/ who like a swan sang out a last funeral lament [θανάσιμον γόον]/ for the dead" (1444–46).

Arrival and death, marriage and murder, the portals of the house and the gates of Hades—these are the foci of Kassandra's inspired perceptions. By elaborating so carefully her exit into the palace, Aeschylus contrasts her deeply tragic awareness with that of Agamemnon, who fails to comprehend what is happening when he walks down the red tapestries to his death.[32] The contrast with Aegisthus in the next play is even more striking, for the doomed tyrant enters the palace boasting, "It is hard to fool a man whose eyes are open" (*Ch.* 854). In her dealings with Kassandra, Klytemnestra also shares some of the blind spots of her two husbands. Her rhetorical excess in welcoming Agamemnon fails to include Kassandra, and her later efforts to cajole the Trojan captive to follow in Agamemnon's footsteps are met with an eloquent silence.

Unlike Agamemnon, Aegisthus, and Klytemnestra, Kassandra has her eyes open to the interactions of history, human agency, and fate. She sees clearly what will happen, and in the face of the known and inescapable she reveals a tragic nobility that sets her apart. Kassandra prays for the impending blow to be sure, so that "I close my eyes at last" (1292–94). We recall the unveiling image with which she began—"No more like a newly wedded bride will my prophecies peek out from under veils." With the fall of the sacrificial blade, the "unveiled" Kassandra no longer will look on the visions that her experience and prophetic powers have forced her to see.

The sacrificial imagery surrounding Kassandra's death cannot help but recall an earlier sacrifice in the play, that of Iphigenia, the death of another young woman on the verge of marriage.[33] Iphigenia is of "a maiden's age" (229), one "still a virgin," literally "unbulled" (ἀταύρωτος 245).[34] Kassandra herself uses the comparison (after inverting the gender) to describe Klytemnestra's rape-like assault of Agamemnon: "Keep the bull (ταῦρον) from the cow" (1125–26), for she "strikes with a black horn" (1127–28).[35] Iphigenia's death serves as a "preliminary offering" (προτέλεια 227) for the ships, the same word used earlier for the deaths of the first Greeks and Trojans at Troy, offered for the marriage of Paris and Helen (60–67). Kassandra views her own death as a prior sacrifice, but not to a wedding; she will provide the "preliminary offering" (προσφάγματι 1278) that precedes the burial of Agamemnon.[36]

Kassandra and Iphigenia are joined by even more striking correspondences. Held over the altar, Iphigenia resembles "a picture [γραφαῖς] straining to speak" (242). At the point of death, Kassandra also compares herself to a "picture" (γραφήν 1329) that will be wiped forever from the slate. To silence her curse on the house, Iphigenia is bound and gagged like an animal wearing a "bit" (χαλινῶν 238). Klytemnestra berates Kassandra as an animal who won't wear the bit (χαλινὸν 1066), because the prophetess refuses to answer her questions. When Kassandra finally breaks her silence, the Chorus tell her to stop because she sings inauspicious lamentations to Apollo instead of the customary paeans (1074–75, 1078–79). We recall that Iphigenia sang paeans when she was young, entertaining the men at her father's table (242–46).

Both Iphigenia (238) and Kassandra (1266–72) cast off garments before meeting their fate, metaphoric undressings that signal the transition from an innocent maiden to a bride of death.[37] In a much-debated passage, Iphigenia "pours [or "sheds"] her saffron-dyed [robes] to the ground" (κρόκον βαφὰς [δ'] ἐς πέδον χέουσα 239). Some think that she disrobes, an action similar to Kassandra divesting herself of her prophetic garb at 1264–72.[38] Others claim that the saffron-dyed article Iphigenia discards is a veil, linking her gesture directly to what follows, for she strikes each of her killers with "shafts from the eye" (240).[39] The image of a gagged but unveiled Iphigenia foreshadows Kassandra, who removes her own metaphorical "bridal veil" to speak to the Chorus.

As attractive as this last reading is, it fails to account for the color of Iphigenia's garment. An Athenian audience would have had a hard time hearing of this "saffron-dyed robe" (κρόκου βαφὰς) without thinking of their own cult of Artemis Braurona, especially given that Iphigenia's sacrifice is linked directly *to* Artemis (134–55).[40] At the Brauronia, prepubescent Athenian girls served the goddess as "bears" and dedicated their saffron (κροκωτός) robes around the time of menarche, part of the cultural and ritual preparation for their eventual marriage.[41] In Euripides' *Phoenissae*, Antigone clearly distinguishes her "veil" (κράδεμνα 1490) from her "saffron garment" (στολίδος κρο-κόεσσαν 1491), both of which she removes to mourn over the corpses of her mother and brothers.[42]

Aeschylus leaves open the precise nature of Iphigenia's actions, encouraging a combination of responses from the audience. She discards her saffron robes much as a young girl does at the Brauronia, bringing her death home to the Athenian audience who would have experienced the maturation rites either personally or through their daughters and female relatives.[43] The "bear" Iphigenia shows her readiness for the onset of menstruation, which will take the ironic, and fatal, form of her own blood being shed. She also assumes the role of an ersatz bride who drops her wedding veil only to look into the eyes of her killers, acknowledging that her marriage will not be realized, except insofar as death is a consummation. Iphigenia's actions anticipate those of Kassandra, who speaks of her own bridal unveiling and who removes and tramples her prophetic robes, returning them to Apollo just as Iphigenia gives hers to Artemis.

Once Klytemnestra appears with the corpses of Agamemnon and Kassandra (1372–1576), the link between the prophetess and Iphigenia is complete. The queen relives the murder of her husband, recounting the blows that culminate with the third in honor of "Zeus below the earth, the savior [σωτῆρος] of corpses" (1387). In this striking conflation of domestic and funeral rituals, Klytemnestra transforms the pouring offered *to* the dead into the blood *of* the dead. She then confuses her husband's fatal "self-offering" with those traditionally poured out at a banquet, the third dedicated to Zeus Σωτήρ, the very libation that Iphigenia would follow by a song at her father's banquet (243–46).[44]

With horrible precision Klytemnestra insists that her pre-banquet "libation" is fitting for the corpse of Agamemnon, a pouring of blood like the one that Agamemnon himself mixed and drank to the dregs (1395–98).[45] If Agamemnon's death provides both the occasion for, and substance of, this libation, then Kassandra is the appetizer for the banquet that follows. Her death, as Klytemnestra puts it, brings "an added relish ["side-dish"] to my bed" († εὐνῆς παροψώνημα τῆς ἐμῆς χλιδῆς † 1447). Earlier Kassandra predicted that she would become the sacrificial victim at Agamemnon's grave (1277–78), and here she provides—in the logic of ritual perversion—part of the flesh consumed at the funeral banquet in his honor.[46] Aeschylus weaves the motif of perverted feasting through the trilogy, but at this point the confusions between banquet and funeral libation, blood and wine, grave offering and sacrificial feast, serve to connect Agamemnon's slaughter of Iphigenia with Klytemnestra's sacrifice of Kassandra.[47]

By linking Kassandra and Iphigenia, Aeschylus brings together the manifold damages wreaked separately by Agamemnon and Klytemnestra, and the audience views their respective fates accordingly. We understand that Agamemnon has to die, in part because of his sacrifice of Iphigenia.[48] Similarly, although the Chorus bewail the dead Agamemnon without mentioning Kassandra (as she herself predicts, 1326–29), Klytemnestra cannot get the Trojan prophetess out of her mind, and neither can we. It is Klytemnestra's murder of Kassandra, not her slaying of Agamemnon, that turns the audience against her. As a result, neither the tapestry scene (with all its theatricality) nor the moment of Agamemnon's death marks the turning point of the play. That occurs in the Kassandra scene, where the prophetess comes to personify the very processes of the trilogy, working out the complex interconnections between past, present, and future.[49]

As we have seen, a good deal of our emotional identification with Kassandra springs from the confusion of her "marriage" and her death, and Aeschylus works this idea through the rest of the trilogy. The first 650 lines of *Choephoroi* are set at the tomb of Agamemnon, and the play begins with belated funeral rites, offered first by Orestes and then by Elektra and the Chorus.[50] Recognizable elements in Athenian funeral practice include the mourners' dedicating a lock of hair (*Ch.* 7, 226), dressing in black (11), pouring offerings at the tomb (87, 538), dedicating garlands (93), lamenting the dead with wailing (γόος [goos] 322, 330, 449, 502) and cries of grief (kōkutos, 150), singing the funeral dirge (thrēnos 334–35, 342), and striking their bodies and tearing their clothing in grief (22–31, 425–28). Orestes regrets that he wasn't present at the ekphora to stretch out his right hand in the gesture of farewell (8–9, echoed at 429–32), and Elektra promises her father that she will offer future pourings and tendance at the grave (486–88).

That these offerings will come from Elektra's "inheritance" or "dowry" (παγκληρίας 486)[51] and will be dedicated on her wedding day (487) serve to connect funeral with marriage rituals. So, too, does the fact that Elektra prays to Persephone (490), the archetypal bride of Hades, for victory. The nexus of wedding-to-death motifs expands if we accept Heyse's and Wecklein's τυχεῖν [from Hermann] με γαμβροῦ θεῖσαν Ἀιλίσθωι μόρον at line 482, meaning "that I find a bridegroom after giving Aegisthus his death blow."[52] Taking a husband seems appropriate for Elektra only *after* she kills the illicit lover of her mother, the corrupter of a royal marriage.[53]

The Chorus of libation bearers develop the connection between marriage and death by presenting mythical examples of female passion that leads to destruction, singling out the perversion of the marriage union (599–601). Their priamel culminates with the women of Lemnos (631–36), who killed their husbands because they took Thracian concubines.[54] The parable points not only to Klytemnestra's murder of Agamemnon, but also to one of her reasons for it, jealous anger over his liaison with Kassandra (*Ag.* 1438–47). Critics often stress the importance of Iphigenia's death in motivating Klytemnestra's revenge, but they fail to acknowledge Klytemnestra's intense interest in her husband's sexual transgressions.

The funeral motifs that dominate the opening of *Choephoroi* reappear with the disguised Orestes at the door of the palace. Announcing his own death, he informs Klytemnestra that Orestes' ashes are waiting for burial in a bronze urn (λέβης 686), the same word used earlier for Agamemnon's bathtub (*Ag.* 1129). At the news of Orestes' death, the old Nurse enters with "grief as her unhired companion" (733), a reference to the practice of employing professional mourners for a funeral. Implied is the contrast between the Nurse's natural grief and that of Klytemnestra, which strikes the Chorus as feigned. In the same way Aeschylus juxtaposes Orestes' offerings at Agamemnon's grave (given out of filial love, 1–9) with those Klytemnestra sends out of fear (employing Elektra and the Chorus as intermediaries, 22–48).

In the climactic confrontation between mother and son, the play returns symbolically to the opening scene, for Klytemnestra finds that Orestes "resembles a tomb" and her appeals to him are like "a vain threnody" (ἔοικα θρηνεῖν ζῶσα πρὸς τύμβον μάτην 926). Her son comes to represent the grave of Agamemnon where Klytemnestra had failed to appease the spirits of vengeance. A marriage to death seems the fitting punishment for her crime, and Orestes vows that she will lie in the same grave with her lover Aegisthus, lest she betray him in death as she betrayed Agamemnon when he was alive (*Ch.* 894–95, again at 905–6).

After the murders, the paired bodies of Aegisthus and Klytemnestra provide a visual counterpart to the oath that the two lovers swore (ξυνώμοσαν), namely to kill Agamemnon and then die together (ξυνθανεῖσθαι 977–79).[55] Kassandra uses the same word (ξυνθανουμένην, *Ag.* 1139) for her impending death at the side of Agamemnon, and Klytemnestra refers to Kassandra as Agamemnon's ξύνευνος or "bedmate" (1442). The ξυν-prefix (suggesting "coupling") provides the lexical equivalent to the physical act of lovemaking and signals their eternal "togetherness" in the grave—marriage to death with a vengeance.

Along with the two bodies, Orestes displays the robes that trapped Agamemnon in the bath. He wonders whether to call them "a net for a wild beast, or a shroud for a corpse/ on its bier" (998–99), confusing the means of death with the covering for the dead.[56] These references to the murders in the previous play, combined with the fact that the murderer stands over his victims, recall the scene where Klytemnestra exults over the corpses of Agamemnon and *his* lover, Kassandra. In both plays an adulterous couple lies wedded in death, while the murderer projects onto their corpses an image of sexual union that motivated (at least in part) the act of vengeance.

Although there is much talk of wives, husbands, and parents in *Eumenides*, marriage and funeral motifs are less prominent. This is understandable in a play where gods and furies take the stage, and where the action shifts from Agamemnon's *oikos* to the sanctuary at Delphi and then to the public world of Athens. Nonetheless, the issue of marriage remains central. The Chorus of Furies are old unwedded maidens (παρθένος 69), and the virgin goddess Athena, although she praises the male in all things, refuses to countenance marriage for herself (τὸ δ᾽ ἄρσεν αἰνῶ πάντα, πλὴν γάμου τυχεῖν 737). Apollo, on the other hand, insists that marital connections take precedence over ties of blood, signaling men's superiority over women. Moreover, he argues in sophistic fashion that the father is the mother of the child. Women are not really parents because Athena (who arose from the head of Zeus) was born without a mother. Some critics claim that Apollo's speech (657–66) represents Aeschylus' view, and so they conclude that the *Oresteia* not only manifests embedded cultural prejudices against women but actually champions misogyny.[57] However, given the importance and interconnection of wedding and funeral rituals in the trilogy, especially in the Kassandra scene, are such conclusions justified?

To begin with, Apollo's own birth contradicts his argument that mothers play a subsidiary role as parents. The famous labor pains of Leto on the island of Delos and Apollo's eventual delivery were celebrated in the Homeric *Hymn to Apollo*, a fact to which the Furies refer when they speak of him as "child of Leto" (ὁ Λατοῦς γὰρ ἴ-/ νίς 323–24). Moreover, the position that mothers were not really parents was neither the popular nor the legal view in the fifth century. The marriage of *homometric* siblings was expressly forbidden in Athens as incestuous, whereas a man could marry a sister by the same father as long as they had different mothers.[58] The Periklean Citizenship Law of 451 limited Athenian citizenship to individuals *both* of whose parents were Athenians.[59] And, not surprisingly, Greek literature gives eloquent testimony to the idea that men and women had children "in common."[60]

If mothers aren't parents, then why does Aeschylus use the pregnant hare devoured with her unborn children as an image for the destruction that results from the Trojan War (*Ag.* 114–20)? Why should Klytemnestra lament the sacrifice of her daughter Iphigenia? Finally, if Apollo's position is right, then Orestes' murder of Klytemnestra raises no serious questions about blood-ties, pollution, and matricide; the Furies have no business haunting Orestes, nor has Orestes any reason to feel haunted; and the dramatic heart of the trilogy—the *Choephoroi*—suffers cardiac arrest.

On closer examination, even the language that Apollo uses to denigrate women proves to do just the opposite. If women are not parents but the *trophos* ("nurse") of the seed, as Apollo argues (*Eu.* 659), then the god inadvertently claims a *cultural* (in addition to a biological) function for the mother with regard to her child.[61] By denying mothers at least an equal role in biological reproduction, Apollo unconsciously champions the place of women on the "culture side" of the nature/culture polarity, a place and role that some scholars claim was denied systematically to Athenian women.[62]

Apollo's biological argument that a woman receives and holds the alien seed of her husband "as stranger/hostess to a stranger/ guest" (ἡ δ᾽ ἅπερ ξένη 660) reappears in slightly different guise in Euripides' *Alkestis* (Chapter 6 pp. 92–95). Exploring the interrelationship between host/guest and husband/wife, Herakles (with conscious irony) disparages Alkestis, the very woman, stranger, and wife whom he restores to Admetus to save his *oikos*. In *Eumenides*, however, the ironies of Apollo's speech go unobserved by the speaker. The god denies women a role as parents of their own children, while unconsciously championing the importance of women as providers of nurture and acculturation.

Apollo further compromises his position by offering a bribe to Athena and her city (667–73). In her response, Athena specifically warns the people of Athens not to allow the court to be corrupted by bribes (693–95, 704), advice the jurors apparently follow as the vote splits evenly between conviction and acquittal.[63] Finally, Apollo's unmarked departure from the theater (at line 753? at 774?) is the ancient equivalent of "slinking off-stage."[64] Silent and unnoticed, Apollo exits as if he knew his argument and his presence were of little ultimate significance in a court where humans must make the difficult decisions. In sum, Apollo's character and his argument against women radiate with something less than the pure white light of Aeschylean approval.

But what remains of the charge of Aeschylean misogyny? In exploring the role and position of women, one of the central concerns of the trilogy, Aeschylus reflects many of the prejudices of his day. However, a more complex and interesting picture emerges than the one that concludes (for example) that Aeschylus "refuses the metaphor of earth and female body, supporting Apollo's view that the female body is not the source of life but, rather, that it is receptacle, a temporary container for the father's seed."[65] We have noted some difficulties in equating Apollo's biological views with those of Aeschylus, and similar qualifications may apply to generalizations about a larger order of cultural misogyny.

The trilogy begins with the "brides" Helen and Klytemnestra shattering the wedding union and bringing violence out of marriage. The attendant "weddings to death" of the bridelike Iphigenia and Kassandra bring home to the audience the cost of that violence, both the destruction of the war wreaked by Agamemnon and the domestic havoc perpetrated by Klytemnestra. We recall that the queen celebrates her triumph by comparing Agamemnon's death-blood to the life-giving rain that falls on the crops in the spring (Ag. 1388–92), an inversion of the forces of life and death that continues until the transformation of the Furies in Eumenides.[66] In a similar way, the libations intended by Klytemnestra to placate Agamemnon's spirit are turned to opposite effect in the kommos of Choephoroi—pourings for the dead give way to the bloodshed of the living, the murders of Aegisthus and Klytemnestra.[67] At the acquittal of Orestes, the Furies in turn threaten to "release from their heart unbearable drops on the land" (782–84, 812–14), pouring out an eternal spring of death against the crops and children of Athens. Once persuaded by Athena to accept a home and honors in her city, however, the Furies change from daemons of death (780–87 = 810–17, 830–31) into spirits of rebirth and regeneration (903–12, 921–26, 938–48, 956–67), the overseers of weddings and childbirth (834–36). They reunite the ideas of life-giving nature and life-giving marriage, singing their blessings on the crops and the land (921–26, 938–47), and on the union of man and woman in wedlock (956–60).[68]

Far from denying significance to women as wives, mothers, and contributors to the prosperity of the polis, the trilogy closes with a ringing affirmation of the importance of marriage and offspring, a celebration that incorporates the Furies into the city and its rituals.

As Loraux reminds us, "La victoire d'Oreste n'est pas le dernier mot de la trilogie, et . . . le principe féminin y conquiert finalement place dans la cité: la tragédie n'est pas une tribune de propagande."[69] The Furies' traditional power over blood-ties and bloodshed now expands to include prerogatives of marriage (that cross bloodlines) and childbirth (that continue them), breaking through the destructive pattern of marriage to death that features so prominently earlier in the trilogy. To be sure, the process of restoration and the reunion of male and female is only barely achieved. No easy solution could follow such horrifying acts of bloodshed without trivializing the intricate causal network that makes the murders of Agamemnon and Klytemnestra necessary.

Aeschylus emphasizes the ongoing nature of the struggle and the need to accommodate more than a single perspective, by having Athena sound increasingly like the Furies at the close of the play, even as the Furies abandon their refrain of vengeance for the blessings of the *Eumenides*. Recall that their post-verdict confrontation is a battle between two contending modes of expression. After Orestes' exit, the Chorus of Furies burst out in angry lyrics, followed by a conciliatory speech (in normal iambic trimeter) from Athena. That pattern is repeated four times (778–891), until the Furies finally accept Athena's offer and join her in dialogue meter, making the transition to Eumenides ("Kind Spirits"). At the end of the play, however, the pattern is reversed. While the Chorus sing in full lyric their blessings on Athens and her people, Athena moves from dialogue meter into anapests, as if drawn toward the Furies' mode of expression. In her "half-lyric," she lauds their retributive impulses and praises their vengeful intractability as both necessary and good for the city. The Furies are "spirits mighty, implacable, quick to anger," as they "order the lives of men" (928–31). "In the fearsomeness of their faces," Athena adds, "I see great gains for my people" (990–91). In her counterpoint to the benisons of the Eumenides, Athena echoes the Furies earlier in the play: "There are times when fear is good/ watching over the minds of men . . ." (517–18). As Harris concludes, the Furies accept Athena's offer "not simply because they are bribed to bless rather than curse, but because they are allowed to remain essentially unchanged."[70]

The intricate relationship between performative modes and contrapuntal voices underlines the fundamental nature of the struggle that Aeschylus chose to dramatize. His trilogy remains of signal importance to our understanding the complex dialectic between men and women, *oikos* and *polis*, justice and vengeance, kinship and civic loyalties that emerged in fifth-century Athens. The *Oresteia* seems to suggest that the best that can be hoped for is a provisional resolution of these tensions, one that must be fought for again and again. The interconnections between marriages and deaths, between wedding motifs and funeral rites, play a crucial role in bringing that perception to its full, and fully problematic, dramatic life.

Chapter 4

THE BRIDE AND GROOM OF DEATH

SOPHOKLES' *ANTIGONE*

IF KASSANDRA is the unveiled bride in *Agamemnon*, then the heroine of Sophokles' *Antigone* is a full-fledged bride of Hades. Scholars acknowledge the prominence of the "marriage to death" motif in the play but frequently in a dismissive fashion: "It cannot be maintained that by this metaphor and the motifs related to it the meaning of the play is, so to speak, summed up or exhausted. . . . For thereby nothing or, at least, nothing much, is said about the great and central themes. . . ."[1] Few would claim that focusing on the bride of Hades *topos* will "exhaust" *Antigone*. However, we can recover some of the play's sheer theatrical power by exploring the importance of this motif as a structuring principle, understanding the wedding-funeral polarity as part and parcel of the more celebrated oppositions in the drama.

Unlike the *Iliad* and Sophokles' *Ajax*, where the importance of burying the dead gradually dominates the action, *Antigone* emphasizes the issue from the start. In her opening dialogue with Ismene, Antigone proclaims her willingness to die in order to bury Polyneikes: "As a loved one I will lie with him, a loved one" (φίλη μετ' αὐτοῦ κείσομαι, φίλου μέτα 73). The exchange continues in this strangely erotic vein:

> ISMENE: You have a warm heart for chilling [ψυχροῖσι] tasks.
> ANTIGONE: But I know that I will be pleasing to those whom I ought to bring pleasure [ἁδεῖν].
> ISMENE: If you can, but you are in love [ἐρᾷς] with the impossible.[2] (88–90)

After she is arrested for attempting the burial, Antigone again employs the discourse of passion to justify her actions: "Hades longs for [ποθεῖ] these rites" (519).[3] As her dialogue with Kreon continues, the erotic vocabulary opens up to include political and ethical concerns reflecting the conflicting positions of the two antagonists:

> KR. An enemy is never a friend, not even when he dies.
> (οὔτοι ποθ' οὑχθρός, οὐδ' ὅταν θάνηι, φίλος.)
> AN. It is not my nature to join in hate, but in love.
> (οὔτοι συνέχθειν, ἀλλὰ συμφιλεῖν ἔφυν.)

KR. Then go below now, if you must love, and love
the dead. While I am alive, no woman will rule me.
(κάτω νυν ἐλθοῦσ', εἰ φιλητέον, φίλει
κείνους· ἐμοῦ δὲ ζῶντος οὐκ ἄρξει γυνή.) 522–25

Kreon's politically oriented definition of friend, φίλος (*philos*), and enemy, ἐχθρός (*echthros*), is strikingly at odds with Antigone's traditional understanding of *philos* as kin, someone linked by blood and hence ultimately not subject to the political category of "friend or foe."[4] Antigone maintains the Greek sense of family as the primary community against Kreon's novel, transpolitical standard that condemns anyone who considers *philos* more important than country (182–83).[5]

The new ruler introduces his political criteria by comparing the city to a ship that carries everyone, making its survival more important than any individual on board (187–90).[6] However, Kreon's estimation of the *polis* is not as objective as it sounds, for the hold of his "ship of state" has a special place for male privilege and power: "If she [Antigone] undermines my authority with impunity, then I am no longer the man; she is" (484–85). Kreon later insists, "While I am alive, no woman will rule me" (525). His zealous belief that loyalties of blood must be subordinated to those of the *polis* proves, on examination, to mean the subjection of the citizenry to his personal authority as a male.

For Kreon, women's inferior position in the public sphere should be mirrored in the marriage relationship. When Ismene reminds him that by sentencing Antigone he condemns his own son's fiancée (568), Kreon is unmoved, boasting that "there are other arable fields" (ἀρώσιμοι γὰρ χατέρων εἰσὶν γύαι 569) for Haimon to plow. The trope compares women to the earth that must be dominated, a common image for (conjugal) intercourse, and one that echoes the Athenian formula that marriage is undertaken for "the sowing of legitimate children."[7]

Far from expressing concern for marriage and offspring, however, Kreon manifests an excessive desire for political control, particularly in his idée fixe that women must be excluded from public influence and confined to the private, domestic sphere. If not, they become subversives, rebellious citizens who "shake their heads in secret and won't hold their necks, as they should, under the yoke" (291–92). Kreon again employs an image of control when he warns Antigone that "a small bit can tame the wildest horse" (477–78), and he locks Ismene and Antigone in the *oikos* so they will not "roam free" (579) like wild animals. In both conception and practice, political rule for

Kreon takes the form of a tyrant dominating his people and a man subjugating women.[8]

As a manifestation of his political power, Kreon denies Antigone her traditional role in preparing her brother's corpse for burial, including bathing, dressing, and mourning the body (26–30).[9] In her final speech Antigone characterizes these rituals as obligations she owes categorically to her natal family. She recalls how she buried her parents Oedipus and Jokasta, washing and dressing their corpses and pouring offerings at the tomb (ἐπεὶ θανόντας . . . ὑμᾶς ἐγὼ/ ἔλουσα κἀκόσμησα κἀπιτυμβίους/ χοὰς ἔδωκα 900–902).[10] Barred from performing these duties for Polyneikes, Antigone finds herself stripped of wedding rites as well. Choosing a punishment to match his misogyny, Kreon condemns her to the maimed ritual of a marriage to death. It is dramatically fitting that the tyrant delivers this sentence in the presence of Antigone's fiancé, his own son Haimon.

When the young man enters, the Chorus wonder if he comes "grieving/ over the death of his affianced Antigone,/ in anguish at the loss [lit. 'deception'] of his marriage bed" (627–30). Instead of dwelling on the personal costs of Kreon's policy, however, Haimon stresses its *public* consequences, assuring his father that no marriage is worth more to him than Kreon's "good governance" (638). With that in mind, Haimon is compelled to report that the Theban citizens consider Antigone a heroine, not a criminal (688–700). He implores his father to swerve from his destructive course—to bend like a tree in a torrent, not remain rigid and be uprooted (712–14); to slacken sails in a gale so as not to risk capsizing (715–17); to have the wisdom to listen to sound counsel, even if it comes from a youth (719–23). Kreon rejects the advice out of hand, warning Haimon not to lose himself in the pleasures of a woman: "the embrace grows cold [ψυχρὸν]/ when an evil wife is bedmate" (650–51). The image of a frigid embrace (recalling the "chilling task" at 88, above) leads Kreon to command that Antigone "go marry someone in Hades" (653–54).

Having made explicit her fate as a bride of death, Kreon berates his son for surrendering to a "woman/wife" (the word γυνή is repeated), accusing him of "fighting on the side of a woman" (740), of being "bested by a woman" (746), of "pleading only for that [woman]" (748), and, perhaps worst of all, of "being slave to a woman" (756, Jebb's lineation). Kreon's wrath at Haimon's attachment to the feminine brings death and weddings together in his mind, and again he pronounces Antigone's sentence: "She will die straightaway before your eyes, at the side of her bridegroom" (760–61).

In the course of this scene, Haimon emerges as a most sympathetic character. Loyal to his father and ruler, gracious under attack, admirable in his self-control, full of sound advice, Haimon is a model son and citizen. To his father's charge that he has allied himself with a woman, he responds pointedly, "Yes, if *you* are a woman (εἴπερ γυνὴ σύ), for my concern is for you" (741). There is more here than a clever retort, for Haimon suggests that he is siding with his father *by* siding with Antigone. If Kreon rejects her (or so Haimon implies), then the ruler himself will suffer, for she occupies a valued, and valuable, position in the *polis* (692–700, 733).

In the logic of the dramatic events, Haimon's apparently counterfactual hypothesis—"if *you* are a woman [but of course you are not]"—points to an unrealized connection between men and women that Haimon himself seems to embody. Kreon needs to be more like the "womanly" Haimon if he is to rule well, but instead he denies women their place in the state. As Taplin puts it, "Antigone is surely the model of the woman who sees right through the sterility and the destructive argumentation of male force. And Haimon might yet prove the model of the man who can speak the same language as Antigone."[11]

But ruling as a process of inclusion is precisely what Kreon rejects, substituting for it a conception of power as personal possession: "Must I rule for others or for myself?" (736) and "Doesn't the city belong to the one who rules?" (738). In frustration, Haimon draws the logical conclusion that his father "would rule well over a desert land [ἐρήμης], alone [μόνος]" (739). His judgment proves strangely prophetic, for Kreon decides to bury Antigone alive in "some desert place [ἐρῆμος] where no mortal goes" (773), where she will be free to "honor Death" (777–80). The tyrant banishes his subject to solitary confinement in the only environment over which, according to his son, he is fit to rule.[12] By the end of the play, Kreon will find himself presiding over just such a desolate world, alone among the dead.

The dramatic fulfillment of similar figures of speech occurs at key moments in the play, but nowhere more effectively than when Haimon joins Antigone in a "marriage to death." After Kreon pronounces that Antigone will die at the side of her groom, Haimon abruptly departs. When we next hear of him, we learn that *he* has killed himself at the side of his bride. Explaining the clash of father and son, the Chorus blame human resistance to Eros for stirring up strife "between those who share blood," (ξύναιμον 793–94).[13] The word echoes Kreon's dismissive comment that Antigone take her appeal to Zeus ξύναιμον, "the lord of shared blood" (658–59). On both occasions ξύναιμον suggests Haimon's name, with the common root αἶμα (*haima*), "blood." The sanguinary play on words turns deadly when the Messenger reports the young man's suicide: Αἵμων ὄλωλεν·

αὐτόχειρ δ᾽ αἱμάσσεται 1175, literally "the one named Blood has died, his blood shed by his own hand." Name and action merge, as Haimon is caught in the crosscurrents of the shared blood that ties him to Kreon and the shared bed that would unite him with Antigone.

Haimon's death confirms the Chorus's fear that marital passions ("the longing/ from the eyes of a bedded/ bride" 795–97) can dissolve even the closest bonds of blood. The Chorus allude to the tension between the centrifugal demands of exogamous marriage and the centripetal forces of natural kinship, opposing tendencies never fully resolved in fifth-century Athens.[14] Indeed, Antigone blames her desperate fate on marriages that lie at both extremes (858–71). She first considers a wedding diametrically opposed to the outward-looking, kin-fragmenting liaisons feared by the Chorus, namely the accursed union of her father (and half-brother) Oedipus and mother Jokasta. Self-reflexive in the extreme, that marriage joined bloodlines *already* the same, a kind of hyper-endogamy of monstrous proportions. Antigone contrasts her parents' incestuous marriage with the one that her brother Polyneikes made with the daughter of the Argive Adrastos. This wedding of ostensible enemies—Argive and Theban—proved so "hyper-exogamous" that it led to the Argive invasion of Thebes, the deaths of Polyneikes and Eteokles, Kreon's edict that the traitor must not be buried, and, ultimately, Antigone's own marriage to death.[15]

In her final scene (806–943), Antigone appears as a bride to be escorted to her new home, Hades. Here, Sophokles follows the tripartite pattern of the Greek wedding outlined in Chapter 1—*enguē* (betrothal), *ekdosis* (preparations culminating in the move to the groom's house), and *gamos* (consummation, preceded by the bride's unveiling). As the last male relative of Oedipus and Jokasta, Kreon acts as Antigone's (and Haimon's) *kurios*.[16] He has arranged her marriage, telling his son to "let her go marry someone in Hades" (μέθες/ τὴν παῖδ᾽ ἐν Ἅιδου τήνδε νυμφεύειν τινί 653–54), a kind of *enguē* with the powers below.[17] As for the transferal of the bride to her new home, the Chorus speak of Antigone's "final journey to the bridal chamber (θάλαμος) where all end in sleep (παγκοίτην)" (804–5). However, this *ekdosis* is without "wedding hymns" (813) "nor any bridal song to crown the nuptials" (οὔτ᾽ ἐπὶ νυμ-/ φείοις πώ μέ τις ὕμνος ὕ-/ μνησεν 814–16). Antigone's procession is to the underworld, where she "will marry Death" (Ἀχέροντι νυμφεύσω 816).

Antigone reiterates the fact that her wedding and funeral are one and the same: "Oh tomb, bridal chamber, my ever-wakeful/ dwelling underground, I go to you/ to join my own kind, where Persephone/ receives the vast number of the dead" (891–94).[18] Echoing the Chorus, Antigone conflates her bridal *exagōgē* ("leading out") with the *ekphora* of her corpse to the grave: "I walk my last road. . . . Hades, where all end in sleep, leads me still living to the river of Death" (τὰν νεάταν ὁδὸν/ στείχουσαν . . . μ' ὁ παγ-/ κοίτας Ἅιδας ζῶσαν ἄγει/ τὰν Ἀχέροντος/ ἀκτάν 807–13). She is like a traveler who never arrives, caught in the liminal state between living maiden and dead bride: "I go to the tomb-like enclosure of the grave" (848–49) as "a resident alien, neither among the living nor the dead" (850–52). Antigone again compares herself to a resident alien amongst her dead kin, one who is "cursed, without a proper marriage" (867–68). She repeats this refrain in the speech that follows her *kommos*: "And now forcefully by the hand Kreon leads me,/ denied a marriage bed, a marriage song, a proper wedding,/ a share in the raising of children" (916–18). Without family or friends to lament her departure (881–82, 919–20), Antigone sings for herself the very wedding hymn and funeral dirge that Kreon has denied her.

If Kreon as Antigone's *kurios* has "betrothed" her to death, and if the journey to her place of entombment constitutes a perverse bridal procession, then there remains the *telos* of this twisted wedding, the *anakaluptēria* (unveiling) followed by the *gamos* (sexual union). Both take place symbolically in the Messenger's account of the events in Antigone's marriage chamber/tomb. Addressing the Chorus and Eurydike (wife of Kreon and mother of Haimon), the Messenger reports that Kreon performed the belated burial rites for Polyneikes, then raced to the "hollow, stone-bedded bridal chamber of the young girl and Hades" (λιθόστρωτον κόρης/ νυμφεῖον Ἅιδου κοῖλον 1204–5). "Funeral cries" (κωκύματα) emanate from "the inner chamber that lacks burial rites" (ἀκτέριστον ἀμφὶ παστάδα 1206–7).[19] There he discovers Haimon mourning over the corpse of Antigone, who lies strangled in the "linen noose" (μιτώδει σινδόνος 1222) by which she has hung herself. Some commentators believe that the σινδών refers to Antigone's veil, opening up the possibility that she "unveiled" herself before taking her life.[20] In Sophokles' *Eurypylos* and Aeschylus' *Nereiads*, the word σινδών also is used for the "shroud" or "winding sheet" of a corpse.[21] The instrument of Antigone's hanging suggests both the veil that reveals the bride and the funeral shroud that conceals the dead.

After her *anakaluptēria*, Antigone achieves symbolic physical union with her fiancé. Haimon lies on Antigone's corpse and "embraces her, bemoaning the loss of his bride and marriage bed" (τὸν δ' ἀμφὶ μέσσηι περιπετῆ προσκείμενον,/ εὐνῆς ἀποιμώζοντα τῆς κάτω φθορὰν/ . . . καὶ τὸ δύστηνον λέχος 1223–25). When Kreon interrupts the scene, begging his son to leave the world of the dead, Haimon directs a wild blow at his father before turning the sword on himself.

The description of his death is erotically charged, suicide as a form of sexual consummation. Haimon drives the sword into his body, then "embraces/ the maiden softly in his arms/ and, panting for breath, releases a sharp gush/ as drops of blood fall on her pale cheek" (ἐς δ' ὑγρὸν/ ἀγκῶν᾽ ἔτ᾽ ἔμφρων παρθένωι προσπτύσσεται· καὶ φυσιῶν ὀξεῖαν ἐκβάλλει ῥοὴν/ λευκῆι παρειᾶι φοινίου σταλάγματος 1236–39). The details—a lover's embrace, heavy breathing, the gush of liquid, drops of blood, pale white skin—suggest both the seminal emission of male orgasm and the defloration of a virgin on her wedding night.[22]

For his part, Kreon has shrunk from all-powerful tyrant and authoritative *kurios* to a voyeur, helplessly gazing on the intimacies of his son's death. In their first confrontation, Kreon reminded Haimon that there were other fields to plow and urged him to "spit Antigone away" (653). In the cave Haimon answers his father's pleas by spitting in his face (1232). Haimon then makes good Kreon's prediction that "you will never marry her while she is still alive" (750), carrying out his own threat that "in dying she will destroy someone else" (751). The final tableau in the sepulchral bridal chamber recapitulates Antigone and Haimon's wedding to death: "Wretched corpse lies with corpse, fulfilling marriage rites in the house of Hades" (κεῖται δὲ νεκρὸς περὶ νεκρῶι, τὰ νυμφὰ/ τέλη λαχὼν δείλαιος ἔν γ᾽ Ἅιδου δόμοις 1240–41).[23]

On hearing the Messenger's news, Eurydike slips silently back into the palace—her abrupt departure mirrors that of Haimon at 765—where she follows her son's example by stabbing herself with a sword. Unmentioned before her entrance at 1180, Eurydike appears late in the play and speaks the fewest lines of any named character in extant tragedy.[24] Nonetheless, her actions repay close examination. The timing of her introduction and the speed with which she is dispatched contribute to the sense that Kreon's *oikos* is collapsing almost faster than events can be reported. But there are other, thematic reasons for the peculiarities of her entrance, exit, and summary death. That Eurydike appears only to hear the Messenger's speech and then returns to the palace without a word, underlines the fact that she plays no part in initiating the tragic conflicts of the play. However, her innocence (like that of Haimon) does not free her from suffering, for Kreon's inflexibility destroys loved ones (*philoi*) and family (*oikos*) as if from within.

To emphasize the inner springs of destruction, Sophokles uses the same "self-directed" αὐτός compound for the deaths of Haimon and Eurydike—"with his own hand he bloodies himself" (αὐτόχειρ δ' αἱμάσσεται 1175), and she stabs herself "with her own hand (αὐτόχειρ 1315). Similar compounds describe Oedipus' "self-detection" (αὐτοφώρων 51) and "self-blinding" (ἀράξας αὐτὸς αὐτουργῶι χερί 52); Antigone's incestuous, "self-generated" birth (αὐτογέννητ᾽ 864–65); Eteokles' and Polyneikes' internecine struggle (αὐτοκτονοῦντε 56, πληγέντες αὐτόχειρι 172); Antigone's "self-sibling" relationship (αὐτάδελφον) with Ismene (1) and Polyneikes (503, 696); and Antigone's "self-accomplished" actions in burying Polyneikes (αὐτόχειρα 306) and her parents (αὐτόχειρ 900), motivated by her "own set of principles" (αὐτόνομος 821) and "self-will" (αὐτόγνωτος 875). By applying the αὐτός-prefix to the suicides of Kreon's wife and son, Sophokles links their fate to that of the accursed, "self-generated" couple Oedipus and Jokasta, and also to their admirable if self-destructive daughter, Antigone.

As reported by the second Messenger, Eurydike cursed her husband, charging him with murdering his sons, and then crowned her malediction by committing suicide at the altar dedicated to Zeus *Herkeios*, Zeus "of the household enclosure" (1301–5).[25] Eurydike signals the death of the family by polluting the locus of domestic cult, which normally received offerings on behalf of the *oikos*.[26] Kreon refers to that altar specifically when he sentences Antigone:

> Although she is my sister's child, closer in blood
> than all who gather at the altar of Zeus Herkeios,
> still she and her blood-sister [ξύναιμος] will not escape
> the ultimate penalty. (486–89)

Later, Kreon tells Haimon to let Antigone make her fruitless appeals to "Zeus ξύναιμος," the "lord of shared blood" (658–59), the same Zeus worshiped in the household. Neither *philos* nor *oikos* seem to matter to the master of the house. As a result, Eurydike, the "all-mother" (παμμήτωρ 1282) and overseer of key aspects of domestic cult, sacrifices herself at the family altar.

By introducing Eurydike only to have her learn of her son's death and kill herself at the household altar, Sophokles highlights the centrality of the *oikos* and the essential role played by women in guaranteeing its survival. In her final speech, Antigone herself laments that she has been denied this experience: "I will have no share/ in married life or in motherhood and raising children" (917–18). Although these sentiments have troubled critics who see Antigone only as a rebel (leading some to advocate wholesale excision of the speech), we should remember that Antigone approaches the corpse of Polyneikes maternally, "crying bitterly/ like a mother bird when she sees her nest/ orphaned, empty of its nestlings" (423–25). It is both dramatically fitting and emotionally compelling that Antigone turns her thoughts to the human connections that have been denied her, what

Murnaghan describes as the "loss of a full life containing not only close and properly honored family ties but the experiences of marriage and motherhood as well."[27]

In this light, Eurydike appears as a maternally realized "double" of Antigone, a wife and "all-mother" (1282) who meets a comparable end. And yet Eurydike is the last person we would expect to associate with Sophokles' heroine. In the brief glimpse we get of the queen, she is the model of female and matronly propriety: quiet, self-effacing, bound to the *oikos*, busy with ritual matters reserved for women, loathe to interfere in the public world of men. Eurydike explains her boldness in appearing at all, having unbolted the doors of the women's quarters so that she might offer prayers to Athena. Hearing the outcry of the household, she faints in the arms of her handmaids, and only then does she go outside to hear the Messenger in person.[28] Contrast Antigone, whose very first action in the play is to draw Ismene "outside the gates of the house" (18). Antigone willfully disobeys Kreon's proclamation regarding Polyneikes, and she challenges the ruler to his face, leading Kreon to lock her and Ismene "inside the house where they will/ behave as women must and not roam freely" (578–79). In both their spatial and political realities, Antigone and Eurydike seem poles apart.

However, Eurydike withdraws indoors at the news of Haimon's death (1246–50) only to emerge from the house with a vengeance. "She is there for you to see," the Chorus tell Kreon; "she is no longer in the inner recesses [of the house]" (1293). Appearing on the *ek-kuklēma*, Eurydike's corpse interrupts Kreon's dirge for Haimon, a shocking intrusion into her husband's world.[29] Draped over the household altar, her body provides striking evidence of the ritual perversion and pollution that has ravaged the *oikos*.[30] The tyrant's efforts to subordinate women—to keep them from "roaming free" (579), to hide them away as he "hides" Antigone in the cave (774)— fail in the end. In different ways, both Antigone and Eurydike disrupt the public world of Kreon.

Having denied burial to Polyneikes, Kreon now must carry the corpse of his own son "in his arms" (διὰ χειρὸς ἔχων 1258).[31] The scene takes the form of a funeral procession in which Kreon sings the dirge,[32] mirroring Antigone's bridal/funereal exit some three hundred lines earlier. As Kreon himself describes it, the stage-picture resembles "a significant memorial" or "tomb" (μνῆμ᾽ ἐπίσημον 1258).[33] Grief piles on grief when he learns that his own marriage has ended with the suicide of his wife. Eurydike died "keening," κωκύσασα (*kōkusasa* 1302) for *both* her sons, Haimon and Megareus (1303–4). Heretofore unmentioned, Megareus sacrificed himself so that Thebes would not fall to Polyneikes and the Argives, an event dramatized in Euripides' *Phoenissae* (911–1018). In Euripides' version, Kreon tries to save his son from the oracle that says he must die, only to have his son choose death behind his back.[34] Sophokles, however, makes the tyrant responsible for Megareus' death,[35] and Kreon stands before us at the end of *Antigone* as the destroyer of his entire family.

The series of mourning cries, κωκυτοί (*kōkutoi*), trace out the chain of events that culminates in this final image.[36] The Messenger reports that Eurydike thrust in the blade when she heard the "sharply wailed cry" (*oxukōkuton* 1316) of her son Haimon. It was his "lamentations" (*kōkumatōn* 1206) for the dead Antigone that drew Kreon's men to the cave, an intervention that led to Haimon's suicide. Indeed, Eurydike's lament for her sons brings to pass Teiresias' prediction that Kreon would soon hear "funeral laments (*kōkumata* 1079) in your own home." These lamentations all have a common source, Kreon's decree forbidding anyone to "utter cries of grief" (*kōkusai* 28, repeated at 204) over the corpse of Polyneikes. As these laments come back to haunt him, Kreon abandons his threnody for his wife and son, replacing the dirge with a plea that he be led away to die (1317–44).

Behind the closing section of *Antigone*, we hear the echoes of the prophet Teiresias' pronouncement to Kreon:

> You hurl down below one who belongs above,
> wrongly making the tomb a home for a living soul,
> while to a corpse that belongs to the gods below you
> deny proper ritual, the rites of the dead, all that is holy. (1068–71)

Teiresias had asked what prowess there was "in killing someone [Polyneikes] who is already dead?" (1030) The question now turns back on Kreon, who cries out that the news of his wife's suicide "slays again a man already dead" (1288). With the body of his wife at the palace entrance and the corpse of his son before him, Kreon has returned to a house that is less a dwelling for the living than a resting place for the deceased. As one whom Hades has destroyed (1284–85), Kreon is now "a being less than nothing" (1332), doomed to survive in an *oikos* of death.

We can only guess how Sophokles staged the closing scene, but Kreon twice asks to be led away into the house (1322, 1328–31), and it seems likely that his wish was granted.[37] Sophokles may have left the corpses of Haimon and Eurydike on stage after the *exodos*, a tableau that proclaims the inversion of upper and lower worlds, reminding the audience that an unburied corpse began the tragedy.[38] Perhaps the presence of the two suicides left alone in tableau—a dead son and bridegroom, a dead wife and mother—would recall the third suicide, Antigone, whose body has been left to lie forever in her "bridal chamber of death."

A play that focuses from the start on how to rule the *polis* ends with the destruction of the *oikos*. By repressing any opposition to his rule, and by failing to value the domestic and ritual contribution of women, Kreon has undermined the validity of his transpolitical standard.[39] We witness the reverse process at work in the *Oresteia*, where the salvation of the house of Atreus is subsumed in the foundation of civic institutions, particularly the court of the Areopagus. In Aeschylus' view, the survival of the court and the prosperity of Athens depend on the inclusion of the Furies in the *polis*, and their incorporation in the ritual life of the *oikos* as guarantors of marriage and childbirth.[40] In *Antigone* Kreon achieves the opposite result, denying funeral rites and perverting the wedding ritual. His wife is dead, his family destroyed, he has no sons left to give in marriage and no way of guaranteeing the continuity of his line or the stability of political rule in Thebes. With the exception of Euripides' *Bacchae* and possibly *Medea*, no tragedy ends more bleakly.[41]

That we find this negativity compelling is due in no small part to Sophokles' manipulating the motif of the marriage to death. A ritual aimed at establishing, fostering, and preserving the *oikos* becomes the means of destroying it utterly. As if imitating the cruel precision of Kreon's punishment, the perverted wedding of Antigone involves Haimon, and through him Eurydike, and through them both, Kreon himself. The final participant in this process is the theater audience, although the means by which we are implicated do not lend themselves to objective analysis. But surely Reinhardt is right that the peculiar manner of Antigone's death helps explain our empathy for her: "The fullness of Antigone's death invests her life with human fullness. . . . By contrast, Creon ends as the personification of nothingness."[42]

Antigone's suffering, and that of Haimon and his mother Eurydike, is the dramatist's coin for counting the cost of Kreon's misrule, and (at least in the latter two cases) of making Kreon himself feel that cost. But the metaphor is inadequate, for the confusion of marriage and funeral provides more than the currency of the play. It would be more accurate to say that here we find the social and personal, the ritual and emotional, *body* of the play, against which the blows of embattled human conflicts are directed and through which they are felt.

Under the influence of Hegel, critics have construed *Antigone* as a series of polar oppositions—between written (human) and unwritten (divine) laws, the ruler and the ruled, political responsibility and individual rights, the duties owed to the state and those owed to the family, and the divergent worlds of men and women.[43] By measuring the tragic results of these antagonisms in terms of weddings and funerals, Sophokles suggests that the two rituals belong to *each* side of the oppositional pairs, like a river that "joins" its two banks. As outlined in the Introduction, the public and private worlds overlapped on these important ritual occasions, suggesting that Athenians viewed the purported oppositions as more mutually informing than simply antithetical.[44] However, Kreon's edict prohibiting the burial of Polyneikes shatters that unitary view, driving a wedge between public and private, state and family, men and women. The dramatic reverberations are measured by the confusion of marriages and funerals, rituals that otherwise negotiate these apparent contraries.

As described in Chapter 1, a Greek marriage involved reaching out beyond immediate blood-kin to incorporate an outsider and so guarantee the future of a new (or renewed) *oikos*. Extending the family through nuptial ties of kinship, the *kēdos* relationship opened up new duties and opportunities in both the private and public spheres. Burial involved a counter movement, the return of a corpse (in the case of a male) from the public sphere back into the private, as the *oikos* took back the dead as one of its own. If either rite is perverted—and both are in *Antigone*—then the tensions between public and private, family and *polis*, eventually erupt with tragic consequences.

Denied the woman's traditional role in burial rites, Antigone is forced to adopt the untraditional role of rebel against the state. And yet she does so by being radically conservative. Confronted with Kreon's edict, she gives total allegiance to brother and natal family, becoming (in effect) solely a daughter and sister. Antigone abandons any hope of fulfilling the outward reaching roles of wife and mother, denying her crucial transition as a bride moving to establish a new *oikos*. For his part, Kreon insists that Haimon honor blood-ties to his father at the expense of the young man's (potential) marriage-ties to Antigone, *precisely* what Antigone does vis-à-vis her own natal family. Haimon rebels against his father (not, like his fiancée, against his father's edict), and the young man dies trying to forge the marriage link with Antigone against his "natural" ties to Kreon. As for Eurydike, she kills herself on the household altar as a means of reasserting ties of blood with her son Haimon, rejecting her marriage-ties with her husband Kreon. And Kreon, in the end, finds himself bereft of both blood- (Haimon) and marriage-ties (Eurydike).[45]

The perversion of weddings and funerals exposes fault lines deep within the city, disrupting the normal commerce between men and women, between public and private, and between *oikos* and *polis*. Moreover, as Teiresias informs Kreon, the maimed rites snap the already tenuous link between mortal and divine spheres. Implied is a homology between the human rituals of weddings and funerals, and ritual sacrifice that links humans with the gods. In this regard, the conflicts in the play between contingent and divine ("unwritten") laws find their point of dramatic contact in the confused rituals of weddings and funerals.

Returning to Kamerbeek's judgment (quoted at the beginning of the chapter) that by the motif of the marriage to death "nothing or, at least, nothing much is said" about the great themes of the play, we recognize at best a superficial truth. Nothing much is *said*, but a great deal is communicated. At the end of the play, Kreon, the new ruler of the *polis*, appreciates the ultimate importance of his *oikos*: "My son, I unwittingly killed you/ and you too [wife], ah! wretched me, and I don't know/ where to look, where to lean" (1340–43). Kreon is left to perform the task he forbade at the outset—to bury *philoi*, but ones who have come to view him as the enemy.

When Antigone undertakes the burial of her brother early in the play, she strives to maintain the ongoing ritual life of her *oikos* before joining Haimon in creating a new one. The ritual duties that face Kreon, however, signal the failure of his marriage, the destruction of his household, and the end of any hope for its renewal in the shared bed, and shared blood, of Haimon and Antigone.

Chapter 5

FROM DEATH BED TO MARRIAGE BED

SOPHOKLES' *TRACHINIAE*

LIKE *Antigone*, *Trachiniae* vividly contrasts the worlds of men and women. An oft-noted feature of the play is the fact that the two principals, Deianeira and her husband Herakles, never meet onstage.[1] However, Sophokles goes to great lengths to introduce people and objects that link the two characters, even using the same actor to play both roles.[2] As a result, the radically different experiences of men and women gradually come together and even merge during the course of the drama. One of the chief means by which this crossover is effected involves the interplay of weddings and funerals, and in its closing scene *Trachiniae* presents the clearest example in tragedy— with the possible exception of Euripides' *Alkestis*—of one rite generating another.

For all its dramatic and poetic ironies, Sophokles' dramaturgy in *Trachiniae* resembles the construction of a composite picture by adding new pieces to the puzzle, which eventually bring the image into focus. We might contrast the workings of *Oedipus Tyrannus*, where a pattern already clear to the audience is only belatedly revealed to the protagonist. In *Trachiniae*, however, the oracle that Herakles will die at the hands of a creature already dead (1159–63) is not introduced to the audience until the hero's death is well in train, and only some one hundred lines before the play ends. Herakles perceives an inevitability in his fate that the spectators have only just learned about. Searching for order behind the additive events in the tragedy, many critics follow Herakles' lead and focus on the late-breaking oracle.[3] However, the play's dramatic coherence may lie elsewhere, at the level of ritual, in particular the pattern of wedding-to-funeral-to-wedding that shapes the overall plot.

In the prologue Deianeira relates her marriage directly to her unhappy life, and twice to her death. She begins with the maxim that one cannot know how life will turn out until death makes it clear, and then she immediately contradicts herself. A troubled courtship taught her early that her life would be hard and ill-fated, "without having to descend to Hades" (4–5) to find out. As a girl she "suffered from marriage" (νυμφείων ὄτλον/ ἄλγιστον ἔσχον 7–8) more than any other Aetolian maiden. Her first suitor was the monstrous river-god Achelous, whose bestial form led her to pray for death rather than share "such a marriage bed" (τῇσδε κοίτης 17). Deianeira's morbid fear of her wedding introduces the link between marriage and death that is developed through the play, culminating in the final scene when Sophokles presents a mirror-image of Deianeira's situation at the opening: Herakles lies on his death-bed, victim of a bestial intrusion (via Nessus' poison) into his marriage, while he forces his son to undertake what seems to be a monstrous wedding.

Deianeira describes how Herakles saved her from a union with Achelous and took her as his own bride, the first of several instances where a wife is won "by means of combat" (εἰς ἀγῶνα . . . μάχης 20).[4] Herakles' rescue brought her marriage and children but bred "fear upon fear" (28) in her heart. Her long-absent husband visits only rarely, "like a farmer of a distant field who sees it once when he sows and once when he harvests" (31–33). The simile brings to mind the Athenian wedding formula that sanctions "the sowing of legitimate offspring," and we hear a poignant echo in Deianeira's anxiety over Herakles' absence, which she likens to "the bitter pangs of child-birth" (πικρὰς/ ὠδῖνας 41–42). The husband/father stays away from his children, while the wife/mother feels his absence as if enduring again the pain of parturition.[5]

Deianeira resembles a poor bird longing (ποθουμέναι 103) for her absent mate; she is unable to "put her longing [πόθον] to sleep [εὐ-νάζειν]," nor can she stop her tears, brought about by her "husband-less bed" (εὐναῖς ἀναν-/ δρώτοισι, 106–10). The noun πόθος (*pothos*) often refers to longing for a marriage partner or for the deceased,[6] and its repetition suggests that Deianeira suffers in her marriage like one who mourns the dead. Although the Chorus point out that some god always saves Herakles from the "house of Hades" (120–21), De-ianeira's premonitions of her husband's death remain. She even con-fesses that when Herakles left on his last journey, he told her that if he failed to return after fifteen months she should take back her dowry as if he had died (161–62).

That period has elapsed, and a Messenger arrives to announce that Herakles lives. The Chorus celebrate with a short, lively lyric: "Let the house prepared for marriage raise the shout of triumph with cries from the hearth" (ἀνολολυξάτω δόμος/ ἐφεστίοις ἀλαλαγαῖς/ ὁ μελ-λόνυμφος 205–7). The "house ready for marriage" welcomes the hus-band's return to his wedded wife, but another possibility suggests itself. Among the women Herakles has captured is the girl Iole, who will join the *oikos* as the hero's new bride.[7]

The Chorus call on the men to raise a paean to Apollo, and on the unmarried girls, παρθένοι (*parthenoi* 211), to sing in praise of Artemis, who holds "a torch in each hand" (214) and is accompanied by the Nymphs (215). Praising the music of the *aulos*, the Chorus end their song with reference to a dance for Dionysus (216–20). The details are confusing,[8] but the explanation for the particular immortals who are invoked—Apollo, Artemis, the Nymphs, Dionysus—may lie in their connection to weddings. The Nymphs were associated with nuptial bathing and fertility and received bridal offerings, as did Artemis, who oversaw female rituals involving menarche and was appealed to during pregnancy and childbirth. The goddess frequently is depicted (with a torch in each hand) on black-figure scenes of "heroicized" wedding processions, as is her brother Apollo (often with a lyre), symbolizing the role of music in the wedding ceremony (figure 5). Dionysus also figures on such processional scenes, suggesting the festive nature of the event—or perhaps, as here, an illusory sense of happiness and liberation.[9]

As if cued by these divinities linked to wedding processions, the captured maidens of Oechalia enter down the *eisodos* in their own procession (στόλον 226), led by the herald Lichas.[10] Deianeira immediately sympathizes with these female prisoners-of-war, particularly Iole whom she identifies as unmarried (ἄνανδρος 308). Lichas explains that Iole suffers "from the labor pangs (ὠδίνουσα) of her heavy burden" (325), the same word that Deianeira uses to describe her longing for Herakles (42). Marriage for a Greek woman was intended to lead to childbirth, but Deianeira's labor pains are for her absent husband, Iole's for her absent home.

Deianeira learns that Herakles sacked Oechalia because he wanted the girl "as a secret bed [mate]" (κρύφιον . . . λέχος 360). Iole has been "led here as a wife for Herakles" (δάμαρτ᾽ ἔφασκες Ἡρακλεῖ ταύτην ἄγειν; 428), the phrase parodying Lichas' greeting of Deianeira as "wife of Herakles" (δάμαρτά θ᾽ Ἡρακλέους 406). In fact, Deianeira displays an uncanny likeness to the captive girl who has undermined her marriage: "I felt pity to see her, for her beauty has ruined her life" (464–65). Earlier, Deianeira made the same observation about herself when *she* was the potential bride, fearing that "my own beauty might someday bring me pain" (25).

The Chorus also link Deianeira to Iole, singing of the ineluctable power of Aphrodite, who always "carries off the victory" (497).[11] Under the influence of the goddess, Herakles has "carried off" Iole as his war-bride, just as years before, compelled by the same erotic force, he won Deianeira from Achelous. In that victory, Herakles tore Deianeira away "like a calf from her mother" (529–30). On one level she is simply a "prize heifer" who goes to the winner, but we also recognize the trope that compares the bride to a young animal weaned from her mother, perhaps taken away to be slaughtered.[12] The simile is apt, for in *Trachiniae* marriage involves the forceful removal of women from the security they have known: "uprooted" (39, 240), pulled from their home soil (144–50), and plucked like a flower when young, only to be discarded when old (547–49).[13] For both Iole and Deianeira, marriage is the disruption of the natural world, inextricably linked— as the battles with Achelous and the sack of Oechalia suggest—with death.

Although drawn to the captive Iole, Deianeira fears she will be displaced by the young woman who obtrudes onto her marriage. She wonders if Iole is still a "maiden" (κόρην) or if she has been "yoked" (ἐζευγμένην 536), and then imagines herself sharing the marriage bed with a new bride (539–40). Deianeira asks whether any wife could "have in common with another woman the same lovemaking?" (κοινωνοῦσα τῶν αὐτῶν γάμων 546), admitting her fears that Herakles will come to be called Iole's "husband" (πόσις 550) rather than her own.[14]

In her distress, Deianeira divulges a second battle fought over her, when the Centaur Nessus attempted rape while ferrying her across the river on the journey home with Herakles. In that struggle, the wedding ritual itself also was under attack. Deianeira was still "a young girl" (557) when, "sent by my father, I first followed Herakles as his bride" (562–63). Given away by her *kurios* (the *ekdosis* of the wedding ceremony), Deianeira is sexually assaulted during the *eisagōgē*, the physical transferal to her husband's home.[15] Both the attempted rape and Nessus' subsequent death occur "in the middle of the crossing" (μέσωι πόρωι 564), suggesting an interruption in the rite of passage from maiden to wife.

The prominence of the Centaur in this near-violation of the bride repays examination.[16] The background myth is the famous battle between the Lapiths and the Centaurs at the wedding of the Lapith leader Perithöos (see Chapter 2 pp. 38–39). Invited as guests, the Centaurs attempt to abduct the bride Hippodameia and her bridesmaids, but they are defeated by the Lapiths and driven out of Thessaly. The earliest surviving version occurs in the *Odyssey*, where the suitor Antinöos relates the story to Odysseus (disguised as a beggar, *Od.* 21.289–311). Graphic scenes of the battle were depicted in the (lost) murals by Polygnotos in Athens (ca. 470), and the story was popular in architectural sculpture. It appeared on the south metopes of the Parthenon (compositions that influenced the centauromachy in red-figure vase-painting), on the sandals of Pheidias' cult statue of Athena Parthenos, on the shield of his bronze Athena Promachos, on the west pediment and frieze above the *opisthodomos* of the Theseion, and on the metopes of the temple of Poseidon at Sounion.[17] The centauromachy also was sculpted on two famous temples in the Peloponnese, the west pediment of the Temple of Zeus at Olympia (by 458/57) and the interior frieze of the temple at Bassae. A particularly dramatic episode from the Bassae frieze shows a Lapith woman clinging to an idol of Artemis, while a Centaur lasciviously pulls off her garment, a horrific parody of the *anakaluptēria* at which the bride "exposes herself" to her husband.[18]

The violent rupture of the Lapith wedding by the Centaurs is mirrored in the assault by Nessus in *Trachiniae*. Moreover, just as Herakles kills the bull-man Achelous in the contest for Deianeira's hand, so he must slay the horse-man Nessus who threatens to violate his bride as he brings her to her new home. In the former case, the fatal aspects of the wedding operate only in Deianeira's and the Chorus's memory (1–27, 503–30). In the latter case, however, they remain physically present in the poisoned blood that the dying Centaur maliciously offers Deianeira, convincing her of its efficacy as a love potion. She has kept it in a "well-hidden place in the house" (578–79) and decides now to use it to regain Herakles' affections.

By applying the Hydra poison/Centaur blood to the robe she sends Herakles, Deianeira resurrects the violent history of her own wedding. As a result, wife, husband, and their go-between Lichas die. The process is well in train when Hyllus returns to the stage to report the horrific *pathos* of Herakles in the poisoned robe. He tells his mother how Herakles killed Lichas, the bearer of the gift, and then "cursed the ill-mated bed and the marriage he shared with you, for they destroyed his life" (791–93). Marriage is fatal not only to Herakles but also to Deianeira, who has decided that if harm comes to her husband "then carried on by the same impetus I will die with him" (συνθανεῖν 720).

With his son's assistance, Herakles is ferried (πόρθμευσον 802) back to the mainland, his body placed "in the middle of the boat" (ἐν μέσωι σκάφει 803). The details recall Nessus' ferrying of Deianeira ('πόρευε 560) and his attempted rape "in the middle of the crossing" (μέσωι πόρωι 564). The middle-point is also where Aphrodite stood (ἐν μέσωι 515) to umpire the battle between Achelous and Herakles, and "the middle of the marriage bed" (ἐν μέσοισιν εὐνατηρίοις 918) marks the spot of Deianeira's eventual suicide. We noted in Chapter 4 the play of betwixt and between in *Antigone*, where Kreon denies Antigone a place among the living, depriving her of a husband and the transition from maiden to wife, and wife to mother. The various midpoints in *Trachiniae* also suggest this liminal zone where opposites interpenetrate and even replace each other. Nessus' ferrying Deianeira across the stream during the *eisagōgē* of her wedding leads to near-rape, poison, and death. Years later those past events press themselves on the present, and they lead in turn to the ferrying of the fatally poisoned Herakles back to the mainland. With a hint of Charon transporting the dead across the river Styx, Herakles' passage initiates the funeral rites that close the play.

The suicide of Deianeira accelerates the shift in focus from saving a marriage to preparing for a funeral. The Nurse reports her death in a *kommos* with the Chorus, and the catechistic form of their exchange (863–95) may reflect an early pattern of Greek funeral lament.[19] The Chorus conclude that "this bride without a wedding has given birth, has borne a great curse [lit. "Fury"] on the house" (ἔτεκ᾽ ἔτεκε μεγά-λαν/ ἀνέορτος ἅδε νύμφα/ δόμοισι τοῖσδ᾽ Ἐρινύν 893–95). The offspring of the union of Iole and Herakles is none other than the suicide of Deianeira and the death of her estranged husband.[20]

In the messenger speech that follows, the Nurse exposes the intimate connection between Deianeira's marriage and her death. Deianeira sees her son Hyllus in the courtyard preparing a "hollow bed" (901–2)—that is, a litter and funeral bier—for his father. As if inspired by his act, Deianeira rushes to the marriage chamber (*thalamon* 913) and makes Herakles' bed, an activity traditionally linked to a wife preparing to have sex with her husband.[21] She then sits "in the middle of the bed" (918) and bids farewell to it and to her bridal chamber, forsaking them for another place of rest (920–22). Tearing off the "golden pin" that holds her *peplos*, she "undresses" and stabs herself with a sword (923–26). As with the blinding in *Oedipus Tyrannus* and the death of Haimon in *Antigone*, the sexual overtones of Deianeira's suicide are unmistakable.[22] Hyllus enters and mourns over her body, "covering it with kisses, and/ groaning as he lay side by side with her" (938–39). The marriage chamber becomes the site of bloodshed, Deianeira's suicide takes on aspects of her wedding night, and, "orphaned of both father and mother" (942), Hyllus bemoans his loss like an impassioned lover.

The arrival of Herakles moves Deianeira's suicide to the background, even as it strengthens the link between marriage and death. The Chorus compare the lamentations of Herakles' escort to the cries of "the sharp-sounding nightingale" (963), alluding to the story of Procne, Philomela, and Itys (Chapter 3 p. 46). Although the parallels are hardly exact, Philomela's betrayed marriage and its fatal results fit the pattern of Sophokles' play, especially Herakles' rape of Iole and the subsequent, if unintentional, punishment executed by his wife. Earlier Deianeira realized that Iole would dwell in the house with her (ξυνοικεῖν, *xunoikein* 545), and now Herakles uses the same word to characterize the garment fixed to his body, a robe that "dwells with" him (*xunoikoun* 1055). Commonly applied to married couples who establish their *oikos* together (Chapter 1 p. 18), the word links estranged husband and wife by suggesting the mutual catastrophe that their wedded union has become.

Crying out to be left "to my final sleep" (ὕστατον εὐνᾶσθαι 1005),[23] Herakles begs Hades to provide him "a bed on which to lie forever" (εὔνασον, εὔνασον μ᾽ 1042). Unaware that Deianeira meant no harm and has killed herself as a result of her error, Herakles unleashes a savage verbal attack on his wife (1036–38). As one who battled the giants, Centaurs, and wild beasts, Herakles bewails the ignominy of dying at the hands of a woman (1058–63). A mere female who fought "without a sword" (φασγάνου δίχα 1063), Deianeira has accomplished what none of Herakles' other opponents ever achieved.

The ironies are remarkable, for those in the audience are well aware that Deianeira herself has taken up the "two-edged sword" (ἀμφιπλῆγι φασγάνωι 930) to end her *own* life. By using a weapon of male combat, she introduces the bloodshed of the battlefield into the marriage chamber. Just the reverse happens to Herakles, for the mixture of Centaur blood and Hydra venom has made its way from the "secret recess" in the house (578–79, 686–89) to find the hero in the field. There the love potion destroys Herakles as if from within, offering no chance for him to fight back. The polarities between the male and female worlds noted at the start of the play begin to reverse themselves and to merge, as it were, from opposite directions.

Herakles' arrival on stage differs radically from what we would expect of the triumphant hero lauded earlier in the play. Carried in on his deathbed and longing for the sleep of Hades (1004–5 and 1040–43), Herakles begins to resemble Deianeira who has converted her marriage bed into her bed of death by the act of suicide.[24] He bemoans his unheroic end, "torn to shreds," κατερρακωμένος (*katerrakōmenos* 1103). The participle occurs nowhere else in Greek literature, but the root noun *rakos* means a "ragged or torn bit of cloth," a domestic image seemingly not fit for the death of a hero. In the same vein, Herakles describes himself as "sacked" (ἐκπεπόρθημαι 1104) like a city. Although the simile is drawn from male combat, it is now the warrior who has been plundered and destroyed, transforming Herakles into a victim like Iole, whom Herakles himself seized as a warbride when he captured Oechalia.[25]

In his suffering Herakles behaves in ways he finds horrifyingly similar to those of a woman:

I groan and weep
like a girl (*parthenos*). No one could ever say
they saw me act this way before.
I always followed my evil fate without mourning it.
Such a man once, now I am found to be a woman.[26] (1071–75)

Lying on his death bed/funeral bier, this "womanized" Herakles uncovers his wracked body: "I will show you my affliction by lifting the veil./ Look! all of you, gaze at my wretched body" (δείξω γὰρ τάδ᾽ ἐκ καλυμμάτων./ ἰδού, θεᾶσθε πάντες ἄθλιον δέμας 1078–79). The unveiling of a girl (*parthenos* 1071) brings to mind the ritual *anakaluptēria* of the marriage ceremony.[27] Herakles relieves his anguish by sharing it, revealing his tortured body like a bride exposing herself to her husband on their wedding night.

The *anakaluptēria* serves as an important symbol for the revelations of Kassandra in *Agamemnon* and figures in the hanging of the heroine in *Antigone*. In *Trachiniae*, Herakles' unveiling on his death bed recalls Deianeira weeping and groaning in her bridal chamber, "undressing" on her marriage bed before she runs herself through with a sword. Just as violence and death infect the courtship and wedding of Herakles and Deianeira (via Achelous and Nessus), so husband and wife reenact aspects of the wedding ritual as they prepare to die.

Although Herakles feels humiliated at his womanly suffering, the dramatic rendering of his *pathos* valorizes rather than discredits his response. Sophokles achieves this result in no small part by his sympathetic and poignant treatment of Deianeira. Up to this point, the character of this "most appealing of Sophoclean women" differs fundamentally from that of Herakles, generally perceived to be "one of the most unpleasant characters in Greek tragedy."[28] Although the transformation is hardly complete, the change in Herakles from an aggressive and brutish male to a more sensitive and (relatively) passive sufferer increases the audience's sympathy for him.[29] In the process, the apparently rigid distinctions in the drama between men and women, between husband and wife, begin to blur.

It is a critical commonplace that Herakles' behavior changes once he understands that the oracle governing his life has come true. Herakles realizes that he has been "slain by the dead" (as the oracle predicted) through the poisoned blood of Nessus. The old prophecy that his toils would cease only meant that he would die, because death signals the end of suffering for all (1159–72). In spite of critical attention focused on the revelation of divine principle,[30] the oracle (revealed only now to the audience) functions dramatically in a more immediate way. It serves as the catalyst to final *actions*, actions that are of key importance to understanding what has gone before.

Herakles ceases to wish for death (as he has done at 1000–1002, 1015–16, 1031–33, 1085–88) once he knows that death is imminent. Instead, he extracts a formal vow from his son to obey his last wishes (1174–90), including the fulfillment of his funeral rites. In some sense the entire scene constitutes the *prothesis*, for Herakles sees himself as already dead ("the light is no longer with me" 1144), and his body has been laid out, covered, and then uncovered for all to see. The trip to Mt. Oeta is the *ekphora*—Hyllus speaks of "bearing," φορᾶς (*phoras* 1212) the body—and once on the mountain the still-living Herakles will be cremated on a great pyre. He orders that the last rites be accompanied by "no tears or sounds of grief" (ἀστένακτος κἀδάκρυτος 1200), a prohibition that may reflect the fact that Herakles once prided himself on "not making sounds of grief" (ἀστένακτος 1074). As he is carried off, Herakles' last words are a self-exhortation to hold back cries of physical pain (1259–63). It is as if the hero already has mourned his death, in the manner of a woman who traditionally sings the funeral lament and whom he fears he now resembles.

As well as settling his "last rites" (τελευτὴ . . . ὑστάτη 1256), Herakles arranges for the wedding of his son Hyllus and his war-bride Iole.[31] Critics advance two different reasons why Sophokles insists on this marriage—to satisfy the demands of legend, or to reveal further Herakles' character of "passionate self-regard."[32] Given the importance of marriage and funeral motifs in the play, might not the purpose of this death-bed wedding arrangement have more to do with the rites themselves than with the demands of an obscure myth or the need to reassert Herakles' brutishness? Let us consider the scene through the lens of ritual and see if the encounter between father and son comes into clearer focus.

If the scene were designed to show Herakles at his monstrous worst, why does he spend so much time (1176–90) securing Hyllus' oath to obey his last wishes? Concern for an oath is rather refined behavior for a man who hurled his guest Iphitus from the towers of Tiryns (270–73, 357), sacked Oechalia out of lust for a girl (351–55, 359–74, 431–33, 476–83), and dashed the brains of his loyal messenger Lichas without waiting to learn his innocence (772–82). Although Herakles threatens to curse his son in the underworld (1201–2) and to disown him in this one (1204–5), the hero centers his appeal on the oath: "After I have died, if you want to act/ with proper piety, remember the oath you have sworn your father/ and take this woman as your wife" (1222–24).[33] By reason of that oath, should Hyllus renege, "the curse of the gods/ will await you" (1239–40). Finally, Herakles calls on the gods to witness that his wish for his son's marriage is "not impious, since you will bring pleasure to my heart" (1246). The idea that this pain-wracked human could find even metaphorical pleasure lends Herakles a sympathetic quality he lacks elsewhere in the play, and Hyllus acquiesces to his father's wish.

Through the pain and threats and remonstrances, the original audience would have seen Herakles acting as *kurios* of both his son and Iole, arranging a marriage to ensure the survival of the *oikos*.[34] This fact helps to account for an apparent digression earlier in the scene, when Herakles asks that his mother Alkmene ("the in-vain bride of Zeus" 1148–49) and his other children come from the house. As the eldest son Hyllus explains, the family is scattered (1151–56), and there is no one else to witness the hero's dying words. Hyllus is all that remains in Trachis of Herakles' family, to whom we can add Iole as Herakles' new "bride." The *oikos* is fragile, and the *kurios* is on his death bed. A funeral and a wedding are in order.

It would be wrong to suggest that Herakles arranges this wedding out of compassion, understanding, or love, either for Iole or Hyllus.[35] On the other hand, Sophokles emphasizes throughout the play the inability of Herakles and Deianeira to see the outcome of their actions (in this regard, they remind us of Oedipus and Jokasta in *Oedipus Tyrannus*). In a world of blind decisions and tragic results, the survival of the *oikos*—the irreducible unit of Greek social identity—may represent the best that human striving can hope to achieve.

The final scene of *Trachiniae* mirrors the close of other Sophoklean plays in its concern for the *oikos*, measured by prospects of future weddings and funerals. At the end of *Antigone*, for example, the devastation of the *oikos* is total, with no possible marriage for the future. Kreon must bury his wife Eurydike and son Haimon, the child who could have maintained the *oikos* had he married Antigone as planned. In *Oedipus Tyrannus* the wife (mother) Jokasta lies dead within the palace, and the blind husband (son) Oedipus embraces his incestuous daughters, in anguish over their prospects for marriage (1489–1502), fearing they will "waste away, barren and unwedded" (1502). In *Ajax* the world of the *oikos* is more distant, but the play still shows Ajax's wife Tekmessa and small son Eurysakes tending his corpse (1168–70). In the closing sequence, Eurysakes, Teukros (Ajax's brother), and friends exit together to perform the funeral ritual for the hero—bathing and laying out the body, preparing a funeral pyre, bearing the corpse, and digging the grave (1402–17).[36] The *oikos* survives, insofar as the family's obligations to its dead *kurios* are fulfilled in a ritually appropriate way. At the end of *Oedipus at Kolonus*, the survival of the *oikos* does not seem likely (the future strife between Polyneikes and Eteokles looms large), but the familial responsibility for burial is observed as fully as possible given the circumstances of Oedipus' death. Antigone and Ismene accompany their living father to "the marble tomb," they bathe him in preparation for his death, they clothe him in burial attire, and they wail for him as if over a corpse (1595–1609, 1620–22).[37]

At the end of *Trachiniae*, both funeral and wedding rituals are set in motion, a fact that mitigates some of the bleakness that modern critics ascribe to the drama.[38] When critics do find the negativity "balanced," they tend to hear intimations of Herakles' apotheosis on the funeral pyre, intimations more argued over than agreed upon.[39] Instead of slipping into despair, or searching beyond the text for its opposite, or settling for the trendy conclusion that Sophokles celebrates "the predicament of continual uncertainty" and actively pursues "interpretive scattering,"[40] we might do better to reconsider the interconnection between marriage and death that informs the action. Perhaps here we can find a clue to the tone at the end of the play.

Marriage in *Trachiniae* is a particularly brutal affair, springing from combat and leading to death. A bride is like a young animal pulled from her mother, a tender plant uprooted from protective soil, or—as in the case of Iole—a war-prize seized at the razing of a city. To cap that brutality, the play ends with a wife lying dead in her marriage chamber and her physically tortured husband preparing to be burned alive on his funeral bier. Their deaths reveal the terrible effectiveness of the hidden poison of the Centaur, and the even greater destruction generated by erotic desire. Deianeira hears how *eros* compelled Herakles to wreak havoc on Oechalia (354–68, 431–33), and she admits the force of that passion in driving her to use Nessus' potion (630–32, seconded by the Chorus at 860–61).[41] Against this background of fatal passion and violence, Herakles' deathbed demand that Hyllus wed Iole seems far less harsh. Young and innocent, the couple bear no responsibility for the destruction that has brought them so improbably together. The proposed union is markedly *without* eros; given the play we have just seen, such a marriage appears in a not unfavorable light.

The final exit enacts the *ekphora* of Herakles' "living corpse" as he is borne off for cremation and burial. The procession includes "foreign men" (964) from Euboea, the Old Man, the Chorus of Trachinian women, Hyllus, and possibly even Iole.[42] The act of escorting Herakles out of the theater integrates male and female worlds, consolidating a community in the face of disaster. The co-operative nature of the funeral rites and the promise of a new wedding give the play a sense of ritual closure. In fact, the arrangements for the marriage of Hyllus and Iole may remind us of the opening scene of the play, the prologue delivered by Deianeira, reminiscing about her wedding to Herakles. If the arguments in this chapter have merit, then by that imaginative return Sophokles inscribes more of an upward spiral than the proverbial full circle.

Chapter 6

THE BRIDE FROM THE GRAVE

EURIPIDES' *ALKESTIS*

N O GREEK PLAY more fully combines wedding and funeral motifs in its plot, language, and staging than does Euripides' *Alkestis*. In the prologue, the figure of Death (Thanatos) actually takes the stage, and later Alkestis expires in the only scene of natural death in extant tragedy. Preparations for her funeral, the *ekphora* to the grave, and the return of the mourners after the burial constitute the main action, accented by references to the marriage of Alkestis and Admetus that the funeral ritual calls to mind. Following Herakles' miraculous intervention, the closing scene takes the form of a second wedding, a reunion of Admetus and his resurrected wife.

By conflating the two rituals, Euripides not only validates the roles of woman and wife as understood by his contemporaries, but he also suggests new models for appropriate *male* behavior in the character of Admetus. With the introduction of Herakles as Admetus' guest, the play juxtaposes the institution of marriage (joining male and female) with that of the guest-host relationship, ξενία (*xenia*, binding male to male). The action extends and complicates both relationships, encouraging the audience to consider new attitudes toward marriage that go beyond the reigning norms of Athenian culture.

Euripides constructs the play around a set of departures and returns, a framework that emphasizes the journey common to both weddings and funerals. In terms of stage action, a wife (and mother) leaves the house, dies, and is borne away to burial, only to be rescued, reunited with her husband, and returned to the house. Her *anodos* works several variations on the Persephone story, and in the end Alkestis' return shares in the Eleusinian promise of rebirth and fertility.[1] As Herakles puts it, "I will go down to the sunless home of Korē [Persephone] and her lord . . . and I will bring Alkestis up" (851–54).

The *anodos* pattern taps into the human desire to challenge, and even conquer, the finality of death. The theme is sounded many times in the play, with references to Asklepius (who tried to bring mortals back to life), to Orpheus (whose song could win over Death), and to Persephone herself.[2] Unlike these myths, however, the resurrection of Alkestis is tied intimately to the social institutions of marriage and family. In place of death as a disease to be cured by a healer (Asklepius), or as a separation to be bridged by art and *eros* (Orpheus), or as a metaphor for the rupture of the bond between mother and daughter (Persephone and Demeter), *Alkestis* focuses on the loss and return of a wife, and the corresponding breakdown and reestablishment of the *oikos*.

The arrival of Thanatos in the prologue—his only personal appearance in tragedy—is the first of many ways Euripides dramatizes the concrete fact of Alkestis' death and revival. Embodied as a "bogeyman," death emerges as a force that can be fought and physically defeated, as Apollo predicts (65–69). Physical presence is not limited to Thanatos himself, for the underworld is presented consistently as a counter-residence to that of the living, with halls, gates, and inner chambers, the "house of Hades" ("Αιδου δόμους 25) that Alkestis will inhabit.[3] When Admetus returns home after Alkestis' funeral, the door of the palace façade that he is loathe to enter seems to stand for the hidden world below rather than the house of the living.[4]

In the parodos, the Chorus gather before the palace in anticipation of Alkestis' death, responding to the signs that a funeral is in the making: the sound of lamentation within the house, indications of the preparation of the body, a container of water at the entrance to purify those who enter and leave, and cut hair at the front door (86–90, 94, 98–104).[5] The Chorus want assurances that Alkestis has died before they crop their hair, change into black mourning dress, and begin the ritual lament (215–17), duties mandated by Admetus (425–27) and performed when he and the household carry out the funeral rites. When Admetus returns to the stage after Alkestis' death, his hair is shorn and he wears black (512), signs of mourning that the Servant and Herakles later point out (818–19, 826–28).

Outward signs of death are matched by the report of preparations within the house. Making the earliest appearance of a messenger in tragedy (at line 136), Alkestis' handmaid describes how her mistress performed the ritual duties normally left to the survivors. She bathed with river-water, then donned her funeral clothing and adorned herself (159–69), actions similar to those performed by a bride before her wedding. Indeed, even as she prepares for death, Alkestis finds herself inexorably drawn to her marriage bed (175–95). Thinking first of her own wedding night and then of the new bride who might replace her, she breaks into tears and throws herself repeatedly onto the bed. Finally she embraces her children and bids farewell to the household servants, stretching out her right arm (193–94) in the gesture also used by mourners to salute the deceased.[6] Preparing to die for her husband, Alkestis draws together the ritual activities of both wedding and funeral.

When she emerges from the house with her family, Alkestis initiates one of the strangest scenes in ancient drama. Not only does she succumb "naturally" on stage, but she actually dies twice, once in a monody and a second time in speech.[7] By exploiting the medium of lyric and that of spoken dialogue, Euripides finds the appropriate form to capture the exceptional nature of her sacrifice. Experiencing Alkestis' death through these different modes, the audience feel more fully the poignancy of her loss and, in turn, find her ultimate revival all the more compelling.[8]

In her opening monody (244–72), Alkestis calls on the sun, the sky, the earth of her homeland, and her "bridal bed" (νυμφίδιοι τε κοῖται 249) for the last time. She visualizes her death in terms of a scene found on white-ground lekythoi that shows a woman being taken off to death like a bride being led by her husband (Chapter 2 p. 35). Alkestis sees Charon approach to ferry her over the river Acheron (252–56), and she cries out three times that someone leads her down into the halls of the dead, with dark eyebrows and wings—Hades (259–62). This is the terrifying road she now travels (263), leading to the shadow-night of death (268–69). The iconography of her imagined passage to the underworld, coupled with her farewell to the bridal bed, links Alkestis' marriage and her death. They are journeys along the same path, although heading in opposite directions.[9]

As if in response to Admetus' plea that she "come back up" (277), Alkestis goes through the process again, abandoning lyric for dialogue meter. Like Kassandra in *Agamemnon*, Alkestis presents a more logical (but no less affecting) account of her actions, and weddings are one of her chief concerns. She imagines the marriage offers she could have attracted as Admetus' widow if she had allowed her husband to die (285–86), but she confesses no desire to live without him, nor does she want her children to grow up orphaned of their father. She makes Admetus promise not to marry again lest a new wife become an unloving stepmother to the children (304–9) and so ruin their daughter's prospects for marriage (313–16). Alkestis laments that she will not be there to serve as *numpheutria* at her daughter's wedding or help her through childbirth (317–19).

During Alkestis' two "deaths," Admetus strives desperately to share his wife's experience. He responds in dialogue meter until the last section of her monody, at which point he shifts to anapests, trying to bridge the widening gap between himself and Alkestis by approximating her mode of expression. Admetus begs her not to betray him (275), a wish he has made before (202, 250) and one that underlines the painful absurdity of his situation, because *his* betrayal of her is more to the point.[10]

After Alkestis' final speech, Admetus again tries to match his wife, this time by making a speech of his own. He grants her request never to remarry and then goes her several better. He will mourn not for a year but for a lifetime (336–37), outlawing any revels and music in the house (343–47). He vows to have an image sculpted of Alkestis to lie in his bed, an effigy he will embrace, caress, call by Alkestis' name, hold in his arms. . . . Then, catching himself, Admetus insists that all this will prove but "a cold pleasure" (348–53).[11] However, the hyperbole returns when he wishes for the power of Orpheus to charm Persephone and Hades, for neither Kerberus nor Charon would stop him from bringing Alkestis back to life (357–62). Admetus shifts strategies again, asking his wife to ready a home for him below so that they can "dwell together in marriage" (*sunoikēsousa*) and lie forever "side by side" (364–67).

Admetus' speech is pathetic and a little absurd. In essence, he proposes three different means to achieve a "marriage to death." The first plan involves living out his own life as if he were dead, dedicating himself to his deceased wife and taking comfort in her image sculpted in stone. He next dreams that he might emulate Orpheus and rescue Alkestis through song, without acknowledging the mythical poet's ultimate failure to bring his wife Eurydike back from Hades.[12] Admetus' third strategy is to reestablish his marriage with Alkestis after he dies, making their union eternal in the underworld. To this end he even suggests that she take him with her to Hades (382–83), a proposal that renders meaningless the very sacrifice Alkestis is making on his behalf.[13] In his inflated attempts to rival his wife, Admetus fails to grasp what Alkestis has done for him and his family, and he offers what hardly could prove a comfort to her as she expires.

In response to his mother's death, the young Eumelos sings a short monody as he, too, tries to call Alkestis back to life. The intrusion in lyric of an otherwise silent character is remarkable,[14] and the simplicity of the child's observations contrasts with Admetus' convoluted efforts. The son tells his father "you have married in vain, in vain" (ἀνόνατ᾽ ἀνόνατ᾽ ἐνύμφευσας 412), because Admetus did not reach the end of old age with his wife. Without her, the boy knows that "the house is destroyed" (ὄλωλεν οἶκος 415). Pointing to the lesson that Admetus will learn, the child portrays Alkestis' death in terms of a lost marriage and a ruined household.

Admetus announces the preparations for the funeral *ekphora* (422), and Alkestis' body is taken offstage. Admetus specifies the mourning observances for the citizens: shorn hair, black garments, the banning of music for a year, even clipped manes for the horses who also must go into mourning (425–31).[15] Later Herakles comments on Admetus' cut hair (512), indicating that the actor changed mask or wig during the intervening ode, at which time he and the Chorus also donned black mourning garb, as the text of 922–25 makes clear.[16] The body of Alkestis is borne from the palace at 606, but the arrival of Pheres, Admetus' father, interrupts the procession. After an acrimonious encounter between father and son (a scene we will discuss later), the *ekphora* continues with the mourners, led by Admetus, bearing the corpse of Alkestis to the grave.

To highlight the importance of the funeral procession, Euripides has the Chorus follow Admetus out of the theater. On only four other occasions do the Chorus vacate the orchestra during the course of a tragedy.[17] By having them do so here, Euripides emphasizes both the *ekphora* to the grave—a mark of the esteem earned by Alkestis—and the desolate procession home after the funeral, conveying in a fully theatrical fashion the sense of loss, particularly as it affects Admetus.

Before Alkestis' death, Admetus seems like a verbally extravagant coward, piling up guarantees about the future while refusing to confront the present or the past. After the funeral, all this changes. Admetus returns to the empty orchestra filled with a sense of bereavement: he confronts a vanished past that is, paradoxically, now present before him. He interprets the journey back as a wedding procession turned upside down—one "without the bride" (ἁμαρτεῖν/ πιστῆς ἀλόχου 879–80; also at 870, 876–77), where "dirges have replaced the marriage hymn,/ and black mourning garments are worn instead of the festive white" (νῦν δ' ὑμεναίων γόος ἀντίπαλος/ λευκῶν τε πέπλων μέλανες στολμοὶ 922–23).[18] In place of marriage torches and the throng of revelers on their wedding night (915–18), Admetus comes home with a Chorus of mourners to "a bridal bed desolate of marriage" (λέκτρων κοίτας ἐς ἐρήμους 925). The "hateful procession" (στυγναὶ/ πρόσοδοι 861) makes its way from the dead bride's "grave-home" (δώματα 867) to the groom's house, a dwelling "bereft" (χήρων μελάθρων 861–62) and uninhabitable. Now the palace façade signals the absence of Alkestis: "Empty shape of my house," Admetus calls out, "how can I enter you,/ how can I make my home here?" (912–13). He is now an outsider in his own *oikos*.

The simple but effective contrast between arriving with his bride on their wedding night and returning without her from the tomb moves Admetus closer to the sympathetic space previously occupied by Alkestis. He finally understands that her death means the loss of the one thing that would give his life meaning, and his thoughts naturally turn back to their wedding, the event by which Alkestis herself measured her sacrifice. Although Admetus links marriage to death and wedding to funeral in expressing his grief, he no longer sounds as strident and rhetorical as before. Facing an empty house, he wishes he could dwell with his wife in the tomb (864–68), and he regrets that he was prevented from "lying together in death with my noble wife" (μετ' ἐκείνης/ τῆς μέγ' ἀρίστης κεῖσθαι φθίμενον 898–99).

Just as Alkestis experiences her death first in lyric and then in speech, so Admetus goes through his grief twice, first in the *kommos* described above and then in a speech on his own. He fully admits the impossibility of his position, and he "finally understands" (ἄρτι μανθάνω 940) that death is preferable to the life that now faces him (935–40). As Vellacott puts it, "The woman loses her life but gains immortal glory, while the man keeps his life but loses everything that makes it worth keeping."[19] The household is "desolate" (ἐρημία 944), filled with signs of Alkestis' absence: the empty bed, her vacant throne, the unwashed floors, the children at his knees weeping for their mother, the servants mourning their dead mistress (946–49).[20] Outside the house things are no better, for in public Admetus faces a double curse. His widowed status will lead maidens (amid the clamor of gossip) to jockey to become his new wife (950–52), while his enemies will mock him for being so cowardly as to "flee Hades/ by giving up the woman he had married to death" (ἣν ἔγημεν ἀντιδοὺς ἀψυχίαι/ πέφευγεν Ἅιδην 956–57).

In the final ode, the Chorus remind Admetus of the necessity of death and the honors that will accrue at the gravesite of Alkestis. Worshipers there will call on her "blessed spirit," μάκαιρα (*makaira*) δαίμων (1003), an appropriate address for one honored in cult (see 445–54) but also a phrase that recalls the *makarismos* blessing for newlyweds.[21] The wedding motif is no accident, for immediately following the Chorus' praise of her tomb the veiled Alkestis enters with Herakles, and the dramatic transformation of a funeral to its nuptial opposite is under way.

By rescuing Alkestis from the dead, Herakles restores Admetus to life almost as much as he does his wife. Their reunion assumes the ritually appropriate form of a second wedding, drawing on the vocabulary and iconography of contemporary practice.[22] Dressed and adorned to highlight her youth (1049–50), the "new bride" (νέα γυνή) stands veiled before the groom.[23] Acting like her guardian (*kurios*), Herakles gives her over to her new husband who takes her by his right hand (1113–18) and leads her to their implied destination, the "marriage chamber" (*thalamon* 1055). The wedding ritual that informed their respective expressions of loss now reunites Admetus and Alkestis, bringing the play to a close.

But this is a wedding with a difference. By forcing Admetus to accept an unknown wife against his will, Herakles reverses the traditional roles in which the *woman* is the reluctant party, entrusted by her *kurios* to a partner whom she has little or no say in selecting. Just like a bride, Admetus has been cut off from his mother and father and handed over to an apparent stranger, all too aware of his dependence on his old/new wedding partner. He protests in vain that by accepting the veiled woman and leading her into the house he will "betray" Alkestis (1059, 1096), recalling his earlier exhortations that Alkestis not "betray" him by dying. He is doubly distressed because the young stranger reminds him so much of his wife. Given that the audience knows she *is* Alkestis (Apollo's prophecy at 64–69 and Herakles' promise at 840–60 make that clear), Admetus' eventual betrayal of his vows seems more ironic than tragic.[24]

Dale observes that the play "is permeated by a grave irony of plot," and her unintentional pun proves quite apt.[25] Alkestis earlier tells Admetus that "time will soften you" (381); Herakles repeats the phrase (1085), savoring the irony along with the audience, for the authoress of the phrase is standing with him, veiled and unrecognized. To a certain extent Admetus is caught living out the ironies implicit in his name, Ἄδμητος, close to the adjective ἀδμής/ ἀδ-μῆτος, "unbroken," "untamed," or "unwedded" (usually applied to women).[26] He is called by name over twenty-five times, and the non-negated cognate δάμαρ, "wife," is used ten times, always for Alkestis.[27] Trying to live up to his name, Admetus squirms against the inevitable, and those in the theater audience delight in the struggle. We want him to give in, for the inevitable no longer signifies his wife's death but quite the opposite, the renewal of their marriage and restoration of their *oikos*.[28]

Nowhere does Euripides imply that Admetus has developed morally to the point that he *deserves* his wife back.[29] However, there is little doubt that he changes after the funeral, and in a play built on dramatic reversals such a change is credible. To understand Admetus' transformation, we must walk a thin line between conceptions of tragic character built on psychology and sentiment and those that deny inner consistency in favor of changing "rhetorical situations."[30] In a sense the approaches are complementary—Admetus appears in very different circumstances following his wife's death and funeral, *and* he presents a more compelling figure who admits to suffering and loss. Euripides emphasizes the shift in character by introducing it in a second parodos, as if the play were beginning again.

To appreciate more fully what Alkestis has come to mean to Admetus, let us consider the earlier scene in which Pheres interrupts the funeral *ekphora*, precipitating a bitter quarrel with his son. Much has been written about the merits of each position, but insufficient emphasis has been placed on the upshot: Admetus rejects his natal family, counting Alkestis "alone/ as my mother and father" (646–47). This dependence on his spouse puts Admetus in an anomalous position, similar to that of a young woman who leaves her parents for the new "lordship" of her husband.[31] As we have seen, in the final scene of the play Admetus again undergoes the experience of a bride, forced to accept the mate selected by her *kurios*.

Finding it unconscionable that neither his mother nor father will die for him, Admetus vows to withhold the social and ritual responsibilities expected of a son. He tells his father to "beget other sons so that you won't run short,/ children who will care for you in your old age and, when you die,/ will cover your body and lay out your corpse./ For these hands of mine will *not* bury you" (662–65). Admetus' threat would have made an impact on the audience in Athens, where parents strongly desired to be buried by those in their *oikos*, particularly their own children, and were deeply concerned that subsequent rites be observed at the grave.[32] It is in this light that we should view Admetus' parting shot at Pheres: "Go keep house with your wife!/ Grow old without children, as you deserve,/ even while your child is alive" (734–36). The word that Admetus uses for "wife," *xunoikēsasa*, literally means "one who shares the house," recalling the sine qua non of Greek marriage—cohabitation as a means of guaranteeing offspring and establishing an *oikos*. By withdrawing from his parents' household, Admetus in effect "disestablishes" it. With the loss of his only child, Pheres is *kurios* over a fractured home, and he faces his eventual death without the guarantee of filial attendance at the grave.

The scene between father and son is even more disturbing when we recall that it is played before the corpse of Alkestis.[33] The words of both men ultimately run up against the fact that Alkestis has died for Admetus and her body awaits burial. Useful here is Kenneth Burke's concept of the "scene/agent" ratio, the degree to which the scene or background (here, the funeral ritual) "contains" or controls the actions of the dramatic agents.[34] On the surface the ratio seems irrelevant, for father and son quickly shift from honoring the dead to uttering bitter recriminations that show little respect for what Alkestis has done. At a deeper level, however, each man relentlessly exposes the other as the cause of the corpse being there in the first place. For her part, Alkestis did not die desiring such a rift; on the contrary, she meant to ensure the survival of Admetus' *oikos* and the living continuity of Pheres' line.[35]

In a sense, Alkestis' corpse unites the quarreling men by representing synecdochally the *destruction* of their respective households. Pheres loses his son and, too old to beget a new one, departs knowing that his own flesh and blood will never oversee *his* funeral. Admetus' *oikos* also suffers a symbolic death, so great is the impact of Alkestis' loss. The Servant cries out that "not just Alkestis, but all of us have been destroyed" (825), and Admetus returns from the grave saying, "I envy the dead, I long to be among them" (866). Apparently outside the exchange between father and son, Alkestis' corpse proves to lie at its center.

It is fitting that the scene closes with Admetus' repudiation of his natal family (737–38) and his resumption of the funeral rites for his dead wife. By coming to value his marriage with Alkestis over ties of blood, Admetus recognizes that the marital "stranger" can replace natural kin. In fact, on several occasions Admetus and others refer to Alkestis as "foreign," ὀθνεῖος (*othneios*), and an "outsider," θυραῖος (*thuraios*). Admetus bitterly attacks his father for "letting this/ 'foreign' [*othneian*] woman die for your son" (645–46).[36] Herakles asks if the house mourns "a foreigner [*othneios*] or a blood-kin," and Admetus answers "a foreigner [*othneios*], but she was in other ways [than ties of blood] pure necessity to the house" (532–33).[37] Misled by Admetus, Herakles chastises the household servant for overdoing grief for an "outsider" (*thuraiou* 778). Repeating that the dead woman is an "outsider" (*thuraios* 805), Herakles fails to see why the death of a "foreigner" (*othneiou* 810) should stop his revels. The Servant responds that the woman who died was too much an "outsider" (*othneios* 811), and it slowly dawns on Herakles that the household's grief does not reflect sorrows for some "outsider" (*thuraiōn* 814). Admetus has covered up the truth in the name of hospitality, claiming he was performing "funeral rites for an outsider" (*thuraion kēdos* 828). Ashamed of his behavior in a house bereft of its mistress, Herakles decides to bring Alkestis back from the dead.

The use of *othneios* and *thuraios* to describe Alkestis conveys the literal truth that a wife is "foreign" (not related by blood) to her husband and that she originates (of necessity) "outside the door." Overlooking the ironic way these terms are mustered, some critics conclude that the play devalues women and supports the view that wives are insignificant to the family. However, the dramatic characters purposefully use "outsider" and "foreigner" to obscure the deeper truth that Euripides is at pains to demonstrate,[38] namely that the woman who died has shattered such literal distinctions, proving herself absolutely integral to the *oikos*. Moreover, Herakles' anger at Admetus only makes sense if he is *misled* by the original description of the dead woman. As for Admetus, he comes to realize that his wife

Alkestis is anything but a foreigner. After all, she has taken the place of his father and mother, a fact he is ready to herald far and wide (734–38).

When Herakles returns with the veiled woman in the closing scene, he confronts Admetus with his earlier deception—"You didn't tell me that the woman laid out for burial/ was your wife, but you opened your home to me as a guest,/ pretending that the grief was for an outsider [*thuraiou*]" (1012–14). Herakles then gives Admetus a taste of his own medicine. He camouflages his match with Death by calling it an "all-comers athletic contest" in which oxen went to the winners and "a woman was thrown in as a bonus" (1025–32). Again, some critics infer from this characterization of women (a prize subordinate even to cattle!) that Euripides (via Herakles) engages in culturally accepted misogyny.[39] However, the context indicates just the opposite, for the hero is dissembling when he denigrates the woman he has rescued. In so doing, Herakles replicates Admetus' earlier deception, when he verbally undervalued the woman who died by portraying her as "outside the family."

Herakles describes the veiled woman as chattel that Admetus must keep for him until he returns from his labors (1020–34). However, the maiden's status changes when Herakles points out that he won her by "much effort" (1025) and "with [great] labor," σὺν πόνωι (*ponōi*, 1035), in a contest that was "worth the trouble" (*ponon* 1027). The repeated word—*ponos*—is the common term for Herakles' famous labors for Eurystheus (so used at *Alk.* 481, 487, 499, 1149); similarly, the word *contest*, ἀγών (*agōn*), describes the games in which he won Alkestis (1021, 1026, 1102, 1141) but elsewhere refers to his twelve great tasks (489, 504). We are encouraged to view Herakles' winning this purported slave as on par with his famous labors, and it is not surprising that he refuses to entrust the woman to a servant (1111) but will give her up only to Admetus' right hand (1113–19). Only after Alkestis' unveiling does Admetus realize who she is: "Do I truly look on my wife?" (γυναῖκα λεύσσω τὴν ἐμὴν ἐτητύμως; 1124). "Do I see my wife?" (εἰσορῶ δάμαρτ᾽ ἐμήν; 1129). "Oh beloved eyes and form of my wife!" (ὦ φιλτάτης γυναικὸς ὄμμα καὶ δέμας 1133). Alkestis is restored to Admetus, but in a way that transvalues her role as wife and asks of the husband that he live up to that new evaluation.

Some critics assert that Admetus' hospitality to Herakles constitutes his greatest virtue, and it is a virtue rewarded.[40] Others see Admetus' commitment to *xenia*, the guest-host relationship, as evidence of male chauvinism, revealing this purported "virtue" to be a culturally disguised form of sexism.[41] Both interpretations fail to do justice to the way the drama unfolds. They ignore the transformative power that Euripides derives from the interplay between weddings and death, and they overlook the important parallels that are revealed between the male bond of *xenia* and the male-female bond of marriage.

Herman examines how the *xenoi* relationship resembled and complemented kinship-through-marriage, two institutions less mutually exclusive than might first appear. Neither followed from birth, and a "ritualized friend" could undertake the obligations of providing the daughters of deceased *xenoi* with dowries so that they could marry. In Herman's words, "acting at one and the same time as quasi-kin and allies, [ritualized friends] provided what can best be described as a supplement to the potential of the family group."[42]

The concept of *xenia* was not simply an abstract model for noble (male) behavior, but a concerted effort to unite *oikoi* against a potentially hostile world. There emerged an unwritten contract between men (as *kurioi* of their households) that a guest was a sacred trust and reciprocal hospitality was expected.[43] Alkestis' willingness to die on behalf of her husband introduces those same values into the *oikos*, exposing Admetus—and the audience—to a radical and problematic conception of marriage, one that demands an exchange and a reciprocity so complete as to extend to the grave. In this respect, Alkestis' death calls out unprecedented action from Herakles on behalf of his host Admetus, a battle with Death itself to restore the wife to her husband.

Before these two forms of "ritualized integration" come together in the final scene, Euripides explores their apparent incompatibility in the disjunction between Admetus' hospitable treatment of Herakles and the mourning due his dead wife. The Servant contrasts the behavior of his drunken charge to that of the mourners in the house:

> The flame of wine surrounded him [Herakles], warming him up,
> and he crowned his head with myrtle and howled
> off-key. There were two melodies going—
> he sang away, oblivious to the grief
> of Admetus' house, and we servants wept
> for our mistress, hiding our tears from the guest. (758–63)

While Herakles drinks the undiluted liquor of "the dark mother" (μελαίνης μητρὸς 757, i.e., "grape"), the Servant mourns a woman "who was mother [μήτηρ]/ to the entire household" (769–70). His master "too, too much honors his guest" (ἄγαν ἐκεῖνός ἐστ᾽ ἄγαν φιλόξενος 809), a judgment with which Herakles concurs once he learns the truth about Alkestis' death: "*Even then* you welcomed me as a guest?" (ἔπειτα δῆτά μ᾽ ἐξενίζετε; 822). Herakles sympathizes with Admetus ("What a marriage partner you have lost!" 824), but the Servant corrects him by pointing out that her loss extends to the entire *oikos* (825). Eating, drinking, wearing wreaths, and talking of love are fitting for a wedding banquet or symposium, but, as Herakles admits, they are grossly out of place in a house that mourns its mistress (826–32). Although angry at Admetus for failing to confide in him (832–33, 1010–18), he expresses loyalty to a friend who would welcome him even while mourning such a wife (855–60, 1147–48). Out of hospitality Admetus opened his house; in reciprocity, Herakles restores the house by recovering Alkestis.[44]

In the final scene Herakles bids Admetus "take the hand of the stranger" (ξένης 1117), the same word for "stranger/guest" (*xenos*) used for Herakles (and Admetus as host) throughout the play.[45] He instructs Admetus to "lead the woman inside" (ἀλλ᾽ εἴσαγ᾽ εἴσω τήνδε· 1147), a phrase frequently applied to a groom "leading in" his new bride.[46] Herakles links this nuptial command directly to his exhortation that Admetus "remain just and continue to honor your guests" (καὶ δίκαιος ὤν/ τὸ λοιπόν, Ἄδμητ᾽, εὐσέβει περὶ ξένους 1147–48). Arrowsmith's freer rendering brings out the connection between the bonds of *xenia* and those of marriage: "in the future treat your guests and those you love/ as they deserve."[47]

For reasons of purity and pollution (1143–46), Alkestis remains silent at the end of the play, but what would we expect her to say?[48] Given the bluster of Admetus before she dies, Alkestis wields far more power here as a potential voice than if she were to speak. Although she returns to the role of wife, in the process her husband is exposed to experiences not unlike her own, and indeed most women in Athens. In the manner of a newly wedded bride, Admetus is forced to abandon his natal family and live dependently on his spouse.

In his despair after the funeral, Admetus wishes he had never wed: "I ought never/ to have married, nor made a house and home with Alkestis./ I envy those who never married [ἀγάμους], who never had children [ἀτέκνους]" (880–82). He repeats the sentiment, claiming that he would prefer to have lived "without children, and unmarried" (ἀτέκνους/ ἀγάμους τ᾽ 887–88).[49] To avoid the pain of loss, Admetus would abandon all dependency on others and dwell "as one alone" (μία γὰρ ψυχή 883), unconsciously echoing the words of his father who insists that men "live one life, not two" (ψυχῆι μιᾶι ζῆν, οὐ δυοῖν 712).[50] Pheres means that no reprieve from death is open to humans, that we only live once; Admetus means that we are better off living alone. The play suggests that both father and son are wrong. Through the ties of marriage and *xenia*, Admetus brings two "outsiders" into the *oikos* and the results are miraculous. The play ends with the departure of a friend and the reunion of a bride and groom at the door of their home. By *not* living as "one alone," Admetus in effect manages to live twice. The idea of a "marriage to death" takes on new meaning in *Alkestis*, a morbid conceit converted to the promise of a second life.

Chapter 7

TORCHING THE MARRIAGE

EURIPIDES' *MEDEA*

MEDEA is an excessive play, even for Euripides. Brutally wronged by Kreon and Jason (who claim to represent the rational Greek order), Medea manipulates the civilized forces that have been turned against her to fashion a revenge of chilling precision. Her poisoned gifts to Jason's new bride convert the wedding ritual into murder, and Medea caps her vengeance by slaying her own innocent children. At the close of the play, she appears transcendent and triumphant in the chariot of her father Helios. Screaming out her hatred for her grief-stricken husband, Medea denies him access to his dead sons while she looks forward to a new life, and a new marriage, in Athens.

It is doubtful that the Athenian audience had seen anything like it. For sheer horror, the story of a mother intentionally killing her children is hard to surpass, but in the telling Euripides exposes—as nowhere else in Greek tragedy—the bleak situation that commonly faced women in the ancient world.[1] Medea recounts what she has had to endure as a foreigner, a wife, and a mother (222–48), concluding that she would prefer three times over to face the dangers of battle rather than the perils of childbirth (248–51). Continuing with the imagery of war, Medea compares her lot as foreign wife to that of a captive seized at the sack of a city (λεληισμένη 256).[2] The married state Medea describes is akin to the situation in contemporary Athens where an ordinary bride could feel like a stranger in a new country.[3]

Discarded by her husband, Medea has no place to turn. Her position mirrors that faced by foreign wives after the enactment of Perikles' Citizenship Law of 451/50. Limiting citizenship to those children *both* of whose parents were Athenian, the law discouraged Athenian males from marrying foreign wives and led to the dissolution of at least some marriages with non-Athenians.[4] If the law was not retroactively applied to children born of mixed marriages before 451/450, then its impact on such preexisting marriages would have been strongest circa 432 B.C., near the time of *Medea*'s first production. At that point a "mixed" son born just after the law was passed would have reached the age of eighteen without political franchise, and a "mixed" daughter would have arrived at marriageable age with little hope of finding an Athenian husband.[5]

Ubiquitous in the play, the language and circumstance of weddings often reveal a funereal after-image. The Nurse reports that Medea and her husband are estranged, for Jason "is bedded down in a royal marriage,/ marrying the daughter of Kreon" (γάμοις 'Ιάσων βασιλικοῖς εὐνάζεται,/ γήμας Κρέοντος παῖδ' 18–19). The Chorus sing of Medea as a "bride" (νύμφα 150) who desires that "unapproachable bed of love" (τᾶς ἀπλάτου/ κοίτας ἔρος 151–52), who strives after "the end [or "ritual completion"] of death" (θανάτου τελευτάν 153). Her rival Glauke is a new wife writ large: a "bride" (νύμφαν 163, νύμφη 1003, 1179), a "newly yoked bride" (νεοζύγου/ νύμφης 804–5), a "wretched bride" (κακόνυμφε 991), the "newly wedded" daughter of Kreon (νεο-γάμου 324, νεοδμήτου 623) who, with her "bridegroom" (νυμφίωι 514) Jason, has joined together as "newlywed" (νεωστὶ νυμφίοις 366) in a "newly forged marriage" (νεοδμῆτες γάμοι 1366). Medea tells Kreon to "marry off" his daughter (νυμφεύετ' 313) but attacks Jason for arranging "this marriage union of yours" (γαμεῖν γάμον 587). She plans to make that "wedding bitter and mournful" (πικροὺς . . . καὶ λυγροὺς . . . γάμους 399) and considers setting fire to the "bridal house" (δῶμα νυμφικὸν 378). She warns Jason that "by marrying you will come to mourn the marriage" (γαμεῖς τοιοῦτον ὥστε θρηνεῖσθαι γάμον 626), and the characters repeatedly refer to the new marriage-bond (kēdos) between the families of Jason and Kreon, the same word used of "mourning rites for the dead."[6]

The breakup of her marriage with Jason is only the first blow to hit Medea. Brusquely interrupting her colloquy with the Chorus, Kreon informs Medea that she has been banished from Korinth. By apprising the audience of her exile some two hundred lines earlier (reported by the Tutor, 70–71), Euripides marshals our sympathies for the protagonist who mistakenly believed that the worst had befallen her. Already marginal in a male world and betrayed by her husband for a new bride, Medea learns that she is to be excluded categorically from the life of the *polis.*

She strives to have her exile rescinded (294–315), presenting herself to Kreon as obedient and reasonable, even to the point of discussing the dangers of sophistic education. At the critical moment, however, Medea abandons rational argument, shifting to rapid stichomythic exchange and assuming the posture of a suppliant (324). Because supplication is an admission of weakness, the picture of Medea kneeling before Kreon is emblematic of the situation of women in the Greek world.[7] Not surprisingly, Medea's overt acknowledgment of her inferior position succeeds where arguments do not, and Kreon grants her one more day in Korinth.

As if motivated by the encounter between a dominant male figure and an abject Medea, the Chorus address the oppression of women directly in the first stasimon.[8] They assail the fact that their gender has been denied the gift of song (424–26), preventing them from answering the charges of men (426–30). If the situations were reversed, "honor would come to women" (419) instead of "ill-sounding fame" (420). The Chorus's language evokes poetic models that underline women's artistic powerlessness: the Ionicisms of ὑμνεῦσαι ἀπιστοσύναν ("singing of woman's faithlessness" 423) may point to the misogynist verses by the Ionian poets Archilochus, Hipponax, and Semonides, and the phrase ὤπασε θέσπιν ἀοιδάν ("he gave [the gift of] godlike song" 425) is taken almost directly from *Odyssey* 8.498, where Odysseus praises the bard Demodokus.[9]

Being denied poetic access does not stop the Korinthian women from denouncing the perfidy of men who gainsay the oaths they have sworn to the gods (415–16). We recall the condemnations of Jason's dishonesty by the Nurse (21–22), Medea (160–63), and the Chorus itself (169–70, 206–12), who repeat the charge in the second antistrophe—"The gift [grace] of oaths has departed, no longer does respect/ for oaths remain anywhere in Greece" (439–40). The stage is set for the arrival of the quintessential oath-breaker, Jason.[10]

The first stasimon begins with an image of sacred rivers flowing backward and heading upstream, a dream of a new dispensation in which honor might come to women by women. With nauseating self-righteousness, Jason offers his own reversal of the natural order, inverting almost everything we have come to consider true in the play. He claims that he is marrying Glauke for Medea's sake and for the good of the children (550–51, 595–97), denying that self-aggrandizement and erotic desire play any part (555–56). He refuses to admit that Medea saved his life or that he has caused her pain, and he concludes that if children could be born another way, there would be no need for the female sex at all and men could be spared an unnecessary evil (573–75).[11] Jason's last comments are egregious, particularly when we recall how Medea valorized a woman's struggle in giving birth over the traditional heroism associated with battle (250–51). She has borne her husband two sons, confirming and validating their marriage, as she herself points out (489–91) and as Jason tacitly admits (557–58).[12] Nonetheless, he blithely prepares for another wedding night, arguing that Medea should be happy because things have turned out so well for her (601–2).

The chief benefit Jason claims he obtained for Medea is that he rescued her from cultural obscurity (539). If not for me, Jason boasts, "you would have no *logos*" (οὐκ ἂν ἦν λόγος σέθεν 541), where *logos* means "language," "culture," "repute."[13] Being among Greeks and their culture makes Medea count, even though Jason flouts the very customs that might give his claim some value. Instead of a civilizing influence, the *logos* has been used to strip Medea of family, home, and city.[14] She protests that Jason employs language not to serve justice but to justify, to "cloak well" (περιστελεῖν 582) the wrongs he has committed.[15] Compare Aristotle on the function of *logos* a century later:

> But speech (*logos*) is designed to indicate the advantageous and the harmful, and therefore also the right and the wrong; for it is the special property of man in distinction from the other animals that he alone has perception of good and bad and right and wrong and the other moral qualities, and it is partnership in these things that makes a household (*oikia*) and a city-state (*polis*).[16]

Far from providing for such a partnership, Jason and Kreon use *logos* to destroy Medea's household and drive her from the city.

As the first stasimon (410–45) makes clear, Medea is a woman trapped in a culture that denies her a public and a poetic voice. But Euripides' tragedy is no meditation on female powerlessness, for Medea bursts the mold of passive victim with explosive fury. Emerging as the author of her own story, Medea at times gains our sympathy —when she learns from Kreon of her exile, or when she faces her husband for the first time and he shamelessly denies that she saved his life. We admire Medea's ability to use the limited means at her disposal to gain a reprieve from Kreon; we do not protest when she thinks of killing Jason and his new bride; and we approve when she secures sanctuary in Athens from Aegeus. However, the attitude in the audience shifts radically when she reveals that she will kill her own children (792).[17] We share the horror of the Chorus (811–13, 816, 818, 844–65, and 996–1001) and hope, as they do (1251–70), that Medea will change her mind or that something will stop her.

The mythical tradition encouraged the original audience to respond in this way, for in all probability the version that Medea intentionally kills her sons was an Euripidean innovation. The Athenians in the theater of Dionysus expected the Korinthians to murder the children, and Euripides leaves that dramatic possibility open until the last minute when we hear their offstage deathcries (1271). Even after the fact, the unknowing Jason fears that his children will suffer violence at the hands of the Korinthians, *not* from Medea (1301–5).[18]

Given the way that Euripides handles the material, those in the audience not only welcome Medea's reservations about infanticide but expect them to prevail. Twice in her second scene with Jason, Medea nearly reveals her authentic self, weeping when she realizes that her actions entail the death of her own children (899–905, 922–32).[19] Ironically, the closer she comes to betraying herself, the more she regains the audience's sympathy. When the children return from their gift-giving embassy, Medea reconsiders her decision in a climactic speech to which the play has been building (1021–80). Nowhere in Greek tragedy is an inner debate so fully dramatized and the pull of competing choices conveyed with such immediacy.[20] But what exactly are those choices, and how is the confusion of marriage and funeral rituals relevant? A closer look at the speech in its dramatic context will help us toward an answer.

As the Chorus predicted (860–65), the sight of the children causes Medea to weep and renounce her plan, at least momentarily. She wonders why, in order to hurt their father, she should "bring on herself twice the evils" (δὶς τόσα κτᾶσθαι κακά; 1046–47). The phrase recalls Hesiod's advice to "pay back double" (δὶς τόσα τείνυσθαι *Op.* 711) a friend who was like a brother but who turns on you and wrongs you by word or deed.[21] Medea inverts the maxim, realizing that by taking revenge against Jason—a "friend" who was once like a brother (implied at line 257)—she will punish *herself* twice as much as her guilty husband. Medea introduces the possibility that the heroic notion of vengeance to which she adheres may constitute her greatest enemy.

Recognizing that the evils (κακοῖς 1046) she visits on Jason through her children are nothing compared to the evils (κακά 1047) she inflicts on herself, Medea abandons her plan (1044, 1048). But the thought of her enemies' laughter changes her mind, and she calls her hesitation "cowardice" (κάκης 1051). The words κακοῖς, κακά, κάκης end their respective lines, and the accumulation of evils reaches its climax at the end of the speech. "Conquered by evil" (νικῶμαι κακοῖς 1077), Medea sends her children inside the house. She knows the "evil" (κακά 1078) that she is doing and that she will suffer,[22] but her desire not to be mocked overwhelms her, a feeling she identifies as "the cause of the greatest evils for men" (μεγίστων αἴτιος κακῶν βροτοῖς 1080). With this second triad—κακοῖς, κακά, κακῶν—ringing out at the end of her speech, neither Medea nor the audience can view the triumph of avenger over mother as a victory.[23]

In reaching her decision, the presence of the children highlights the enormity of the violence that Medea intends. Euripides could have had the Tutor announce that Glauke accepted the gifts and that the children were back home, inside the house. Medea could then consider what to do and why, without having to contend with the physical presence of her victims. Instead, the "smiles" (προσγελᾶτε and γέλων 1041) of her sons lose out to the "laughter" (γέλωτ᾽ 1049) of her enemies. Medea calls her reasons for abandoning infanticide "soft" (μαλθαχοὺς 1052), the same adjective she uses to describe the "soft skin" of her children (μαλθαχὸς χρὼς 1075). The "sweet image" (γλυκεῖα φροντίς 1036) of a life together with her boys—ruined in Korinth (1035) but possible in Athens (1045, 1058)—becomes the "sweet kiss" (γλυκεῖα προσβολή 1074) that she must reject in order to carry out her plan. Awakening her sense of touch, smell, taste, and sight, the children "come to life" via Medea's response, only to become the victims she must destroy.

If Medea bids farewell not only to her children but to her maternal instincts as well, then we expect some expression of loss in terms of the specific expectations of a Greek wife and mother, some indication beyond the commonplace that she will miss her sons when they are dead. Having juxtaposed marriage and death earlier in the play, Euripides now works out the macabre interplay of weddings and funerals in detail, focusing particularly on the mother's role as the overseer of her children's nuptials.

Medea mourns that she will not arrange the wedding of her sons, prepare the bridal chamber and bed, and hold up the traditional marriage torch (1026–27).[24] Time and again in Euripides, mothers refer to this torch-bearing role. Jokasta laments that Polyneikes' marriage in Argos kept her from lighting the wedding torch and her son from taking the nuptial bath and processing with his bride through Thebes (*Ph.* 344–49).[25] In *Iphigenia in Aulis*, Klytemnestra wonders who will hold the marriage torch for Iphigenia when she weds Achilles, and she grows furious at Agamemnon for interfering with her part in the ritual (*IA* 731–41). Alkestis mourns the fact that she will not be there to dress her daughters for their wedding or help them during childbirth (*Alk.* 317–18), and Admetus laments her death by recalling their nuptial procession with marriage torches and wedding songs (*Alk.* 915–25). In *Ion*, Kreusa reveals the bleakness of her "wedding" with Apollo, for no marriage torches led her to the bridal bed where she eventually gave birth to, and later abandoned, her child (*Ion* 1474–76).[26]

As well as mourning the non-wedding of her sons, Medea grieves that they will not care for her in her old age, nor will she receive funeral rites at their hands (1032–34). As discussed in Chapter 6, Greek parents placed great value on being cared for in their old age and then buried by their children when they died. Medea herself claims that burial by loved ones is something "desired by all people" (ζηλωτὸν ἀνθρώποισι 1035).[27] Without the rituals of wedding and funeral, a mother's efforts are "in vain" (ἄλλως), Medea's first word in lines 1029 and 1030.

Although she will sacrifice these rituals with her children, Medea helps to prepare the wedding and funeral of Jason's new bride, Glauke. She tells Jason in their second meeting, "I should have taken part in your plans/ and seen them through, and stood by your wedding/ and taken pleasure in tending to your bride" (886–88). Medea speaks like a *numpheutria*, the mother who helps her daughter get ready for the ceremony.[28] From wife of Jason to surrogate mother of his new bride, Medea manipulates the social and ritual roles available to her, just as in her farewell to her children she realizes that these maternal duties are the ones she will miss the most.

Medea arranges for gifts to be sent via her children to clothe the new bride, identifying the finely wrought robe and golden headpiece as φερναί, both "dowry" and "wedding presents" (956).[29] When the young boys leave bearing caskets with the gifts inside, the audience may have recognized a theatrical version of gift-bearing scenes frequently depicted on Attic vases, either part of the wedding procession itself or the gift-giving occasion (*epaulia*) that followed the next morning.[30] Medea insists that the children deliver the gifts directly into the hands of "the prospering (*makariai*) bride" (957), a nicely ambiguous command given that the *makarismos* blessing was offered not only to newlyweds but also to the recently deceased. For Medea, Glauke is both a prosperous new bride and one of the blessed dead.[31]

The Chorus imagine Glauke donning Medea's gifts, where the wedding crown will prove "an ornament of Hades" (τὸν Ἅιδα/ κόσμον 980–81), and the robes will make her a "bride for those below" (νερτέροις δ᾽ ἤδη πάρα νυμφοκομήσει 985).[32] When Medea bids farewell to her children, she also conjures the moment that Glauke as bride (νύμφη) puts on the fatal crown (στέφανος) and wedding dress (πέπλοισι 1065–66), exploiting the similarities between adorning a bride and dressing a corpse for burial.[33] Even as she mourns the lost marriage and funeral rituals of her sons, Medea arranges a fatal wedding for her rival.

The conflation of the two rituals culminates in the Messenger's horrific account of the death of Glauke and Kreon. He describes how the children and their father enter "the marriage house" (νυμφικοὺς δόμους 1137), and Glauke turns away in disgust at the sight of Medea's children.[34] She "veils her face," προυκαλύψατ᾽, (*proukalupsat'* 1147), the opposite gesture to that of the bridal *anakaluptēria* performed before her husband. But the splendor of the gifts overcomes Glauke's disdain, and she eagerly tries them on, arranging the crown in her hair as she sits and looks at herself in a mirror. The details mesh closely with scenes of bridal preparation popular on red-figure vases after 440 B.C. In these compositions, a woman sits in her chamber and prepares for her wedding, accepting gifts, trying on clothes and jewelry, and admiring the effect by looking in a mirror.[35] Gazing at her reflection, Glauke "smiles at the lifeless image of her own body" (ἄψυχον εἰκὼ προσγελῶσα σώματος 1162). The scene snaps into focus, for the mirror captures a fifth-century wedding about to turn into its opposite. We noted in Chapter 2 the presence of bronze mirrors in the grave goods of women and, more strikingly, the prominence of funerary stelai that bear the sculpted image of the deceased woman sitting and holding a mirror.[36] While Glauke and her household see a happy bride dressed for her wedding, the Messenger, Medea, and the audience know that the mirror reflects a potential corpse adorned for her funeral.

Glauke catches on fire and runs through the chamber trying to shake off the crown, but her efforts only make the fire "give off twice as much light" (1194). Mixing with the flames, "blood drips from the top of her head," and her flesh "flows away from her bones like pine tears" (1200). The macabre comparison of flesh and blood to the pitch that drips from burning pine has specific relevance to the wedding ceremony. Recall that in her farewell to the children, Medea regrets that she will not be able to hold up their nuptial torch. Now she works a ghastly inversion of this ritual practice, turning Jason's new bride into her own wedding brand, burning brighter and brighter until she expires.[37]

Medea's contribution to the marriage celebration is not over, for the Messenger recounts how Kreon enters and throws himself on his daughter's body, προσπίτνει νεκρῶι (1205), meaning "he falls on" or "he embraces the corpse." After enfolding the body in his arms, Kreon kisses it (1206–7), and the sexual language soon merges with the funereal, for Kreon's grief takes the form of "threnodies and wailings" (θρήνων καὶ γόων 1211). He wonders aloud, "Who has made me an old tomb (τὸν γέροντα τύμβον 1209) orphaned of you?" and then he cries in despair, "May I die together with you" (συνθάνοιμι σοι 1210). As if trapped by his own rhetoric, Kreon becomes what he only intended as a figure of speech. He struggles to free himself from the dead girl's counter-embrace (1216), but her wedding dress clings like ivy to a bay tree (1212–13), and Kreon rips his skin from his bones as he tries to pull away. His self-portrayal as an "old tomb" proves all too accurate, and his prayer to die with his daughter is granted sooner than he desires. After their "terrible wrestling" (δεινὰ . . . παλαίσματα

1214), father and daughter "lie together in death" (κεῖνται δὲ νεκροὶ 1220).[38]

Euripides magnifies the horrific impact of Glauke's murder by having Medea exploit signal aspects of the wedding ritual: she contributes to the gift-giving ceremonies by sending bridal adornments and dowry, she precipitates a momentary reveiling of the bride, she helps with the nuptial preparations by providing the garments and coronal worn on the occasion, she ignites a human wedding torch, and she even arranges a perverse consummation of Glauke's marriage by providing her a male to embrace and lie with in death. But Medea also attends to Glauke's funeral, clothing and crowning the corpse for burial, providing a family member to offer the lament over the body, and even erecting a kind of burial marker (Kreon's "old tomb"). Medea's revenge is hideous not only for the physical suffering it unleashes, but also for the poetic refinement with which it subverts the ritual patterns familiar to the Athenian audience.

Preparing to extend her vengeance by killing the children, Medea braces herself with warlike encouragements, exhorting her heart to "arm itself" (ὁπλίζου 1242) and "not grow cowardly" (μὴ κακισθῆις 1246). She addresses her own right hand—"Take up the sword,/ take it!" (1244–45). The hand that signifies sworn oaths (21–22, 492–95), supplications (496, 745–55), and reconciliation (899, 1141) now becomes an instrument of violence.[39] Medea's double imperative and vocative indicate that she gestures at this point, and she may have raised her right hand in militant fashion (befitting the warrior she has become) and then converted that gesture into the ritually appropriate farewell to the dead, the "right-hand farewell" of male mourners known from vase-painting (figure 7).[40] Adrastos makes this sign when saluting the corpses of the Seven (Eur. *Supp.* 772), and the Servant wishes he could do the same at Alkestis' funeral (*Alk.* 768). Because the gesture seems to have been reserved for men, its use here would be all the more telling, marking the emergence of Medea as a male warrior in both language and physical action.

The murder of her children completes the process of Medea's "male-ification" that began when she first countenanced infanticide (764–810). She yearns to be the conquering hero over her foes (765); she wants to pay her enemies back (767); she construes Korinth as hostile territory (781) and will not leave her children there to be insulted by the enemy (782); she cannot endure the thought that they will laugh at her as well (797); she takes delight in proving herself hard on her enemies and kind toward her friends (809).[41]

Following that strident speech, the Chorus respond with an ideal, "feminized" view of the city of Athens, only to contrast it in the second half of the stasimon with a war-torn city victimized by Medea's violence (824–65).[42] Initially, this "ode to Athens" reflects the erotic, women-centered lyric epitomized by Sappho, who often queries the system of values found in epic.[43] But the second half of the ode shatters this vision of Athens: in place of "stepping lightly through the air" (830), Medea offers deadly blows against her children (851); for garlands of roses (841), the Chorus sing of blood and slaughter (φόνον 852, φονεύσῃς 855, φόνου 862, φοινίαν 864); the lovely waters of the river Kephisus (835) will be polluted by Medea's crime (846–50); the peace-loving songs of the Muses (830–32) give way to unheeded pleas for mercy (851–55); instead of Harmonia, the daughter of the Muses (832), or Aphrodite (836) and her sons the Erotes (844), we hear of Medea "the child destroyer" (παιδολέτειραν 849).[44]

It is this crazed warrior that the city of Athens will receive, and who appears on high at the close of the play. But even as Medea ascends to that part of the Greek stage usually reserved for the gods, we realize how far she has fallen. As Cunningham puts it, "The final scene of the play presents visually and strikingly the dehumanizing effect upon Medea of what she has done."[45] For all her knowledge of the future— she predicts Jason's death (1386), the establishment of a cult in Korinth (1379–83), and her own marriage to Aegeus in Athens (1384–85)[46]—Medea is controlled by the past, particularly by her dread of being mocked by an enemy. As she tells Jason, "you were not about to dishonor my bed/ and lead out your life in pleasure by laughing at me" (1354–55). She reins in her regrets over killing the children— "the pain I feel brings me profit so long as you don't laugh at me" (1362). To Jason's incredulous "You killed them," Medea responds, "To cause you pain" (1398).

Medea denies Jason's request to mourn over his sons and bury them (1377–81), and she rejects his appeal to hold their bodies one last time (1399–1404, 1411–12). Stripped of his arrogance, Jason becomes more and more like the Medea who earlier struggled with her decision in the presence of the children. Jason calls his sons "most beloved" (φίλτατα 1397, used twice by Medea at 1071); he yearns to kiss them (1399–1400, as does Medea at 1071, 1074); and he longs "to touch the soft skin (μαλακοῦ χρωτὸς) of my sons" (1403, echoing Medea's ὦ μαλθακὸς χρὼς at 1075).[47] Unable to ease his grief by tending to his dead sons, Jason wishes that he had never been a father at all (1413–14). In these (his last) lines, Jason reaches the same conclusion that the Chorus do when Medea decides on infanticide, namely that it would be better never to have offspring (1090–1115).

Given the transposition of attitudes of Jason and Medea, we catch the bitter irony in Medea's insistence that *she* keep the dead bodies and bury them in the "sanctuary of Hera" (1379), the goddess traditionally associated with marriage.[48] At Hera Akraia in Korinth, Medea will initiate "rites" (τέλη 1382) to expiate the murder of the children.[49] Far from securing a resolution to the upheavals of the play, the institution of a ritual in honor of Hera guarantees a locus *in perpetuum* for the conflation of weddings and funerals that has so guided Medea's revenge.[50]

Medea taunts Jason with the prophecy that his death will be caused by a piece of the Argo, constituting the "bitter final rites of my marriage" (πικρὰς τελευτὰς τῶν ἐμῶν γάμων 1388), again playing on the double meaning of *teleutē* as "end" and "ritual completion." The play's language has come full circle, for the Chorus first sing of Medea as a bride who desires that "unapproachable bed" (τᾶς ἀπλάτου/ κοίτας), striving after "the end/completion of death" (θανάτου τελευτάν 150–53). Between these two "ritual ends," a vicious pattern of marriage and death has been revealed— the wedding rites of Glauke lead to her (and her father's) gruesome murder; the children born from the marriage of Medea and Jason are killed by their own mother; a distraught father is unable to bury the sons whom he now realizes he loves.

And Medea? As Mead writes, "The woman we have known throughout the play is no longer there. A hard and embittered creature has taken her place."[51] That creature heads for Athens, the city where the play was performed, there to join Aegeus (1384–85), the Athenian ruler who offered her asylum. At the time of his unexpected entrance, Aegeus showed a benevolence that mirrored the audience's own acceptance of Medea, a woman victimized by political exile, brutal sophistry, and conjugal rejection.[52] By the end of the play, however, Athens will receive a very different Medea, one who brings war into the household, a "child destroyer" (παιδολῆτορ 1393) who justifies bloodletting by appealing to a "heroic" code that enemies must not laugh at her.

The horrifying precision with which Medea converts marriage into death—and maternity into child-murder—shatters the validity of the heroic ideal she uses to justify her actions. When doing harm to enemies so as not to be laughed at becomes the reason for killing one's loved ones, when an abused woman inverts her traditional roles at weddings and funerals and so converts her home into a battlefield, then the play challenges the ideological roots of the culture. For it is to this ideology that Medea succumbs, denying the Chorus's hope that one day women will tell a different, and perhaps better, story.

Herein lies the importance of Athens as Medea's final destination and home. Far from representing a place of escape beyond the conflicts of the play, Athens receives a Medea who is a monstrous image of the city's own values.[53] Euripides indicates that the excesses of the play are not restricted to an imaginary *mythos* but stand squarely before his contemporaries in the audience.

In the spring of 431 (the year of *Medea*'s first production), a full-scale war between the Athenian empire and Sparta and her allies was imminent, and major hostilities between Athens and Korinth (in the Spartan camp) already had broken out. Although no one could have imagined the destructiveness of the Peloponnesian War, something of its cost—especially to noncombatants—could have been surmised from the unprecedented scale of the fighting that had already taken place.[54] We get a suggestion of the impending violence in the ode to Athens (*Med.* 824–65), where Euripides juxtaposes the portrait of a peaceful, feminine city with the bloody picture of murdered children. Medea's valorization of childbirth over warfare (248–51) conveys a similar opposition, but one that she abandons as the play unfolds. Estranged from her society and herself, Medea increasingly adopts the language, ethos, and actions of a warrior. In the process, her infanticide takes on unmistakable aspects of the male art of war, reflecting the oncoming conflict between Athens and Sparta.[55]

With what specificity *Medea* communicated this connection is, of course, impossible to determine. As we have seen, the play also grapples with issues familiar to the daily life of the *polis*: the destructive effect of men's public aspirations on the family, the importance of children to both private and public spheres, the conception of the *oikos* as people and not property, the differing relationships between women and men and their offspring.[56] However, given the historical moment of the play's first production, the story of a twisted warrior coming from Korinth to Athens must have struck a disturbing chord in the original audience of 431 B.C.

Reading *Medea* in this way emphasizes the social and political contexts that inform the play. In *After Virtue*, Alasdair MacIntyre describes a similar approach to the plays of Sophokles, although his comments are no less applicable to Euripides:

> What is at stake in Sophoclean dramatic encounter is not simply the fate of individuals. . . . [I]t is the outcome for the Greek community which is in the balance. . . . Hence in some important sense the community too is a dramatic character which enacts the narrative of *its* history.[57]

In *Medea*, the rituals of weddings and funerals serve as cornerstones of community self-definition, but they also provide the fulcrum and lever with which Medea undermines it. With ruthless logic Euripides exposes the limitations of his society and its values, presenting a powerful image of the forces that could lead to its collapse. Perhaps the very bleakness of the picture encourages the audience to imagine, and create, a better one.[58]

Chapter 8

FOLLOWING PERSEPHONE

EURIPIDES' *SUPPLICES* AND *HELEN*

D EVELOPED MOST FULLY in the Homeric *Hymn to Demeter*, the story of Demeter and Persephone offered the principal mythical paradigm for the association of death with marriage. Focusing on Persephone's abduction by Hades and separation from her mother, the *Hymn* exposes the suffering that male domination causes women, and the disaster that results if women, in turn, deny their life-giving powers. By "hiding" the fruitful seeds "under the earth,"[1] Demeter forces Zeus to allow her daughter Persephone to return to the light. Persephone's *anabasis* ("going up") mitigates the finality of the underworld and the bleakness of winter, infusing the myth with the vitalizing force of comedy.[2]

In *Supplices*, however, the Persephone story provides the background for a collective *katabasis* ("descent"), where the rejuvenation of the natural world is colored by violence and future destruction displaces the hope of vernal return.[3] In *Helen*, the Persephone story (mutatis mutandis) also provides the mythic template. Here Euripides juxtaposes a funeral ritual with the promise of rebirth and remarriage, only to stain that promise with bloodshed, darkening what many critics view as a romance, "an elegant, irrelevant and lovely marvel."[4]

SUPPLICES: MARRIAGE, DEATH, AND THE CYCLE OF VIOLENCE

Set at Eleusis, *Supplices* evokes the famous Mysteries that honor Demeter and Persephone, as well the lesser ritual known as the Proerosia, offered each year in anticipation of the fall plowing. Both rites give hope of renewal and rebirth—the Mysteries on a spiritual plane, the Proerosia more literally down to earth.[5] The play opens with Aethra making this "preliminary/ sacrifice for the land's tillage" (28–29), but the circumstances under which she performs the Proerosia are extraordinary. She stands before the altar of Demeter, surrounded by the mothers of the famous Seven against Thebes who "bind her" with their suppliant wands (32). Together with Adrastos, king of

Argos, the Chorus supplicate Aethra to intervene on their behalf and persuade her son Theseus to recover the corpses of the Argive Seven from the Thebans who have denied them burial.

Through the opening scene, the Eleusinian setting is never forgotten. The altar where Aethra stands "imprisoned" (102–3) is "the holy hearth of the twin goddesses, Demeter and Korē" (33–34). The suppliants acknowledge that their request does not fit the sanctuary (63–65), and Adrastos reiterates that they have come not to celebrate "the mysteries of Demeter/ but to bury the dead" (173–74). When Theseus rejects their appeal, Adrastos prepares to leave, invoking "the torchbearing goddess/ Demeter" (260–61) to witness the failure of their supplication. The Chorus, however, "rise from the holy floor of Persephone" (271) and make a final appeal for help. They so affect Aethra that, still bound at "the holy hearth of Demeter" (290), she persuades Theseus to change his mind and recover the Argive dead.[6]

The Mysteries represent a symbolic conquest over death, but the suppliants come to Eleusis for precisely the opposite purpose, to consign corpses eternally to the underworld, to "bury the dead" (θάψαι νεϰϱούς). The phrase rings out like a leitmotiv through the play, and the word *corpses*, νεϰϱοί (*nekroi*), receives added emphasis as the first or last word in eighteen different trimeter lines.[7] Visually, *Supplices* is overwhelmed by corpses as well, for the recovered bodies are paraded through the orchestra as part of the longest funeral sequence in tragedy (798–954). In addition to the laments at the *prothesis* and *ekphora*, Adrastos delivers a full-scale funeral oration (857–917) on the model of those given annually in Athens to honor Athenian soldiers who had fallen in battle.[8] The bodies of the Seven then are carried out of the theater for cremation, followed by a *second* procession through the orchestra (1114–82), a cortège of the ashes of the dead borne by their sons.[9]

In between these funeral obeisances, Euripides launches an even more daring assault on the rites associated with Eleusis. Evadne, the wife of Kapaneus, unexpectedly appears on high and leaps into the burning pyre of her husband in an unprecedented union with the dead. If the scene (980–1113) had been omitted by a befuddled Byzantine scribe, not even the most enterprising scholar would have noticed a lacuna, for no one even mentions Evadne before her entrance. The Chorus sing a formally balanced ode mourning their dead sons who have been borne off for cremation (955–89). Shifting suddenly into anapests, the women point to the pyre of Kapaneus, which they describe as θαλάμας (*thalamas*, "hollow, recessed place," 980), etymologically connected to *thalamos* ("marriage chamber"). They next spot Evadne, the wife of the dead hero, climbing the rocks above the pyre. Most commentators presume that she stands on the *theologeion* (a platform on the "roof" of the wooden *skēnē*-façade), although it is possible that she ascends along part of the *cavea* itself.[10] From this elevated position Evadne sings a monody, and then, after a brief exchange with her father who tries to stop her, she leaps to her fiery death.

As far as we know, nothing like this ever took place in fifth-century tragedy before or after *Supplices*, and it would be hard to find a more theatrically daring moment in the history of the stage.[11] Out of the blue, Evadne interrupts the funeral ritual for the Argive Seven, willfully determined to reconstitute her marriage by means of suicide. She evokes her wedding to Kapaneus in her monody (990–1030) and then reenacts it as if for the first time. She recalls the auspicious day and glorious night when "the city of Argos towered tall with songs in honor of my marriage" (ἁνίκα < > γάμων/ τῶν ἐμῶν πόλις Ἄργους/ ἀοιδαῖς εὐδαιμονίας/ ἐπύργωσε 995–98). In place of that song-filled journey to her new *oikos*, Evadne now follows her (dead) husband who leads her *away* from their home (1000–1001). Gone is the torchlit wedding procession (993–94),[12] for Evadne now pursues "the light of the pyre and the tomb" (πυρᾶς φῶς τάφον 1002). She sees in her husband's cremation her own "ritual end" (τελευτὰν 1012), suggesting both marriage and funeral rites.[13] In fact, Evadne is wearing her wedding dress (1054–58), not the black mourning garb of the Chorus. When her father Iphis rebukes her for appearing in such garments at the funeral of her husband (1054), she counters by insisting that she is arranging a new marriage: "Let the wedding-torch [be lit] and the marriage proceed!" (ἴτω φῶς γάμοι τε˙ 1025).[14]

Above all, Evadne imagines her death in terms of the consummation of the wedding night. She longs for "the pleasure of dying together with a loved one who has died" (ἥδιστος γάρ τοι θάνατος/ συνθνήισκειν θνήισκουσι φίλοις 1006–7), a sentiment she repeats: "I will lie in death, dying together with my husband" (πόσει γὰρ συνθανοῦσα κείσομαι 1063). The union she anticipates with Kapaneus is unabashedly erotic, "mingling-in-love my body with my husband's in the flames" (σῶμά τ᾽ αἴθοπι φλογμῶι/ πόσει συμμείξασα φίλωι 1019–20), "my skin touching my husband's skin" (1021). Her father Iphis has come fearing that she "passionately longs to die with her husband" (θανεῖν ἐρῶσα σὺν πόσει 1040), and Evadne's last words proclaim her joy that she will "burn together" (συμπυρουμένωι 1071) with her husband. The repetition of συν-words (suggesting physical togetherness) underlines Evadne's fatal combination of marriage, sex, and death.

Befitting the Eleusinian setting, Evadne situates herself within the frame of the Persephone myth, hoping to arrive at "the marriage chamber [*thalamos*] of Persephone" (1022). But Evadne reenacts Korē's marriage to Hades as if in a parabolic mirror. Whereas Persephone is "taken below" by force while gathering flowers in a meadow (*h.Cer.* 1–18, 425–33), Evadne willingly makes her descent from high up on a barren rock. Persephone cries out to her father Zeus to no avail, for he approves of Hades' abduction (*h.Cer.* 3, 30, 78–80); Evadne refuses to heed her father who begs her *not* to join her husband. Just as Demeter searches for Korē, so Iphis makes his way to Eleusis to find his child (*Supp.* 1038). But Euripides reverses the pattern of Demeter's reunion with her daughter, for Iphis fails to sway his child from her decision to dwell below. Demeter races to rejoin Persephone "like a maenad" (*h.Cer.* 386), while Evadne abandons her father and rushes toward her death "like a bacchante" (ἐκβακ-χευσαμένα 1001). The torches that the goddess carries to search for Persephone (*h.Cer.* 47–48 and 61, referred to at *Supp.* 260–61) give way to Evadne's imaginary wedding torches and the real flames of her husband's pyre. In place of the return and regeneration symbolized by the myth and sanctuary of Eleusis, the play offers an irreversible "marriage to death."

Why does Euripides include this coup de theatre? Why should a suicidal wedding occur so unexpectedly at this point in the play? Let us reconsider the attention lavished on death, funerals, and the dead, examining the ways that weddings are invoked and confounded against the background of the Persephone myth. Returning to the Evadne scene, we then will be able to show how its radical disruptiveness brings Euripides' play into dramatic focus.

To achieve the burial of the Seven is the explicit goal of Adrastos and the Chorus, and it is sought after, supplicated for, debated, and fought over. Once the bodies are recovered, the dead receive a funeral oration and two processions, the second more elaborate than the first. Playing no part in these rituals, Evadne's suicide actually interrupts them by bringing death unexpectedly onto the stage.[15] Recall that the play begins with the static situation of unburied corpses, then moves toward the actual (but reported) battle fought over the dead bodies, where the Athenian army led by Theseus "harvests" the enemy, "snapping necks like stalks/ and cropping the helmets on their heads like ears of summer corn" (716–17).[16] The reported events and past tense keep the killing at a distance, but not so Evadne's self-immolation. Here, the waste of death becomes palpable—someone is there, and then that someone is gone. Death is suddenly present as an animate force, the activity of *dying* and *killing*, rather than something mourned over (as in the opening scene) or reported (as in the battle between Athens and Thebes). The progression from death to dying is particularly shocking when the victim is a noncombatant, someone who doesn't have to die but chooses to leave a world already awash with blood.

To understand the Evadne scene, we also should consider the links between marriage and death forged earlier in the play. Theseus condemns the Argive Adrastos for marrying his two daughters to foreigners and so embroiling his city in the disastrous assault on Thebes (131–45, 219–37), a charge echoed by the Chorus (832). Theseus speaks of Adrastos' "passion for such a marriage tie" (ἔρωτα τῆσδε κηδείας 137), the same *kēdeia* between Thebes and Argos arraigned by Antigone in *Antigone* and by Jokasta and Kreon in *Phoenissae*.[17] As noted in Chapter 4, Thebes is plagued by the hyper-endogamy of incest (Oedipus and Jokasta), and the excessive exogamy of marriage ties with a foreign enemy (Polyneikes and the daughter of Adrastos). Because the focus of *Supplices* is on Argos and Athens, not on Thebes, Evadne's suicide owes little to the incest of Oedipus. However, her wedding to death does result directly from the *kēdos*-relationship established by the marriage of Polyneikes to an Argive, an event that led to the expedition of the Seven against Thebes.[18] Without that war, Evadne's husband Kapaneus never would have mounted the walls of Thebes and been struck down by Zeus' lighting-bolt, and Evadne never would have climbed the crags of Eleusis to leap into her husband's funeral pyre.

In the aftershock of his daughter's suicide, Iphis condemns marriage and children as the source of suffering (1080–91). The idea is introduced earlier by the mothers of the Seven (786–93)—had they remained "unyoked" (ἀπεζύγην 791, μήποτ' ἐζύγη 822), they never would have given birth to the sons whose corpses they must lament (again at 918–23). Iphis desires a second youth and second old age in which to rectify the mistakes of his first life, chief among them his "passionate desire for children" (παίδων ἐραστὴς 1088).[19] Having discovered what it means to lose his daughter, he would live again only to rid himself of the pain of that loss.[20]

Iphis introduces a Möbius-strip of apparent possibilities that wind back on themselves. What does it mean to desire a second incarnation if in that rebirth no future generation will follow in the form of children? Why desire a future existence at all? The question of a second life—metaphoric if not actual—recalls the impulse that drew the initiates to the Eleusinian Mysteries, the desire to obtain some purchase on the afterlife, reflected in Persephone's return from Hades:

In spring when Earth puts out her multitudinous sweetly
scented blossom of flowers, up from the glooming murk
you will rise again, a marvel to gods and to men who die.[21]

(*h. Cer.* 401–3)

The link between the return of spring and the hope of mitigating the
horror of death was central to Eleusinian cult (*h. Cer.* 480–82), for the
Mysteries implied that the uninitiated would suffer after dying.[22]
Seen in this context, Iphis' desire for a second life devoid of children
paradoxically *denies* the promise of the Mysteries, where the idea of
fertility merges with the desire for future life and the return of spring,
if not literally offspring.

The Eleusinian backdrop and mythological frame force the audience to consider the idea of return and renewal even as its possibility is negated. The incongruity of mourning and burial rituals
in a sacred place associated with fertility and regeneration makes
explicit the tension between the drama and its setting. Evadne imagines that she is following Persephone as a bride of Hades, but her
actions categorically deny the myth's redemptive promise of revival
and reunion.

There is, however, one cycle to which the play gives new life—the
fatal cycle of vengeance and martial violence. As he leaves the stage,
Iphis hopes that his own death will come soon: "Old age should make
way for the young" (1113). And so it does, for at that very moment the
secondary Chorus of children, bearing urns with the ashes of their
fathers, enter the orchestra. Euripides has prepared his audience to
attend to the message of the younger generation, and what we hear is
ominous. The sons sing of their orphaned status (ὀρφανεύσομαι 1132)
and are joined in grief by their grandmothers (the mothers of the
Seven), in keeping with the funereal mood. However, one son hopes
that as "shield-bearer" (ἀσπιδοῦχος 1143) he will avenge the death of
his father (1142–44). Another prays that "with the help of the gods,
justice may come/ for my father" (1145–46). A mother responds in
muted disagreement, "And this evil still does not sleep./ Terrible
events! Too much lamentation,/ too much grief comes at me" (1146–
48). A third son imagines himself leading a new Argive assault on
Thebes to avenge his dead father (1149–51), while a mother speaks of
the double suffering bequeathed by her son, grief for herself and for
her grandson (1156–57).

It is hardly surprising that the boys' desire for vengeance and
renewed violence receives a muted response from the Chorus. Mothers who have lost sons in a foreign war, they are alive to the pain of

future bloodshed.[23] Nor can the audience be expected to view with equanimity—much less with patriotic delight—the rumblings of new battles, especially at Thebes. The play's opening section establishes the questionable nature of the *first* Argive war on Thebes, and we recall Theseus' original conclusion that intervention on behalf of the suppliants was not justified. When he bows to his mother's arguments, he does so not on the merits of the Argive expedition, but rather to defend the pan-Hellenic norm that burial is due to friend and foe alike.[24] The battle that Athens wages against Thebes is fought expressly *for the bodies*, nothing else. Theseus shows no interest in exacting vengeance, only in securing funeral rites for the dead. With victory won and the way open to seize the city of Thebes, Theseus refuses to press his military advantage, proclaiming instead that "he did not come to sack the town, but only to take back the dead" (723–25).

Theseus is a model of self-control and moderation in the midst of war, and his actions after accomplishing his mission continue to set the example. He begins the exequies for the recovered warriors, washing the bodies, readying the funeral biers, and covering the corpses. In so doing, Theseus himself performs many of the ritual actions normally reserved for the mothers of the dead (762–68). Adrastos is amazed that a man, a general, the leader of the city would undertake such duties—we should recall that the bodies have long been dead and exposed above ground. For Adrastos, even slaves would take on such work "with abhorrence" (762), for cleaning up these rotten corpses is "an awful business, one that is full of shame" (δεινὸν μὲν ἦν βάσταγμα κἀισχύνην ἔχον 767).[25] Adrastos' reaction should answer those critics who interpret Theseus' intervention in the funeral rites as a symbol of the extension of state control over traditional female duties.[26] Rather, as Theseus explains to Adrastos, the women "would die if they saw the bodies all mutilated" (944). Because they have suffered so much, he asks, "Why would you want to inflict them with new grief?" (946).[27]

Rather than promulgating a *polis*-sponsored program to constrain women, Euripides singles out Theseus' willingness to assume a female role, emphasizing that the Athenian ruler transcends the forces of pride that lead others in power to lose their self-control. Earlier Theseus takes the advice of his mother Aethra on a crucial question of policy, reversing his course of action to help the Argive women recover their dead (293–341). When Athens is victorious, he refuses to press the advantage and sack the city of Thebes, prompting the Messenger to praise Theseus in words of particular relevance to the war-torn Athenians of the original audience:

Best to pick such a military leader (στρατηγὸν) [*stratēgon*]
who provides in times of trouble the surest defense,
for he hates the popular tendency of violent overreaching
　　[ὑβριστὴν] where, when someone does well,
he strives to climb to the top of the ladder [κλιμάκων]
and so destroys the prosperity he had at his command. (726–30)

The image of climbing too high brings to mind Kapaneus, who
scaled the walls of Thebes by ladder (κλιμάκων 497) only to be blasted
by the lightning bolt of Zeus (496–99).[28] Kapaneus' rise and fall epitomizes the entire expedition of the Seven against Thebes, a collective
exercise in *hubris*. Adrastos himself admits that a peaceful and fair
resolution had been offered by Eteokles, but the Argives rejected it
and were destroyed (739–41).[29] He sees their error replicated by the
Thebans when they refuse to return the bodies, "falling victim to
their own violent overreaching" (ὕβρις᾽, ὑβρίζων τ᾽ αὖθις ἀνταπώλετο
743). Adrastos concludes that cities must resolve disputes by argument and reason and not by bloodshed (744–49).

With this admission, Adrastos gives sympathetic voice to the case
made earlier by the Theban Herald:

When a people vote to make war,
no one considers that he himself might die
but turns that harsh fate on to another.
But if death were *there to behold* [εἰ δ᾽ ἦν παρ᾽ ὄμμα
　　θάνατος] when the votes were cast,
war-crazed Greece would never destroy itself. [30](481–85)

Although the Herald's argument is suspect (in part because he uses it
to deny the right of burial at 494–95), his comments should not be
rejected out of hand.[31] A common ploy in ancient narrative is to
introduce difficult truths via an unsympathetic character and then
have a major player adopt a similar perspective later.[32]

Considering the end of the play with the Herald's point in mind, we
realize to what lengths Euripides has gone to present images of death
"there to behold." Not only does an array of corpses dominate the
second half of the play, but the suicidal marriage to death of Evadne
virtually explodes onto the stage. Euripides makes every effort to
preclude a failure of imagination in the audience by keeping images
of war-generated destruction before us. In an emotionally powerful—
if verbally muted—way, they evoke the lessons taught by Theseus
and echoed by Adrastos.

And yet, for all their vividness to the audience, the lessons of death
seem to go unheeded by the characters onstage.[33] Holding the ashes of

their fathers who fell in an unnecessary and avoidable conflict, the sons of the Seven proceed as if that truth had never been admitted. Instead, they sow the seeds of future war, and Athena (who appears *ex machina*) waters the ground. On the one hand she insists on formalizing a defensive alliance between her city and Argos (1183–1212), on the other she gives her blessing to the second Argive assault against Thebes and guarantees its success (1213–26). The lessons of Argive arrogance (embodied in the fate of Kapaneus), the reflections of Adrastos, and the moderation of Theseus are all, as it were, simultaneously acknowledged and ignored.[34]

It is hard to believe, as many critics do, that Athena speaks *for* Euripides when she encourages a fresh outbreak of bloodshed.[35] Athens at the time was engaged in the devastating Peloponnesian War, and aspects of *Supplices* indicate that the conflict was integral to the play's composition and reception. Theseus' battle with Thebes over the corpses may reflect the historical refusal of the Thebans to relinquish the Athenian dead after the battle of Delium in November of 424, and the Argive-Athenian defensive alliance clearly anticipates the actual agreement achieved in 420, after the Peace of Nikias in 421.[36]

Di Benedetto points out that performances at the City Dionysia took place not long before the *stratēgoi* (military leaders) were elected for the year. We recall the Messenger's advice that Theseus—with his clearly defined goals and resistance to violent excess—is the kind of *stratēgos* to choose (726–30). It is hard to fault Di Benedetto's conclusion that, at the time of its first production, the play translated into support for candidates other than the war-mongering Kleon.[37] The desire for peace took on even greater relevance if the play were produced (as Collard and others think) in the spring of 423. The tetralogy of which *Supplices* was a part would have been performed only *a few days before* the Athenian assembly met to consider a year-long armistice with Sparta. The Peloponnesian delegates arrived for discussion with the Council before the City Dionysia began, and it is likely that they were in attendance at the theater, joining the citizens of Athens who later would vote on the treaty.[38]

At this point we should consider the specific relevance to the play of a ceremony that preceded the performances. Orphaned sons of Athenians who had fallen in battle were reared at public expense, and when they reached the age of 18 they marched through the orchestra dressed in hoplite armor provided by the city, a gift that bound them to the defense of Athens.[39] In the closing section of the play, Euripides makes a series of references to this preperformance ceremony. Orphaned boys (ὀρφανεύσομαι 1132) process through the orchestra

holding the ashes of their fathers, men who have been given a funeral
oration just as the fathers of the Athenian orphans would have received at the time of their burial. The Argive youths long for the day
when they can bear a shield (ἀσπιδοῦχος 1143) and avenge their war-
slain fathers, just as their Athenian counterparts bore the city's gift of
armor (including the great hoplite shield) in remembrance of their
forebears. Theseus, the leader of the Athenian *dēmos*, urges the boys
"to honor this city, and from son to son/ to pass down the memory of
the things that you obtained from us" (1172–73). Similar sentiments
were offered to the wards of the Athenian state when they were ush-
ered into civic responsibility and adult life in the orchestra before the
tragic performances.[40]

As dea ex machina and protectress of Athens, Athena exhorts the
orphans—once "their beards begin to shadow"—to avenge their fathers by leading a "bronze-clad" army against Thebes (1219–20). Her
call to battle again brings to mind the Athenian orphans who, having
come of age, also come into arms. The message of renewed conflict at
the end of the play merges with the militaristic preperformance spectacle, a fusion of artistic convention, civic practice, and contemporary politics that shaped the experience of the original audience.

Dramatized before them were two broad, but clearly opposed, scenarios for the city: to use battle as a last resort in defense of laws and
customs that were pan-Hellenic in nature, as Theseus does; or, to
surrender to the instincts of violence and vengeance, as the orphans
do and as Athena encourages. Will the spectators support their city's
participation in activities that Euripides has exposed so relentlessly
—hubris, avoidable war, the waste of youth, the endless cycle of
vengeance? Will the hard earned insights of the play be overwhelmed
by the impulse for future conflict? These questions remain at the end,
for the answers are not to be found on the stage but in the lives of the
Athenian audience.

That the leaders and the citizenry, the *dēmos*, could act responsibly
is Euripides' point in having Theseus consult the assembly before
going to war (393–94). A passionate concern for the direction of the
city helps to explain the other "public" aspects of the play, particularly the prominence of political advice, debate, and decision-
making. Initially deferring to men, Aethra forthrightly interjects her
views on a policy question in order to persuade her son to act well for
the city. Theseus changes his position and then emphasizes that
Athenian practice requires him to consult the citizens and follow
their will, which he does (349–57). He engages the Theban herald in a
debate on the relative merits of democracy and tyranny (404–56),
stressing the specific advantages of Athens' form of government, in-

cluding the annual rotation of officers (406–7).[41] Theseus echoes the phrase that opened each meeting of the Athenian Assembly (438–39),[42] and he emerges as a model *stratēgos* (obliquely at 190–92, directly at 726–30). At his behest, Adrastos presents a funeral oration —an essential part of the *patrios nomos*—for "the young men of this city" (i.e., Athens, 843), delivered out to the theater audience.[43] Finally, the relationship between Argos and Athens takes the form of a treaty that was in the air at the time of the play's first performance, anticipating the agreement reached in 420 B.C. (as noted above).

Although fully incorporating this public discourse, Euripides seems doubtful of its ultimate effectiveness, and he relentlessly probes its potential for misuse.[44] The Theban Herald highlights the problems of democratic demagoguery, where a few clever-tongued, self-serving politicians lead the majority astray (412–25). The common man does not have the time to become an expert on issues and therefore is tempted to hand over his vote to the most persuasive speaker. Democracy only appears to be the rule of the people, for power is wielded by the few who manipulate the many.[45] In the funeral oration delivered by Adrastos, Euripides dramatizes the very process that the Herald criticizes. Adrastos constructs a virtuous "Kapaneus" for public consumption and for the edification of the young men of Athens. Gone is the overreaching man of violence struck down by Zeus' lightning bolt, the very epitome of *hubris* (495–99). In his place, Adrastos creates a moderate aristocrat, a Kapaneus who, for all his wealth, "was no prouder than a poor man" (862–63), one for whom "the mean was enough" (866).[46]

Against this politically motivated rewriting of history, Euripides counters with a theatrical rhetoric all his own. The mothers of the dead heroes take no comfort in Adrastos' funeral address, responding to his glowing words with grief and despair (918–24). Their reaction brings us back to our starting point, the unexpected appearance of Evadne. Her scene is so shocking that it cuts through the contradictions and doubletalk that precede it. And yet Euripides makes Evadne's "wedding to death" as aggressively public as any encounter in the play. When she reveals her plan to throw herself on her husband's pyre, Iphis begs her not to say such things "before a crowd" (1066). But Evadne insists, for by her example "all the Argives will learn" (πάντας Ἀργείους μαθεῖν 1067).

Euripides encourages us to contrast the lessons that Evadne teaches with those offered by Adrastos, who closes his funeral oration with some thoughts on education. For him, learning is a process that works subliminally on the young, involving things "they don't fully understand" (ὧν μάθησιν οὐκ ἔχει 915). "When someone learns (μάθηι) something *that* way, it will stay with them till they grow old," Adrastos proclaims (916).[47] Perhaps this observation explains the extraordinary nature of Evadne's suicide. Only something so excessive, so theatrically daring, could shake the fifth-century audience free from the education toward war and aggression they had known from an early age. Evadne's "marriage to death" sets off a dramatic explosion that brings home to the audience what the characters on stage only talk about and then forget.

Evadne's death serves as an unsought, even perverse *proteleia* ("preliminary sacrifice") for the burial rites that follow.[48] However, the young participants in those rites are not content with putting the dead to rest but are keen to renew the cycle of violence. Gone are the offerings to Demeter for bountiful harvest that started the play, and absent too is the wise mother, Aethra, who made them. Gone, too, is the hope of return from the underworld symbolized by the figure of Persephone and the Eleusinian setting. In their place we have a gathering of ashes, an orchestra full of mourning women and future warriors, the patron goddess of the city in her characteristic armor, and, still present as an after-image, the stark and forbidding memory of a wife leaping to join her husband—a theatrical world firmly wedded to death. How closely that stage picture will reflect the world outside the theater constitutes Euripides' implicit challenge to his audience.

HELEN: BURYING AND MARRYING A PHANTOM

Written some ten years after *Supplices* and hard on the disastrous defeat of the Athenian expedition at Sicily,[49] *Helen* follows the version of the myth credited to Steisichorus. There, the heroine never goes to Troy but is replaced by a phantom "Helen," who draws the Greeks and Trojans into a disastrous conflict—all part of Zeus' plan to reduce the world's population.[50] By featuring a shadow Helen, Euripides exposes the insubstantial justifications with which invaders rationalize wars of aggression—applicable not only to the legendary Greek expedition against Troy, but also to the Athenian armada that sailed to Sicily with such high expectations.[51]

The play develops the Persephone theme with great wit and irony, bringing out Helen's likeness to Korē in a variety of ways.[52] Helen is swept up, Persephone-like, while picking flowers in a field (243–47). Hermes—the *psychopompos* ("leader of souls") who negotiates between Hades and the upper world—covers Helen in a cloud and deposits her in Egypt (44–48), a place the Greeks associated with the "ends of the earth" and the infernal world.⁵³ There she wards off the nuptial advances of Theoklymenos, the young Egyptian king, until she is reunited with her husband Menelaus, converting a feigned funeral into a celebration of their remarriage and return to Sparta.⁵⁴ Teukros, the Greek who lands at Egypt early in the play, likens the rich Egyptian palace to the "house of Ploutos," the god Wealth (68–69). But the name also suggests Plutōn, an epithet associated with Hades, who is "rich" because he receives all departed souls.⁵⁵ Teukros refers to the phantom Helen as "daughter of Zeus" (Διὸς κόρης 77, Διὸς κόρην 81), recalling the name Κόρη (Korē), the common appellation for Persephone as offspring of Zeus and bride of Hades.

The Chorus recount Demeter's search for her daughter in the great Demeter ode (1301–68), where Helen takes on both roles in the myth. Persephone was "seized" (ἁρπασθεῖσαν 1312, ἁρπαγὰς 1322) by Hades and taken to the underworld—in the Chorus's version, while dancing with other maidens—just as Helen seemed to be "seized" by Paris (ἀναρπαγὰς 50) but in fact was "taken up" (ἀναρπάσας 246) by Hermes and brought to Egypt where she resists Theoklymenos' efforts to "seize" her (ἁρπαγάς 904). And just as Demeter grieves for Persephone, Helen laments the fate of her own daughter Hermione, separated from her mother and devoid of marriage prospects in Sparta (282–83, 689, 933, echoed by the Chorus at 1478–79).⁵⁶

Euripides has Demeter make her way to Mt. Ida in the Troad (rather than to Eleusis as in the *Hymn to Demeter*), and there she casts her blight on the earth (1323–37). In the folds of this very mountain Paris rendered his judgment that led to the Trojan War (357–59, 676–78).⁵⁷ By conjoining the legend of Persephone with that of Troy, Euripides uses the wedding-to-death theme to highlight the disasters of war. The figure of the grieving goddess Demeter spreading sterility from the mountains above Troy mirrors the grief-stricken Trojan women who lament their loss (194–99, 362–69, 1113–21) and bewail a city that has been reduced to ashes (109, 383–84, 503, 1161–64, 1220, 1560, 1652).

In addition to the mythical frame of the Demeter-Persephone story, *Helen* builds on the ritual foundation provided by weddings and funerals. We hear of the original marriage ceremony uniting Helen and Menelaus (638–41, 1400–1401), and the Messenger relives the celebration in which he himself played a part (722–25). The Coryphaeus forcefully reminds Theoklymenos that Helen's father, acting as her *kurios*, gave her as a bride to Menelaus, not to him (1634–36). The Dioskouroi reconfirm the original wedding by announcing that Helen "will go to her [new/old] home and dwell together [συνοικῆσαι] with her husband" (1655).⁵⁸

Against this real union, Euripides plays off the apparent marriage of Paris and Helen (referred to ten times), a union that leaves Greek widows "lying in their weddingless chambers" (ἄνυμφα δὲ μέλαθρα κεῖται 1125).[59] On several occasions we hear of the wedding of Hermione that may never occur, and we learn that Theoklymenos' sister, the prophetess Theonoe, has reached the age of marriage but has decided to remain "always a maiden" (12–13, 1008). Even more prominent is the wedding that Theoklymenos eagerly pursues with Helen, a union so close to materializing that he orders his underlings to send wedding presents and commands all Egypt to raise the marriage hymn (1431–35).[60]

Balancing these multitudinous weddings are the evidence of a past funeral and the promise of a new one. Located in the center of the orchestra, the tomb of Proteus provides the magnet for the stage action.[61] Helen takes refuge there to avoid Theoklymenos' advances (1–329), and the tomb provides the locus for the eventual recognition scene between her and Menelaus (556–697). There Helen warns her husband that, if Theoklymenos discovers him, "my marriage bed will end up killing you" (807). The couple agree to die at the tomb if necessary (835–50), a suicide pact that Menelaus reveals to Theonoe after he has prayed over the grave, invoking the spirits of Proteus and of Hades (961–76). If Theonoe tells her brother of their plan, Menelaus vows that "streams of blood/ will soak this grave, and we shall lie together/ twinned in death on this carved tomb" (984–86).

Fresh funereal activities break out at other points in the play. Helen sings dirges and threnodies for her dead mother and (apparently) dead brothers, as well as for the many who fell at Troy (164–78). As a bereaved wife, she readies the funeral lament for her absent Menelaus whom she thinks is dead (335–39). Once reunited with her husband, Helen begs Theonoe not to betray them: "If he had died and his body consumed on the pyre,/ I would be offering my tears to his distant ashes./ Now that he is alive, safe, *here*, am I to have him taken from me?" (936–38).

The strongest funereal presence is, however, the mock rite for Menelaus that dominates the close of the play. As if following contemporary practice in Athens, Helen cuts her hair in mourning, changes her white raiments for black, and scars her cheeks with her nails (1087–89, 1186–90). The absent body is to be "shrouded" (1243) and carried on a "covered bier" (1261), precisely the ritual followed in the Athenian *patrios nomos*, where a single bier was borne in the procession to represent all the bodies that could not be recovered from battle.[62] Grave gifts (κόσμον 1062, 1068) are to include flowers and fruit (1265), a common custom in Attic burials, although along with them Helen procures the bronze armor that will serve Menelaus when the time is right.

Helen specifies the importance of having women from the family participate in the rites (1275), and it is in this context that we should understand her bathing and re-clothing of Menelaus (1382–84). As part of the play's "inexhaustible irony,"[63] Helen washes and dresses the "corpse" as she prepares for her husband's reemergence into life.[64] Although Theoklymenos thinks his own wedding is at hand, the funeral of Menelaus restores his union with Helen, even as it signals the approaching wedding of their daughter in Sparta. A "young calf " (1476) left at home, Hermione awaits "the nuptial torches that have not yet been lit" (1477).[65] Perhaps the ritual wedding torches will compensate in a small way for the fact that the phantom Helen "kindled the war at Troy" (συνάψαι πόλεμον 55) and the Greeks burnt the city to the ground. Symbolizing the return of husband and wife as well as the promise of her own marriage, Hermione's wedding torches might even provide the redemptive light that counters the false beacon-fires that lured the Greek fleet to ruin on the voyage home.[66]

Euripides gives us a heroine to warrant such expectations, for Helen remains true to her husband, ready to die to preserve her marriage. She is wracked with grief over the meaningless suffering inflicted at Troy, particularly as felt by the women who mourn the loss of their sons, brothers, and husbands. Helen's response to the cruel ironies of the war opens up the imaginative space for the sentiments of the Chorus, who close their long-delayed first stasimon with a plea for peace:

> Fools who strive for glory in war,
> in the shock of spear against shield,
> senselessly you try to stop
> > the labor of mortal life.
> Must contests of blood decide
> these things? Then strife will
> never leave the human city.
> You see what they won—wedding chambers
> in the Trojan earth,
> > and they could have
> settled it with words, their strife over you.
> > > Ah Helen! (1151–60)

As the fair winds waft husband and wife homeward at the end of the play, the audience may be encouraged to see a movement toward the realization of such a world (at least theatrically), where peaceful resolution replaces the desire for glory in battle, a desire that serves (like the phantom Helen) only an illusion.[67]

Having aroused such hopes, Euripides proceeds to dash them. The promise implicit in the myth of Persephone—given ritual form in the juxtaposition of Menelaus' funeral and Helen's wedding—turns back on itself. The first hint of this development occurs when Menelaus sacrifices a bull and horse as part of his mock funeral: "streams of blood shot out /into the waves" (αἵματος δ' ἀπορροαὶ/ ἐς οἶδμ' ἐσηκόντιζον 1587–88). The verb εἰσακοντίζω literally implies the hurling of spears, hinting at the martial reality that lurks behind the simulated ritual. The "streams of blood," αἵματος δ' ἀπορροαὶ [aporrhoai], recall the three loci of the play—Troy, Sparta, and Egypt—each marked by its river: the streams (rhoai) of the Scamander (53) and Simoeis (250), where countless Trojans and Greeks fell (367–69, 608–10); the reedy-green streams (rhoai) of the Eurotas (124, 162, 492) that await the homecoming of Helen and Menelaus (1465–66, 1491–94); and finally the virgin streams (rhoai) of the Nile (1–3), with its dark-gleaming (179) and shining (462) waters. Through these associations, Menelaus' sacrifice suggests that the blood spilled for the phantom at Troy has spread to waters previously untainted.

Earlier Helen bathed Menelaus in the pure, dewy water of the Nile (1384), preparing this "corpse" to resume its true identity. But the play reveals the darker side of Menelaus' "burial into life," for he emerges in full armor (1606), a warrior ready to slay barbarians just as he did on the plains of Troy. When the boat reaches deep water, Menelaus springs to the attack, urging his disguised Greek comrades to "slaughter, massacre these barbarians, and hurl them/ from the ship into the sea" (1594–95). Rising up with their hidden swords, they join Menelaus in cutting down the unarmed Egyptian rowers who must do battle with ship oars and planks. The Messenger describes the results with Homeric simplicity: "the ship flowed [ἐρρεῖτο (errheito), lit. streamed"] with blood" (1602).[68]

This is not the first time we meet the warrior Menelaus in the play. Earlier, he refuses to countenance separation from Helen: "Leave you! But I sacked Troy for you!" (806). Behind the bitter humor lies the mentality of a soldier who stands committed to his conquests, even when they appear—given the "phantom" reasons for the war—to be an utter waste of life. Menelaus considers any sign of womanly cowardice "unworthy of Troy" (808), and so he refuses to supplicate Theonoe or weep in her presence (947–53). Compare Theseus in *Supplices*, himself a soldier, but one willing to be moved by a woman and to take on a female role, performing the funeral offices for the exposed corpses of the Seven. No such "new man" emerges at the end of *Helen*, for the Menelaus who springs to life out of his own funeral is very much the old conqueror of Troy, back in his element as he cuts down the alien foe (1606–8).

And what of Helen? At the crucial point in the battle, she cries out to her fellow Greeks, "Where is the fame and glory [κλέος] of Troy? / Show it against these barbarians!" (1603–4)—this from the woman who earlier bemoans the fate of the Trojan women, who grieves for the senseless suffering, who admits straight-out (250–51) that the war was fought over nothing.[69] From her feigned wedding with Theoklymenos and the counterfeit funeral of Menelaus, Helen emerges as a true bride of her warrior husband, a battle cry of death on her lips.

In the play's opening dialogue, Teukros prays that Helen of Troy might die and never come back to Greece, but he wishes just the opposite for the (unrecognized) Helen standing before him: "But you, lady, may you always thrive" (163). At the end of the play, the Helen who makes her way home with her husband shows signs of being the wrong one, the Helen whom Teukros wished dead. By calling the spirit that sacked the city of Troy to rise up and kill more barbarians, Helen renounces the lesson she has learned, that the ten-year struggle was a trick, a sham fought over a phantom, death without a human purpose. It is as if the war that Euripides keeps Helen from, that she laments so eloquently during the play, manages to sweep her up after all.

Winnington-Ingram summarizes the relevance of these issues to Athens of the late fifth century:

> When Euripides writes about the Trojan war, he cannot fail often to have had the Peloponnesian war in mind. So here there is an ironic analogy. Greek and Trojan have fought a destructive war—about what? A phantom, a cloud. Was any better purpose served by the war which Athenians and Peloponnesians had been fighting?[70]

The rhetorical and self-aggrandizing phantoms that led Athens to undertake the Sicilian expedition surely are reflected in the underlying premise of Euripides' play. When we consider the near-madness with which Athenians embraced the invasion of Sicily (only to see it end in the worst defeat the city had known), Helen's conversion into a cheerleader for battle sounds a bitterly ironic note. Even more, the Chorus's vision of a world where lust for glory and conquest give way to reason and negotiation takes on immediate, and undeniable, relevance.

Euripides' *Helen* adopts the mythic pattern of return based on Persephone's ascent from Hades. As in *Supplices*, however, the promise of rebirth inherent in the *anodos* structure—a promise underlined by juxtaposing funeral and wedding rituals—falls prey to chauvinism, bloodshed, and war. The funeral-wedding of Helen and Menelaus calls to life the very things that the play has exposed as the source of ruin, epitomized by the "phantom Helen" who reappears at the end to make her way back to Greece. If some members of the audience cheer at Helen's *cri de combat* (as have some critics, in their scholarly fashion), they simply replicate the tragic process and deep-rooted impulses that the play seems so keen to reverse.

Chapter 9

WAR BRIDES AND WAR DEAD

EURIPIDES' *TROADES*

E URIPIDES' *Troades* confronted the audience of 415 B.C. with the brutality of war and the bankruptcy of political power that served no end but its own perpetuation. Even critics reluctant to see contemporary references in tragedy admit that the destruction of the island of Melos in 416 lay in the formative background of Euripides' play. Refusing to submit to Athens, the island carried on as if neutral until an Athenian force invaded, slaughtered the adult males, and enslaved the women and children.

Although the conquest of Melos was of little military importance in the Peloponnesian War, the presence and placement of the Melian dialogue in Thukydides' history emphasizes the incident's symbolic role. Revealed as nowhere else in fifth-century literature is the Athenians' willingness to abuse power and find ready justifications for doing so. The apparently objective tone of the debate, with no discussion of moral right or wrong, suggests the corrupt position that Athens came to embrace. Matters of life and death are discussed solely in terms of self-interest, as if objective advantage and external rewards could be determined without considerations of piety, or the mutability of events, or the cardinal issue of what the Athenian empire *was* whose survival demanded the annihilation of a people.[1] Under the guise of rational discourse, horrors are countenanced, endorsed, and committed, in a manner all too familiar to our own time.[2]

As her child is torn from her to be hurled to his death, Euripides' Andromache speaks for the Melian woman and for countless other victims of "civilized" savagery: "You Greeks invent barbaric evils" (*Tro.* 764). Not surprisingly, *Troades* has produced eloquent critical responses, and modern playwrights have brought its anti-imperialist passions to bear on the barbarisms of their own day.[3] What has remained unexplored, however, is the way in which the confusions of marriage and death inform each of the major dramatic encounters, bringing their distant horror into immediate contact with the audience. By tracing the interplay of weddings and funerals, we can recapture more fully the theatrical power of one of the greatest antiwar plays ever written.

Euripides throws us into the postwar world of fallen Troy, and his focus is almost exclusively on the female victims. The same women who gather when Hektor's body is returned at the close of the *Iliad*— Hecuba, Kassandra, Andromache, Helen—reappear in *Troades* as the central characters. Hecuba's encounters with her two daughters and erstwhile "daughter-in-law" (all three played by the same actor) constitute the main scenes, and Hecuba's young daughter Polyxena, although never appearing on stage, lingers in the background. Captives at the fall of the city, *all* the daughters of Troy—characters and Chorus alike—face some form of marriage to death, a union with the men who slew their husbands or their grooms-to-be.[4]

Through the Greek herald Talthybios, we learn that Kassandra is to become Agamemnon's concubine, "the shadowy wife of his bed" (λέκτρων σκότια νυμφευτήρια 252). Hecuba asks to whom Polyxena "has been yoked" (ἔζευξεν 262), and the Herald responds that her daughter "attends on Achilles' tomb" (264). Talthybios refers cryptically to the sacrifice of Polyxena at the hero's grave, an act that Euripides dramatizes as a twisted wedding with the dead in his earlier *Hecuba*.[5] Hektor's wife Andromache has been claimed by Neoptolemos, the son of Achilles, the man who slew her husband. As for Hecuba, she goes to Odysseus, that paragon of deceit, the man with "the double tongue" (287).

The glow of torches within the palace prompts Talthybios to wonder if the Trojan women prefer death by self-immolation to a life of slavery without their husbands. The audience may recall Evadne's suicide on Kapaneus' pyre in *Supplices*, but here Euripides introduces a figure diametrically opposed to that of a wife mourning her dead husband: the prophetess Kassandra enters holding a nuptial torch in each hand, a madly joyous bride who foresees and celebrates her upcoming wedding with Agamemnon.

Mother and friends have gathered, as is proper for the ceremony, but Kassandra must sing her own wedding hymn and utter the *makarismos* blessing for herself (312–13), words that should come from others.[6] Bearing the bridal torches that ought to be carried by her mother, she upbraids Hecuba for not doing her part, for lamenting the dead Priam instead of celebrating her own union with Agamemnon (315–21). Kassandra urges the festivities to begin, encouraging Hecuba to take her place in the wedding dance and calling on the Trojan women to join in the nuptial hymn (325–40). Kassandra describes the maidens as "lovely-dressed" (καλλίπεπλοι 338), imaginatively transforming the rags they wear into the rich attire appropriate to a wedding. Perhaps she herself wears white, as befits a Greek bride.[7]

Confident in her foreknowledge, Kassandra celebrates her wedding precisely *because* it leads to death. Her attitude reflects the grim irony of the play introduced in the prologue, where the gods Poseidon and Athena arrange for disaster to strike the victorious Greeks on their return home. Breaking off her monody, Kassandra (like her namesake in *Agamemnon*) shifts to dialogue meter and explains that "the glorious leader of the Achaeans, Agamemnon/ will marry in me a worse bride than Helen" (357–58). Hecuba should cease lamenting, "since both my enemies/ and yours I shall destroy by my wedding" (404–5).

By Kassandra's lights, Troy is "more blessed," μακαριωτέραν (*makariōteran* 365), echoing her wedding *makarismos* at 312–13) than the conquering Greeks. The invaders "were not shrouded/ in death-robes by the hands of their wives, but lie here/ in foreign soil" (377–79). Similarly, the old men who died in Greece also lacked proper rites, because their sons were not present to perform them (380–82). The Trojans, on the other hand, received full funeral honors from their loved ones and were buried in their homeland (386–93). Even Agamemnon will not be as fortunate as that, for he will be murdered by his own wife and his corpse disposed of ignominiously (446–67). For this reason, Kassandra is impatient for her wedding to begin: "Make haste, so that as fast as possible I might marry my bridegroom in Hades" (. . . ἐν Ἅιδου νυμφίωι γαμώμεθα 445).

Hecuba never imagined her daughter "would contract a marriage at spear point,/ a captive of the Greeks" (346–47). The wedding torches that Kassandra brings onstage are out of place in a fallen city, and Hecuba wrests them away by claiming she does not hold them properly (348–50). Symbols of the monstrous union between the prophetess and the city's destroyer, the torches indicate how far Troy has fallen,[8] even as they foreshadow the flames that will consume the city at the play's end.

Hecuba would drown out the wedding song with the sound of her own weeping (351–52), and her sepulchral tone fits the true situation. For although Agamemnon will die, so must Kassandra, and her end will mirror that of the Greeks who fell at Troy. She will be cut down in a foreign land, without proper burial, "thrown out naked in a mountain ravine/ to be washed by the melting snows . . . / a gift to the wild beasts to feast on" (448–50). Hecuba also mourns her husband Priam (killed at the household altar, 474 and 481–83), her many sons who have been slain (475–80), and the "maiden daughters I raised/ to be worthy of the most select bridegrooms" (ἃς δ' ἔθρεψα παρθένους/ ἐς ἀξίωμα νυμφίων ἐξαίρετον 484–85), destined now to become slaves and concubines of the Greeks.

As women facing the same fate, the Chorus begin the first stasimon by invoking the Muse, asking her to sing "a new strain" (*kainōn humnōn* 512) that proves to be a "funeral hymn" (*epikēdeion* 514). They tell the story of the Trojan horse wheeled into the city on a "four-footed cart" (τετραβάμονος . . . ἀπήνας 516), the catalyst for the all-night dances that celebrate the end of the war. But out of this ersatz gift to Athena come the Greek soldiers who sack the city, killing Trojan husbands and raping the conquered women:

> Slaughter at the city altars,
> and the headless corpses of husbands
> fill the beds of their young wives.
> They [the women] are now the victors' crown
> worn by the Greeks, bearing them children,
> causing Troy greater pain. (562–67)

Just as Kassandra's wedding hymn celebrates the impending death of husband and wife, so the Chorus' "new strain" changes from a song of victory to a dirge for the lost marriages of Troy.

At the end of the stasimon, Andromache and her child Astyanax arrive on stage "ferried in a foreign wagon" (ξενικοῖς ἐπ᾽ ὄχοις πορθμευομένην 569), borne "on the back of a cart" (ἀπήνης νώτοισι 572). Their entrance recalls that of the Trojan horse, also hauled in on a "four-footed cart" (τετραβάμονος . . . ἀπήνας 516). Instead of hiding the enemies of Troy, however, this wagon holds the spoils of the city's conquest—Trojan riches, Hektor's bronze armor, and his young widow who must sail with a new man back to Greece (573–76). As Andromache mourns her lost marriage with Hektor and prepares to live as Neoptolemus' concubine, the wagon that carries her begins to resemble a marriage cart that bears the bride to her new home.

Hecuba urges Andromache to make herself desirable to her new husband, so that she might rear Astyanax along with any future offspring. But no sooner does Hecuba raise the hope of Troy's survival through her grandson then Talthybios announces the Greeks' decision to hurl Astyanax to his death (699–719). For Andromache, the news is "an evil worse than the wedding" that awaits her with Neoptolemus (720). Her life with her young child is reduced now to a final embrace and the last trace of his "sweet breath of skin" (758). The echo of Medea's farewell to her children (*Med.* 1075) underlines the horror of Astyanax's murder, for the *logos* that condemns these innocent youths represents a world in which barbaric actions are made to appear reasonable and even necessary.

Talthybios warns Andromache to utter no protest lest the Greeks refuse her son burial, leaving her no choice but to urge the Greeks on to the savagery implicit in their verdict: "Take him, carry him, throw him down (ῥίπτετ'), if throwing him (ῥίπτειν) is what you want./ And then eat his flesh" (774–75). She tells them to throw her (ῥίπτετ' 778) into the ship, for "I come upon such a beautiful/ wedding, having lost my own child" (778–79). The anguished bride is taken away to her new husband, while Talthybios leads Astyanax to be hurled from the walls of the dead city. Moved in spite of himself, Talthybios realizes that—in a world where an innocent child can "lose his breath by a vote" (785)—a herald should be without pity or shame.

Left alone with the Chorus, Hecuba begins to beat her head and body in lamentation, the same mourning ritual that Andromache performed for her sister Polyxena (626–27).[9] The Chorus flesh out Hecuba's grief by singing of the first sack of Troy, recounting the wedding of the goddess Aurora (Dawn) to Tithonus, a "marriage bond [kēdos] forged with the gods" (844–45). "Abducting" the Trojan youth in her "golden four-horse chariot" and taking him up to Olympus (855–56), Aurora reverses the journey that Hades makes when he leads Persephone in his chariot down to the underworld. The goddess of dawn bears children to her mortal husband in the "marriage chamber" (thalamois 854), but their union fails to save Troy, for it is Aurora's light that "looked on the destruction of Pergamon" (851).[10] In the end, her four-horse chariot of gold gives way to the four-legged wagon that hauls the Trojan horse into the city, and, finally, to a lowly mule-cart that shunts the war-bride Andromache down to the sea, to be shipped with the other spoils back to Greece.

The failed kēdos of Aurora and Tithonus provides the perfect prelude to Hecuba's encounter with her "daughter-in-law" Helen, "abducted" by Paris in the accursed marriage that destroys the city. Filled with tonal ambiguities and rhetorical flourishes, the debate between the two women presents its own interpretive problems, but one point should be stressed. When Helen wishes to make a speech in her own defense, Menelaus rejects the idea: "I haven't come to hear you talk but to kill you" (905). It is Hecuba who persuades Menelaus to let Helen speak (906–10), confident that in her rebuttal she will prove the bankruptcy of Helen's sophistry and the rightness of her own position.

Hecuba's belief in the efficacy of words is as touching as it is ill-founded, for the scene reveals the futility of rational discourse when events have reached such a stage. We know that Menelaus will welcome Helen back to his marriage bed, no matter how strong are Hecuba's arguments. Her appeal for justice from those who destroyed her city is doomed from the start. Moreover, the very presence of Menelaus gives the lie to Hecuba's claim (seconded elsewhere by

Andromache and the Chorus) that Helen bears sole responsibility for causing the war.[11] Menelaus—and Hecuba's own'son Paris (subject of *Alexandros*, part of the Trojan trilogy)—represents the brutal male world that will wed its "Helens" again and again, with no concern for the havoc unleashed on the innocent.

In bitter contrast to the reunion of the estranged Menelaus and Helen, the Trojan women grieve over their dead husbands and lament the impending separation from their children. As they are shipped off to Greece as chattel, they pray that Helen will never reach Sparta, sailing as she does "in full possession of the golden mirrors, the joy/ of unmarried girls" (1108–9). Although commentators refer to Helen's narcissism, we might consider the passage in light of the prominence of mirrors in Attic wedding iconography. The Chorus may be implying that Helen has symbolically removed all their hopes for a marriage of choice, a point raised earlier by Hecuba (484–85, above p. 130). Because Helen's "hateful wedding" (δύσγαμον 1114) has destroyed the city, the Trojan women pray that she will drown on her voyage home. We know from the prologue that disaster will strike the Greek fleet, but not, ironically, Helen and Menelaus, who are destined to survive and prosper.

The play draws to a close with a series of convulsive images of marriage and death. Talthybios enters bearing the corpse of Astyanax on Hektor's shield, confessing that even he wept at Andromache's farewell to her son (1130–31). She begged her new husband Neoptolemus "not to take the shield to Peleus' hearth/ nor to the very marriage chamber where she was to be wedded,/ but to use it in place of a cedar coffin and stone tomb/ and have the child buried on it" (1138–42). Trying to arrange the funeral of her son even as she is led into slavery, Andromache gives instructions for Hecuba to "wrap the corpse in its burial robes/ and wreaths, as well as circumstances allow" (1143–44).

Talthybios himself offers to bury the body after Hecuba has dressed and adorned it (κοσμήσῃς νέκυν 1147). He already has helped with the ritual, washing the corpse and cleansing its wounds in the flowing streams of the Scamander (1151–52). Moved to perform one of the women's tasks in the funeral rites, Talthybios recalls another "ritually feminized" male, Theseus, who bathes the Argive corpses in *Supplices*. In both cases, the funeral preparations emphasize the physical fact of death, its inescapable reality in a society where corpses were not turned over to professionals but were handled, cleaned, clothed, and buried by family members.[12] Talthybios' earlier confession of pity (758), the fact that he weeps for Andromache (1130–31), and his willingness to assume the woman's role in preparing the body of Astyanax (an ostensible enemy) indicate how fully he is drawn into the emotional orbit of his Trojan victims, one of the few tender moments in the bleak world of the play.[13]

Mourning over her grandson, Hecuba unites marital hopes with funereal grief for the last time: "If only you had died for the city, reaching a ripe age,/ and marriage, and a king's rule like a god,/ then you would have been blessed [makarios], if there is blessedness in such things" (1168–70). The ritual makarismos offered to the groom again is conflated with the blessings for the dead, just as Hecuba's lament recalls the nuptial rites that Astyanax will never know. She calls her attendants to bring out what adornments they can find for the body (1200–1202, 1207–13). Wrapping Astyanax in Trojan robes, she returns to the wedding that might have been: "I cover your skin with a treasure of Trojan robes,/ those that should have been used to dress your body at your wedding/ when you married the finest Asian princess" (1218–20). At that celebration the wreaths and finery would have meant something to Astyanax, but now they cover a senseless corpse, at best a source of empty pride for the survivors (1248–50).

Hecuba remembers how the boy promised to dedicate locks of hair at her tomb, and to bring groups of mourners to the post-burial rites in her honor (1182–84). As often in tragedy, the natural cycle of the young burying the old has been reversed, and Hecuba—bereft of her children and her city—must oversee the funeral of the last young hope of Troy (1185–86). She composes an imaginary epitaph to be carved on the tomb, casting everlasting shame on Astyanax's murderers: "Once upon a time, out of fear for the child buried here,/ Greeks cut him down" (1190–91).[14]

After the body is removed for burial, Talthybios interrupts the women's lamentations for the last time. Arriving with soldiers who bring torches, Talthybios carries out the order to burn the city. Hecuba threatens to hurl herself into the flames, a giant funeral pyre for an entire people (1274–83), recalling the scene where Talthybios saw firelight in the palace and feared the women were planning suicide. Then it was only Kassandra, bearing wedding torches and a prophecy that Agamemnon would couple with death. Now it is the city of Troy that dies, and the women pound on the earth as if to revive the dead spirits of the land they must leave—the walls and towers (1291–99), their own children (1304), the unburied corpse of Priam (1312–14). Hecuba and the Chorus make their way down to the ships and the forced weddings that lie ahead (1326–32), the end of Troy, her final marriage to death.

At the time of the production of Troades, Athens was considering an invasion of Sicily, the disastrous enterprise discussed in Chapter 8.[15] In the ongoing debate on that expedition and the direction of the *polis* in general, the performances in the theater of Dionysus played an important role.[16] In *Troades*, for example, Euripides has a conquering army put men to the sword and sail off with the women as slaves and concubines, just as the Athenians themselves had done the year before at Melos.[17] But as Troy goes up in flames at the end of the play, the audience might have recalled another invasion, one that also razed a great city. Sixty-five years before Melos, the Persians burnt the temples and other buildings on the acropolis of Athens, just above the theater where *Troades* was performed. Could Euripides be pointing out the disconcerting truth that the hubris of the hated Persian aggressors has reappeared among democratic Athenians?[18]

In Aeschylus' *Persians* (721–25, 745–51), the barbarian invaders are punished for "yoking the sea;" the Greeks in Euripides' *Troades* will pay for their zeal in subjugating all-too-human victims. In a notorious act of impiety, Ajax rapes Kassandra, dragging her from Athena's temple "by force" (βίαι, *Tro.* 70). Agamemnon, too, "marries Kassandra by force" (γαμεῖ βιαίως 44), becoming a "second Ajax" (618–19).[19] The Greeks commit other outrages, culminating in the murder of the young Astyanax. For all that separates the historical Persians from the invading Greek army in *Troades* (and, by extension, the Athenians at Melos), the cruelty, arrogance, and argument from empire remain the same.[20]

In such a world—as the prophetess Kassandra tries to convey—the wedding torches of the future only light the way to death, like the torches that set Troy ablaze in the closing moments of the play.[21] In the final lament of the Trojan women, would the Athenian audience hear a trace of the dirges they themselves had sung for their own war dead in the conflict with Sparta? And what of the chorus members who dressed as females and mourned in the persona of women victimized by invasion? How many of these performers would sail off in the upcoming expedition to Sicily and not return? How many men in the audience would do the same? How many women would find themselves—like Hecuba grieving for her unburied Priam—mourning a husband or son or father lost at sea in the naval disaster at Syracuse? Although Euripides could not have known the outcome of the Sicilian expedition, his *Troades* makes it clear that destruction like that at Melos will come back to haunt its perpetrators. Like Agamemnon wedded to Kassandra, or Polyxena to Achilles, the Athens that is mirrored in Euripides' tragedy seems bound to a future of lamentation and death.

CONCLUSION

THE IDEA of marriage to death in Greek tragedy does not serve a single thematic end but rather flows through the plays in varying currents and eddies. A twisted wedding informs important segments of *Agamemnon*, where Helen, Iphigenia, Klytemnestra, and Kassandra (as well as Paris and Agamemnon) all participate in some form of ritual perversion. Alternatively, marriage and death can be integral to the entire plot, as in *Trachiniae*, which culminates in the promise of both a wedding and a funeral. In *Medea*, the conflation of the two rituals exposes an inhuman revenge and the flawed system of values that turns a sympathetic victim into a triumphant monster. In *Supplices*, the wedding-to-death motif is reflected in the Eleusinian background, but it emerges with theatrical power only with the appearance of Evadne. Her suicide plays a crucial role in dramatizing the cycle of violence, where the allure of the dead drags down the living. Wedding and funeral motifs are conjoined from the outset of *Alkestis*, and the inclusion of an outsider—Herakles as *xenos* (guest-friend), Alkestis as *xenē* (stranger, bride)—allows for a Persephone-like resurrection. A similar pattern operates in *Helen*, but there the *anodos* leads to fresh bloodshed, recalling the wasteful violence at Troy. In *Troades*, the grim interplay between marriages and funerals helps convey the depredations of imperialism and foreign war. Although the rituals have some impact on individuals (Talthybios helps with the burial of Astyanax), they seem ultimately powerless in a world of self-justified aggression.

In many instances, the plays use familially defined weddings and funerals to explore the political and social problems facing the city, gauging the well-being of the *polis* in terms of the health of the *oikos*.[1] In the process, women emerge as the vehicles of change and renewal, although—as we would expect of the genre—not without tragic complications. In *Medea*, for example, the Chorus invoke a Muse for the female sex to ensure that *their* story is told, and at moments in the play it appears their wish will come true. Ultimately, however, the protagonist self-destructs as a woman, blotting herself out by adhering to a set of values that replicate the male *logos*, which has cast her aside so ruthlessly. Although constituting her triumph, the "wedding" that Medea arranges for her rival and the murder of her own sons show her to be a twisted Argonaut on her way to Athens, a revelation of particular moment to the Athenian audience who stood poised on the verge of a ruinous war with Sparta.

We meet a more sustained authenticity in Aeschylus' Kassandra. Her clarity in the face of death evokes, and to some extent redeems, the nightmarish sacrifice of Iphigenia. Kassandra knows all too well what the future holds, and her "marriage to death" involves the dramatic confluence of time past and time future, caught between the man who eradicated her city and the woman ("too much like a man") who cuts her down at the altar. Sophokles' Antigone carries the challenge to male authority further, and ultimately she is vindicated. But in resisting Kreon, Antigone must forsake the traditional fulfillments of marriage and family life. This fact emerges strongly in her last appearance on stage and takes final form in her "marriage to death" with Haimon in their wedding chamber/tomb.

Although no fully "liberated" woman appears in these scenarios, it would be unfair to conclude that female characters simply affirm the structures of power that constrained their real-world counterparts.[2] These tragic heroines broaden the horizons of the possible by manipulating the social and cultural norms that give cohesion to the society from which they spring. The playwrights' interest in feminism—to give that ancient concern its modern name—did not extend greatly beyond "the minimal claim that women have been unjustly disadvantaged because of their sex."[3] But given the social, economic, and legal realities of fifth-century Athens, that was no small step, and its reverberations, at least on the stage, were anything but minimal. Instead of viewing the concern over feminist issues as a smokescreen hiding the *real* repression perpetrated against women, we would do better to admit that tragic characters frequently posed radical challenges to traditional ways of thinking and dealing with the world, and women's perspectives and positions (as understood by male playwrights and interpreted by male actors) were central to those challenges.

If tragic women represent unfulfilled potential in and of themselves, their effect on male characters—here we see a clear reflection of the male orientation of Athenian society—greatly extends their influence. Charged with being ruled by a woman, Sophokles' Haimon reveals a disposition that might navigate between the extremes of the play, loyal to his father but equally alive to the mood of the city and the inherent rightness of Antigone's stand. In *Supplices*, Aethra changes Theseus' mind on the issue of retrieving the Argive bodies; by defining his mission in his mother's terms, Theseus resists the temptation to sack the city of Thebes, the very madness that struck the misguided men whose corpses he must rescue. Through his wife's sacrifice on his behalf, Admetus gains a second life in *Alkestis*, only to find that it is not worth living. However, by receiving the strange woman forced on him by Herakles, a "feminized" Admetus validates both the male ties of *xenia* and the male-female bonds of wedlock. In *Troades*, the forced marriages of the captive women and the cold-blooded murder of an innocent child release unexpected compassion in Talthybios, who pities the Trojan captives and even takes the woman's part in washing the corpse of the murdered Astyanax.[4]

In other tragedies, the *rejection* of such behavior and the insistence on traditional male roles generate violent actions that turn on their perpetrators. By sacking the city of Oechalia to seize Iole as his war-bride, Herakles in *Trachiniae* sows the seeds of his own and De-ianeira's deaths. In *Medea*, the protagonist brings war to the house-hold, converting her sons into instruments of vengeance against Jason, and so eviscerating her own maternal feelings. At the death of Astyanax in *Troades*, Hecuba lashes out at the powers that counte-nance such horror: "Ah, you Greeks! You have more to boast of in your spears/ than in your brains. Do you so fear this child/ that you must find new ways to shed his blood?" (*Tro.* 1158–60). Having de-nied compassion to those they have conquered, the Greeks set sail at the end of the play, oblivious to the disasters that await them as they return home to *their* wives and children.

Even in tragedies where violence appears to be rewarded, there is a lingering sense that things are not so simple. In *Supplices*, the first Argive invasion of Thebes is exposed as ill-advised and unnecessary, but the passion to settle the score gradually takes hold of the sons of the Seven, who plan a new campaign. Euripides the realist confronts the short-lived memories of human beings, acknowledging that the cost of foreign aggression must be counted anew by successive gener-ations. His *Helen* reveals the Trojan War to be a sham, waged over a phantom, and yet at the end of the play the war is trumpeted as a model for heroic behavior.

The theatrical *cris de coeurs* connected with marriages and deaths gather particular force around the issue of foreign war, an enterprise that robs the young of their wedding day and brings death and funerals out of season. In particular, the plays of the last third of the fifth century focus on the Greek civil war between imperial Athens and Sparta. As Thukydides reports, the Peloponnesian conflict was not business (or battle) as usual, but something unprecedented in scale, conception, and execution. In his speech to the Assembly, Perikles outlines a radical strategy to guarantee Athenian victory. Instead of a bloody but brief series of hoplite encounters with the Spartans, Athens will fight a protracted conflict, one in which she depends on her navy and avoids pitched land-battles, even abandoning homes and fields to the invader.[5] The citizens who live on farms outside the city gather their possessions and withdraw behind the walls, where they watch the Spartans ravage the land.[6] Even after the plague strikes the overcrowded city, Perikles insists on following the same strategy, and the pattern of Athenian withdrawal and Spartan invasion continues (with some lapses) through 425. We may assume that the Athenians feared the pattern would continue, as it did when the Spartans gained a permanent base in Attica with the capture of Dekeleia in 413.[7]

In this pattern of hostile return and depredation, the Athenians watched their crops being ravaged in the early summer. As Demeter's gift of renewable grain went up in smoke, did they recognize the inversion of the myth of Persephone acted out on their own soil?[8] In Aristotle's account of the funeral oration (*Rh.* 1.7.34, 3.10.7), Perikles compares the death of the young men of the city to "the year being robbed of its spring," imaginatively moving the myth's focus from the world of nature to that of humans. Euripides develops this transformation, for the story of Persephone and Demeter lies behind the *anodos* of the prewar *Alkestis*, then shifts to reflect the pattern of recurrent violence in *Supplices* and the renewal of bloodshed in *Helen*. Persephone's marriage to death takes on increasingly tragic significance for Euripides, as the Peloponnesian War continues and opportunities to end it are squandered, giving way to a cycle of violence.

Clearly, the clash of weddings and funerals offered powerful possibilities for the tragic playwright, from the emergence of female characters who challenge male values to an explicit critique of imperialist aggression. These possibilities complemented those provided by the myths that shaped the dramatic conflicts themselves. Fergusson observes in myth "an ordering of human experience at a level (or in a 'scene') wider, deeper, and more permanent than the rationalized scene and the literal facts of the moment."[9] The tragic playwrights found similar potential in the ritual life around them. To employ a metaphor familiar to the Greeks, wedding and funeral rituals provided a warp to match the woof of traditional mythology, on which was woven the cultural "rug" of Athenian self-expression.

Sharing a timeless quality with traditional myth, these ritual activities stood outside the temporal flux, although each wedding and funeral marked a highly personal transition experienced by the individual participants.[10] By definition, there was no freedom to alter rituals in their social enactment (or they would cease to be rituals), but that constraint did not apply to playwrights. As we have seen, they could juxtapose and transpose elements, confuse and intermingle events, and from these changes create images that disturbed and shocked, criticizing the status quo and opening up radical possibilities. Both myth and ritual enabled the playwrights to challenge the audience's preconceptions of how things were (and how they might be) by manipulating elements of the society that were constitutive of its meaning. In the hands of Aeschylus, Sophokles, and Euripides, the ritual/mythological rug did not sit still but was shifted and even pulled out from under those in the audience, reorienting their perspective and to forcing them to see the world—and themselves—more clearly.

Responding to the anti-art tenant of commercialism ("Give the public what they know"), the South-African novelist and Nobel laureate Nadine Gordimer counters with the claim that "writers—artists of all kinds—exist to break up the paving of habit and breach the railings that confine sensibility."[11] Is it forcing modern concerns on the ancients to suggest that similar thoughts occurred to the tragedians of Athens? If not, then women emerge in Greek tragedy to speak with a difference, and weddings turn into funerals to symbolize their failed hopes, or to highlight the extent of their mistreatment. Maimed rituals reveal a world gone seriously wrong, where the old must bury the young in a sad reversal of the natural order, where dominant modes of thinking and acting prove deadly, where wars of aggression are indiscriminate killers as well as destroyers of ritual life.

To be sure, many events enacted on the tragic stage have the look and feel of the inevitable, of something transparent to the very conditions of human experience. But when we examine the manner in which rituals are used in tragedy, issues of human agency and choice stand out as the determinant ones. Although they drew on traditional mythology and heroes, Aeschylus, Sophokles, and Euripides did not create a world beyond their audience's reach. By incorporating contemporary rituals into the language and action of the plays, they brought these stories home with compelling urgency, forcing their fellow Athenians to confront the world before them. The powerful images of marriages and death, the shocking perversion of weddings and funerals, issued a call to the living. Through their multiple effects, Greek tragedy reveals itself as the subversive prototype of all great theater, a theater in which the audience becomes the subject of inquiry and the site for change.

Appendix A

THE *ANAKALUPTĒRIA*

MANY scholars—including Oakley, Redfield, and Deubner—believe that the *anakaluptēria* took place at the wedding banquet, before the bride and groom left for the groom's *oikos*.[1] There are problems with this view. According to a sixth-century B.C. source, Pherekydes of Syros (*DK* 48), the event occurred on the third day, presumed to be the last day of the wedding celebration, after the bride and groom spent their first night together. To make this information fit with contradictory sources that connect the *anakaluptēria* with the wedding banquet and with gift-giving, Deubner argues that the *archaic* wedding must have taken more than three days. Deubner then claims that the fifth-century A.D. Alexandrian scholar Hesychius (s.v. *anakaluptēria*)—who wrote that the ritual unveiling took place on the third day—must have been using an archaic source. Better to admit, with Montuoro, the confusion in the sources: "I grammatici e lessicografi si contraddicono perché attingono a fonti di età e di ambienti senza coordinare le notizie in base a conoscenze personali degli usi."[2]

To bolster the case for the *anakaluptēria* at the wedding banquet, Oakley (following Deubner, and followed by Sutton) contends that vase-paintings of the wedding procession to the groom's house "uniformly show the bride unveiled," thus indicating the *anakaluptēria* already has taken place.[3] To argue in this manner is, I think, misleading. Time and again painters (especially in black-figure) show the bride and groom together in profile in a chariot or cart headed toward the viewer's right, the bride further from the viewer with her left hand holding out her veil so that it frames her face (figures 4, 1b, 5).[4] What the gesture implies about the temporal sequence of the *anakaluptēria*—whether it has occurred already or whether it will take place after the couple's arrival?—remains a matter of conjecture. All we can assume with confidence is that the iconography—a man, a woman with veil, and a chariot—indicates a wedding procession and establishes a nuptial context for the scene. Similarly, in red-figure, brides with veils are depicted frequently, although usually in processions on foot. Often in these scenes the image of a bride with her head covered is the vase-painter's convention for showing her wearing a veil (figures 2, 3).[5] Again, the fact that she is so depicted does not

establish that the formal unveiling lies ahead, any more than it suggests that the *anakaluptēria* already has occurred.

Returning to Pherekydes and Hesychius, let us assume that Deubner, Oakley, and Sutton are mistaken, and that the *anakaluptēria*
took place in the *thalamos* on the wedding night—a position supported by an increasing number of scholars.[6] If so, then the presence
of the bride at the gift-giving ceremony (*epaulia*) the following morning would be her first public appearance as a formally "unveiled"
wife. This possibility may account for the association of the *anakaluptēria* with giving gifts to the bride mentioned in some sources
(e.g., Pollux 3.36). If this assumption is correct, then at some point the
two uses of the word *anakaluptēria* became confused, one referring to
the private unveiling of the bride before the groom and the other to
the appearance of the "unveiled" bride at the *epaulia*, the formal
reception of gifts (and givers) in her new home. Indeed, the late
second-, early third-century A.D. lexicographer Harpocration (s.v.
anakaluptēria) thought that the *epaulia* and *anakaluptēria* were the
same event. Instead of dismissing his account (as some scholars have
done), we might better understand his use of *anakaluptēria* in the
second sense that I have suggested, the public appearance of the unveiled bride the morning after her private unveiling before her husband. This sequence for the *anakaluptēria* makes better sense of
passages referring to the ritual in tragedy, discussed in Chapter 3
and 4.

Appendix B

MEDEA 1056–80

CRITICS HAVE DISCOVERED in Medea's monologue the key to her changeable character, or exactly the opposite, the manifestation of her unshakeable resolve. That these prejudices strongly influence the discussion of the validity of the last twenty-five lines of her speech should be acknowledged from the start. The complexity of the debate makes it impractical to defend in detail the text as printed (with minor variations) by Kirchhoff, Paley, Prinz, Verrall, Bayfield, Earle, Murray, the Loeb editors, Page, Flacelière, Elliott, and others. However, a brief account should make it clear why the passage in question belongs to the play.

There are four basic positions regarding the authenticity of lines 1056–80: 1) they should be deleted in toto; 2) only lines 1056–64 should be deleted, but the rest of the speech should stand; 3) a shorter deletion of 1059–63 removes the major problems (1062–63 are bracketed by almost all editors as copied from 1240–41); 4) the entire speech should stand. Let me deal briefly with the arguments for each of these positions.

Wholesale deletion, proposed by Reeve and followed by Diggle, Bain, and others, is based on purported staging problems involving the children and a sense that the speech combines illogicality with questionable Greek.[1] If the children withdraw even a little from Medea at 1054, however, no one in the theater would wonder, as Reeve (60) does, "what . . . the children [are] supposed to make of Medea's remarks." We must not expect of Greek tragedy a dramatic realism that is foreign to it. Nor do we need to save the transmitted text by removing the children altogether, as Grube 1941, 160–62 does, leaving Medea to speak to their imagined presence as Macbeth does to his "dagger of the mind."

It is not infrequent in tragedy that a character fails to hear everything that another character says. For example, Oedipus hears Jokasta mention that Laius was killed where three roads meet, but misses her saying that her child was exposed with his ankles pierced and pinned together (S. *OT* 711–30). As to Bain's "rule" that orders to mutes [here, the children] are carried out with little or no delay, it is not followed earlier in the play (*Med.* 89) when the Tutor fails to leave with the children as instructed. And yet on that basis, and "the inconcinnity of Medeia's reasoning," Bain would eliminate 1056–80.[2]

Reviewing the arguments for this whole-scale deletion, Kovacs mounts a strong case for the authenticity of all but 1056–64, quoted here (through 1066):

μὴ δῆτα, Θυμέ, μὴ σύ γ᾽ ἐργάσηι τάδε·   1056
ἔασον αὐτούς, ὦ τάλαν, φεῖσαι τέκνων·
ἐκεῖ μεθ᾽ ἡμῶν ζῶντες εὐφρανοῦσί σε.
μὰ τοὺς παρ᾽ Ἅιδηι νερτέρους ἀλάστορας,
οὔτοι ποτ᾽ ἔσται τοῦθ᾽ ὅπως ἐχθροῖς ἐγὼ   1060
παῖδας παρήσω τοὺς ἐμοὺς καθυβρίσαι.
[πάντως σφ᾽ ἀνάγκη κατθανεῖν· ἐπεὶ δὲ χρή,
ἡμεῖς κτενοῦμεν οἵπερ ἐξεφύσαμεν.]
πάντως πέπρακται ταῦτα κοὐκ ἐκφεύξεται·   1064
καὶ δὴ ᾽πὶ κρατὶ στέφανος, ἐν πέπλοισι δὲ
νύμφη τύραννος ὄλλυται, σάφ᾽ οἶδ᾽ ἐγώ.   1066

("Oh my heart, don't, don't do this deed.   1056
Wretched woman, let them be, spare your children.
Living there [in Athens] with you, they will make you happy.
By the avenging furies that live below in Hades,
no! It cannot be. I will never let my children   1060
suffer violence at the hands of my enemies.
[No way out. I must kill them. Since it is necessary,
I will cut down those whom I brought to life.]
The thing's done, and she will not escape.   1064
Even now the crown is on her head, and in the wedding dress
the royal bride is doomed, I see it clearly.")   1066

Kovacs claims that defenders of these nine lines "have not pointed to any convincing dramatic gains Medea's illogicality makes for the play."[3] One character's illogicality is another's indecision, however, and much of the prejudice against these lines begins with the assumption that Medea never seriously considers changing her mind. Once that assumption is made, however, the game is up—it is extremely difficult to establish "dramatic gains" if one cannot appeal to Medea's struggle over what to do. Kovacs claims "the Medea we have rescued . . . is the same heroic Medea we see in the first half of this speech and elsewhere in the play."[4] Foley advises against playing down "the text's moments of genuine hesitation," only to conclude that "Medea's choice was inevitable from the start." Lloyd-Jones concurs: "The fate of the children has long since been decided; Medea has never seriously contemplated renouncing her revenge, for if she did so, she would not be Medea."[5]

Even with this prejudice, Lloyd-Jones offers the simplest solution to the textual difficulties. Deleting only lines 1059–63 eliminates Medea's peculiar fear that if she fails to kill the children they will somehow suffer harm from her enemies in Korinth.[6] Her thought here does seem illogical, for she has just entertained the possibility of taking her children with her to Athens (1045), a possibility she returns to at 1056–58. Easterling, however, calls lines 1059ff "Euripides' master-stroke"—"the parent becomes convinced of a threat to the children that clinches the feeling that they would be better dead."[7] The observation loses some of its force when we recall that it is *Medea* who will do the killing. Might it not be equally true to observed behavior to find a mother, under similar pressure, grabbing her kids and heading for safety?

With the deletion of 1059–63, Medea moves from thoughts of a future life in Athens directly to the image of Glauke's passion: "Living there [in Athens] with you, they [the children] will make you happy./ The thing's done, and she will not escape./ Even now the crown is on her head. . . ." (1058, 1064–65). Although 1064–65 marks a break in thought, Lloyd-Jones believes that with "a pause in the delivery the asyndeton will cause no trouble . . . the audience will have no difficulty in seeing that the implication of 1064f. must be 'too late.'"[8] However, Kovacs, followed by Foley, strongly objects to the absence of any adversative.[9] If a dramatic pause in delivery is *really* insufficient, we could follow Kvičala's transposition of 1064 to follow 1066.[10] Then the nonconnective καὶ δή (1065) marks the distance between Medea's imagined life with her children in Athens and the fact that "vividly and dramatically, something is actually taking place at the moment,"[11] namely the death of Glauke: "Living there [in Athens] with you, they [the children] will make you happy./ Even now the crown is on her head, and in the wedding dress/ the royal bride is doomed, I see it clearly./ The thing's done, and she will not escape."

We are left with Kovacs's objection that, no matter *where* you put it, line 1064 is not good Greek. I point out only that Lloyd-Jones and others find it acceptable Greek. Again, Kvičala's transposition could help make sense of the line, because the (admittedly implied) subject of ἐκφεύξεται (the royal bride, νύμφη) would now precede that verb. Deletion of the text should be a last resort. Lloyd-Jones seems to execute the least traumatic surgery required to remove a tumor that perhaps has grown bigger in the minds of textual critics than it has on the text of the play.[12]

Appendix C

HELPING FRIENDS AND HARMING
ENEMIES IN *MEDEA*

MEDEA KNOWS that her children's death is not fated, and she herself advances a ready alternative: "I will lead my children out of this land" (1045). She returns to this idea when she tells herself to take the children to Athens where they will live together in happiness (1057–58). However, Medea is controlled inexorably by the specter of her enemies' mockery: "Do I want to earn the laughter of my enemies by leaving them unpunished?" (1049–50).[1] Unlike her reflection three lines before ("Why must I, to cause your father grief, acquire for myself twice the pain?"), the question of her enemies' laughter is rhetorical in the extreme. After the gruesome murder of Glauke and Kreon, the idea that someone might laugh at Medea is hard to credit.

On five other occasions, Medea refers to the fact that she must not be scorned by her enemies (383, 404–5, 809, 1355, 1362), each time using a form of the verb γελάω, "mock." So frequently does Medea put forward this justification for her vengeance that we need to consider the fear of being mocked by an enemy in its larger context. The idea stems from the traditional belief that one should hate ones enemies and love ones friends, mentioned explicitly by Medea at line 809.[2] Basic to the Greek system of values, this position appears to some scholars to be so thoroughly ingrained in Athenian consciousness that it provided the moral equivalent of gravity, an attitude that simply *was*, and, as such, was beyond question or change.[3]

The situation, however, was far more complicated, for we perceive a different relationship obtaining between enemies as early as Homer.[4] In *Iliad* 24, Achilles does not laugh at his mortal enemy Priam but accepts his supplication and grieves with him, even helping to prepare Hektor's body for burial.[5] In Sophokles' *Ajax*, Odysseus refuses to laugh at his humiliated enemy even though the opportunity has been arranged by the goddess Athena (121–27). Again, funeral rites signal a new dispensation, for Odysseus ensures that Ajax's body is given burial against the protests of the Greek camp and its generals.[6] These (and other) challenges to the heroic ideal of helping friends and harming enemies anticipate the radical conception of human interaction proposed by Sokrates in his troubling claim that it is better to suffer evil than to do it.[7]

Granted that the view that one should harm one's enemies and avoid their mockery at all costs was scrutinized in the fifth century, in what way does *Medea* partake of this critique? For critics who view her great monologue as an inner debate between reason and passion,[8] Medea exemplifies *akrasia*, the powerlessness of a person who knows what is right but cannot act on that knowledge. Walsh believes that her character presents a counter-example to the Sokratic "doctrine" of the motivational sufficiency of reason. That is, knowledge of what is right is *not* sufficient to motivate right action but is at the mercy of stronger, pathetic forces that are represented by the word θυμός (*thumos*), used by Medea at 1056 and 1079.[9]

Other critics argue that nothing of the sort happens, for their Medea must be heroic through and through. Rejecting the idea that the monologue constitutes (in Snell's words) "the great scene of decision," they fail to recognize in the speech moments of real doubt and hesitation.[10] For Kovacs, Medea's speech does not present "a process of decision, but . . . the revelation of the cost to Medea of a decision already taken." Therefore, in his view the last lines (1077–80) have nothing to do with realizing a conflict between moral insight and passion. Rather, "Medea's desire for vengeance overcomes not her sense of right and wrong but her prudent desire to avoid pain."[11] For such critics, Medea foresees the unpleasant results of her decision, but she never considers the decision *as such*, nor does she frame her choice in moral terms.

A third, more promising, possibility suggests itself. Agreeing that Medea does not act out of *akrasia* (that is, powerlessness to do what she knows is right), Rickert points out that an agent's *thumos* is inextricably bound up with beliefs and judgments. It is not simply "emotions" but "the faculty in which the hero's passionate attachment to principles resides, which reacts to dishonor, unjust treatment, insult, and mockery by enemies."[12] When Medea says that her *thumos* is stronger than her βουλευμάτων (*bouleumatōn* 1079), she does not mean that her passion is stronger than her reason, but (to paraphrase Rickert) "my commitment to my principles [namely, to take vengeance on my enemies and avoid their mockery] is stronger than any competing claims." This interpretation seems reasonable enough, but Rickert's argument strains belief when she adduces literary and inscriptional evidence to show that the "total destruction" of the perjurer's children or progeny was (or ought to be) the penalty for perjury.[13] For Rickert, infanticide is an effective and *appropriate* form of vengeance for Medea's *thumos* to take.

In this view, Medea (1077–80) voices a conflict between the valued course of killing the perjurer's children and the less valued course of considering the harm to herself and her maternal feelings. Medea recognizes that her actions are "evil," κακά (kaka), but also that she must remain true to her principles, principles that Rickert believes were shared by Euripides' society. However, the fact that an oathtaker might swear that breaking his oath should lead to the destruction of his family does not mean that the *offended party* was the one to exact that punishment. Dover illustrates that the Greeks made an important distinction between "It is just that B should be hurt" and "It is just on the part of A to hurt B."[14]

The problems with Rickert's position are evident once we leave philosophical discussion and return to the play. If we are to see Medea's conflict in normative terms and the values that she ultimately chooses as supported by the drama (at least to some degree), then we might expect a statement or suggestion in the play that such is the case. We get precisely the opposite. The Chorus make no protest when Medea vows to take vengeance on Jason (267) or when she outlines how she will kill Jason, Kreon, and Glauke (373–83). But once she unveils her plan to kill her *children*, the Chorus turn on Medea and their response is unequivocal (811–13).

Not only is the idea (and later the deed) of child-murder rejected by all parties,[15] but Medea's great speech itself constitutes a revelation of the devastating effects of such a course of action. The fact that Medea carries out her deliberations in the presence of the children is critical, for their physical proximity emphasizes a fact so obvious that critics are prone to forget it, namely that the children are Medea's as much as they are Jason's.[16] Killing the children is anything but appropriate, not because they are children but because the assassin is their own mother. The principle of doing "harm to your enemies [ἐχθροί, echthroi]] and good to your friends [φίλοι, philoi]—with the alternative meaning "your own flesh and blood" (as at 809–10)—demands a clear distinction between the two end-terms, "friends" and "enemies." It is this distinction that Medea's revenge tragically ignores. Sophokles' *Antigone* also probes this distinction vis-à-vis Polyneikes, but he is both *philos* to Antigone and *echthros* to Thebes, because he has besieged the city. In *Medea*, the children are not Medea's *echthroi*, but *philoi* through and through.[17]

Medea adheres so blindly to the principle that she must harm her enemies to avoid their mockery that she chooses to slay her own *philoi* in preference to killing her husband, something she had proposed doing at lines 271 and 375.[18] The wish voiced early in the play that Medea might "work against enemies and not friends" (95) has turned on itself, for Medea acts against her enemies *by* acting against her loved ones. Given these considerations, it seems reasonable to conclude that the play condemns Medea's murdering her children and, more importantly, exposes the dangers inherent in the principle that leads her to do it.[19]

NOTES

INTRODUCTION

1. *A Guide to the Collections: Smith College Museum of Art* (Northampton, Mass. 1986), #62, pp. 47 and 104; see also P. Courthion, *L'Opera completa di Courbet* (Milan 1985), #111, p. 78.

2. *Hamlet* 1.2, 176–81. An ancient parallel occurs in *Adelphoi* (11–16), a third-century comedy by Hegesippus. The cook compares his preparations for the two different celebrations: "Whenever I turn my talents to the funeral banquet/, as soon as they come back from the burial/ dressed in black, I take the lid/ off the pot and make the mourners smile/ . . . it's just like being at a wedding." Quoted by Kurtz and Boardman 1971, 146.

3. Van Gennep 1909 and Hertz 1907, 80–86. See the summaries by Morris 1987, 29–39 and Danforth and Tsiaras 1982, 35–38.

4. Rites of passage may require a *series* of rituals to mark fully the transition from one status to another. For example, in some societies a maiden does not fully become a wife until she bears a child, and burial or cremation in itself may demand further obeisances and the passage of time before the dead are truly "dead" to the living. See Danforth and Tsiaras 1982, 117.

5. Even when rituals lose their religious significance—as when nonpracticing Christians participate in a Christian funeral—there is comfort in the formality of the occasion, in the prescriptions for a certain order of events, dress, mode of behavior. At times of loss, the psychological motivations for ritual observance seem as strong (*pace* Durkheim) as the social and symbolic forces. From a social/political perspective, Bloch 1982, 211–30 stresses the role that mourning rituals play in maintaining social and ideological authority. Morris 1987, 33 views such rituals as a way "to socialise other members of the group into accepting an unchanging order of dominance." However, Rosaldo 1989 is surely right to insist on the primacy of an individual's emotional response during rituals of grief and bereavement.

6. Turner 1969, 94–97, 106–13, 165–203; 1982, 28; and 1982a, 26–28, 201–18. He emphasizes the potential for creative change offered by liminal status, whereas van Gennep stresses the danger of such transitional stages. See Douglas 1966, 96.

7. See Gay 1988, 401–2, 410. The idea takes shape in Freud's *Civilization and Its Discontents*, tr. J. Rivière (London 1973, orig. 1930), 38–40, 49, 55–59, 69–70, 74–78, 82, and *New Introductory Lectures in Psycho-Analysis*, tr. W.J.H. Sprott (New York 1933), 141–48. It plays a key role in the posthumous *An Outline of Psycho-Analysis*, tr. J. Strachey (New York 1969, orig. 1940), esp. 5–8, 54–55.

8. Bataille 1962, 20 and 241.

9. For traces of necrophilia in Greek myth, see Humphreys 1983, 48–49 and 163n.4. Cf. Aristophanes' speech in Pl. *Sym.* (192 D–E), the prototype of

love continuing in the afterlife with no hint of the perverse. The god Hephaestus makes the following proposition to lovers:

> Do you desire to be as close to each other as possible, so that you will never be parted day or night? If that's what you desire, I'm willing to fuse and weld you together into one, so that instead of being two you will become one as long as you live . . . and when you die, even in Hades you will be one instead of two, having died a common death.

As Aristophanes puts it, "Hearing such an offer, we know that no one would turn it down or want anything else."

10. Lebeck 1971, 68–73.

11. Seaford 1987; the quotation is from 107, echoed at 109 ("the negative element prevails"), 110 ("one of the negative tendencies . . . has emerged as a triumphant reality"), etc. See also Seaford 1986 and Redfield 1982. Burnett 1983, 224 observes the same tendency in the poetry of Sappho. Arthur 1977, 40n.22 thinks the association of weddings with death reflected not only a general attitude toward marriage but also the high rate of mortality in childbirth.

12. Loraux 1987, esp. 38–42, 63–64; see the rev. by B. Knox, *NY Rev* (April 28, 1988), 13–14. Far from confronting the audience with disturbing images of itself or opening up a space to reexamine the city's values, the tragic wedding-to-death is, for Loraux, subversive of any real subversion.

13. Zeitlin 1965 and 1970; Foley 1985 offers a full bibliography for the study of tragic sacrifice and sacrificial irony. See also E.A.M.E. O'Connor-Visser, *Aspects of Human Sacrifice in the Tragedies of Euripides* (Amsterdam 1987). Part of the limitation of these studies is their concentration on sacrifice per se, rather than the greater ritual or festival context in which sacrifice usually took place.

14. This is not to deny the similarity between weddings and civic festivals, including the sacrifices with which they began and the feasts with which they concluded (see Ch. 1 pp. 12, 14, 18). In some sanctuaries, caretakers in need could hold their weddings in the sacred buildings and even use part of the meat sacrificed there for their wedding feast (*LSCG* 177).

15. For a down-to-earth account of public sacrifices, see Parke 1977, 18–19 and 127–28. Ferguson 1948, 134 gives the number of victims at the City Dionysia. Sacrifices-*cum*-banquets also were offered by (and for) members of the boule, prytany, deme, phratry, genos, and family (in the last case, esp. at weddings and funerals). See Mikalson 1983, 68–70 and 84–85.

16. Rosaldo 1989, 1–21 faults anthropological accounts of bereavement and funerary rituals that mask the emotional aspects of those events with the social scientist's pretensions to objectivity, neutrality, and impartiality.

17. Summarized by Humphreys 1983, 16–17, who reminds us that tragic women often apologize for their overtly public presence. Gould 1980, 57 speaks of the "masculinization" of tragic women without attending to the corresponding "feminization" of at least some tragic men. For the effect that the mistreatment of tragic women had on the oppressor as well as the victim in tragedy, see the excellent discussion by Vellacott 1975, 82–126. Worth

noting is the fact that only one extant tragedy, Sophokles' *Philoktetes*, has no female characters; among lost plays, possibly Euripides' *Palamedes* (see Mason 1959, 89 and Scodel 1980, 61).

18. Zeitlin 1985, 80 suggests that Greek theater "uses the feminine for the purposes of imagining a fuller model for the masculine self."

19. Steiner 1984, 237 finds in Greek tragedy "a constellation of women matchless for their truth and variousness," and he analyzes artistic epigones based on Sophokles' portrayal of Antigone. The influence of other tragic women on later writers and composers can be seen in Gluck's *Alceste*, Cherubini's *Medea*, Strauss's *Elektra*, Racine's *Phèdre* and *Andromaque*, Goethe's *Iphigenia in Tauris*, Harrison's *Phaedra Brittanicus*, Bond's *The Women*, and Wolff's *Kassandra*, to list but a few examples.

20. See Seaford 1990a, 151–53; Blundell 1989, 46–47; and Osborne 1985, 138–39, 152.

21. In tragedy, "domestic crises can be used to delineate public ones, and public crises can be signs of abuses to the domestic sphere," as Foley 1981, 161 writes. See also Zeitlin 1985, 72–73. Aristotle (*Pol.* 1.1260b) explicitly acknowledges the interdependence of *oikos* and *polis*.

22. See Easterling 1988, 109. Cf. Foley 1985, 59, who finds Euripides "insisting on a restoration of ritual to a central place in the politically and socially unstable worlds he creates." Segal 1982, 347 posits a similar goal for Euripidean tragedy itself, providing a point of stability that transcends the very issues raised by the plays: "If the gods themselves spread disorder, the order we need to stay alive lies elsewhere. Perhaps, Euripides suggests, it lies in the work of art that contains but does not resolve the violence." Wolff 1982, 264 also claims that "the compensatory order, which offsets the tragic horrors, is the beautiful order of the dramatic work itself revealed in performance." Missing is any compelling sense of the relationship between Euripides' plays and the world of his audience. His tragedies contain too much passion, anger, and moral outrage to suggest that he wants those in the audience to contemplate only the play and not look *through* it to the world in which they live.

23. Cf. R. Stilling, *Love and Death in Renaissance Tragedy* (Baton Rouge 1976) 1, who aims to "reveal the presence of a single unifying motif . . . running through and linking the major works." Vis-à-vis Shakespeare, a more insightful approach is taken by C. T. Neely, *Broken Nuptials in Shakespeare's Plays* (New Haven 1985).

24. Poole 1987, 12.

25. Absent in my analysis are A. *Danaïd* trilogy, where suppliant maidens are forced to marry their uncles only to kill them on their wedding night, and Eur. *IA*, where Iphigenia is lured to her sacrificial end under the guise of celebrating her wedding to Achilles. Here I direct the reader to Zeitlin 1992; Seaford 1987, 110–19; and Garvie 1969, 211–33 for the *Danaïd* trilogy; and to Foley 1985, 84–91 and 1982a for Eur. *IA*.

26. Levin 1988, 126 and 132; see also 1979, 11–55.

27. Interpretation that fails to consider the practical needs of the theater also ignores what differentiates dramatic texts from others. Critics continue

to read Greek tragedies as if they were novels in verse, or poems on the page, or "texts" to be analyzed, or polysemous writing to be deconstructed. As Kitzinger 1986, 116 gently remarks on Goldhill's deconstructive account of the *Oresteia* (1984), "we lose the activity of hearing and seeing to the activity of reading." Compare the comments by Nussbaum 1986, 70, whose observations on choral lyric extend quite naturally to the plays themselves:

> They are performed by a group working together in word, music, and dance; and they are watched by a group—by an audience that has come together in community . . . and whose physical placement surrounding the action makes acknowledgment of the presence of fellow citizens a major and inevitable part of the dramatic event. . . . [They] experience the complexities of the tragedy while and by being a certain sort of community, not by having each soul go off in isolation from its fellows.

CHAPTER 1

1. The following sources provide useful accounts of weddings and/or funerals. In subsequent notes, I cite these works only when interpretation is more than usually controversial or a specific topic is treated thoroughly. For weddings and marriage, see Oakley and Sinos 1993; Leduc 1992 ("an interpretive and . . . speculative essay"); Patterson 1991; Sealey 1990, 12–49, 151–60; Just 1989, 40–104; Hague 1988; Pomeroy 1988, and 1975, 57–78; Craik 1984; Froning 1984; Cox 1983; Sutton 1981, 145–275, esp. 145–60; Redfield 1982; Modrzejewski 1981; Schaps 1979; Vernant 1973; Lacey 1968, 15–16, 100–124, 138–46, 162–63; Brindesi 1961; Nilsson 1960; Ehrenberg 1951, 193–207; Wolff 1944; Magnien 1936 (to be used with caution); Erdmann 1934 (the fullest treatment); Minto 1919 (a good summary); and Collignon 1904.

For funerals, Thomas 1989, 103–8; Morris 1987, 18–22 (Attic burial customs from sub-Mycenean period to circa 510 B.C.); Garland 1985, 21–37; Humphreys 1983, 13–14, 82–94, 104–11, 144–64; Parker 1983, 32–48, 53–73; Vermeule 1979; Alexiou 1974, 1–23; Kurtz and Boardman 1971, 68–161 (the fullest treatment); Lacey 1968, 80–81, 148–49; Flacelière 1965, 55–82; and McClees 1941, 121–29.

For the legal aspects of marriages and funerals, see MacDowell 1978, 84–109; Harrison 1968, 1–60, 108–15, 132–38 (marriage and succession); Broadbent 1968, 113–239 (laws on death, marriage, citizenship, divorce, dowry, adoption, guardianship, and inheritance); Jones 1956, 174–97 (marriage and succession). For ancient attitudes toward death, funerals, and the afterlife, see Morris 1989, 296–320; Richardson 1985, 50–66 (a good introduction); Bremmer 1983; Danforth and Tsiaras 1982 (for parallels between ancient and modern attitudes); Sourvinou-Inwood 1981; Ehnmark 1948; Rohde 1925; and Grieve 1896, 59–64 (a concise account of tragic weddings and deaths).

2. See Wolff 1944, 44–51; Harrison 1968, 1–6, 18, 21; and Patterson 1991. As Modrzejewski 1981, 241 puts it, "une *ekdosis* sans *engyē* ne fonde pas un mariage légitime; une *engyē* sans *ekdosis* . . . est dépourvue de conséquences juridiques' ("An *ekdosis* without *enguē* does not constitute a legal

marriage; an *enguē* without *ekdosis* . . . is deprived of any legal consequences").

3. For the etymology and use of *enguē*, see Wyse 1904, 289–93; Just 1989, 45–50; and L. Gernet, "Hypothèses sur le contrat primitif en Grèce," *REG* 30 (1917), 249–93 and 363–83 (who argues persuasively that the term refers to the handshake through which the agreement is sealed). Hignett 1952, 344 stresses the legal nature of the *enguē* and notes the inadequacy of "betrothal" as a translation. However, we should be wary of legalists who insist that the *enguē* constituted the wedding; as Patterson 1991, 64–65 n.20 points out, "it is somewhat odd to speak of a wedding with possibly no bride." For guardianship see MacDowell 1978, 86–91.

4. Foxhall 1989, 32; see also Diggle 1970 on Eur. *Phaeth.* 158–59.

5. Foxhall 1989, 38 notes that "the dowry went with the woman," no matter when or why the marriage broke up. Vernant 1973, 59 overemphasizes the public nature of the dowry, calling it "le signe tangible de l'alliance entre les deux maisons." Cox 1983, 431–32 and 485–95 demonstrates the influence that the dowry gave Athenian women over the affairs of their new *oikos*, especially during the Peloponnesian War.

6. The concubine Andromache (Eur. *Andr.* 192) may pun on the word when she asks Hermione (Neoptolemus' wife) "for what 'legally entrusted reason' [τῶι . . . ἐχεγγύωι λόγωι] would I keep you from your legitimate marriage?" In Eur. *IA* 703, Agamemnon rehearses Achilles' pedigree as the future husband of Iphigenia, pointing out that his mother Thetis was "betrothed by Zeus" to Peleus, but "given him in marriage" by her father Nereus (Ζεὺς ἠγγύησε καὶ δίδωσ' ὁ κύριος 703). For dowries in Menander, see Webster 1974, 25. Redfield 1982, 186 (followed by Kurke 1991, 119–25) mistakenly claims that Pi. *O.* 7.1–12 describes the *enguē*. The references to the banquet, toasts "from house to house," the envy of the guests, and the *makarismos* blessing better suit the wedding banquet. See C. P. Ruck and W. H. Matheson, *Pindar: Selected Odes* (Ann Arbor 1968), 52–55.

7. Sutton 1989, 347–51 describes the sole example, the red-figured loutrophoros in Boston (MFA 03.802).

8. The verb ἐκδίδωμι (*ekdidōmi*) can mean "hiring out" or "renting." The commercial language is not surprising—"economics" derives from *oikos*, the household that each wedding established. The founder of a colony was called *oikistēs* ("an *oikos*-maker"), and compounds with that noun are ubiquitous in the vocabulary of colonization (see Casevitz 1985, 75–218; on colonists generally, Malkin 1987). Perhaps there was a comparable sense of risk and adventure in the founding of an *oikos* by marriage. For the use of *ekdidōmi* to signify a father giving his daughter in marriage, see Hdt. 1.196, 2.47; Thuk. 8.21; Eur. *Med.* 288, 309, *Hipp.* 552–53 (Halleran 1991, 113–14), *Andr.* 344, *Supp.* 133, *El.* 249, *Hel.* 933, *IA* 132, 703 (above, n.6), 729; Ar. *Av.* 1635; Pl. *R.* 362b, 613d.

9. Flacelière 1965, 57 and 64–65. Focusing on the genealogical link provided by women, Michelini 1982, 139–40 concludes that "the purpose of marriage, in Greek terms, is to perpetuate the family through such linkings, so that the role of wife and mother is really single, not double."

10. See Roberts 1978, 177–78. A wool basket commonly appears as part of wedding iconography (Roberts 66, 111, 146, 183–84). Two epinetra depict wedding preparations appropriate to their function: *ARV2* 1081.21 shows a woman seated with wool; another (Athens, National Museum 2179, *CC* 1589) depicts a seated woman sewing, with an epinetron on her knee, a wool basket at her feet, and an Eros flying above to suggest the upcoming wedding.

11. Sutton 1981, 158. Ancient sources for this sacrifice include Eur. *IA* 432–39, Poll. 3.38, Hsch. s.v. γάμων ἤθη, and Phot. and *Suda* s.v. προτέλεια.

12. Sources include Eur. *IA* 431–33 and 718–19, *SEG* ix 72, Apollod. *Bibl.* 1.9.15, and Poll. 3.38 (Artemis); *AP* 6.318, D.S. 5.73.2, and Paus. 2.34.12 and 3.13.9 (Aphrodite); D.S. 5.73.2, Plu. *Mor.* 141.27 ("Advice to the Bride and Groom"), and Poll. 3.38 (Hera); *Suda* s.v. προτέλεια (Athena); A. *Eu.* 834–36 (Furies/Eumenides); Prokl. *in Ti.* 5.293 (Ouranos and Ge); Phot., *Suda*, and *EM* all s.v. Τριτοπάτορες (Tritopatores). For discussion of the evidence, see Oakley and Sinos 1993; Bruit Zaidman and Schmitt Pantel 1992, 186–88; Dowden 1989, 2–3, 123; H. King, "Bound to Bleed: Artemis and Greek Women," in Cameron and Kuhrt 1983, 114–15, 120–22; Redfield 1982, 190–91; M. Detienne, "The Myth of 'Honeyed Orpheus,'" in Gordon 1977, 102–3; Burkert 1977, 120–21n.29 and 1972, 62–63; Barrett 1964, 4n.3 and 192–94; and Ch. 2 n.17 of this volume. Regarding the nymphs, see Ch. 5 n.9 and Ginouvès 1962, 269n.3, who views them as "les protectrices par excellence des mariages" ("the guardians par excellence of marriage").

13. Thuk. 2.15.5. For the significance of ritual bathing in the wedding ceremony, see Ginouvès 1962, 265–82; Cook 1940, 370–96; and Kenner 1935, 109–54.

14. Regarding head-coverings as veils, see App. A; for nuptial *stephanoi*, see Reilly 1989, 419–20. The wedding garments may have been white, judging from Eur. *Alk.* 922–23 and (by implication) *Supp.* 1054 and *Hel.* 1088, 1186–87.

15. See App. A, esp. n.6. To be rejected out of hand is E. Keuls, *The Reign of the Phallus* (New York 1985), 107, who claims that the unveiling "probably took place after the signing of the marriage contract. On that occasion the groom gave the bride some presents. . . ." As noted above, the presence of the bride was not required at the *enguē*, and there is no evidence for written contracts before the Hellenistic period; see Jones 1956, 178 and W. V. Harris, *Ancient Literacy* (Cambridge, Mass. 1989), 69.

16. For wedding dances and music, see for example *Od.* 23.133–36, 297–99; Eur. *IT* 1143–52; Ar. *Thesm.* 972–76; and modern discussions by A. Kauffmann-Samaras, Ἡ μουσικὴ στὸ γάμο τῆς ἀρχαίας Ἑλλάδας, *Archaiologia* 14 (Feb. 1985), 16–28; Huddleston 1980, 108–11; Webster 1970, 73–76; and Lawler 1964, 51. Regarding the nuptial *makarismos*, Snell 1931, 74–75 and Seaford 1987, 106n.5 list literary references, and McDonald 1978 examines Euripides' use of the term. Hague 1983, 141n.11 claims that the *makarismos* was not offered to the bride, but she overlooks evidence from tragedy (Eur. *Med.* 956–58, *Tro.* 310–12, *Ph.* 344–46, etc.).

17. See Griffith 1989, 57; Hague 1983, 134–35; Burnett 1983, 232–33n.5 and 305n.69; and B. Snell, *Gesammelte Schriften* (Göttingen 1966), 85–86.

Fr. 412 of S. *Mysoi* may refer to the music at the wedding banquet of Auge and Blephus (Sutton 1984, 79–80). For types of wedding songs, see Garvie 1969, 228–30; Muth 1954; Smyth 1900, cxii–cxx; and Jebb 1893 on *Ant.* 813ff. I use *hymenaioi* for songs during the banquet and procession, and "epithalamia" for those sung outside the bridal chamber (both the "serenades" on the wedding night and the morning "waking songs"). Technically, however, as Muth 1954, 43 states, "*Hymenaios . . .* verhält sich zu *Epithalamion* wie das logische Genus zur Species" ("logically, *hymenaios* is related to *epithalamion* as genus is to species"). Burnett 1983, 216–24 examines parallels between these songs and Sappho's wedding lyrics, as does J. M. Snyder, *The Woman and the Lyre* (Carbondale, Ill. 1989), 31–33.

18. *exagōgē* is used for marriage at H. *Il.* 13.379, B. 11.103 (with some irony), Eur. *Hel.* 590 (punning on its nuptial sense), and *IA* 693. For *eisagōgē* and weddings, see Hdt. 5.40, 6.63, and *Alk.* 1112 (again with irony). Forms of the verb ἄγω (*agō*, "I lead") for taking the bride to her new home occur at A. *Pr.* 539 and S. *Tr.* 857–58; in the middle, ἄγομαι (*agomai*, "I lead away for myself"), at *Od.* 14.211, Hes. *Th.* 410, Hdt. 1.59, 2.47.

19. By substituting a two-wheeled chariot (linked to warfare and the Olympic games) for the four-wheeled cart, vase-painters lifted the scene above the mundane. Moreover, bride and groom appear physically more impressive standing in a chariot than sitting in a cart. For wedding processions, see App. A n.4; Boardman 1952, 34 and 39; H. L. Lorimer, "The Country Cart in Ancient Greece," *JHS* 23 (1908), 132–51; and E. Gerhard, *Auserlesen Griechische Vasenbilder* Vol. 4 (Berlin 1858), 81–87 and pl. 312.1,2. Processions on foot (χαμαίπους, Poll. 3.40) are popular in red-figure painting, but the scenes usually are set inside the house (Sutton 1981, 177).

20. For torch-bearing mothers, see D. von Bothmer, "New Vases by the Amasis Painter," *AK* 3 (1960), 73; W. A. Becker, *Charicles*, tr. F. Metcalfe (London 1899), 486; and Ch. 7 p. 102 of this volume. Vase-paintings showing musicians in the wedding procession are comparatively rare, leading Sutton 1981, 194–95 to conclude that they may be professionals hired for the occasion.

21. Erdmann 1934, 258, from scholion to Eur. *Ph.* 344; see also Sutton 1989, 339. Redfield 1982, 189 (from Poll. 3.41) thinks the *nympheutria* led the couple to the marriage chamber, but the presence of a torch-bearing woman awaiting the couple on Attic vases makes the groom's mother the more likely candidate. If the *nympheutria* was an agent of the *bride's* family (Sutton 1981, 194), then it is hard to imagine that she would guide the married couple inside the home, especially if it were not "new." For example, if the patrimony of the groom's father had not been divided, the newlyweds might join the paternal or joint-fraternal household before establishing their own (Broadbent 1968, 149–50).

22. Redfield 1982, 188 compares this to the modern custom of throwing rice. A similar rite marked the introduction of a slave and an adopted child into the *oikos*, both cases of an outsider becoming an insider. See Pl. *Tht.* 160e; also Richardson 1974, 231–32 and Gould 1973, 97–98. For the *katachusmata* in Pindar, see Carson 1982, 123–28.

23. Brueckner 1907, 80–84. However, locations such as "the marriage chamber," "the hearth," and "women's quarters" may have operated more in the imagination than in reality. Greek houses were not large, much of the activity took place in the courtyard, and archaeological remains indicate that there was no permanent hearth (portable braziers probably were used). This should caution against overly structural interpretations of domestic space, such as J-P. Vernant, "Hestia-Hermès," L'Homme 3[3] (1963), 13, who describes the hearth in this way: "Fixé au sol, le foyer circulaire est comme le nombril qui enracine la maison dans la terre. Il est symbole et gage de fixité, d'immutabilité, de permanence" ("Fixed to the ground, the circular hearth is like the navel that roots the house in the earth. It is the symbol and pledge of fixity, of immutability, of permanence"). For correctives, see M. H. Jameson, "Domestic Space in the Greek City-State," in Domestic Architecture and the Use of Space, ed. S. Kent (Cambridge 1990), 92–113; and "Private Space and the Greek City," in The Greek City from Homer to Alexander, ed. O. Murray and S. Price (Oxford 1990), 171–95.

24. Plu. Mor. 138D, 279F, and Sol. 20.4. Plutarch believed that the ancient bride nibbled on a quince to freshen her breath and speech! See also Sutton 1981, 153–54, 323. For wedding cakes, see Flacelière 1965, 64. Similar cakes appear on the "Totenmahl" grave reliefs, another instance of the overlap in wedding and funeral rituals; see P. M. Fraser, Rhodian Funerary Monuments (Oxford 1977), 102–3n.100.

25. For this last possibility, see C. A. Faraone, "Aphrodite's Kestos and Apples for Atalanta: Aphrodisiacs in Early Greek Myth and Ritual," Phoenix 44 (1990), 219–20, 230–38. In a tour de force, Burnett 1983, 267 and n.102 connects the apple/quince with the apples in the stories of Atalanta and the Hesperides, and with the apple of virginity in Sappho 105V. The "apple of discord" makes an ironically fitting gift for Strife to give at the marriage of Peleus and Thetis. Other explanations for apples at weddings involve their (purported) resemblance to female breasts; see Griffith 1989, 58 and D. E. Gerber, "The Female Breast in Greek Erotic Literature," Arethusa 11 (1978), 203–4.

26. H.Cer. 371–74, 393–400, 411–13; Richardson 1974 on 372. See also B. Lincoln, Emerging from the Chrysalis: Studies in Rituals of Women's Initiation (Cambridge, Mass. 1981), 85.

27. The term θυρωρός occurs in Sappho 110, explained by Hsch. (s.v.) and Poll. 3.42 as the guard at the door, although the practice may not have been common in the fifth century. Scholars frequently give too much credence to late sources, such as the account (Zen. 3.98) that a boy, ἀμφιθαλής ("with both parents living"), wore a crown of thistles and acorns, carried a winnowing basket (λίκνον) full of bread, and moved among the wedding guests saying, "I escaped the bad, I found the better." However, Zenobius was a Greek living in Hadrianic Rome, and Nilsson 1960, 243–50 argues persuasively that the practice was Roman, not Greek, a late imitation of the Mysteries.

28. Richardson 1974, 26–27. Besides unveiling, initiates carried torches and received the makarismos blessing, elements in common with the wedding ritual. See Burkert 1987, p. 93 and figures 1, 3, and 4 there.

29. Magnien 1936, 116 notes that a Greek wife was characterized by words involving "bed"—sometimes directly, λέχος (*lechos*, "bed"), as at Eur. *Hel.* 475, 590, 638, 784, 974, 1634, but more frequently with the copulative α, such as ἄλοχος (*alochos*, from *lechos*) and ἀκοίτης/ἄκοιτις (from κοίτη, *koitē*, "lying-down place"); compounds with ὁμο, "same," such as ὁμόκοιτις, and ὄμευνος, ὄμευνις, ὁμευνέτης, ὁμευνέτις (εὐνή, *eunē*, "bed"); and constructions such as κοινόλεκτρος ("shared bed"), etc. See also Motte 1973, 225n.56 and Willink 1989, 53nn.33 and 39. The Greeks conceived of marriage in terms of a physical reality, not simply as a state of being or a social role.

30. Virginity was not an issue when a hetaira married, or when a widow or divorcée remarried, a common enough practice (Thompson 1972). Nor was it impossible for a young woman to have intercourse before marriage. Dionysiac festivals provided an opportunity, as in Eur. *Ion* when Xouthus admits to premarital sex with a "Delphic maiden of free birth" at such an all-night celebration (Owen 1939 on *Ion* 552). Dover 1968 on *Nu.* 532 notes that παρθένος (*parthenos*) is not a biological word for "virgin" but a cultural term for "unmarried." Clark 1989, 21 and Just 1989, 66–70 point out that interest in a woman's chastity had more to do with the legitimacy of offspring than with sexual purity per se.

31. Harrison 1968, 2, 6–7. The word *gamos* had a range of meanings, from "marriage" to "sexual intercourse"—see L. Robert, "Sur des inscriptions d'Ephèse," *RevPhil* 41 (1967), 77–81. For *gamos* as the consummation of the marriage, see Poll. 3.37–38; Clem.Al. *Strom.* liv II, c 23; and the arguments of Redfield 1982; Sutton 1981, 150; Flacelière 1965, 62; and Wolff 1944, 48–50. Lacey 1968, 110 and MacDowell 1978, 86 fail to distinguish *ekdosis* from *gamos*, which in their view is an inclusive term for wedding. Harrison 1968 (6, 18, 21) uses *ekdosis* and derivatives as virtually synonymous with *gamos* (so *EM*, s.v. γάμος). Flacelière 1965, 61 uses it for the "actual wedding ceremony."

32. See Lambin 1986, 71–72; Burnett 1983, 218–19, 224n.34; Huddleston 1980, 60–63; Smyth 1900, cxv–cxvi. The scholiast to Theok. (Idyll 18) rationalizes the epithalamia as a means of drowning out the cries of the virgin bride when her husband deflowers her. Ribald jesting and insults (αἰσχρολογία) were part of other initiatory rites, particularly the Eleusinian Mysteries. Richardson 1974, 23 and 213–17 gives a full account.

33. See Poll. 3.39–40; Hsch., *Suda*, and *EM*, all s.v. ἐπαύλια; Harp. s.v. ἀνακαλυπτήρια; and Eustath. on *Il.* 24.29. See also Brueckner 1907, 91–112 and Deubner 1900.

34. Patterson 1991, 59. For *sunoikein/xunoikein* as "living together in marriage," see Just 1989, 43–44, 62–63; Lacey 1968, 110; and Broadbent 1968, 159–60. It is so used (with cognates) at A. *Th.* 188, *Ch.* 1005; Eur. *Alk.* 734, *Med.* 242, 1001, 1385, *HF* 68, *IT* 524, 915, *Hel.* 1655; and Ar. *Pax* 708. Foxhall 1989, 34 lists Attic sources showing marriage as a partnership (esp. Arist. *EN* 1162a 16–33). Patterson 1991, 61 insists that "Athenian marriage was not simply the transfer or 'exchange' of women, but the process through which a man and a woman set up a common household (*sunoikein*), whose purpose was a productive and reproductive *koinōnia* [community]."

Thompson 1972, 223–25 shows that widowed/divorced men often remarried even though they already had produced a male heir for the *oikos*. Isager 1981, 82–84 notes the rarity of permanent bachelors and spinsters in Athens. For a view of Greek marriage that emphasizes its constraints on women, see Carson 1990, with correctives by Cohen 1992, 156–58.

35. Sealey 1990, 21; Cole 1984, 236–37; Sutton 1981, 157; A. Andrewes, *The Greeks* (New York 1967), 84–86; Flacelière 1965, 64; and Jones 1956, 178.

36. For the Citizenship Law, see Patterson 1981; Whitehead 1977, 149–53; and Broadbent 1968, 167–70 (who prints the sources and useful comments). D. M. MacDowell, *Andokides On the Mysteries* (Oxford 1962), 152, believes that on the third day of the Apatouria new members were registered in their phratry, including new wives as well as newborn children. See also Harrison 1968, 6. Isaios (3.73 and 75; see Wyse on 3.73.6–7 and 3.76.1) indicates that a father might present his daughter to his phratry to establish her legitimacy, an act comparable to enrolling a son in the phratry, or so interpreted by R. J. Bonner, *Aspects of Athenian Democracy* (Berkeley 1933), 134–35, and Hignett 1952, 60n.2. See also M. Golden, " 'Donatus' and Athenian Phratries," *CQ* 35 (1985), 9–13, and Hedrick 1987, 136.

37. See Patterson 1991, 66n.30 and "The Epikleros in Athens" (delivered at CAMWS meeting, April 1990); Sealey 1990, 29–30, 157; Just 1989, 83–89; and Redfield 1982, 184–85 (on the bilateral basis of Athenian kinship). Karnezis 1972, 227 suggests the complexities in his definition of *epiklēros*: "A single, legitimate (or adopted) woman, whether a minor or of age, who had no father, paternal grandfather, great-grandfather, homopatric brother, or fraternal nephew, was an epikleros."

38. See Foxhall 1989, 43; Schaps 1979, 29; and Lacey 1968, 141–42.

39. Osborne 1985, 127–28; Karnezis 1972, 207; and Lacey 1968, 145–46. Menander exploits the comic possibilities of failing to take these preventive steps in *Aspis*, where a greedy old uncle claims a young heiress for his wife.

40. Is. 3.64; see Schaps 1979, 28.

41. Lacey 1968, 16 describes the *oikos* as "a living organism which required to be renewed every generation to remain alive; it supported its living members' needs for food and its deceased members' needs for the performance of cult rituals." Raepsaet 1971, 94–99 and 109 concludes that procreation per se was motivated (and rationalized) by the sense that childbearing was a law of nature, that prosperity entailed progeny, that bearing and raising children was patriotic, that offspring would care for their parents in old age, and that they were necessary to perpetuate the cult of the dead, both at the funeral and at subsequent rites (see Is. 1.10, 2.10, 6.5, and 7.29–30). Even a grown man who had been sold into prostitution by his father was compelled to bury him (Aeschin. 1.13; Broadbent 1968, 137). Also, Athenians scrutinized candidates for office on the basis of whether they had honored their parents' graves (X. *Mem.* 2.2.13).

42. See Eur. *Alk.* 662–68, *Med.* 1033–34, *Hec.* 430, *Supp.* 174–75, *Tro.* 388–90, 1185–86. Tragedies feature the inversion of the generational pattern of burial, particularly where a father offers funeral rites for his son (traceable to H. *Il.* 24), as at S. *Ant.* 1257–75, Eur. *Hipp.* 1458, and *Ph.* 1310–21. Kroesus

prefers peace to war (Hdt. 1.87.4): "In the former, sons bury their fathers, but in the latter, fathers bury their sons." Other cross-generation burials in tragedy include grandfather burying grandson (*Ba.* 1216–26, 1298–1300) or grandsons and daughter-in-law (*HF* 1360–64, 1419). A mother offers funeral rites for her child or children in *Med.* 1378–81; *Hec.* 508, 609–18, 1287–88; *Supp.* 1114–68; and *Rh.* 983; and a grandmother buries her grandchild at *Tro.* 1141–55.

43. Kurtz and Boardman 1971, 143. Humphreys 1983, 13 and 153–54 argues correctly that the rites constituted "a memorial-cult, rather than ancestor-*worship.*" Thomas 1989, 103–8 observes in fifth-century Athenian literary sources a shift away from the aristocratic ideal of tracing the dead back to (legendary) ancestors and toward the democratic practice of stressing service to the *polis* and links with the recent past. Lacey 1968, 77 observes that exiles lost not only burial by their loved ones, but also access to the burial place of their forebears. Jacoby, 1944, 51–52 imagines the displeasure among Athenians when battle casualties were left in foreign soil, and Lattimore 1962, 199–201 describes epitaphs of those whose bodies could not be buried because they died at sea.

44. From a fragment of Pherekydes in Jacoby, *FGrH* 3,119. See also *Theognidea* 699–718 and comments by T. Hudson-Williams, ed., *The Elegies of Theognis* (New York 1978, orig. 1910), 221. Sophokles refers indirectly to the Sisyphus story at *Ph.* 624.

45. Frisk 1960–72, s.v. κῆδος.

46. Connor 1971, 15n.20 and Miller 1953, 46. Garland 1985, 137 examines the various meanings of the word-group *kēdos* and—citing R. F. Willetts, *The Law Code of Gortyn* (Berlin 1967), 19—notes that "the first reference in Greek literature to *kēdestēs* is of a bridegroom's father who has to light the funeral pyre of a dead bride." See *AP* 7.712 (Erinna), below n.72.

47. For women's prominence in funerary rites, see Havelock 1981, 108–15. Preparations and display of the body took place in the home, returning the dead to the world where women had their greatest influence. The pattern continues in modern rural Greece:

> Given the sexual division of labor that exists in rural Greece, caring for other people in life (which involves feeding, washing, and keeping company), as well as caring for them in death (which involves the performance of all the appropriate death rites), is a task performed exclusively by women. It is the women of a family who actually fulfill the family's obligations to its dead. [Danforth and Tsiaras 1982, 119]

Before drinking the hemlock, Sokrates (Pl. *Phd.* 115a.2–116b.7) prepares for his own funeral by bathing and changing his clothes, ostensibly to save the women the trouble.

48. In the case of the *kurios* of the house, for example, this group would include his grandmother, mother, wife, daughter(s), sisters, nieces, maternal and paternal aunts, female cousins, and daughters of female cousins. For the role of the *anchisteia* in funerals, see D. 43.62–65 ("Against Makartatos") and F. B. Jevons, "Greek Burial Laws and Folk-Lore," *CR* 9 (1895), 247–50.

49. We observe in A. *Ag.* (esp. 1541–59) the struggle over who will bury

Agamemnon's corpse. Sophokles works a variation on the desire to possess a corpse so as to accrue future advantage in *OC* 389–411, 581–667, and 1518–55.

50. See Kurtz 1984, 314–25 and Brooklyn 1981, 36–43. Havelock 1981, 111–12 thinks that the "division of labor" between men and women encouraged the emotional release exhibited by female mourners. Humphreys 1983, 20 conjectures that a reason for the number of female roles in tragedy is that Greek culture allowed women a wider range of emotional expression than men. That fact was exploited by arranging for the appearance of women in Athenian lawcourts, where their emotional outbursts could be calculated to move the jury. See Humphreys 1986, 72–73 and 90.

51. Durkheim 1925, 557–75. I owe many of the observations in this section to Seaford 1989.

52. Burkert 1972, 53.

53. Consider the early Nazi funerals that created "martyrs" for the cause, or the fact that IRA displays at funerals in Northern Ireland frequently are banned. In S. *Ant.*, a lone woman throwing dust on her brother's corpse is viewed as a political threat; see Steiner 1984, 150–51, 296. Margarethe von Trotta's film "Die bleierne Zeit"("Marianne and Juliane" in the U.S.) draws on *Ant.* in its fictionalized account of Gudrun Ennslin, a Baader-Meinhof member whose body was not returned to her family for burial after she died (killed by police?) in prison.

54. That dawn had not yet broken for the interment is suggested on two vases by the Sappho Painter (Kurtz and Boardman 1971, pls. 36–38, and Vermeule 1979, fig. 17, p. 21). See also Kurtz and Boardman 1971, 144–45 and Garland 1985, 33 and 143.

55. A. E. Harvey, "The Classification of Greek Lyric Poetry," *CQ* 5 (1955), 168–72, distinguishes the various funeral laments, expanded by Alexiou 1974, 102–14. See also Thomas 1989, 104–5.

56. Kurtz and Boardman 1971, 96–99; my summary of Athenian burial practice draws heavily on their account, pp. 68–141. See also Morris 1992, 116–18, 140–41.

57. The classic study remains Jacoby 1944; his date of 465/64 for the institution of the practice is confirmed by W. K. Pritchett, *The Greek State at War*, Vol. 4 (Berkeley 1985), 94–124 and 249–50, and accepted by Fraenkel 1950 on *Ag.* 435, Page 1959, 323, Collard 1975 on *Supp.* 857–917, and others. Loraux 1986, 28–30 and 56–72 faults Jacoby's account, only to reach virtually the same conclusion on the same evidence. H. Strasburger, "Thukydides und die politische Selbstdarstellung der Athener," *Hermes* 86 (1958), 20–25, thinks a date just after the Persian Wars more likely, altered to the late 470s by Clairmont 1983, 2–15. See also Tyrrell and Brown 1991, 189–95; Shapiro 1991, 644–47; and D. W. Bradeen, "The Athenian Casualty Lists," *CQ* 19 (1969), 145–59.

58. I am indebted to Morris 1989a for many of these observations. Loraux 1986, 28 wrongly implies that public grave monuments were splashy affairs compared to private markers, arguing that state tombs "were exempt from the constraints imposed by the general rule of austerity." Cf. Morris 1992, 132–34, 141–42; and Shapiro 1991, 647.

59. An interpretation put forth by Alexiou 1974, 21–23; Loraux 1986, 42–56 and 328–36; Foley 1989a; and Shapiro 1991. The possible connection between purported sumptuary legislation and the institution of the *patrios nomos* complicates matters, but two correctives are overdue. Loraux insists that Athenian public burial displaced traditional *thrēnoi* of the private funeral; however, in the annual civic rite, "the procession is accompanied by anyone who chooses, whether citizen or foreigner; and the female relatives of the deceased are present at the funeral and make their lamentation" (Thuk. 2.34.4). Loraux 1986, 24 interprets this to mean that women were "tolerated only at the graveside, not in the cortège," hardly the obvious meaning. Moreover, she emphasizes the "prohibition against bemoaning the combatants" (p. 41), but we find on examination precisely the opposite—lamentations not only preceded the *epitaphios* but also followed it. Perikles bids his audience depart only "after you have made the fitting lamentations, each for his own dead" (Thuk. 2.46.2, ἀπολοφυράμενοι echoing ὀλοφυρόμεναι, the lamentations of the women that precede the funeral address). Similarly, at the end of Lysias' funeral oration (2.81), the speaker concludes, "It is necessary that we follow our ancient custom and respect our ancestral law by lamenting (ὀλοφύρεσθαι) those we are burying." So, too, Demosthenes (60.37) ends his *epitaphios* by enjoining his listeners to "take their fill of lamentation" (ἀποδυράμενοι) before they depart. Finally, the *patrios nomos* could not impinge on private funerals that *never took place*. Previously, there were no formal burials for those who fell in war; their corpses (or ashes) had been buried on the battlefield.

60. Kurtz 1975, 136. Hellenistic graves provide the earliest material evidence for the custom of burying an obol with the dead, payment for Charon to row the corpse over the river Styx. Aristophanes refers to the practice (*Ran.* 140, 270), but he speaks of two obols and may be joking about the price of a ticket at the City Dionysia—theatre-going as a veritable trip to Hades! See Morris 1992, 105–6 and Kurtz and Boardman 1971, 166 and 211.

61. See Kurtz and Boardman 1971, 145, 200–201, 215; Lorimer 1931; and Ch. 3, this volume, p. 50.

62. Garland 1990, 44, 147–48; and Parker 1983, 36.

63. O. Murray, "Death and the Symposion," in *AION*(arch) 10 (1988) 250; Garland 1985, 145–46; Kurtz and Boardman 1971, 92, 139, 214, 234, 277; and Ch. 3, this volume, pp. 51–52.

64. For the *makarismos* of the dead, see Garland 1985, 8–10, 134–35; and McDonald 1978, passim. P. W. Harsh, *A Handbook of Classical Drama* (Stanford 1944), 461n.61, notes the *double entendre* at Eur. *Med.* 957, where Glauke is both "a happy bride" and one of the "blessed dead" (Ch. 7, this volume, p. 103).

65. Such self-reference—the "vase-on-the-vase"—emphasizes the ritual use of the vessel (Ch. 2, this volume, p. 31). Flowers on tombs are mentioned in epitaphs (Lattimore 1962, 129) and at S. *El.* 896; Eur. *Tro.* 1144, 1247, *Or.* 1321–22, etc. At *Hec.* 126–27, the tomb of Achilles is "coronalled" (στεφανοῦν) not with flowers but with the blood of Polyxena.

66. Kurtz 1988, 147.

67. See Richter 1961, esp. 2–7.

68. Morris 1992 (145–55) and 1989a. For the interpretive problems and a critical evaluation of Morris 1987, see the review by S. C. Humphreys, *Helios* 17 (1990), 263–68 (esp. 267).

69. Johansen 1951, 151; even the sitting position in Attic reliefs does not necessarily designate the deceased (37, 149). Lullies 1960, 83 reasons that if all the characters face the same direction, they belong to the same sphere and the stele emphasizes union after death. If one character looks away, however, separation from the living becomes the dominant message.

70. Kokula 1974, 182–83 concludes that the so-called loutrophoroi-hydria were reserved for male graves and loutrophoroi-amphora for female. On this basis, only one-sixth of the surviving marble loutrophoroi marked the graves of unmarried women; the rest were erected at the graves of unmarried men. See also Boardman 1988; Osborne 1985, 134; Garland 1985, 72–73, 87; D. Peppas-Delmusu, "Monumento Sepolcrale di un Guerriero," *ArchCl* 25–26 (1973–74), 529–38 and pl. 91–96; Kurtz and Boardman 1971, 149–52, 161; Panofsky 1964, 20–21; and Beazley 1932.

71. See Barrett 1964 on *Hipp.* 1423–30, who wonders (p. 4) whether this might be "a fusing of marriage-custom with mourning-custom."

72. For wedding themes on tombstones and in funeral epigrams, see E. N. Lane, "*PASTOS*," *Glotta* 66 (1988), 102–5, 112–14; and Lattimore 1962, 192–94. Note the epigram attributed to Erinna (*Greek Anthology*, Loeb Vol. 2, 7.712) that quotes the epitaph of a young bride Baukis, whose new "father-in-law lit her funeral pyre/ with the very torch that burned at her wedding hymn./ And you, Hymenaios, changed that tuneful wedding song/ to the wailing voice of lamentation." J. W. Day, "Early Greek Grave Epigrams and Monuments," *JHS* 109 (1989), 23–24, explores the "archaic idea that encomium for a dead man and his grave monument are analogous means of recording, even reiterating his funeral." By returning the onlooker to the funeral, the grave stele and epitaph emphasize the centrality of the ritual itself to Greek thinking about the dead.

73. In some essentialist way—emotive, anthropological, even spiritual—the rituals of weddings and funerals never fundamentally changed their (admittedly manifold) meanings for the fifth-century Athenian men and women who performed them. On the basis of the literary and archaeological record, Morris 1989, 313 can detect "no analytically significant change in individual attitudes toward death between the eighth and the fifth century."

CHAPTER 2

1. See Schnapp 1988, 574. A full study of attribute and gesture in Greek tragedy (akin to Neumann 1965) would be helpful, perhaps modeled on D. Bevington, *Action Is Eloquence: Shakespeare's Language of Gesture*, (Cambridge, Mass. 1984). Kaimio 1988 limits her discussion to gestures of physical contact.

2. See App. A n.4.

3. Sutton 1981, 164–215, 235. See also App. A n.4. For an overview of

loutrophorous shape and function, see Shapiro 1991, passim (funerary); Webster 1972, 105–8; H. Gericke, *Gefässdarstellungen auf griechischen Vasen* (Berlin 1970), 59–63.

4. *ARV²* 1102.2, *Para* 451, *Add²* 329, and *ARV²* 1127.18, *Para* 453, *Add²* 332. For the possible confusion between wedding and funeral processions in these scenes, see R-M. Moesch, "Le Mariage et la mort sur les loutrophores," *AION*(arch) 10 (1988), 135–37.

5. Attic red-figure pyxis, Berlin Staatliche Museen, inv. 3373, reproduced in Deubner 1900.

6. *ARV²* 512.13 and 1657, *Para* 382, *Add²* 252; S. Karouzou, *CVA* Grèce 2 (Paris 1954), 14, identifies "la couronne des jeunes mariées." See also W. Zschietzschmann, "Die Darstellungen der *Prothesis* in der griechischen Kunst," *MDAI(A)* 53 (1928), 17–47.

7. As on the black-figure loutrophoros (NY 27.228), published by G.M.A. Richter, *BMMA* 23 (1928), 393–96, and the red-figure loutrophoros in Paris, *ARV²* 184.22 and 1632, *Para* 340, *Add²* 187 (see Lissarrague 1992, 164–66). In an imaginative sense, the funeral bath may have constituted the dead youth's nuptial bath. We find mythological references to young women "marrying Hades" and to mortal youths snatched up by goddesses to be their consorts—death envisioned as a wedding to an immortal. See Vermeule 1979, 164–69; Roberts 1978, 178–80; and sources in n.22 (below).

8. *CVA* Grèce 1, Hg, pl. 8.1 (Athens NM 12947). Similar logic explains the presence in infant graves of small wine vessels (*choes*) that depict children. At the annual Anthesteria festival, an Athenian youngster would receive such a *chous*. When the vessel was buried with a child, it presumably evoked the festival that the young boy would never live to enjoy.

9. Kurtz 1975, 64–65 and Beazley 1932, 15. According to Shapiro 1991, 639–44, these vases (and those with scenes alluding to funeral games) reflect a heroicizing impulse that dropped out of private funeral iconography with the institution of the *patrios nomos* (see also Ch. 1 n.57, this volume).

10. Marble loutrophoroi were carved fully in the round, or in relief on a stele. Kokula 1974, 2–3, 182–83 distinguishes two-handled loutrophoroi-amphorai (used for unwedded men) from three-handled loutrophoroi-hydriai (marking graves of unmarried women, Ch. 1 n.70, this volume). See also Davies 1971, 361–62.

11. Johansen 1951, 54–60, 148–51. G. Davies, "The Significance of the Handshake Motif in Classical Funerary Art," *AJA* 89 (1985), 627–30, 639, thinks that some scenes show the reunion of the dead in the underworld. The gesture on grave reliefs also may represent an oath taken by the survivor, perhaps linked to the inheritance after the death of a married woman. The dying Alkestis makes Admetus swear not to remarry and dispossess her children (Eur. *Alk.* 299–308, 328–31), and much is made of the link between right hands and sworn oaths in *Medea* (Ch. 7 p. 105, this volume).

12. Kokula 1974, 77–101, 181–83.

13. In Vernant and Vidal-Naquet 1988, 99.

14. Kokula 1974, 182–83 and Boardman 1988, 175 and 179 conclude that far more male than female graves were marked with marble loutrophoroi (Ch.

1 n.70, this volume). Marriage/remarriage patterns in Athens (Ch 1 n.34, this volume) also support the conclusion that a wedding was viewed as central to male (as well as female) experience, an opinion shared by Bruit Zaidman and Schmitt Pantel 1992, 71–72.

15. See Loraux 1981a, 40–41. Late-fifth-century Attic grave reliefs had a strong domestic flavor: "Even when the dead is portrayed as a warrior, very often he is shown taking leave of a family group containing women and small children. The atmosphere of the reliefs is private and non-heroic, and the same is true of classical epitaphs" (Humphreys 1983, 105). Women also feature prominently on vase scenes depicting warriors departing for battle, closely linking herocizing, martial images with those of the *oikos*. See Lissarrague 1992, 172–76.

16. "A symbolic wedding present"—Harl-Schaller 1972–75, 170. See also Boardman 1958–59; Robinson 1936, 507; and C. H. Smith, *British Museum Catalogue of Vases*, III (London 1896), 366–67. On the Eretria Painter epinetron (*ARV²* 1250.34 and 1688, *Para* 469, *Add²* 354) depicting Alkestis (inscribed) in her bedroom, women place sprigs and flowers in a loutrophoros and lebetes gamikoi.

17. See L. Burn, *The Meidias Painter* (Oxford 1987) 82. According to Kahil 1983, 243, loutrophoroi used on the wedding day were dedicated to the sanctuaries of Nymphē and of Aphrodite Pandemos on the south slope of the Akropolis, whereas the various Attic sanctuaries of Artemis received offerings of "pyxides, the epinetra, the lebetes gamikoi used for the 'day after.'" See also her "Quelques vases du sanctuaire d'Artémis a Brauron," in *Neue Ausgrabungen in Griechenland*, AK Beiheft 1 (1963), 27.

18. *ARV²* 1475.1, *Para* 495, *Add²* 381.

19. *ARV²* 833.45, *Add²* 295. In the Eretria Painter pyxis (*ARV²* 1250.32, Ch. 1 n.10) showing preparations for a wedding, two lebetes gamikoi appear on which *also* are painted wedding scenes.

20. See Kurtz 1984, 320n.68, 231n.74; Webster 1972, 108; and R. Lullies, "Attisch-Schwarzfigurige Keramik aus dem Kerameikos," *JDAI* 61–62 (1946–47), 74 (#78,#79) and pl. 23. A fourth-century fragment (Kenner 1935) depicts a louterion (like a lebes gamikos on its stand) itself decorated with a grave scene. Boardman 1952, 30–32 traces the connection between Eretrian high-necked grave amphorai and the lebes-gamikos shape. Occasionally a lebes may have been used to hold water for purifying the mourners after a burial; see Shapiro 1991, 635n.37 and 647n.121 and Ch. 1 p. 28, this volume.

21. Boardman 1958–59, 161n.40.

22. "As a wedding of the deceased with the god of death"—Harl-Schaller 1972–75, 170. See also Thimme 1964, 21–22; H. Kenner, "Flügelfrau und Flügeldämon," *JÖAI* 31 (1939), 94–95; Rose 1925; and A. von Salis, "Die Brautkrone," *RM* 73 (1920–24), 211–15.

23. Kurtz 1975, xix, 133, and 136. For a synopsis of funeral iconography found on these lekythoi, see Shapiro 1991, 649–55.

24. Rubbing the body with oil was common before exercising and after bathing, a means of cleansing the skin and protecting it from the sun. See Flacelière 1965, 104, 147–48.

25. Kurtz 1984, 321 and 1975, xix, 74, 77, and 136. Lullies and Hirmer 1960, 88 trace the importance of oil in burial rites, culminating in the marking of graves with stone or marble lekythoi, often decorated with reliefs on the model of marble loutrophoroi. The number of strigils (oil-scrapers) found as grave-gifts further testifies to the importance of oil; see Kurtz and Boardman 1971, 102, 208–9.

26. Kurtz 1975, xix.

27. Reilly 1989; quotation at 431.

28. Ch. 1 p. 14. Sutton 1981, 242–52 describes forty-five red-figure vases where a groom takes his bride by the hand or wrist.

29. *ARV*[2] 670.17, *Add*[2] 278.

30. *ARV*[2] 1237.14. Cf. the mutual clasping in the *dexiōsis* handshake on Attic grave reliefs (above n.11). Also compare the hydria fragment (*ARV*[2] 263.42) from an Attic grave that shows Hermes *psychopompos* ("leader of souls") leading a heavily cloaked man by the hand where the dead man reciprocates Hermes' clasp. Although the detail may be inconsequential, I know of no illustration where Hermes takes hold of a woman and her hand grips his in response.

31. V. Tusa, *Odeon ed Altri "Monumenti" Archeologici* (Palermo 1971), 360–61 and pl. VIIb.

32. *ABV* 363.37, *Para* 161, *Add*[2] 96.

33. *ARV*[2] 446.266, *Para* 375, *Add*[2] 241. See Kurtz 1975, 140; Haspels 1930, 437; and E. Gabrici, "Il Santuario della Malophoros a Selineute," *MonAnt* 32 (1927), 333.

34. See Ch. 3 p. 50 and n.37. For marriage and sacrifice in *IA*, see Foley 1985, 68–78 and 84–92, and 1982a. In *Hec.*, Polyxena describes herself as a young calf torn from her mother—an image used elsewhere for a bride (Ch. 5 pp. 74–75)—as she is led off to be sacrificed (205–10). She imagines the royal match she might have made (351–53, 365–66), preferring to dedicate her body to Hades (368) rather than to live as a concubine. "Without marriage or wedding hymn" (ἄνυμφος ἀνυμέναιος) she "will lie in Hades" (416–18). Preparing to wash Polyxena's corpse and lay out the body, Hecuba calls her daughter "a weddingless bride and a married virgin" (νύμφην τ' ἄνυμφον παρθένον τ' ἀπάρθενον 612).

35. The change may reflect a relaxation in sumptuary laws, allowing families to commission larger-scale monuments (Kurtz 1975, 136). However, Morris 1992 (128–55) and 1989a argues that sumptuary laws played little part in this pan-Hellenic change in funerary practice. Harrison, 1977, 421 thinks that the shift (in Athens) may signal a return to older, more traditional forms of reverence for the dead after the plague in 430/429. Clairmont 1983, 2 and 277n.2 believes that stone stelai *continued* to be erected in the Kerameikos during the first two-thirds of the fifth century.

36. Kurtz 1975, 225.

37. See S. Karusu, "'ΕΡΜΗΣ ΨΥΧΟΠΟΜΠΟΣ," *MDA1(A)* 76 (1961), 91–106 and *Beilage* (i.e., "supplement") 58–63, for representations of Hermes in this role. Also H. Diepolder, *Die Attischen Grabreliefs* (Berlin 1931) pl. 13.1, and Conze #1146, pl. 242, 243c.

38. A krater by the Alkimachos Painter (*ARV*² 532.44, *Add*² 254) shows Hermes leading a young woman with covered head XEK, preceded by a woman holding two torches and followed by a Silenus carrying a chest. Schefold 1981, 299–300, pl. 435 identifies the scene as the marriage of Hermes to the daughter of Dyrops. Others think it illustrates the *anodos* of Persephone, including C. Bérard, *Anodoi* (Institut Suisse de Rome 1974), 133–34; Haspels 1930, 443; and Minto 1919, 72. For scenes of Hermes escorting Persephone *without* the XEK gesture, see Bérard 1984, 129–42 and pl. 15.50–51, 16.53, 17.59–61, 18.63, 19.71.

39. See H. Götze, "Die Attischen Dreifigurenreliefs," *RM* 53 (1938), 189–280 and pl. 32–38; H. A. Thompson, "The Altar of Pity in the Athenian Agora," *Hesperia* 21 (1952), 60–74; and E. B. Harrison, "Hesperides and Heroes: A Note on the Three-Figure Reliefs," *Hesperia* 33 (1964), 76–82, and 1977, 421 (noting the influence of the three-figure reliefs on Attic funerary art). Ridgway 1981, 209 compares Eurydike on the Orpheus reliefs with Myrrhine on the marble lekythos grave monument (Ch. 2 figure 10, this volume), which shows "the deceased being led away by a more active and frontal, but not entirely dissimilar, Hermes."

40. The Quirinal relief (Berlin, Staatliche Museen 709) is the best example, showing Hermes "dancing" with the three nymphs: the left hand of the god takes the right wrist of the first nymph, and the gesture is repeated by each subsequent pair. C. Edwards, "Greek Votive Reliefs to Pan and the Nymphs," diss. NYU 1985, 37, notes that the nymph whom Hermes leads XEK is tightly wrapped in her *himation* and "lowers her head as if the dance was [*sic*] a solemn occasion." See also Ridgway 1981, 210.

41. Sutton 1981, 183–84 and 1989, 344–47, 351; also Lissarrague 1992, 152–54. S. Schama, *The Embarrassment of Riches* (New York 1987), 420–27, observes a comparable shift in the rise of "companionate" wedding portraits in seventeenth-century Holland, marking "a fresh moment in the history of European marriage."

42. See, e.g., C. Sourvinou, "The Young Abductor of the Locrian Pinakes," *BICS* 20 (1973) 17; and Jenkins 1983.

43. See Ch. 5 pp. 75–76, this volume. P. DuBois, *Centaurs and Amazons* (Ann Arbor 1982), 27–32, interprets Centaurs as the negation of marriage.

44. See the lebes gamikos in Baltimore (Robinson 1936) with the *epaulia* on the body and Apollo pursuing Daphne on the pedestal; the *epinetron* (*ARV*² 1250.34, above n.16) with one side depicting the marriage of Alkestis, while a band running over the end shows Peleus wrestling Thetis; the red-figure *krater* in Boston with the upper frieze split between Peleus chasing Thetis and an indoor scene showing a seated bride holding a mirror in the presence of other young women (Boston MFA 1972.850); etc. Perhaps the scene of Peleus and Thetis (note also figure 5) points toward the violent results of their eventual marriage—Eris' gift of the apple of discord that disrupts the ceremony and leads to the Trojan War (see Ch. 1, n.25), and the fate of Achilles, offspring of the union between mortal and immortal—in contrast to the ordered calm of a traditional wedding scene. Cf. the red-figure amphora (Ch. 5 n.16) that juxtaposes a decorous version of the wedding of

Peleus and Thetis with the Centauromachy that disrupts the wedding-feast of Perithoös and Hippodameia. Roberts 1978, 178–80 discusses the appropriateness on wedding and funeral vases of scenes depicting the rape of Oreithyia by the god Boreas, and of Kephalos by the goddess Eos. S. Kaempf-Dimitriado, *Die Liebe der Gotter in der attischen Kunst*, AK Beiheft 11 (Berlin 1979), 16–21, 36–42, and 47–53, presents a survey of comparable abductions in tragedy. C. Sourvinou-Inwood, "A Series of Erotic Pursuits," *JHS* 107 (1987), 136–47 and 152–53, explores the polysemic interplay between abduction and marriage on Greek vases.

45. See P. A. Clement, "The Recovery of Helen," *Hesperia* 27 (1958), 47–73, and L. B. Ghali-Kahil, *Les Enlèvements et le retour d'Hélène* (Paris 1955). For Paris leading Helen XEK, see Ghali-Kahil pls. III.3, IV; for Menelaus recovering Helen XEK, see XLII 2, LXXXII 1 and 2, LXXXV 1 and 2, LXXXVI 1 and 2, and LXXXVII 3. Ghali-Kahil thinks the last five show the wedding of Menelaus and Helen, but the fact that Menelaus is armed makes this unlikely.

46. See *ARV*² 406.1, *Para* 371, *Add*² 232, and *ARV*² 459.2, *Para* 377, *Add*² 243, where Agamemnon (inscribed) personally takes the girl XEK. For the image of the "mourning/sulking Achilles," see *LIMC* s.v. "Achilleus" 107–14 and pls. 103–5, 110–12; Johansen 1967, 164–80; and K. Bulas, *Illustrations antiques de l'"Iliade"* (Paris 1929), 2–5. Achilles calls Briseis his "wife" (ἄλοχος, *Il*. 9.336), and we learn that Patroclus had vowed to persuade Achilles to marry her formally (*Il*. 19.291–99).

47. For *Ion* as comedy, see Knox 1970. The prominence of Eleusis in the play strengthens the parallels with the *Hymn to Demeter*. Not only is Kreousa's rape modeled on Persephone's, but her search for her lost child also links her to Demeter. See Rehm 1985, 351–53, and N. Loraux, "Kreousa the Autochthon: A Study of Euripides' *Ion*," in Winkler and Zeitlin 1990, 201–3.

48. Panofsky 1964, 21; Thimme 1964; and Kurtz and Boardman 1971, 138.

49. Athens, National Museum 3472. Other grave reliefs depicting a seated woman with hand on veil (it is often unclear if the image is one of veiling or unveiling) include Munich Glyptothek W491 (Mnesarete), and Conze #67, 70 (Melitta), 79 (Kallisto), 78, 81, 82, 99 (on a marble lekythos), 109 (Pamphile and Demetria), 161 (Menekrateia and Meneas), 162 (Melite), 163 (Gome), 274 (Eirene), 281, 297 (Archestrate), 304; standing women with veil gesture, Conze #803 and 804. On the metope at Selinus, Hera holds out her veil with her left hand, while a seated Zeus takes hold of her XEK. The metope is reproduced beautifully by V. Tusa, *La scultura in pietra di Selinunte* (Palermo 1984), pl 12, 15–16, who describes Hera's gesture as "tipico della sposa," noting that Zeus wears a *stephanē*, which also points to a wedding (120–21). See also Burkert 1977, 132. For Hera's unveiling on the Parthenon frieze, see Pemberton 1976, 115–16 and pl. 17.4.29–30.

50. Andromache faints at the news of Hektor's death, and "dark night covered her eyes" (H. *Il*. 22.466), a formula normally reserved for warriors dying in battle. As she falls, she loses her κρήδεμνον (*krēdemnon*), the head-dress/wedding veil given her by Aphrodite on the day she married Hektor (22.468–72). Her action foreshadows the destruction of Troy, for the word

krēdemnon also refers to the crenellations atop the fortification walls, the city's symbolic "headdress." Hecuba also throws off her veil, καλύπτρη (*kaluptrē*), at the sight of Hektor's body (22.405–7), and the Trojans cry out as if Troy has fallen. H. L. Lorimer, *Homer and the Monuments* (London 1950), 385–86, concludes that "the city is perhaps compared to a captive woman whose veil is torn off by her captor." See also Nagler 1974, 10–11, 45–54. In the *Hymn to Demeter*, *krēdemnon* refers both to the towers of the city of Eleusis (151) and to the head-covering veil that Demeter rips apart on hearing of Persephone's abduction (41). For visual representations of veiling as covering the head, see App. A. n.5.

51. Barrett 1964 on *Hipp*. 1459–61 shows that Hippolytus expires at 1459, and that Theseus covers his corpse. Euripides may be alluding to his earlier *Hippolytus*, which acquired the name *Kalyptomenos* ("Veiled") because the hero covered his head in shame at Phaedra's advances. See Taplin 1978, 94–95; B. Goff, *The Noose of Words* (Cambridge 1990), 14; and Halleran 1991.

52. P. E. Easterling, "Euripides in the Theatre," *Pallas* 37 (1991), 52–53.

53. Johansen 1967, 156–57 (on *ARV*² 746.3).

54. See Ch. 1 p. 17. The pomegranate is found on funerary sculpture such as the Attic stele (Berlin Staatliche 1531 and NY Met. 11.85, Richter 1961, #137), where a *korē* stands holding a flower alongside a taller male holding a pomegranate. A pomegranate also is held by free-standing *korai*, including Acr. Mus. 593, 677, and 680 (G.M.A. Richter, *Korai* [London 1968], #43, 59, and 122). In the first instance, the maiden not only has a pomegranate in her left hand but also holds a wreath or *stephanē* in her right, attributes of both funerals and weddings.

55. *ARV*² 754.13, *Add*² 285; Kurtz 1975, 205 (pl. 22.1,2).

56. National Museum 1938; Kurtz 1975, pl.36.3.

57. *ARV*² 754.14, *Add*² 285.

58. Noted at Ch. 2 p. 40. See Conze #157, #310, #360 (a marble lekythos), #813 (standing woman); the marble lekythoi published by H. N. Fowler, "An Attic Grave Relief," in Mylonas 1951, 588–89 (pl. 54), and by M. B. Comstock and C. C. Vermeule, *Sculpture in Stone* (MFA Boston, 1976), #40, pp. 30–31; and Kurtz and Boardman 1971, 138.

59. A bride holding a mirror is depicted on several lebetes gamikoi: Baltimore *CVA* 2, pl. 50 (Robinson 1936); in New York, *ARV*² 1098.35, *Add*² 328; *ARV*² 1080 in London; two in Berlin, *ARV*² 841.70, *Add*² 296 and *ARV*² 1225.1; two in Athens, *ARV*² 582.1 and *ARV*² 1179.3, *Para* 460, *Add*² 340. Women with mirrors in a wedding context occur on other vase shapes: see E. Zevi, "Scene di gineceo e scene di idillio," *MAL* 6 (1938), 306, 324–26, and fig. 3; also the red-figure krater in Boston (MFA 1972.850, above n.44), the kylix in Malibu (Getty 82.AE.38), an oinochoe (*ARV*² 1207.26bis, *Add*² 345), and a small hydria (*ARV*² 1212.7, *Add*² 347). Sutton 1981, 203 observes the rise from circa 440 B.C. of strictly feminine toilette scenes in nuptial contexts. For marriage scenes on pyxides, see Roberts 1978, 4, 178.

60. See Robinson 1936, 509 and n.3, and N. T. de Grummond and M. Hoff, "Bronzes in the Mediterranean," in *A Guide to Etruscan Mirrors*, ed. de Grummond (Tallahassee 1982), 37–38, who cite the frequency of mirrors on

white-ground lekythoi and funerary reliefs, and the popularity of bronze mirrors as grave gifts. See also Congdon 1981, 12–14; S. P. Karouzou [Karusu], "Attic Bronze Mirrors," in Mylonas 1951, 566; and K. Schefold, "Griechische Spiegel," *Die Antike* 16 (1940), 11–37.

61. For example, a woman bearing torches can signal a nuptial scene: see *ARV*[2] 899.146, *Add*[2] 303; Robinson *CVA* 2 (Walters/Baltimore) pl. 49; Sarajevo *CVA* 32.3; the loutrophoros in H. Hoffman, *Ten Centuries That Shaped the West* (Houston 1970), 406; Tübingen 5 *CVA* Tf. 6.6 and pp. 24–25; *ARV*[2] 1031.51, *Add*[2] 317; *ARV*[2] 1102.2 (above n.4); and *ARV*[2] 539.40. Roberts 1978, 182–84 notes that the presence of a door can make the nuptial aspects clearer.

62. Scholars increasingly admit the anachronism of tragic references to wedding and funeral rituals vis-à-vis the heroic period in which the plays ostensibly are set. On A. *Ag.* 435, see Jacoby 1944, 44 and n.30; Page 1959, 323; and Fraenkel 1950 on 435. For Eur. *Supp.* 947–49 and 1123–26, see Collard 1975 on 947–49a and Diggle 1970 on *Phaeth.* 158–59. For tragic threnodies, see Pickard-Cambridge 1962, 107; Collard 1975 on *Supp.* 794–954; Brown 1987 on *Ant.* 1257–1353; and Ch. 4 n.32, this volume. For marriages (esp. dowries), see Jebb 1892 on *Tr.* 161ff.; Barrett 1964 on *Hipp.* 625–26; and Page 1938 on *Med.* 956. Regarding the Athenian-specific nature of the visual iconography of marriage and funeral rites, see Kurtz 1975, xx, 132, and Brooklyn 1981, 96. Roberts 1978, 4–5 notes that the lebes gamikos, loutrophoros, and pyxis shapes—all of which show "a striking interpenetration of wedding and funeral matter"—were rarely exported outside of Greece. The same holds for white-ground lekythoi with funerary iconography, which had the most restricted market among vases of that shape. Kurtz 1975, 131 reasons that "the specialized iconography rendered it intelligible only to those familiar with Athenian rites of death and burial." Pattern- and black-bodied lekythoi, on the other hand, had a wide provenience in Greece and abroad.

CHAPTER 3

1. Those who focus on corrupted sacrifices include Zeitlin 1965 and 1966; Burkert 1966, 119–20; P. Vidal-Naquet, "Chasse et sacrifice dans l'*Orestie*," *PP* 129 (1969), 401–25 (= Vernant and Vidal-Naquet 1988, 141–59); F. T. Griffiths, "Girard on the Greeks/ The Greeks on Girard," *Berkshire Review* 14 (1979), 24–29; and Foley 1985, 56. Other elements of inverted ritual involve inappropriate hymns and appeals to the gods—see J. A. Haldane, "Musical Themes and Imagery in Aeschylus," *JHS* 85 (1965), 37–40; above, p. 46; and below, n.20. Comparatively little has been done on the perversions of weddings and funerals; see Lebeck 1971, 48–49, 68–73; and Seaford 1984.

2. Fraenkel 1950, and Denniston and Page 1957, on *Ag.* 65; Zeitlin 1965, 465–66; Lebeck 1971, 69–73, 186–88; and Burkert 1972, 62–63 and n.20. For the martial/nuptial *proteleia* in Eur. *IA*, see Wolff 1982, 253; and Borghini 1986.

3. Seaford 1987, 124.

4. *kalumma* also is used for the bridal veil at Eur. *IT* 372 and funerary coverings at S. *El.* 1468. See Seaford 1984, 253.

5. Ch. 1 p. 22.

6. Denniston and Page 1957 on *Ag.* 744ff. argue unconvincingly that the Chorus do *not* identify Helen with the Furies, translating νυμφόκλαυτος Ἐρινύς as "a Fury bewept by the bride" [i.e., Helen]. J. C. Hogan, *A Commentary on the Complete Greek Tragedies: Aeschylus* (Chicago 1984), 68, correctly observes that Aeschylus substitutes the effect (vengeance) for the cause (Helen), "and then the effect is incarnated as a demonic agent."

7. See Seaford 1987, 128; Jenkins 1983, 138; Ch. 2, this volume, p. 30; and App. A. The scenes almost always feature the heroicizing substitution of a chariot for a cart. For other references to the wedding cart in tragedy, see Eur. *Supp.* 994, *Hel.* 639, 723 (Ch. 8 p. 112, 122), and possibly *Tro.* 568–76 (Ch. 9 p. 131). D. Thompson, "The Persian Spoils in Athens," in *The Aegean and the Near East*, ed. S. Weinberg (New York 1956), 287, argues that Agamemnon does not arrive in a chariot (the common view), but in a Persian-styled "throne wagon." Although Agamemnon's rejection of Eastern-style pomp (*Ag.* 919–21) argues against a recognizably Persian cart, the term ἁμαξήρη θρόνον (used of the vehicle at *Ag.* 1054) indicates a wagon with a seat (θρόνος). The other term describing Agamemnon's cart is ἀπήνη (906), technically a four-wheeled carriage used for traveling (see Jebb on *OT* 753). Although Denniston and Page 1957 on *Ag.* 782; Taplin 1977, 303–21; and Seaford and Jenkins (above) all assume a chariot, the text indicates a vehicle like that used in actual Athenian weddings. If Aeschylus *did* use a chariot, the association with a wedding would still hold, but only in the "heroicizing" fashion of black-figure scenes.

8. The veiled Alkestis, Admetus' "new bride," is called *xenē* (Eur. *Alk.* 1117, Ch. 6 p. 95); Deianeira refers to Iole as *xenē*, (S. *Tr.* 310, 627), the second time knowing she is Herakles' "auxiliary" wife; in Ar. *Thesm.* (888–91, parodying Eur. *Hel.*), Menelaus (played by Euripides) calls Helen (Mnesilochus) *xenē*, and she responds that (s)he is being forced to marry. At *Eu.* 660–61, Apollo calls a wife/mother a "stranger" (*xenē*) who guards the seed of the "stranger" (*xenos*) husband/father (above, p. 55).

9. See Ch. 1 p. 17 and n.22.

10. To Seaford's list (1987, 111n.58) add A. *Kares* (or *Europa*) *Fr.* 50 (99) 6; Eur. *Supp.* 220 and *Hel.* 1654; and perhaps A. *Pr.* 579, because the suffering to which Zeus "yokes" Io (ἐνέζευξας) arises when the god himself becomes "a bitter suitor for [Io's] hand in marriage" (πικροῦ . . . τῶν γάμων/ μνηστῆρος 739–40). For marriage as a yoke that *both* parties wear, see A. *Pers.* 139, Eur. *Med.* 242, and Arist. *Pol.* 1253b9–10. For spouse as "yokemate" (σύζυγος), see Sappho fr. 213.3, A. *Ch.* 599, and Eur. *Alk.* 314 (Gentili 1988, 76 and Patterson 1991, 49 and n.36). Unwedded girls are "unyoked of marriage" (Eur. *Hipp.* 1425, *Ba.* 694), as are unmarried men (*Med.* 673, *IA* 805, *Kresphontes* 66.23 [Austin 1968; see also Harder 1985, 66–67]). Iphis (*Supp.* 791) wishes he had remained "unyoked in marriage," *pace* P. T. Stevens, *JHS* 97 (1977), 76; see Ch. 8 p. 114.

11. Seaford 1987, 111–12 and n.62, and 1986, 52–53; ἐξαίρετον ("select") is linked to brides at Eur. *Tro.* 485 (Ch. 9 p. 130).

12. Fraenkel 1950 on *Ag.* 1207. Apollo's ruin of Kassandra is attested at

1072–87, 1202–13, 1256–57, and 1264–76. Kovacs 1987 argues that Kassandra was raped by Apollo, received her prophetic gift, and then denied the god children. Although he errs in claiming that Kassandra is punished for pride (334), Kovacs's main argument (330–33) is convincing: Apollo's "wrestling" with, and "breath of pleasure" on, Kassandra (Ag. 1206) means that the god forced her sexually, as Apollo does with Kreusa at Eur. Ion 881–96. Kassandra also was raped by Aias (son of Oileus) at the sack of Troy. See M. Davies, The Epic Cycle (Bristol 1989), 62–79; C. Vellay, Les Légendes du cycle troyen (Monaco 1957), 277–81; J. Davreux, La Légende de la prophétesse Cassandre (Liege 1942), 12–13; Alcaeus fr. 298 in Lobel and Page, 1955; and H. Lloyd-Jones, "The Cologne Fragment of Alcaeus," GRBS 9 (1968), 125–39. The scene was popular on Attic vases (Johansen 1967, 39 and Schefold 1978, 258).

13. The image suggests Sappho's comparison of eros to a "flame that runs up under the skin" (31.10). In A. Toxotides, we find the "burning (φλέγων) eye of a young woman—she who has tasted man" (Fr. 134 [243]). Klytemnestra boasts that Aegisthus "kindles the fire of my hearth" (Ag. 1435–36), a sexual/domestic double entendre, as Pomeroy 1975, 98 notes. For the destructive "flame of eros" in S. Tr., see Parry 1986, 108–11.

14. Klytemnestra is ἀνδρόβουλον (Ag. 11), "manlike in thought."

15. Legalisms abound in the Oresteia, but we find a special correspondence between witnesses and victims. The dead testify to their own bloodshed (Thyestes' children here, the ghost of Klytemnestra at Eu. 103), and the living bear witness to the fatal suffering of others until they, too, become victims (Kassandra, Orestes in Ch.). The Greeks at Aulis witness the eagle that feasts on the pregnant hare (109–20), a premonition of their own deaths at Troy as the "young" of Greece (825–26). Agamemnon bears witness to the false "mirror of companionship" (831–40), unaware that his own wife is deceiving him. Aegisthus testifies to the crimes of Atreus after helping to kill Atreus' son Agamemnon (1583–1609), then moves from witness to victim when he is slain by Orestes, another child who grows up an avenger.

16. Lebeck 1971, 68. Kassandra asks if Klytemnestra "will really accomplish the end" she has in mind (τόδε γὰρ τελεῖς; 1107), and then wonders "how shall I describe that end?" (πῶς φράσω τέλος; 1109).

17. The word bedmate (ξύνευνος) often refers to wives (Ch. 1 n.29); Klytemnestra later uses it for Kassandra (1442).

18. Seaford 1984, 248–49. Recall that Sokrates (Pl. Phd. 115A) also takes his funeral bath before he dies in order to save the women the trouble of bathing his corpse.

19. See Garvie 1986 on Ch. 686 and Foley 1985, 41. Mourning Agamemnon, the Chorus lament that he occupies "the lowly bed of a silver-walled bath" (Ag. 1539–40), the word for bathtub here (δροίτης) later signifying Agamemnon's funeral bier (Ch. 999). The word occurs again at Eu. 633; see Seaford 1984, 250.

20. A "blasphemous paradox," as Fraenkel 1950 on Ag. 645 puts it. See above n.1, and D. Clay, "The Daggers at Agamemnon 714–15," Philologus 110 (1966), 128–32; Kannicht 1969 on Hel. 176–78; and Collard 1975 on

Supp. 975–76. Generically, a paean was a song of healing, praise, triumph, or thanksgiving; the Chorus properly address Apollo as "Healer" (Παιᾶνα) at *Ag.* 146.

21. Sophokles dramatized the legend in his lost *Tereus*; see Sutton 1984, 127–32. Drawing on Ovid's version in *Metamorphosis*, Shakespeare uses the myth to bloody effect in *Titus Andronicus*.

22. See the perceptive comments by Ahl 1984, 182–84. Marriage-to-death resonances from the nightingale's song occur elsewhere in tragedy. In Eur. *Hel.* 1107–25, the Chorus ask the nightingale to join their threnody for the enslaved Trojan women, for Helen whom Paris (apparently) abducted in a "fatal marriage" (1120), and for the Greeks who died leaving their wives "lying in marriageless chambers" (1125). The Chorus compare Herakles' cries of pain to the strains of a nightingale at S. *Tr.* 962–64 (Ch. 5 p. 77). Elektra mourns like a nightingale, calling on "the halls of Persephone" and the god Hermes to help avenge the "stolen marriage beds" of her troubled house (S. *El.* 107–18; also 147–52, 239–42, and 1074–80). For other tragic references to the Procne-Philomela story, see Kannicht 1969 on *Hel.* 1107–12, to which add Eur. *HF* 1021–27, *Rh.* 546–50, and ?*Kresphontes P. Oxy.* 27.2458 fr. 2 col. II (line 83) + Michigan Papyri inventory no. 6973 (line 41) reconstructed by S. Bonnycastle and L. Koenen. For the link between nightingales and death generally in Greek literature, see D. W. Thompson, *A Glossary of Greek Birds* (Oxford 1936), 16–22; A. S. McDevitt, "The Nightingale and the Olive," in *Antidosis*, ed. R. Hanslik, A. Lesky, and H. Schwabl (Vienna 1972), 230–33; and N. Loraux, *Les Mères en deuil* (Paris 1990), 87–100.

23. See Johansen-Whittle 1980 on A. *Supp.* 58–67 and 68–72; A. H. Sommerstein, "Notes on Aeschylus' *Suppliants*," *BICS* 24 (1977), 68; and T. Gantz, "Love and Death in Aischylos' *Suppliants*," *Phoenix* 32 (1978), 280–81.

24. Ps. Aeschin. *Ep.* 10.3. See Gernet 1968, 41–42.

25. See Fraenkel 1950 on *Ag.* 1180. The dawn wind and bridal veils may recall the veils that Helen abandons when she sails "down the winds of a Zephyr" to Troy (*Ag.* 690–93, above, pp. 43–44), exchanging one marriage for another.

26. "The marriage ritual is, in all its details, a struggle against secrecy"— Sissa 1987, 116. Cf. the Danaids' rending of their veils (A. *Supp.* 120–21), suggesting their ultimate rejection of marriage (see Sommerstein, above n.23).

27. See Ch. 1 pp. 17–18. Fraenkel 1950 on *Ag.* 1191 notes that δώμασιν ("house") often specifies "bedrooms," linking the band of Furies more closely to wedding celebrants. In A. *Danaïds*, Danaus(?) refers to the "waking-song" in the "clear light of the sun" for his newly wedded daughters, all of whom (save one) have killed their husbands that very night (*Fr.* 24 [43]). In Eur. *Phaeth.* 228–44, the Chorus (Merops' daughters?) enter singing the wedding hymn for Phaethon and his new bride; at that moment the groom's corpse, still smoldering from Zeus' thunderbolt, is being hidden offstage by his mother Klymene. See also Nagy 1979, 198–200.

28. The verb κομίζω ("lead inside, escort, bring in") is used for leading a bride into her new home at Eur. *Alk.* 1028–29, 1063–64, 1110; *IA* 145–49, 428–39, 905–8 (Iphigenia as bride and as sacrificial victim). In its middle form, the verb is used at And. 1.127 and Is. 8.8 for a *kurios* taking his daughter back after the death of her husband. Forms of the verb also are used for recovering a corpse and preparing it for burial: A. *Ch.* 682–85 (Orestes' ashes); S. *Aj.* 1047–48 (Ajax's corpse); *El.* 1113–14 (Orestes' ashes); Eur. *Hipp.* 1261–62, 1264–67 (the dying Hippolytus); *Andr.* 1158–60, 1263–64 (Neoptolemus); *Supp.* 24–26, 126, 272–73, 494–95, 631–33, 754, 1185–86 (the bodies/bones of the slain Argives); *HF* 1420–22 (the children's corpses); *Hec.* 671–73 (the body of Polyxena, but really Polydorus); *Tro.* 1200–1201 (funeral gifts for Astyanax); *El.* 959–60 (Aegisthus, although no burial is implied); *Ph.* 1315–21 (Menoikeus) and 1627–28 (Eteokles); and Hdt. 4.71 (the Scythian custom of conveying corpses on wagons). Escorting a (surrogate) bride and (future) corpse is combined in Eur. *Hec.*—Odysseus is the "conveyor" (κομιστήρ 222) who "leads" (κόμιζ' 432) Polyxena to be sacrificed at Achilles' tomb so the Greek ships might return home from Troy (534–41), the reverse of A. *Ag.* 218–47 where Iphigenia is sacrificed so the fleet can sail for Troy (see below n.33).

29. Taplin 1977, 299–300, and figure 6, this volume.

30. Earlier Klytemnestra speaks of her delight at "opening wide the gates" (πύλας ἀνοῖξαι 604) to welcome Agamemnon home.

31. The verb κωκύω (s.v. *LSJ*), "wail" or "shriek," is applied specifically to the ritual lament over the dead and is used only of women in epic and tragedy. The name Kokytus—the "river of death" where Kassandra mourns (1160)—derives from this lament.

32. Dodds 1960, 27 writes that "what the King chose blindly . . . , Kassandra chooses with full knowledge, yet by a free act of will." See also S. L. Schein, "The Cassandra Scene in Aeschylus' *Agamemnon*," *G&R* 29 (1982), 11–16. Taplin 1977, 317–22 and Rehm 1988, 282n.81 analyze Kassandra's growing insight as realized dramatically through her series of false exits.

33. According to tradition going back to the lost *Kypria*, Agamemnon lures Iphigenia to Aulis under the guise of a betrothal to Achilles; see Conacher 1967, 250–53 and Cunningham 1984, 10. Iphigenia's "wedding" turns her from bride into sacrificial victim in Eur. *IA* (Ch. 2, this volume, n.34); a similar approach may have informed S. lost *Iphigenia* (Sutton 1984, 65). Denniston and Page 1957 on *Ag.* 227 believe that Iphigenia's deceptive betrothal to Achilles is ignored by Aeschylus, but Zeitlin 1965, 466 and 493 finds traces of the story and points out other similarities between Iphigenia and Kassandra (470–73).

34. The word occurs elsewhere in drama only at Ar. *Lys.* 217, 218, where it means "living a life without [marital] sex." See Henderson 1987 on *Lys.* 217.

35. Aeschylus' Io, also driven mad by a god, describes herself as a "horned maiden" (βούκερω παρθένου *Pr.* 588), alluding both to Zeus' rape and to her transformation into a cow.

36. See Denniston and Page 1957 on *Ag.* 1278.

37. Note their likeness to Polyxena, who removes her *peplos* from her

shoulders before being sacrificed at Achilles' tomb (Eur. *Hec.* 557–80). Born to be "the bride of kings" (*Hec.* 352), Polyxena takes leave of her mother (402–31) and covers her head while being led away by Odysseus (432), actions that resemble the *eisagōgē* of a bride to her new home. However Polyxena is "without nuptials and without wedding hymn" (ἄνυμφος ἀνυμέναιος 416). "I dedicate my body to Hades" (Ἄιδηι προστιθεῖσ᾽ ἐμὸν δέμας 368), she proclaims, accepting a marriage to death that recalls Aeschylus' Iphigenia and Kassandra.

38. See W. Headlam, *Agamemnon of Aeschylus* (Cambridge 1925, orig. 1910), 63; Fraenkel 1950 on *Ag.* 239; Sourvinou 1971; T.C.W. Stinton, "Iphigeneia and the Bears of Brauron," *CQ* 26 (1976), 11–13 (= Stinton 1990, 186–89). Others believe that her garments flow naturally toward the earth as she is lifted over the altar, including H. Lloyd-Jones, "The Robes of Iphigeneia," *CR* 2 (1952), 132–35; Denniston and Page 1957 on *Ag.* 239; and Lebeck 1971, 81–84. Regarding Kassandra, Fraenkel 1950 on *Ag.* 1264f argues convincingly that she discards her robes as well as her staff and fillet.

39. See Cunningham 1984; D. Armstrong and E. Ratchford, "Iphigenia's Veil," *BICS* 32 (1985), 5–10; and Seaford 1987, 125–26. Iphigenia's "shaft from the eyes" (ὄμματος βέλει 240) is the counterpart to the "soft shaft from the eye" (μαλθακὸν ὀμμάτων βέλος 742) with which Helen wins Paris, bringing on "the bitter completion of the marriage ritual" (ἐπέκρανεν/ δὲ γάμου πικρὰς τελευτάς 744–45). Cf. A. *Toxotides* (*Fr.* 133 [242]): "For pure maidens with no experience of the marriage bed, the glance [βολή] of their eyes looks down in shame."

40. See P. Perlman, "Plato *Laws* 833C–834D and the Bears of Brauron," *GRBS* 24 (1983), 125–26; Kahil 1983, 237–38; Ar. *Lys.* 219–20, 641–47; and Eur. *IT* 1461–67. Also, Iphigenia is lifted over the altar "like a goat" (232), the animal sacrificed to Artemis at the Brauronia; see H. Lloyd-Jones, "Artemis and Iphigeneia," *JHS* 103 (1983), 93, and Osborne 1985, 162–63.

41. See Dowden 1989, 9–47; Seaford 1988, 119–20; Sourvinou-Inwood 1988, 127–35; Osborne 1985, 161–72; Cole 1984, 242–44; Perlman (above n.40); A. Henrichs, "Human Sacrifice in Greek Religion," in *Le Sacrifice dans l'antiquité*, Fondation Hardt Entretiens 27 (Geneva 1981), 207–8; Parke 1977, 139–40. A disrobed Iphigenia strengthens the link to the Brauronia, for the vases (*krateriskoi*) dedicated there often depict young initiates in the nude.

42. Discarding her veil (like a bride) and her yellow robe (like a Brauronian "bear"), Euripides' Antigone symbolically abandons her youth. Like Iphigenia and Kassandra, however, her future is with the doomed or the dead. In place of marriage to Haimon (*Ph.* 1586–88, 1635–38), Antigone chooses to bury Polyneikes' corpse and suffer with her father (1656–82).

43. I assume that women attended the theater in fifth-century Athens, a position supported by J. Henderson, "Women and the Athenian Dramatic Festivals," *TAPA* 121 (1991), 133–47, and Podlecki 1990. As Podlecki notes, the idea that women could *not* attend dramatic performances goes back to Böttiger in 1796 and reflects contemporary German proprieties, a prudery antithetical to the inclusive nature of Dionysiac cult. As to the percentage

of Athenian girls initiated at the Brauronia, Vidal-Naquet 1977, 179–80 believes it was very small. However, Sourvinou-Inwood 1988, 75n.61 and 111–14 argues that the numbers were far more significant, and that the maturation rite (at least symbolically) was performed by all girls. The rite was organized by tribe, and those selected to participate were seen as representatives of their age group. Simon 1983, 86 goes further, claiming that the whole citizen population sent their daughters.

44. See Fraenkel 1950 on *Ag.* 1395f and Lebeck 1971, 60–63. D. W. Lucas, "ΈΠΙ ΣΠΕΝΔΕΙΝ ΝΕΚΡΩΙ, *Agamemnon* 1393–8," *PCPhS* 15 (1969), 60–68, distinguishes libations (σπονδαί) from pourings (χοαί), the former having no part in funeral rites. According to Lucas, Klytemnestra may allude to the practice of dousing sacrificial victims with libations. However, reference to the "third offerings" to Zeus (see Fraenkel 1950 on *Ag.* 1387) blurs these distinctions, conflating libations of wine, pourings over sacrificial victims, and liquid offerings for the dead.

45. Seeking poetic as well as personal justice, Orestes adopts this figure of speech when he promises the Furies the blood of Aegisthus (and presumably of Klytemnestra too) for their third libation; see Garvie 1986 on *Ch.* 577–78.

46. See Fraenkel 1950, and Denniston and Page 1957, on *Ag.* 1278. Klytemnestra inverts other aspects of Agamemnon's funeral—with fatal irony she has given her husband his final bath, and he lies in "public view," a perverse *prothesis* with the body wrapped in a net-cum-funeral shroud (1382, 1492, 1550). The Chorus refer to the "garland of unwashed blood" (1459–60) that comes from Helen, as if a funeral *stephanos* had been placed on the corpse. Seaford 1984, 248–49 examines these motifs in impressive detail.

47. Perverted feasts include the eagles that devour the pregnant hare (*Ag.* 119–20), the lion cub who grows up to wreak havoc on the herds (730–31), the Greek soldiers who "lap up the blood of kings" (827–28), the feast of Thyestes (1091–92, 1096–97), the plagues that will devour Orestes if he fails to take vengeance (*Ch.* 279–82), the snake drinking its mother's blood and milk in Klytemnestra's nightmare (*Ch.* 530–33, 545–46), the Furies who would suck Orestes' blood (*Eu.* 264–66) and threaten to consume the harvests of Attica (*Eu.* 781–87, 811–17).

48. Winnington-Ingram 1983, 111 notes that the offenses of which Klytemnestra accuses Agamemnon—killing their daughter Iphigenia and taking Kassandra as his concubine—"strike at the status of women in marriage."

49. As Pohlenz 1954, 101 puts it, "Mit der Kassandraszene hat die Tragödie ihren Gipfel erreicht" ("With the Kassandra scene, the tragedy has reached its climax"). See also Knox 1972; Lebeck 1971, 52; and Mason 1959, 84. The Kassandra scene is the longest in *Ag.* (over 250 lines), fully exploiting the modes of lyric and rhetoric available to the dramatist; see Rehm 1992, 86–89.

50. See Garvie 1986 on *Ch.* 22–83. Note also *Ch.* 429–32, 508–11, and 1014–15.

51. The word is used for "dowry" at Eur. *Ion* 814.

52. Although printing Murray's text, Garvie 1986 on *Ch.* 481–82 supports Heyse's and Wecklein's conjecture.

53. Alluded to only here in the *Oresteia*, Elektra's future marriage to Pylades seems to be a traditional element in the story; see Eur. *El.* 1249; *IT* 682, 696; and *Or.* 1092–93, 1658–59.

54. W. H. Race, *The Classical Priamel from Homer to Boethius*, Mnemosyne Supp. 74 (Leiden 1982), 89–90. For the scholarly debate on the order of the strophes, see Garvie 1986 on *Ch.* 585–651.

55. J. H. Kells, "Aeschylus *Eumenides* 213–24 and Athenian Marriage," *CP* 56 (1961), 169–73, thinks their adulterous oath parodies the marriage vows referred to at *Eu.* 217–18; Klytemnestra delivers an even stronger parody at *Ag.* 1431–36.

56. ἄγρευμα θηρός, ἢ νεκροῦ ποδένδυτον/ δροίτης κατασκήνωμα *Ch.* 998–99; for δροίτη as both "bathtub" and "coffin," see R. Pfeiffer, "A Fragment of Parthenios' *Arete*," *CQ* 37 (1943), 29n.6 (the word is used for Agamemnon's bier at *Ch.* 999). A similar confusion operates when Elektra uses ἀμφίβληστρον ("fishing-net," lit. "something thrown around") and καλύμμασιν ("coverings") for the net that trapped her father (*Ch.* 492, 494). The former word suggests both "net" and "shroud" at *Ag.* 1382; the latter means "shroud" at S. *El.* 1468. See Seaford 1984, 252–53.

57. See, for example, C. Paglia, *Sexual Personae* (Yale 1990), 100–101; DuBois 1988, 70–71; Cantarella 1987, 64–65; K. Millet, *Sexual Politics* (Garden City 1970), 112–15.

58. Broadbent 1968, 153–54. For fifth-century assumptions regarding the predominance of males in the reproductive process and challenges to those beliefs, see Garland 1990, 28–29 and Peretti 1956. For the idea that females as well as males produced "seed," see D. M. Halperin, "Why is Diotima a Woman?" 278–79, and A. E. Hanson, "The Medical Writers' Woman," 314n.27, both in Halperin, Winkler, and Zeitlin 1990.

59. Careful consideration of the Citizenship Law undermines the oft-repeated claim that Athenian women were "non-persons" in the *polis*. If women could be designated "Athenian," what rights and duties did that status entail? They did not vote in the Assembly, hold political office, act as jurors in the law courts, or serve in the military. However, women played a traditional and pervasive role in cult worship, performed essential ritual activities at weddings and funerals, and oversaw many aspects of child-rearing and economic/domestic life. Moreover, with the new law of 451, citizenship was passed down through them as well as through their husbands (see Patterson 1981, 135 and 1986, 63). Their new status found its way onto major public monuments, particularly the Parthenon frieze—see E. B. Harrison, "Hellenic Identity and Athenian Identity in the Fifth Century B.C.," in *Cultural Differentiation and Cultural Identity in the Visual Arts*, ed. S. J. Barnes and W. S. Melion (National Gallery of Art, Washington 1989), 50–51, 55, and 61n.96.

60. Europa says "I was yoked in marriage for [or 'to'] the joint partnership of children" (παίδων δ' ἐζύγην ξυνωνίαι), in A. *Kares* (or *Europa*), *Fr.* 50 (99), 6. Lloyd-Jones 1971 (600n.6) and *LSJ* (s.v. ξυνέων) prefer Blass's ξυνάονι ("ownership") to Weil's ξυνώνιαι, but the point holds. The Chorus in Eur. *Ion* denounce Apollo's failure to allow Kreusa "the common good fortune of chil-

dren" (κοινὰν τεκέων τύχαν 1101). The idea that men and women were equal biological parents occurs at Eur. *Ph.* 940–44, when Teiresias proclaims that the sacrifice to save Thebes must be of a pure-blooded Theban on *both* his mother's and father's side. Cf. Gagarin 1976, 103 who claims "the view that the male is the sole true parent is also Apollo's one convincing argument"[!].

61. Bacon 1982, 149–50; see also Patterson 1986, 56.

62. For example, Zeitlin 1978, 167 states that "the Apollonian argument is the hub of the drama," and she generates a purportedly Aeschylean (Apollonian?) list of antithetical roles for males and females, including "culture" for the former and "nature" for the latter (171–72). However, in *Choephoroi*, the Nurse (*Trophos*) shows the importance of women rearing and nurturing children independent of ties of blood. She received the baby Orestes from his mother Klytemnestra, she "raised" him (ἐξέθρεψα 750), and she "nursed and cared for him" (τρέφειν 754) when he was too young to communicate his needs. Looking to Athena, Goldhill 1984, 258–59 argues that she transcends (even as she emphasizes) the various polarities that critics point to, particularly the opposition between the sexes.

63. Scholars are divided on the actual count—either six votes for convicting Orestes and five for freeing him, with Athena casting her vote for Orestes and the resultant tie going to the defendant, or the jury votes are evenly split and Athena casts the tie-breaker. For the former, see M. Gagarin, "The Vote of Athena," *AJP* 96 (1975), 121–27, and Tyrrell and Brown 1991, 128–29; for the latter, Jones 1962, 111–13; D. A. Hester, "The Casting Vote," *AJP* 102 (1981), 265–74; and Podlecki 1989a, 211–13. Either way, the verdict *could not be closer*, and Apollo's argument sways Aeschylus' dramatic court no more, perhaps, than it impresses the audience.

64. For Apollo's exit, see Kitto 1961, 89, 93–94; and Taplin 1977, 403–7. Cf. the elaborately worked departures of Agamemnon and Kassandra in *Ag.*, and Orestes' final exit following his longest speech in the play, *Eu.* 754–77.

65. DuBois 1988, 71.

66. Klytemnestra may be parodying the "cosmic marriage" presented by Aphrodite(?) in *Danaïds Fr.* 25 (44), where "love takes hold of the earth to join heaven in marriage,/ and the rain falling from the sexually charged heavens/ impregnates the earth." See J. Herington, "The Marriage of Earth and Sky in Aeschylus' *Agamemnon* 1388–92," in Cropp et al. 1986, 27–33.

67. Epitomized by the Servant's cry, "Those who are dead are killing the living" (*Ch.* 886). See also Lebeck 1971, 80–91.

68. For the triumph of a beneficent natural world in *Eu.*, see Vickers 1973, 419–24. Drawing on Homer (but relevant to the *Oresteia*), W. Berry, *The Unsettling of America* (San Francisco 1977), 123–30, explores the connections between marriage, household, and land, noting the "uncanny *resemblance* between our behavior toward each other and our behavior toward the earth."

69. "Orestes' victory is not the last word of the trilogy, and . . . the feminine principle finally wins a place in the city. Tragedy is not a platform for propaganda." (Loraux 1981a, 58).

70. Grace Harris, "Furies, Witches and Mothers," in *The Character of*

Kinship, ed. J. Goody (Cambridge 1973), 155. See also J-P. Vernant, "Greek Tragedy: Problems of Interpretation," in *The Structuralist Controversy*, ed. R. Macksey and E. Donato (Baltimore 1972), 290–91; Rehm 1985a, 242–43 and 1992, 106–8; Nussbaum 1986, 41–42, 49–50; Sommerstein 1989 on *Eu.* 990–91; and Goldhill 1992, 33–37, 42–45. As Kitzinger 1986, 117 concludes, "the ending of the *Eumenides* does not represent the triumphant celebration of civic stability for which many critics argue" (see also Saïd 1983). To use the purple robes (signifying metic status) like straitjackets to bind the Furies at the end of the play—as Peter Stein did in his much-lauded production of the *Oresteia* in 1981—is to betray Aeschylus' dramaturgy, ignoring the richly earned, if tenuous, balance that the trilogy struggles so hard to achieve.

CHAPTER 4

1. Kamerbeek 1978, 34–35, with similar sentiments from Calder 1968, 400–401:

> The pathetic fourth *epeisodion* (806–943), concerned with the departure of Antigone, need not detain us long. Rather a standard *captatio misericordiae*, the *Hadesbraut*, the scene shows in human terms the unpleasant side-effects of stern decrees. . . . Exit wronged maiden to death in bridal array.

Better discussions of the marriage-death dialectic in the play include Neuberg 1990, 66–69; Loraux 1987, 31–32, 36–38; Brown 1987, 188–91; Porter 1987, 50, 54–57, 61; Scodel 1984, 50–51; Leinieks 1982, 79–80; Sorum 1981–82, 206–9; Segal 1981, 179–83 and 1964, 58–59; Musurillo 1967, 45–46; Méautis 1957, 209–10; Goheen 1951, 37–41; and Reinhardt 1947, 80–83.

2. Echoing this sentiment, the Chorus proclaim that "no one is so foolish as to be in love with [ἐραῖ] dying" (220).

3. For the erotic significance of the noun πόθος ("longing") and verb ποθέω ("long for"), see Ch. 5n.6.

4. For *philos* as "close blood relations," see Else 1976, 30, 35n.23, and 1957, 349–50. Bowra 1944, 76–77 describes the sanctity of the familial *philos*-bond for the Greeks.

5. Blundell 1989, 106–30 and Nussbaum 1986, 51–82 analyze this conflict in detail. See also Winnington-Ingram 1983a, 245; Kamerbeek 1978 on *Ant.* 522 and 523; Connor 1971, 49–52; Knox 1964, 75–116; and Segal 1964, 62–63. Goldhill 1987, 67 takes up the civic appropriation of "the emotionally and morally charged terminology of the family . . . to express the citizen's relations to the city and its laws," and Patterson 1990, 61 points out that "the Classical Athenian polis structured itself on the model of the family." Leinieks 1982, 74–76 traces the principle "of family affection (*philia*) as the basis of good government" developed in the fourth century, noting that *Antigone* is the earliest surviving text that alludes to the idea. Kreon "indicates his complete misunderstanding of the principle by assuming that there is a potential conflict between family affection and the welfare of the city." Ehrenberg 1954, 55–61 lays out the parallels between Kreon's state absolutism and the political message of Perikles. Note in particular the erotic dic-

tion in the latter's exhortation that Athenians "gaze on the power of the city every day and become her lovers" (Thuk. 2.43.1; see Immerwahr 1973, 27–28).

6. Perikles voices a similar sentiment in Thuk. 2.60.3; see Knox 1983, 13–17.

7. For other comparisons of marital sex to plowing in tragedy, see S. *OT* 270–71, 1211–12, 1257, 1485, 1497–98; Eur. *Tro.* 135, *Ph.* 18. In A. *Niobe*, Europa describes Zeus' extramarital "plowing" that led to their "joint ownership of children" (*Fr.* 99, 5–9). Sokrates (Pl. *Cra.* 406B) derives the name of the virgin goddess Artemis from ἄροτον μισεῖ, "she who hates plowing" (i.e., sexual intercourse). See also DuBois 1988, 72–73. For the marriage "formula" of "sowing legitimate children," see Kamerbeek 1978 on *Ant.* 569; *I.G.* 14.1615; and Men. *Dysk.* 842–43, *Mis.* 444–46, *Pk.* 1013–14, *Sam.* 726–27, *Fr.* 682 (Körte and Thierfelde 1959), *Fab. incert.*, 29–30, and *Fr. dub.*, 4–5 (Sandbach 1972).

8. For Kreon as tyrant, see R. Bushnell, *Prophesying Tragedy: Sign and Voice in Sophocles' Theban Plays* (Ithaca 1988), 53–55; Podlecki 1966, 359–71; Bowra 1944, 72–75. Cf. M. Ostwald, *From Popular Sovereignty to the Sovereignty of Law* (Berkeley 1986), 156–57, who finds Kreon sympathetic and not at all tyrannical. So, too, Sourvinou-Inwood 1989, 139 who argues that Kreon generally "speaks the polis discourse," and that his position consistently exemplifies the kind of democratic patriotism that was at one with his Athenian audience. Nussbaum 1986, 60 provides the compelling corrective: "The play is about Creon's failure. . . . Only an impoverished conception of the city can have the simplicity which Creon requires."

9. Summarized by Knox 1964, 87. Regarding Kreon's decree, it seems to have been standard Athenian practice to refuse burial *on Attic soil* to traitors and those guilty of sacrilege. See Thuk.1. 126.12 and 138.6; X. *HG* 1.7.22; Dinarchus. *Against Demosthenes* 77; Pl. *Lg.* 909B–C; Lycurg. *Against Leocrates* 113; Plu. *Mor.* 833A, 834A and *Phoc.* 37.2; Ael. *VH* 4.7; and the law establishing the second naval confederacy, in M. N. Tod, *A Selection of Greek Historical Inscriptions*, vol. 2 (Oxford 1948), no. 123. My thanks to James Diggle for these references; see also his rev. of Kovacs's *The Heroic Muse* in *AJP* 110 (1989), 361. Against this practice, however, was the pan-Hellenic custom that the dead were owed burial *somewhere*, indicated at S. *Ant.* 450–60, 1070–73, *Aj.* 1342–45; and Eur. *Supp.* 308–12, 526–36, 538–41, 670–72, a compulsion that was magnified if the dead were kin (e.g., S. *Ant* and *OC* 1409–13). Parker 1983, 33 and 43–48 discusses the issue in terms of avoiding pollution. Cerri 1982, 121–31 contrasts the law (νόμος) for traitors (burial outside of Attica) with a decree voted on by the Assembly (ψήφισμα) that condemned a man to death without burial.

10. When Kreon finally has Polyneikes buried, the corpse is "washed with the sacred bath" (λούσαντες ἁγνὸν λουτρόν 1201) before cremation, burial, and the erection of a funeral mound.

11. Taplin 1984, 16. To help the audience identify Haimon with Antigone, Sophokles may have used the same actor to play both roles. See McCall 1972, 142 and M. Croiset, *Histoire de la littérature grecque* Vol. 3 (Paris 1891), 237.

W. J. Ziobro, "Where Was Antigone? *Antigone* 766–883," *AJP* 92 (1971), 81–85, argues that Antigone returns to the stage on Haimon's exit at 765, which would make this casting impossible. However, most editors have Antigone return to the stage at 801–5 after the short choral ode to Love, allowing an actor enough time to make the change.

12. Kreon uses the same phrase when issuing his final order that Antigone be left "alone" (μόνην) and "deserted" (ἐϱῆμον 887). Antigone also refers to her future life immured in the cave as "bereft [ἐϱῆμος 919, lit. "deserted"] of friends/loved ones."

13. As Kitto 1959, 167 puts it, "We cannot fail to suspect that it is Kreon who has set himself in hopeless opposition to this god [Eros], and the sequel will confirm this suspicion." See also Winnington-Ingram 1980, 97.

14. See Osborne 1985, 135–41 and Seaford 1990a.

15. The marriage of first cousins was not considered abnormal in ancient Athens, so the union of Haimon and Antigone (first cousins, as Jocasta and Kreon were siblings) would have seemed natural. On Polyneikes' marriage, see Bayfield 1902, xii–xiii and Winnington-Ingram 1980, 143n.74, a subject that recurs in Eur. *Supp.* (Ch. 8 p. 114). Seaford 1990b analyzes the incest-exogamy opposition in the context of Antigone's entombment, a symbol for her radical attachment to her natal family.

16. Kreon assumes power in Thebes on the basis of *anchisteia* (174), the fact that he is the closest surviving male relative of Eteokles and Polyneikes, and so also of Antigone. Sophokles does not specify whether Kreon betrothed Antigone to Haimon or if Eteokles acted as her *kurios* and gave her away, as at Eur. *Ph.* 756–60 (see Kamerbeek 1978, 7). In either case, with Eteokles' (and Polyneikes') death, Kreon would become Antigone's legal guardian.

17. Hdt. 9.111 uses a form of the same verb μεθίημι ("let go," "dismiss") for a husband's formal dismissal of his wife prior to his marrying another woman.

18. For the thematically rich confusion in Antigone's burial place—cave/grave/bedroom—see Vermeule 1979, 54–55 and Sourvinou-Inwood 1988a, 169–71.

19. Teiresias uses ἀϰτέϱιστον ("without grave offerings" 1071) to describe Kreon's treatment of the corpse of Polyneikes. See Jebb 1900 on *Ant.* 1070f and (with Kamerbeek 1978) on 1207.

20. See Jebb 1900 on *Ant.* 1222, and Loraux 1987, 10, 31.

21. Pearson 1917, *Fr.* 210 l.67; A. *Nereiads Fr.* 73 (153). Fine linen (σινδών) also swathed Egyptian mummies (Hdt. 2.86).

22. Compare the description of Oedipus' self-blinding after Jokasta hangs herself in the "the bridal chamber" (τὰ νυμφιϰὰ/ λέχη 1242–43), "lamenting over her marriage bed" (1249). Oedipus bursts through the doors "bending the hollow bolts" (ἔϰλινε ϰοῖλα ϰλῇιθϱα 1262), a possible double entendre because ϰοῖλον can mean "a cavity in the body." Standing in the bedroom before his dead wife, Oedipus rips out the pins that hold her clothes (1268–69), and then "struck the joint/socket" (ἔπαισεν ἄϱθϱα 1270) of his eyes. Aristophanes uses the verb παίω ("strike," "hit") for sexual intercourse, and the noun ἄϱθϱα (socket) can mean genitals (Hdt. 3.87, 4.2). Having undressed his

wife for the last time, Oedipus achieves the climax of his sexual nightmare with a gruesome outpouring of blood. Unlike the self-blinding that cuts Oedipus off from others, Haimon's death establishes a union with Antigone, albeit one of "tragic destruction rather than guaranteed bliss" (Goheen 1951,40).

23. Because the noun *corpse* (νεκρός) is grammatically masculine, Sophokles leaves open the possibility that the fulfilled rites are not those of Haimon but of Antigone, or of them both: "the wretched [corpse] lies on corpse, coming upon his/her wedding rites in the house of Hades."

24. Except for Pylades in A. *Ch.*, who speaks only three lines. Aegisthus delivers twice as many lines in *Ch.* as Eurydike in *Ant.*, and even his servant has more lines than she.

25. Brown 1987, Bayfield 1902, and Jebb 1900, all on *Ant.* 1301, agree that the altar of Zeus Herkeios is meant, referred to by name at 487 (for textual problems see Müller 1967 on 1301–3). According to Prokl. *Chr.*, Priam was slain at the altar of Zeus Herkeios during the sack of Troy, the locus classicus for the destruction of a family. See T. W. Allen, ed., *Homeri Opera* (Oxford 1912, rpt. with corr. 1946), 107–8; *Hesiod, The Homeric Hymns, and Homa-rioa*, tr. II. G. Evelyn-White (Cambridge, Mass. 1936), 521; and Eur. *Tro.* 481–83. In the *Odyssey* the minstrel Phemios considers seeking asylum at the corresponding altar in Odysseus' courtyard on Ithaka (22.333–37). A public altar to Zeus Herkeios stood in the sanctuary of Pandrosos adjacent to the Erechtheion on the Athenian Akropolis, part of the complex of sacred precincts dedicated to the archetypal family of Athens, the Erechtheids; see Cook 1940, 243. C. Sourvinou-Inwood, in "Further Aspects of Polis Religion," *AION*(arch) 10 (1988), 271–72, overestimates its role in weakening the *oikos* cult.

26. Other loci for family cult include the "hearth" (most likely portable rather than permanent, as noted in Ch. 1 n.23) and the gravesites of family members; see Burkert 1977, 255–56 and Mikalson 1983, 70, 83.

27. Murnaghan 1986, 207 (and 195–96); see also Blundell 1989, 134–35; Podlecki 1989, 282–84; and Gellie 1972, 45–46.

28. Eurydike conforms to Perikles' advice for *widows* in the funeral oration (Thuk. 2.45.2): "Great will be your glory if you are found not inferior to your nature; and the greatest of all is hers who is least spoken of by men, whether for praise or blame." The translation is by Wilkinson 1979, 56 who presents an interesting analysis (47–78) of ancient attitudes toward women's liberation.

29. Brown 1987 on *Ant.* 1257–1353 emphasizes the unexpected appearance of Eurydike's corpse, interrupting Kreon's grieving and then compounding it; see also his comments at pp. 223–24.

30. There is every reason to believe the *ekkuklēma* was used, so we may presume that Eurdyike's body would lie on or near the altar, a possibility that Seale 1982, 105–7 fails to consider.

31. That Kreon carries Haimon's corpse is indicated by the repetition at 1297, ἔχω μὲν ἐν χείρεσσιν ἀρτίως τέκνον, "I just now held my child in my arms." It is appropriate—and perfectly Sophoklean—for Kreon literally to be burdened by the dead as he moves through the *eisodos* to the center of the

orchestra. Buxton 1984, 10 and 25; Kamerbeek 1978 on *Ant.* 1258; and Müller 1967, 265–66 agree that Kreon carries Haimon's body onstage. Seale 1982, 105 cannot decide between this possibility and the consensus that the corpse was carried in by (undesignated) attendants, the latter view urged by Knox 1968, 755, and Jebb 1900 (stage directions at 1256) and repeated by most translators.

32. Brown 1987, 223 points out the similarity between Kreon's mourning and Athenian funeral rites. For the forms of tragic lamentation and their close relationship to fifth-century practice, see Hutchinson 1985 on *Th.* 822–1004; Brown 1977, 48–50, 54–55, 58, 61–75; Lawler 1964, 44–45; Pickard-Cambridge 1962, 107; Broadhead 1960, 310–17; and Ch. 2 n.62. For a reading of *Ant.* that uses the *patrios nomos* and "the discourse of funeral oratory" as the interpretive paradigm, see Tyrrell and Brown 1991, 204–15.

33. The word μνῆμα is used for a tomb or a memorial for the dead at *Il.* 23.619, Hdt. 7.167, and frequently in tragedy; it signifies a coffin at Eur. *Or* 1053. The adjective ἐπίσημον—from σῆμα, a common word for grave, tomb, burial mound—can mean literally "bearing an inscription." See Vermeule 1979, 45.

34. There Megareus has the name Menoikeus; see Bayfield and Jebb on *Ant.* 1303, and A. C. Pearson, *Euripides, Phoenissae* (Cambridge 1909), xxiii. For the sacrifice of Menoikeus in Eur. *Ph.*, see Foley 1985, 106–12, 132–46.

35. The change is so striking that Méautis 1957, 226–27 labels Eurydike's accusation against her husband "manifestement faux." Steiner 1984, 245–47 stresses that Eurydike views her husband as "Kreon παιδοκτόνος" (1305), "Kreon the child-killer." Haimon lives to have a son (Maion) in Homer (*Il.* 4.394); in Euripides' lost *Antigone*, Maion is the offspring of Haimon *and* Antigone (Webster 1967, 181–84). By diverging from these versions, Sophokles deepens the disaster of Kreon's family and highlights his role in its destruction.

36. See Struck 1953, 333 and A. T. von S. Bradshaw, "The Watchman Scenes in the *Antigone*," *CQ* 12 (1962), 208.

37. Kreon probably leaves during the choral *exodos* (1347–53). Seale 1982, 107 claims that "there is not [*sic*] exit, no final procession, just the final comment of the Chorus that we have witnessed a lesson in late learning." More dramatically fitting is to have Kreon enter the *oikos* he has destroyed, while the Chorus exit out the *parodoi* as they speak their final lines.

38. As there was applause in the ancient theater, we may assume some form of curtain call during which performers could move as actors and not as dramatic characters. This would allow the "removal" of the corpses at the end of A. *Ag.* and *Ch.*, when the *ekkuklēma* may not have been available and the use of supernumeraries to remove the bodies would have been awkward.

39. These aspects of *Antigone* continue to inspire writers with a political conscience. E. Anne Mackay, "Fugard's *The Island* and Sophocles' *Antigone*," in *Literature and Revolution*, ed. D. Bevan (Amsterdam 1989), 160, observes that "any society in which Antigone surfaces should look long and hard at the conflicts which give rise to her resuscitation. She has become the ominous hallmark of an oppressive and dehumanized regime."

40. Finley 1966, 2–4 compares *Antigone* and the *Oresteia* on the possibility for civic conciliation and inclusion. See also M. A. Santirocco, "Justice in Sophocles' *Antigone*," *Philosophy and Literature* 4 (1980), 180–81.

41. As Steiner 1984, 193 observes, "Creon is left in hideous solitude. There is around him . . . nothing but familial devastation." See also Gellie 1972, 30 and Goheen 1951, 90.

42. Reinhardt 1947, 93.

43. See *Hegel on Tragedy*, ed. A. and H. Paolucci (New York 1962), 62–74 (from *The Philosophy of Fine Art*); also Steiner 1984, 1–106; Segal 1964, 46–51; M. Heidegger, *An Introduction to Metaphysics*, tr. R. Mannheim (New Haven 1959), 146–65, 171; Reinhardt 1947, 64–66; and the extensive bibliography compiled by D. A. Hester, "Sophocles the Unphilosophical: A Study in the *Antigone*," *Mnemosyne* 24 (1971), 11–59. For the limitations of Hegel's reading, see Stern and Silk 1981, 318–23.

44. See above, n.5 and Cox 1992. The failure to entertain this possibility hobbles the interpretation of Sourvinou-Inwood 1989, which purports to remove modern perceptual filters from our reading of the play.

45. My analysis owes much to Neuberg 1990, esp. 74–75.

CHAPTER 5

1. Gellie 1972, 53–54, 73, and 78 finds the pair "so close to their respective temperamental extremes that any dialogue between them must have been a travesty of communication." See also Poole 1987, 71–72; Silk 1985, 3; Sorum 1978, 64; and Segal 1977, 119–23. T. F. Hoey, "*Trachiniae* and Unity of Hero," *Arethusa* 3 (1970), 18, reads the play as "the *tragedy of a house* whose two essential components never meet."

2. On the ties between the two, see Easterling 1981, 58 and Segal 1977, 155–58. For the single actor, see Jouan 1983, 72–73; Fuqua 1980, 76–77n.186; and McCall 1972, 142, 162.

3. Easterling 1981, 58–59 quotes Pound's translation (line 1174), "what/ SPLENDOUR,/ IT ALL COHERES" and approves his judgment that "this is the key phrase, for which the play exists." See E. Pound, *Sophokles, Women of Trachis* (New York 1957), 50n.1. My view is closer to that of Mason 1985, 17 and 93–96, and Kraus 1991, 94–95, who stress the lack of such coherence. As for audience expectation, March 1987, 65–77 shows how Sophocles *altered* key elements in the myth: Nessus' death, the love charm, Deianeira's character and motivation, and the manner and meaning of Herakles' demise.

4. The Chorus call Deianeira "fought over" (ἀμφινεικῆ 104) and later refer to the "fought-over (ἀμφινείκητον) eyes of the bride" (527), who watches Achelous and Herakles battle for her. As well as Deianeira and Iole, Tekmessa in S. *Aj.* is a bride won by combat; for other such Sophoklean brides, see the fragmentary *Aechmalotides* (*The Captive Women*), *Amphitryon*, *Andromeda*, *Chryses*, *Hermione* (obliquely—see Fr. 185), *Iobates*, *Lemniae* (*The Women of Lemnos*), *Mysoi* (*The Mysians*), and *Oenomaus*.

5. Deianeira's "life-giving and life-sustaining functions as the keeper of the house are heavily underscored in her language" (Segal 1977, 126), and

images of birth and child-rearing recur throughout. As well as her "labor pains" for Herakles, Deianeira "nurses" (τρέφω 28) fears for him. The Chorus sing that "the Sun slays and despoils the gleaming/ Night who gave it birth, and Night/ in turn puts the blazing sun to its [death] bed" (94–96), suggesting "a murderous sexual cycle" (Wender 1974, 6) in the alternation of night and day. Nessus mixes his blood with "the offspring [or "nursling," θρέμμα 574] of the Hydra"; see A. A. Long, "Poisonous 'Growths' in *Trachiniae*," *GRBS* 8 (1967), 275–78. After Deianeira's suicide, the Chorus sing that Iole "gave birth, gave birth/ to a dreadful Fury in the house" (893–95).

6. See Vermeule 1979, 154 and V. Ehrenberg, "Polypragmosyne," *JHS* 67 (1947), 66. *Pothos* as longing for bride, wife, or husband also occurs at *Tr.* 368 and 431 (Herakles for Iole), 631 (Deianeira for Herakles), 632 (*pothoumetha*) and 1142 (Herakles' possible longing for Deianeira); elsewhere at A. *Ag.* 414 (Menelaus for Helen) and *Pr.* 654 (Zeus for Io); Eur. *Alk.* 1087 (Admetus for a new wife), *Med.* 623 (Jason for his new wife), *Herakl.* 299 (if genuine, a man's passion to marry someone beneath him), *Tro.* 891 (Menelaus for Helen), *IA* 555 (Chorus of women for a reasonable match) and 1410 (Achilles for Iphigenia). *Pothos* as longing for the dead occurs at A. *Pers.* 62, 133, 136 (wives longing for their husbands, presumably dead), and Eur. *Hel.* 1306 (Demeter for Persephone) and *Tro.* (Andromache and Hecuba for Hektor). The word is used for Oedipus' longing for *death* at Eur. *Ph.* 330. Aristophanes combines erotic and morbid meanings in Dionysus' "longing" for the dead Euripides (*Ran.* 53–69).

7. Later the Chorus specify Deianeira's fear of "the harm/ rushing toward her home/ because of the new marriage" (841–43).

8. Are they singing a song for a sacrifice (ἀνολολυξάτω 205), a paean (210–212, 221), or a dithyramb (references to Dionysus, ivy, and the aulos, 216–20)? See Easterling 1982 on *Tr.* 205–24.

9. Regarding the Nymphs, the word νύμφη means both "bride" and "nymph," a divinity associated with springs and fresh water. Lloyd-Jones 1971, 569 (on A. *Semele*) notes that "the nymphs are patroness of marriage and childbirth. . . . This is why brides and women who had just given birth performed a ceremonial ablution in the water of a particular spring conse-crated by their city to this purpose" (see also Ch. 1 n.12). For combinations of Apollo, Artemis, and Dionysus on scenes of the wedding procession, see *LIMC* s.v. "Apollon" #840–53, "Artemis" #1245–57 and 1281–85, and "Di-onysos" #515–16. Add *ABV* 335.5; *MMA* 98.8.9; *ABV* 330.1, *Add²* 89; Bérard 1984, fig. 135; *CVA* Fiesole 1, 20.4; D. M. Buitron, *Attic Vase Painting in New England Collections* (Fogg Art Museum, Harvard 1972), 24; the hydria in J. Mertens, *Attic White Ground* (New York 1977), pl. 5.3,4. On mythologizing versions of the wedding procession (App. A n.4), Artemis often holds a torch in each hand where she "joue le rôle de la *nympheutria*," ("plays the role of the bride-helper") as Kahil puts it (*LIMC*, s.v. "Artemis," p. 744). For Artemis and marriage, see also Ch. 1 p. 14, Ch. 3 p. 51, and Lissarrague 1992, 150. Why Apollo carries his bow (*Tr.* 208–9) rather than his nuptially appropriate lyre may be explained by the later reference to Herakles' bow (265), a gift from Apollo.

10. Deianeira later refers to the "abundant train" (πολλῶι στόλωι 496) of captive women; see Kamerbeek 1963 on *Tr.* 225–26 and 495–96. She also uses στόλος for the journey she herself made when sent by her father to be Herakles' bride, 562–63.

11. In the ode Aphrodite "acts as umpire" (ῥαβδονόμει 516), giving an uneasy sense that the game in which she is always victorious has been fixed from the start.

12. See Seaford 1986, 52–54, 58.

13. Seaford 1986, 50–53 and 1987, 111–12 and nn.62–65 lists passages that compare a newly wedded bride to a tender plant that is plucked or felled; add *h.Cer.* 66, where Demeter describes Persephone (abducted by Hades) as a "sweet shoot." Danforth and Tsiaras 1982, 96–99 and Alexiou 1974, 32–42, 159, and 195–201 quote later Greek laments that compare the dead (often unwedded girls) to plants, flowers, and trees. Nagy 1979, 174–93 discusses the trope in terms of archaic lamentation and hero cult.

14. Winnington-Ingram 1980, 75 stresses the erotic basis of Deianeira's fears ("this is a tragedy of sex"), but there is something particularly *marital* about her concerns. The language used by and about Deianeira highlights the potential anguish of a bride and wife (above n.5). In this regard, Wilamowitz-Moellendorff 1923, 357 is right—"Deianeira ist eine Athenerin." ("Deianeira is an Athenian [woman]").

15. Ch. 1 p. 14. See D. Armstrong, "Two Notes on Greek Tragedy," *BICS* 33 (1986), 101–2.

16. According to Detienne 1972, 166–67, Ixion and the race of Centaurs for which he was responsible represent the negation of marriage. DuBois 1979, 35 highlights stories that demonstrate the Centaurs' "hostility to legal marriage." See also G. S. Kirk, *Myth* (Cambridge 1970), 152–62. For visual representations of Nessus' death and their relation to *Tr.*, see C. Dugas, "La Mort du centaure Nessos," *REA* 45 (1943), 18–26. Pindar (*P.* 9.30–66) tells of the "good" Centaur Cheiron who reverses the pattern of his fellow horsemen. With wise counsel he stops Apollo from raping the virgin-huntress Kyrene and persuades the god to marry her instead. See E. Robbins, "Cyrene and Cheiron," *Phoenix* 32 (1978), 91–104, and Kurke 1991, 127–34. Cheiron features prominently on an Attic red-figure amphora (NY, Levy Collection) that contrasts a proper marriage ritual with one disrupted by Centaurs. The main field shows the wedding of Peleus and Thetis, featuring a decorous procession on foot to the marriage chamber. The Centaur Cheiron holds a torch in each hand to guide the newlyweds, pointing to his later role as educator of Achilles, the offspring of this famous marriage. In marked contrast to this civilized wedding, the shoulder of the amphora depicts the Centauromachy at the marriage feast of Perithoös and Hippodameia. See D. von Bothmer, *Glories of the Past: Ancient Art from Shelby White and Leon Levy Collection* (NY 1990), 168–71, no. 121.

17. On the Polygnotos paintings, see R. B. Kebric, *The Paintings in the Cnidian Lesche at Delphi* (Leiden 1983), 33–35 and n.117, and Robertson 1975, 240–42, 256. The Theseion mural innovatively set the centauromachy at the wedding feast itself, discussed by J. P. Barron, "New Light on Old

Walls," *JHS* 92 (1972), 20–33, 44–45, and S. Woodford, "More Light on Old Walls," *JHS* 94 (1974), 158–65. On the Parthenon metopes, see Robertson 1975, 297–98 and F. Brommer, *Die Metopen des Parthenon* (Mainz 1967), pl. 146–239. For their influence on comparable scenes in vase-painting, see K. A. Schwab, "A Parthenonian Centaur," in *Greek Vases in the J. Paul Getty Museum* Vol. 2 (Malibu 1985), 89–94. Robertson 1975, 312 discusses the centauromachy on the Athena Parthenos sandals and the Athena Promachos shield, and Fuqua 1980, 23–26 deals with the Theseion sculpture. For the Poseidon temple at Sounion, see L. Burn, "The Art of the State in Late Fifth-Century Athens," in *Images of Authority*, ed. M. M. Mackenzie and C. Roueché, *PCPhS* Supp. Vol. 16 (Cambridge 1989), 73.

18. For Olympia, see Robertson 1975, 280–84, and B. Ashmole and N. Yalouris, *Olympia: The Sculptures of the Temple of Zeus* (London 1967), pl. 62–142; for the Bassae frieze, see Robertson 1975, 357–58. C. Hofkes-Brukker, *Der Bassai-Fries* (Munich 1975), 54–55 reproduces the scene of the disrobed Lapith woman.

19. Easterling 1982 on *Tr.* 863–95. Alexiou 1974, 131–51 (followed by Brown 1977, 61–64) discusses the relationship of antiphonal structure to antithetical thought in Greek lament (referring to *Tr.* 874–80 and 881–95 at p. 137). See also Willink 1986 on *Or.* 960–1012, and his "The Parodos of Euripides' *Helen* (164–90)," *CQ* 40 (1990), 77–78, where he imagines the Chorus entering silently during Helen's strophe, fitting their steps to the rhythm of her lament, and then providing in the antistrophe the proper "antiphonal" element to her dirge. A call-and-response pattern also "seems to be a constant in Greek wedding-songs," as K. J. Dover notes in *The Greeks and Their Legacy* (Oxford 1988), 220; see also Huddleston 1980, 30–35, 78–80.

20. Well treated by Easterling 1982 on *Tr.* 893–95.

21. See Kamerbeek 1963 on *Tr.* 896–946 and Easterling 1982 on *Tr.* 915–16. Deianeira's suicide is notably bed-ridden: δεμνίοις 915, εὐνατηρίοις 918, λέχη 920, ἐν κοίταισι ταῖσδ᾽ εὐνάτριαν 922.

22. See Ch. 4 p. 65. As Winnington-Ingram 1980, 81n.28 reminds us, "for a woman to strip herself half-naked on the marriage-bed—as she had often stripped herself for Heracles—and stab herself in the belly is very suggestive indeed." Parry 1986, 109 calls her suicide "a gruesome erotic parody." For other tragic deaths in the *thalamos*, see Loraux 1987, 22–24.

23. Printed by Erfurdt, Schaefer, Wunder, Hermann, and Jebb.

24. For other beds becoming biers, see Seaford 1984, 251.

25. The active form of the verb πέρθω (the collateral form of πορθέω) is used for Herakles' sack of Oechalia at 244, 364–65, 433, 467, and 750. See Segal 1977, 117.

26. Easterling 1981, 59 points out that Herakles' description "reminds us of the helpless *parthenos* earlier in the play." The word is used of Deianeira at 148, of Iole at 1219, and of the Chorus of women at 211 and 1275. Loraux comments on aspects of the feminized hero in "Herakles: The Super-Male and the Feminine" (in Halperin et al. 1990, 28–29, 38–39); in 1981a, 61–64, she suggests that the image of Herakles suffering on a bed is meant to evoke a

woman in labor (an unlikely *parthenos*!). However, ancient birthing tended to be in the sitting position, using a birthing stool or other means, noted by Garland 1990, 70–74. Loraux's assumption that parturition in the supine position is—or was—"natural" reflects the prejudices (and convenience) of the modern medical profession rather than the wishes of women giving birth.

27. See Seaford 1986, 56–57; καλύμματα is used for bridal veils at A. *Ag.* 1178 and Eur. *IT* 372. Silk 1985, 9 observes that "Heracles fights monsters and takes on their monstrousness; faced with woman [Deianeira and her robe], he becomes a woman."

28. Winnington-Ingram 1980, 74 and 83, speaking for many critics of the play.

29. "To find H. repellent does not mean that we should withhold from him the pity he demands. The pathos of 1089ff. is indeed extraordinary" (Winnington-Ingram 1980, 83n.32). This is underlined by Hyllus' graphic description of the robe's effect (767–71, 777–78, 786–90) and by Herakles' physical presence from line 971. Carne-Ross 1979, 81 notes the similarity in Deianeira's and Herakles' language as each faces death.

30. Kitto 1959, 194, for example, sees in the oracle the workings of "the eternal law of the universe."

31. The play is full of τέλος (*telos*) words (see Ch. 3 p. 43), suggesting the fulfillment the play ultimately achieves, the deaths of Deianeira and Herakles, and the wedding rites of Hyllus and Iole: lines 26, 36, 79 (twice), 155, 167, 170, 174, 286, 742, 824, 825, 917, 1149, 1171, 1187, 1252, 1256, 1257, and 1263.

32. Easterling 1982, 10–11. Jebb 1892 on *Tr.* 1224 argues the importance of the legendary union, but literary references to the wedding of Hyllus and Iole are rare and, in any case, not binding on either playwright or audience. That the wedding demonstrates once and for all the "negative Herakles" is claimed (albeit for different reasons) by H. F. Johansen, "Heracles in Sophocles' *Trachiniae*," *C&M* 37 (1986), 53–54; Easterling (above); Foley 1981, 158–59; Galinsky 1972, 49–51; Ronnet 1969, 97–99; Kitto 1966, 170–72; Whitman 1951, 119; and Murray 1946a, 121–23. Winnington-Ingram 1980, 85 believes that the scene reveals Herakles' "erotic passion for Iole, still alive in him, which could not bear to think of any other male body in contact with hers . . . except that of his other self, his son." Hoey 1977, 286 discovers the Oedipus complex in reverse, "since it is enjoined by the father that his son possess his bride," an idea followed by Carne-Ross 1979, 87.

33. The last phrase quoted—προσθοῦ δάμαρτα (1224)—means "to take *as wife*." See Segal 1977, 135; Fuqua 1980, 60; and De Wet 1983, 219–26. δάμαρτα also is used for Herakles' wife Deianeira at 406, and of Iole at 428 and 429. J. K. MacKinnon, "Heracles' Intention in his Second Request to Hyllus," *CQ* 21 (1971), 33–41, champions the counter-view that Herakles intends only concubinage, followed by McCall 1972, 161n.20 and Stinton 1986, 98n.105. MacKinnon's case is far too legalistic, and his claim that the slave Iole is unworthy of becoming Hyllus' wife overlooks the fact that she *is* the princess of Oechalia, daughter of King Eurytos. Schol. *Tr.* 354 (= *FGrH* 3 F 82a) attests an earlier version by Pherekydes in which Herakles captures Iole

to provide a bride for his son in the first place. Note also Achilles' intended marriage to his "warbride" Briseis (*Il.* 9.336, 19.291–99); see also above, n.4.

34. Deianeira is dead, and as Iole's new "husband" Herakles acts as her *kurios* as well. Lawcourt speeches often refer to dying husbands who arrange a future marriage for their wives—D. 20.33, 27.5, 30.22, 36.8, 57.41; Plu. *Per.* 34.5 (see Pomeroy 1975, 64). As Sorum 1978, 67 and 70 notes, Herakles tries to "collect his scattered family" and to "reestablish the two families he has destroyed." Foxhall 1989, 28n.22 stresses that it was the *recreation* of households, not their *continuation*, that was perceived as essential. See also Segal 1977, 152.

35. Bowra 1944, 142–43 is one of few who appreciates the anomaly of the wedding arranged from the death-bed: "Sophocles could have omitted such a detail which is not of fundamental importance to the plot. Since he introduces it, he must have meant it to be significant." Bowra then goes wildly astray—"The great hero still loves Iole, for whom he has done so much and for whom, in a sense, he dies. . . . Hyllus must marry her because he can be trusted to care for her." The play hardly sustains such romanticism, and Bowra's reading has been rejected. Sadly, his intuition that the arranged wedding is crucial has been obscured by the judgment that Herakles is nothing but a human brute.

36. Blundell 1989, 103–4 notes that Ajax's funeral is "characterized as a cooperative endeavour by the repeated use of verbs compounded with *sun-* or *xun-*, which indicated joining or sharing in an activity." See also Easterling 1988, 91–98, who offers a masterful reading of the funeral scene in *Ajax*.

37. Although the "marble tomb" does not refer to Oedipus' grave, the detail reinforces the sense that Oedipus is about to die. Earlier Polyneikes begs his sisters to give him funeral rites if Oedipus' curse should come true (*OC* 1405–13).

38. "Die Trachinierinnen enden dumpf, wie sie begannen" ("The *Trachiniae* ends in gloom, as it began")—Reinhardt 1947, 63. For Whitman 1951, 121, the end is all "doubt and suffering. . . ." R. M. Torrance, "Sophocles: Some Bearings," *HSCP* 69 (1965), 304, sees "the irrationality of human misery" in "the darkest imaginable colors." Hoey 1977, 279 finds "more broken pieces left behind" than anywhere else in Sophokles.

39. On Herakles' purported apotheosis, see Hoey 1977 (bibliography at nn. 5–11). Easterling 1981, 64–74 insists that the apotheosis is evoked; Stinton 1986, 74 and 84–99 offers a careful and persuasive rejoinder. The marriage of Herakles and Hebe ("Youth") after his apotheosis also seems to have no place in the play. For the Herakles-Hebe myth elsewhere, see H. *Od.* 11.601–4, Hes. *Th.* 950–55, Eur. *Herakl.* 849–51 and 910–18, *HF* 637–72 (by implication), and *Or.* 1686–88. In the visual arts, see *LIMC* s.v. "Herakles," #3330–43; R. Vollkommer, *Herakles in the Art of Classical Greece* (Oxford 1988), 37–39; and F. Brommer, "Herakles und Geras," *AA* 1952, 60–73. *If* Herakles' apotheosis and union with Hebe were so "present" as to need no overt reference in the text, then the play's funereal ending points to *two* weddings—Hyllus and Iole in Trachis, and Herakles and Hebe in the heavens.

40. B. Heiden, *Tragic Rhetoric: An Interpretation of Sophocles' Trachiniae* (New York 1989), 151, 161.

41. Winnington-Ingram 1980, 333 observes that "Heracles is in fact betrayed by a lust comparable to that of the centaur he killed." In 1983a, 240 he writes that "the central unifying theme of *Trachiniae* is the power of sex." Other critics who single out *erōs* as the root of the tragedy include I. M. Linforth, "The Pyre on Mount Oeta in Sophocles' *Trachiniae*," *CPCPh* 14 (1951), 260–61, 265–67; C. Segal, "The Hydra's Nursling: Image and Action in the *Trachiniae*," *AC* 44 (1975), 612–17; Fuqua 1980, 39–43 and n.104; and Parry 1986, 108–9. The idea may have been prominent in Sophokles' lost *Phaedra* (Fr. 684; see Sutton 1984, 103). Insofar as Herakles is a victim of uncontrollable eros, he represents a kind of male Phaedra, but one free to seize the object of his desire. For Phaedra, there is no such outlet and she must turn in on the *oikos* and, finally, on herself.

42. For the possibility that Iole is present at the end of the play (deemed unlikely by Seale 1982, 208 and Easterling 1982 on *Tr.* 1275), see R.W.B. Buxton, *The Chorus in Sophocles' Tragedies* (Oxford 1980), 81–82 and Hoey 1977, 288–89.

CHAPTER 6

1. J.-P. Guépin, *The Tragic Paradox* (Amsterdam 1968), 120–42, traces the Persephone paradigm in *Alk.* and other Euripidean tragedies. See also Foley 1992 and 1985, 86–89, and Lattimore 1964, 52–53 and 70–71.

2. For the idea of cheating death in the play, see Gregory 1991, 19–49; E. M. Bradley, "Admetus and the Triumph of Failure in Euripides' *Alcestis*," *Ramus* 9 (1980), 112–27; Nielsen 1976, 92–102; Dale 1954 on *Alk.* 579; and Jones 1948, 51–52.

3. See also *Alk.* 73, 126, 436–37, 457, 626, 851–52, 867; Vermeule 1979, 35–37; and Roberts 1978, 182–85. Euripides also exploits the confusion between Hades as physical place and as metaphor for death in *HF*, esp. at 296–97, 426–35, 1101–5.

4. *Alk.* 861–63, 911–13, 922–25. See P. Riemer, *Die Alkestis des Euripides*, Athenäum Monografien 159 (Frankfurt/M 1989), 131–38, and Burnett 1965, 243, 251.

5. This is the only evidence for the practice of leaving cut hair at the door of the deceased.

6. Alkestis' Servant later regrets that he could not perform the same ritual salute—"I did not stretch out my right hand, wailing my grief/ for my mistress" (768–69). See Ch. 1 p. 24 and Ch. 7 p. 105.

7. See S. E. Scully, "Some Issues in the Second Episode of Euripides' *Alcestis*," in Cropp et al. 1986, 139–40; J. McCaughey, "Talking About Greek Tragedy," *Ramus* 1 (1972), 30–31, 43–44; and L.H.G. Greenwood, *Aspects of Euripidean Tragedy* (Cambridge 1953), 131–37.

8. See Conacher 1988 on *Alk.* 244–79 and Burnett 1971, 28. Gregory 1991, 31 argues that the shift in modes echoes the "confusion of categories" that arises from the play's central premise, namely that the finality of death can be negotiated.

9. Alkestis' cry, "Someone leads me away" (ἄγει μ' ἄγει τις, ἄγει μέ τις 259)

is answered when Admetus begs Herakles to "lead her" inside the house (αὐτὴν εἴσαγ᾽ 1112). Although the verbal echo would go unnoticed in performance, the *action* of Admetus leading Alkestis back as his bride is another matter, reversing the *ekphora* earlier in the play when Alkestis' corpse is borne out of the house (606–10) and out of the theater (741–46).

10. This raises questions about Apollo's offer to Admetus (Conacher 1988 on *Alk*. 250 and Smith 1960, 130). It seems that once Admetus agrees to a substitute, he cannot go back on his decision, even though his wife is the only one willing to make the sacrifice. See Vellacott 1975, 100–101 and A. Lesky, *Alkestis, der Mythus und das Drama* (Wien 1925). However, Conacher 1967, 337–38n.23 and L. Méridier, *Euripide* I (Paris 1956), 52–53, think that Admetus must have had *some* say in allowing Alkestis to die (hence his fear of public rebuke, and Pheres' barbs at his cowardice).

11. Poole 1987, 140–42 aligns this passage with the conversion of Shakespearean women into icons, an idealizing process that resembles the transformation of a living woman into a corpse. Schnapp 1988, 569–71 views Admetus' "sculptural program" in terms of the ancient idea that a statue "contained" part of what it represented.

12. In the version current in Euripides' day, I assume that Orpheus looked back and lost his love. See Dale 1954 on *Alk*. 357–62; Rose 1959, 259; and L. Burn, "Honey Pots," *AK* 28 (1985), 103n.47. This would make Eurydike the "perpetual bride of Hades," as Detienne (Gordon 1977, 101) puts it. For the view that the fifth century knew only a successful Orpheus, see M. Grant and J. Hazel, *Gods and Mortals in Classical Mythology* (New York 1979), s.v. "Orpheus," and C. M. Bowra, "Orpheus and Eurydice," *CQ* 46 (1952), 118–20. In either case, Admetus' wish remains only that, for he clearly possesses *no* Orpheus-like gifts. See Smith 1960, 133n.12, and C. Segal, *Orpheus, The Myth of the Poet* (Baltimore 1989), 155–59.

13. The Chorus (228–30) remark that the loss of such a wife would make a husband commit suicide, precisely what Admetus *cannot* do if Alkestis' death is to have any meaning. Cf. Burnett 1965, 245–46, who views Admetus' rhetoric sympathetically.

14. In Eur. *Andr*. 504–36, the heroine and her (otherwise silent) child share a lyric passage.

15. Vermeule 1979, 58–62 and 91–93 examines the link between horses and funeral rites. Admetus' extension of mourning practices to the equine world ("cut manes") may have struck the original audience as risible. Cf. the spontaneous grief of the immortal horses of Achilles who weep at the death of Patroclus, standing immobile like a funerary stele (H. *Il*. 17.426–40).

16. A comparable change occurs in Eur. *HF* 442–43 when Amphitryon, Megara, and the children return from the house dressed for burial. The Queen changes into mourning clothes for her reentry at A. *Pers*. 598, as does Helen in Eur. *Hel*. 1087–89, 1186–90. The famous drag scene in Eur. *Ba*. not only involves dressing Pentheus as a woman, but also putting on his funeral garb (857–58; see Seaford 1984, 252). Something of the reverse happens in Eur. *Supp*. 1054–59, when Evadne appears in a wedding dress, out of place in the midst of funeral rites (Ch. 8 p. 112).

17. In A. *Eu.* the Furies pursue Orestes out the *eisodos* (231); when they reenter (244), the scene has shifted from Delphi to Athens. In S. *Aj.* the Chorus leave to track down the hero (814), enabling Ajax to enter in solitude for his suicide. In Eur. *Hel.* the Chorus accompany Helen into the palace to consult Theonoe (385), allowing the shipwrecked Menelaus to arrive at an empty stage. The Chorus of Trojan sentries leave the orchestra at *Rh.* 564 so that Diomedes and Odysseus can enter undetected. V. Castellani, "Notes on the Structure of Euripides' *Alcestis,*" *AJP* 100 (1979), 487–96, elaborates on the "two-act effect" achieved by vacating the orchestra, the first act ending in burial and the second in a wedding.

18. Confusing marriage hymn with funeral dirge is a principal means of conflating the two rituals in tragedy: A. *Ag.* 707–10 (Ch. 3 p. 44), *Pr.* 553–60; S. *Ant.* 806–16, *OT* 420–23, *Phryges fr.* 725(?); Eur. *Supp.* 990–1008, *Phaeth.* 227–44 (a marriage hymn just before the discovery of the groom's corpse), *Tro.* 331–52; and the parody of Eur. *Andromeda* at Ar. *Thesm.* 1034–41.

19. Vellacott 1975, 102. On Admetus' belated learning (parodied at Ar. *Lys.* 1008), see Conacher 1988 on *Alk.* 935–61; Musurillo 1972, 286; and Dale 1954, xxv.

20. The detail of the unwashed floor (αὐχμηρὸν οὖδας 947) strikes moderns as incongruous and even humorous, suggesting a prissily refined Admetus. There is more humor in tragedy than often admitted, but not, I think, here. In a speech from the lost *Melanippe Desmotis* (Page 1950, 112–13 [13a5–7]), Euripides writes: "Women manage homes and preserve/ the goods from abroad. A house where there is no/ wife is neither clean nor prosperous." A similar idea lies behind Admetus' comment in *Alk.*, where the poet evokes realities of daily life in Athens, a city with dazzling public buildings but relatively primitive private dwellings. As Herakleides Kreticus put it, "The whole city [Athens] is dry, not well-watered, badly laid out on account of its antiquity. Most of the houses are mean, the nice ones few" (*Die Reisebilder des Herakleides,* ed. F. Pfister [Vienna 1951], 72). The word Admetus uses, αὐχμηρός, "unwashed" or "squalid," also can mean "parched," implying lack of water. Getting water, cleaning house, and washing clothes are referred to frequently in tragedy (I exclude references to bathing): A. *Ch.* 755–60 and his *Hydrophoroi* (*Water-Carriers*) or *Semele* (possibly a Sophoklean play by the same title); S. *Nausikäa* or *Plyntriai* (*Washerwomen*; see Sutton 1984, 84–85); Eur. *Hipp.* 121–29, *Andr.* 166–67, *Hec.* 363, *El.* 74–78, 107–9, 140–41, 309, *Ion* 102–6, 112–23, 144–50 (cleaning the temple precinct), *Hel.* 179–83, *Kyk.* 29–33, *Phaeth.* 55–58, and *Hyps.* 1.ii.16–18 (see also Page 1950 on *Hyps.* 31–33).

21. Ch. 1 p. 14.

22. See Foley 1992, 138–39; M. R. Halleran, "Text and Ceremony at the Close of Euripides' *Alcestis,*" *Eranos* 86 (1988), 123–29; and Buxton 1987, 167–78.

23. Although not explicit in the text, Alkestis' veil is assumed for several reasons: 1) Admetus doesn't recognize his wife (although he notes a striking resemblance, 1066–67); 2) he determines her youth from her clothing and adornments, not her face (1049–50); 3) there is a specific moment when he

looks away without recognizing her (1118) and then turns back to see Alkestis (1121–23). Most commentators and translators have Herakles remove the veil, but there is no reason Alkestis should not do so—the *anakaluptēria* was one of the few prerogatives of the bride at her wedding.

24. See Smith 1960, 142. R. Hamilton, "Prologues, Prophecy and Plot," *AJP* 99 (1978), 293–301, questions the predictive value of Apollo's prophecy, but his argument in this case is unconvincing. Cf. Rivier, 1972, 131 and Musurillo 1972, 277.

25. Dale 1954, xxv.

26. This is the poetic form for ἀδάματος, the negative of the verb δαμάζω, "tame" or "break in," used by Homer for a woman "made subject to her husband." The noun δάμαρ, a poetic word for wife, derives from the verb.

27. At *Alk*. 46, 227, 296, 612, 930, 934, 953, 1126, 1129, 1131. Séchan 1927, 10; Conacher 1967, 332; and Foley 1985, 88 link "Admetus" to ἀδάμαστος (*adamastos*)/ἀδάματος (*adamatos*) ("inflexible"/"unconquered"), attributes of the god Hades. But the word is not used of Hades in the play (perhaps a hint at 980–81); the pun on Admetus' marital status seems more lively and to the point.

28. Critics who emphasize Admetus' resistance to Herakles include Grube 1941, 144; U. Albini, "*L'Alcesti* di Euripide," *Maia* 13 (1961), 5; and Burnett 1965, 251. Those who think he gives in too soon include T. Pandiri, "*Alcestis* 1052 and the Yielding of Admetus," *CJ* 70 (1974–75), 50–52; Nielson 1976, 99 (the scene is "a bitter farce"); and Seidensticker 1982, 150–52 (emphasizing Admetus' betrayal). Those in the audience, however, are "in-the-know" as they watch Herakles' deception, fully aware of the pattern of return that informs the action (Lattimore 1964, 70–71). Tragic bitterness belongs to a different kind of play.

29. Cf. Wilamowitz-Moellendorff 1916, 91–93; Séchan 1927, 35–44; Jones 1948, 50–55; and Musurillo 1972, 285–86 and n.18, all of whom think that Admetus has earned the miracle.

30. Important voices in this debate include C. Garton, "Characterisation in Greek Tragedy," *JHS* 77 (1957), 247–54; Jones 1962, 29–46; Dale 1969, 139–55 (orig. 1959) and 272–80 (orig. ca. 1950); Gellie 1972, 201–22; P. E. Easterling, "Presentation of Character in Aeschylus," *G&R* 20 (1973), 3–19, and "Constructing Character in Greek Tragedy" in Pelling 1990, 83–99 (see also essays there by Halliwell, Goldhill, and Silk); J. Gould, "Dramatic Character and 'Human Intelligibility' in Greek Tragedy," *PCPhS* 24 (1978), 43–67; Winnington-Ingram 1980, 5–8; D. J. Conacher, "Rhetoric and Relevance in Euripidean Drama," *AJP* 102 (1981), 3–25; Goldhill 1986, 167–98; and Podlecki 1989, 279–94.

31. See Humphreys 1983, 62.

32. Kurtz and Boardman 1971, 147 state that "assurance of proper performance of annual [commemorative] rites was reason enough for a man to adopt a son." See Isaios 2.10, 36, 46; 6.64–65; 7.29–30 (noted in Ch. 1 p. 22); also J. W. Hewitt, "Gratitude to Parents," *AJP* 52 (1931), 33, 42. The Chorus in Eur. *Supp.* lament that their fallen sons will not be able to tend to them in their old age (γηροβοσκόν 923), Antigone in Eur. *Ph.* mourns that her dead

brothers cannot care for Jokasta in her last years (ὦ γηροβοσκὼ μητρός 1436), and Medea bemoans the fact that her children will not live to care for her when she is old nor perform her funeral rites when she dies (*Med.* 1032–34).

33. The first in a distinguished line of scenes where a corpse is present but "forgotten"—cf. the wooing scene in *Richard III* 1.2 (parodied in Brecht's *The Resistible Rise of Arturo Ui*); the final scene in *Othello* (not only Desdemona's corpse, but later Emilia's as well); the closet scene in *Hamlet* (after the murder of Polonius); etc.

34. Burke 1969, Introduction and 3–20.

35. Alkestis conceives of her death as a duty to her husband (153–55, 180–81, 283–85) and children (287–88). On the familial motivation for her sacrifice, see Vellacott 1975, 101–2; E. Valgiglio, *Il Tema della Morte in Euripide* (Torino 1966), 100, 111; and Smith 1960, 136–38. Burnett 1971, 35 points out that "husband, children, house and marriage make up a single ideal concept which her death will save." Alkestis does not die for "love," if one means romantic feeling for Admetus. See F. R. Adrados, "El Amor in Eurípides," in *El Descubrimiento del Amor en Grecia*, ed. F. Galiano, J.S.L. de la Vega, and F. R. Adrados (Madrid 1985), 186–88; C.M.J. Sicking, "*Alceste*: Tragédie d'amour ou tragédie du devoir?" *Dioniso* 41 (1967), 155–74; and generally P. Walcott, "Romantic Love and True Love: Greek Attitudes to Marriage," *AncS* 18 (1987), 5–33.

36. Admetus finds their disinterest in dying for him so unnatural that he wonders if he really *is* their child (636–41).

37. *LSJ* define the term ἀναγκαῖος here (s.v. II.5) as "related by blood." This is surely wrong, although the word *can* bear that meaning. Because it carries the undertone of ἀνάγκη ("necessity"), I translate it here as "pure necessity."

38. The single exception occurs when Admetus confronts his father with the fact that Alkestis made a sacrifice one would expect only from a blood relation (645–56); see Jones 1948, 53.

39. Euripides was no misogynist. See Pomeroy 1975, 107 and J. R. March, "Euripides the Misogynist?" in Powell 1990, 63.

40. Mikalson 1991, 78–79 and Burnett 1965, 249–51. For the importance of *xenia* generally, see Herman 1987, passim; M. Scott, "*Philos, Philotēs* and *Xenia*," *AClass* 25 (1982), 1–19; O. Murray, *Early Greece* (Sussex 1980), 50–52.

41. Humphreys 1983, 41–42, following D. Gerin, "Alceste ou l'Inversion des rôles sexuels" (unpublished); my thanks to Mme Gerin (of the Cabinet des Medailles, Bibliothèque Nationale) for sending me a copy. Loraux 1987, 28–30 argues that Alkestis' sacrifice recoils on Admetus by feminizing him, assuming that the process entails nothing but his humiliation.

42. Herman 1987, 22–29 (quotation at 29), 120–21; however, he makes limited use of dramatic material and fails to mention *Alk.* R. Scodel touches on the replacement of Admetus' natural *philoi* (parents) by *xenoi* (Alkestis and Herakles) in "Ἀδμήτου Λόγος and the *Alcestis*," *HSCP* 83 (1979), 61.

43. See, for example, A. *Ch.* 702–3. A violation of that trust—such as Paris' abduction of Helen from his host's home (*Il.* 3.51–54, A. *Ag.* 61–62)—caused a convulsion in the social order and was punished accordingly. G.

Glotz, *La Solidarité de la famille* (Paris 1904), 317n.3, lists other poetic and dramatic examples. In *Alk.*, once Herakles leaves Admetus' house he faces a most inhospitable welcome, for his intended host in Thrace, Diomedes, feeds his "guests" to man-eating horses (483–90).

44. Several years later, Euripides again portrayed the hero as restorer of the *oikos*, rescuing his *own* family from death (*HF*). In the terrible reversals of that play, however, Herakles kills his wife and children after being struck mad by Hera.

45. ξένος (*xenos*) and compounds describe Herakles as guest and Admetus as host over twenty-five times in the play.

46. Ch. 1 p. 14.

47. Arrowsmith 1974, 93; his note on 1472–73 (his lineation) is exemplary.

48. O'Higgins 1993, 78, 92–95 and Rabinowitz 1989 view Alkestis' silence as a symbol of the misogyny they find consistently represented in Greek tragedy (but see above, n.39). Cf. Burnett 1965, 255n.24, who argues persuasively that Alkestis must remain mute for us to believe that she actually had died. Buxton 1987, 173 and E. P. Trammell, "The Mute Alcestis," *CJ* 37 (1941–42), 144–50 stress the importance of silence and ritual purification, but Buxton's claim that this reflects a formal part of the Greek wedding ceremony is dubious. Closer to the mark is Dale 1954 on 1146, who emphasizes the advantage of a silent Alkestis in terms of "drama, poetry and good taste." She is wrong (as is O'Higgins 1993, 93) only in assuming that Euripides had but two actors at his disposal in the play, and therefore was compelled to have a nonspeaker play the veiled Alkestis. In Euripides' tetralogy of 438 B.C. (which included *Alk.*), at least one of the other plays—*Telephus*—required three actors; see Webster 1967, 44–48 and M. Heath, "Euripides' *Telephus*," *CQ* 37 (1987), 277–80. With three actors at hand, why wouldn't Euripides have used them all in the final scene of *Alkestis*?

49. For the "despair" motif—no marriage, no children, no grief—see Ch. 7 p. 106 and Ch. 8 p. 114.

50. Cf. the proverb φιλία ἐστὶ μία ψυχὴ ἐν δύω σώμασιν ἐνοικουμένη ("*philia* is one soul dwelling together in two bodies"), in G. H. Opsimathes, ΓΝΩΜΑΙ (Leipzig 1884), 19, quoted by Burnett 1965, 255n.21. The play recuperates the description of Alkestis as "both living and dead" (ζῶσαν . . . καὶ θανοῦσαν 141), as one "who both is and is no more" (ἔστιν τε κοὐκέτ᾽ ἔστιν 521).

CHAPTER 7

1. Cf. the reductive conclusions reached by Cantarella 1987, 66: "Euripides confirms with utter certainty the old commonplace of the woman as 'scourge, infamous race, unspeakable misfortune' for whoever cannot manage to escape her evil influence." So, too, S-E. Case, "Classic Drag: The Greek Creation of Female Parts," *Theatre Journal* 37 (1985), 327, steamrolls over the play's complexities: "Feminist practitioners and scholars may decide that such plays [*Medea, Lysistrata*] do not belong in the canon—that they are not central to the study and practice of theatre."

2. Kassandra describes Helen as λεληισμένης (Eur. *Tro.* 373), albeit seized "willingly and not by force." Iole in S. *Tr.* (Ch. 5 pp. 73–74) is a new bride literally captured at the sack of a city.

3. See Reckford 1968, 337 and 354; Redfield 1982, 181–201; and Jenkins 1983, 137–46. M. Visser, "Medea: Daughter, Sister, Wife and Mother," in Cropp et al. 1986, 152, emphasizes Medea's loss of both natal and conjugal families.

4. This situation may provide the backdrop for the exchange at 591–97. Medea accuses Jason of spurning a "barbarian marriage," and he responds by claiming advantages of power previously denied him. One of Jason's few defenders, R. Palmer, "An Apology for Jason," *CJ* 53 (1957), 49–55, claims that Jason realizes the implications of the fifth-century Athenian law and acts accordingly. For other ideas about the law's relationship to *Medea*, see Mead 1943, 15–20; E. M. Blaiklock, *The Male Characters of Euripides* (Wellington 1952), 21–22; Snell 1960, 124; Reckford 1968, 346n.26; Davies 1977–78, 111–12; and Ch. 1 p. 18.

5. Those who insist the law was retroactive argue that, in the absence of birth registers, "the only effective way to put the law into effect was to instruct demes and phratries that *from the date when the law was passed* they were not to admit any candidate who was not of Athenian parentage on both sides" (Humphreys 1974, 92). See also Davies 1977–78, 107 and D. Whitehead, "Women and Naturalisation in Fourth-Century Athens," *CQ* 36 (1986), 109n.3. By this reasoning, a son born to an Athenian and his foreign wife in 467 B.C.—sixteen years before the citizenship law was passed—would find himself suddenly ineligible to enroll as a citizen. However, Hignett 1952, 345 and Broadbent 1968, 170 argue that so grossly unfair an arrangement could never have been adopted. Moreover, as Hedrick 1987 points out, "It is only natural that issues of heredity be debated *at birth* [my emphasis] in the context of a kinship organisation such as a phratry rather than at eighteen in the context of a geographic entity such as the deme." See also Ch. 1 n.36, this volume.

6. *kēdos* (or cognate) occurs at 76, 367, 400, 700, 885, and 991.

7. Medea still kneels fifteen lines later (as ἱκέτευσά, "supplicating," at 338 suggests). Gould 1973, 85–86 and 94–95 describes supplication as placing oneself completely at another's mercy with the understanding that the gods protect anyone who takes this desperate step. See also Michelini 1987, 175–76; Collard 1975 on *Supp.* 8–11a; Dover 1974, 199; Vickers 1973, 438–94 (476–78 for *Medea*); and L. Pearson, *Popular Ethics in Ancient Greece* (Stanford 1962), 94, 136–37.

8. G. B. Kerferd, *The Sophistic Movement* (Cambridge 1981), 159–62, notes that revolutionary theories about women's status and rights were in the air at the time of *Medea*'s first performance.

9. See Page 1938 on *Med.* 423; Elliott 1969 on *Med.* 421–22 and 424–25; and H. Lloyd-Jones, *Females of the Species: Semonides on Women* (London 1975), 14, 18–20, 25–29. Verrall 1883 on *Med.* 420 notes the Homeric parody in the line "Muses . . . *abandon* your song" (421), fitting in a play that questions "heroic" values.

10. Dover 1974, 248 characterizes oaths as a means of involving the gods as witnesses. Medea attacks Jason as an oath-breaker at 492–95, 511, 698, 801–2, and 1392; see Boedeker 1991; Mikalson 1991, 82–84; Vickers 1973, 282–86; and Burnett 1973, 13–14.

11. Echoed by the misogynist Hippolytus (Eur. *Hipp.* 618–24).

12. See Osborne 1985, 138–39. At Eur. *Supp.* 54–56, the Chorus tell Aethra, "You bore a son, making your bed [or "marriage"] dear to your husband," a sentiment repeated at Lys. 1.6–7.

13. C. H. Kahn, "The Origins of Social Contract Theory," in *The Sophists and Their Legacy*, ed. G. B. Kerferd (Weisbaden 1981), 94–99, examines the role ascribed to *logos* in the rise of Greek civilization. M. Heidegger defines *logos* as "the laying out that gathers" and "the essence of saying as thought by the Greeks," in "Logos (Heraclitus, Fragment B 50)," *Early Greek Thinking*, tr. Krel and Capuzzi (San Francisco 1984, orig. essay 1951), 59–78.

14. The inability of *logos* to rectify injustice may be part of Euripides' point. Although Jason and Medea's first encounter can be characterized as a law-court scene (Collard 1975a, 61–63; Elliott 1969 on *Med.* 475–95; and Page 1938 on *Med.* 476), at its conclusion no pretense remains that this form of problem solving can redress the wrongs (Solmsen 1975, 28).

15. Describing the civil war in Kerkyra, Thuk. 3.82.4 reveals the disastrous results when words are twisted to mean their opposite and serve only the ends of power. The White House christening Nicaraguan "Contra" terrorists as "Freedom Fighters" provides a modern parallel (Ch. 9 n.2). Re περιστελεῖν, Medea uses it in its literal sense (1034), grieving that her children will not "cover" or "dress" her corpse when she dies.

16. Arist. *Pol.* 1.1.10–11, tr. H. Rackham (Cambridge, Mass. 1949).

17. Critics have tried to determine when this black light first dawns on Medea. Schlesinger 1966, 42 locates the moment when she hears Kreon say that, next to his children, he loves his homeland most (329): "Sie empfängt hier die erste Anregung zum Kindermord" ("Here she first gets the idea of infanticide"). But Kreon's line is part of a stichomythic exchange and nothing in Medea's response indicates any such realization. Euripides was perfectly capable of externalizing the thoughts of a character if he felt it important to do so. He did not, and therefore Medea's announcement of her new plan at 792 comes as a shock, marking a radical shift in which the audience along with the Chorus begin to turn their sympathies away from Medea.

18. Earlier versions had the Korinthians slay the children to revenge Kreon's death (spreading the rumor that Medea killed them) or, in a variation in which Medea ruled Korinth, she slew her children by accident while trying to make them immortal. See Lesky 1972, 217–18, and 1967, 143; Page 1938, xxii–xxiv; and A. E. Haigh, *The Tragic Drama of the Greeks* (Oxford 1896), 289–90. The case for the anteriority of Neophron's lost *Medea* (in which Medea kills her children) is made by E. A. Thompson, "Neophron and Euripides' *Medea*," *CQ* 38 (1944), 10–14; B. Manuwald, "Der Mord an den Kindern," *WS* nf. 17 (1983), 27–61; and Michelini 1989, 115–35; and refuted by Kovacs 1993, 49 and McDermott 1989, 9–24. See also T. V. Buttrey, "Accident and Design in Euripides' *Medea*," *AJP* 79 (1958), 13–14.

19. Conacher 1967, 194 contrasts the wavering Medea with the cold-blooded avenger who emerges after the Aegeus scene:

> If this is the Medea which we are to watch without relief to the play's end, then both the Chorus and ourselves have been the dupes . . . for yielding our sympathy and interest. Fortunately, however, it is the air of cold inflexibility which is false: a cloak of desperate resolution hiding the maternal anguish as well as a device by which the dramatist may, in the end, present the anguish more effectively.

20. Lesky 1967, 146. Snell 1960, 124 observes how the scenes are constructed to lead up to the monologue. The authenticity of lines 1056–80 has been challenged recently. See App. B., where I argue that the speech (with minor deletions) is both original and essential to the play.

21. Dover 1974, 184 calls Hesiod's principle "a head for an eye," and Blundell 1989, 30 notes that it "adds an element of retribution to the financial model of restitution."

22. Reading τολμήσω at line 1078 with Kovacs 1986, 352; see also Foley 1989, 71n.36.

23. See Burnett 1973, 21–23, Walsh 1979, 297–98; and Foley 1989, 79–83. For a fuller discussion of "helping friends and harming enemies" in *Medea*, see App. C.

24. Diggle, following Burges, prints λούτρα for λέκτρα at 1026, preparing the bridal bath rather than the marriage bed; in either case, Medea refers to the wedding ceremony.

25. Plutarch (*De Exilio* 606F–607A) lambastes Euripides' Jokasta for carrying on as if her son would not find a nuptial bath and someone else to bear his wedding torch. The passage suggests what five hundred years can do to ideas of ritual *participation*.

26. See Ch. 8 n.65.

27. The linguistic parallels between *Med.* and *Alk.* are exact: Medea's children will not be able "to care for me in my old age,/ and to cover [my corpse] when I die" (γηροβοσκήσειν τ᾽ ἐμὲ/ καὶ κατθανοῦσαν . . . περιστελεῖν 1033–34); Pheres must father new sons to "care for your old age and cover [your corpse]/ when you're dead" (γηροβοσκήσουσι καὶ θανόντα σε/ περιστελοῦσι, *Alk.* 663–64).

28. Page 1938 on *Med.* 887. The play never mentions the woman who is Glauke's mother and Kreon's wife.

29. Schaps 1979, 99.

30. See Ch. 1 p. 18 and App A. p. 142. Medea's gifts must have been carried in a container, because the robe and crowns act on contact (787–88). For gifts borne during the wedding procession, see the Group E amphoras *ABV* 134.15 and 141.1, *Add*[2] 38; the black-figure column crater (Bérard 1984, #135); and the red-figure vases listed in Sutton 1981, including W.13 (figure 1b, this volume), 27, 29, 31, 34, 52, and 53(?). See also the red-figure loutrophoros ca. 420 B.C. in *AR* 14 (1967–68), 59 and fig. 19. For red-figure scenes depicting the *epaulia*, see Sutton 1981, 210–11, 364–69.

31. Ch. 1 nn.16 and 64. Earlier, Medea sardonically calls herself *makarian* ("blessed" 509) for having Jason as a husband.

32. Verrall 1883 on *Med.* 957 notes that the phrase κόσμον [*kosmon*] φέρειν ("to offer adornment") is used for both wedding and funeral gifts; it occurs at Eur. *Alk.* 613 for gifts buried with the dead, and *kosmos* alone refers to grave goods at *Alk.* 149, 618, and *Hec.* 578. At *Alk.* 161 *kosmos* is used for the ornaments Alkestis wears with her funeral dress; Hecuba adorns the corpse of Astyanax with *kosmoi* (*Tro.* 1200, 1208), and Helen weaves such a garment for the dead Klytemnestra (*Or.* 1431–36). Periander (Hdt. 5.92.7) strips beautiful *kosmoi* off the women he brings to the Hera temple and burns them as offerings to his dead (and naked) wife.

33. στέφανος and πέπλος refer explicitly to "funeral crown" and "burial dress" at Eur. *Tro.* 1143–44, 1220, and 1223; see Lee 1976 on *Tro.* 1221–23. Megara dresses and crowns her sons for their impending death and burial at *HF* 329, 525–26, and 548–49.

34. Glauke "turns away her pale cheek" (1148) out of loathing for the children, the same gesture Medea makes to hide her distress at the thought of killing them (923). Other details connect the two "brides"—both exhibit "wrath" (ὀργή) before their husband (Glauke at 1150, Medea at 870), and Jason advises Glauke to control her "passionate spirit" (θυμός 1152), the very thing Medea cannot do (1079). In the mock reconciliation, Medea advises her children to exchange "enmity for friendship" (ἔχθρας ἐς φίλους 897); when Glauke initially spurns the children, Jason tells her to "consider as friends [φίλους 1153] the same people your husband does." His injunction that she not be "hostile to friends" (δυσμενὴς . . . φίλοις 1151) echoes Medea's boast that she is "well-intentioned to friends" (φίλοισιν εὐμενῆ 809). The parallels turn Glauke into a kind of mirror-Medea, her gruesome demise anticipating the metaphoric death of the protagonist.

35. Sutton 1981, 49, 196–212, 337 and Webster 1972, 216–22.

36. See Ch. 2 p. 41. Of special interest is the bronze caryatid mirror from Korinth, c. 450–40, in Congdon 1981, 196 and pl. 84. The caryatid that supports the mirror herself holds a mirror and gazes at her image. This detail in *Medea* proved memorable: a Lucanian hydria (late fifth century) by the Policoro Painter (#286 Taranto) shows Medea in her dragon-chariot, to the left the seated Glauke *holding a mirror*, and below the Tutor, the two dead children, and Jason brandishing a sword. See N. Degrassi, "Il Pittore di Policoro," *BA* 50 (1965), 9–10 and figs. 8, 11, 12; also J. Henle, *Greek Myths: A Vase Painter's Notebook* (Bloomington 1973), 110–11.

37. The metonym "pine" (πεύκινον δάκρυ 1200) for "torch" also signals wedding torches at *Alk.* 915 (πεύκαις σὺν Πηλιάσιν). For the treatment of pine to accumulate resin for torches, see *Dictionary of Greek and Roman Antiquities*, 2nd ed. (London 1878), s.v. *taeda* 1039a. Heiner Müller (*MEDEA-MATERIAL*) expands the trope of a bride becoming wedding torch, in *Hamlet-Machine and Other Texts for the Stage*, tr. C. Weber (New York 1984), 128–33.

38. Wrestling frequently occurs as a sexual metaphor, as at A. *Ag.* 1206. The erotic overtones of Kreon "dying together with" Glauke (συνθάνοιμί 1210) recall Agamemnon and Kassandra in *Ag.* (1438–47), Klytemnestra and Aegisthus in *Ch.* (ξυνθανεῖσθαι 979, also 894–95, 906), Antigone and Haimon

in S. *Ant.* (1237–41), Evadne and Kapaneus in Eur. *Supp.* (συνθνήισκειν 1007, also 1019–1030, and συνθανοῦσα 1063), and Helen's wish to die with her husband in *Hel* (ξυνθάνοιμ' ἄν 1402). R. Hirzel, *Der Selbstmord* (Darmstadt 1966, orig. 1908), 18–26, 85–88, identifies both the flight from marriage and the desire for physical union in death as motivations for suicide in Greek tragedy. Other references to "lying together in death" occur at *Il.* 23.83–92 and *Od.* 24.76–77 (Achilles and Patroclus), S. *El.* 1165–70 and Eur. *Or.* 1051–55 (Elektra and Orestes), and *Alk.* 363–68 (Admetus and Alkestis).

39. See S. Flory, "Medea's Right Hand," *TAPA* 108 (1978) 71, and Kaimio 1988, 29. The word *hand* (χείρ) occurs over thirty times in *Medea*; the right hand is specified five times.

40. At the same moment Medea urges herself to forget her sons for the day "and mourn them later" (κἄπειτα θρήνει 1249), making the funeral gesture all the more fitting.

41. The word Medea repeats is ἐχθρός (*echthros*), often reserved for personal enemies but frequently applied to military foes, as at S. *Ant.* 10, 522, 1162. See Blundell 1989, 39 and Kells 1973, 9n.1.

42. The contrast of two cities, one at peace and one at war, goes back to the *Shield of Achilles* (*Il.* 18.490–540). Homer's depiction of the peaceful city begins with weddings (nuptial feasts, torchlight processions, marriage hymns), a paradigm for civic concord. So, too, the Chorus of Ar. *Pax* oppose weddings to war (775–80) and call Peace the "mistress of marriages" (976).

43. See Winkler 1990, 162–87; L. Rissman, *Love as War: Homeric Allusion in the Poetry of Sappho* (Königstein 1983); and J. D. Marry, "Sappho and the Heroic Ideal: ἔρωτος ἀρετή," *Arethusa* 12 (1979), 71–92. For echoes of Sapphic vocabulary in the ode, see Rehm 1989, 106n.32.

44. Euripides also links the Muses with peace at *Supp.* 488–91 (see Collard 1975 on *Supp.* 489–91), indirectly at 882–87, and at *Kresphontes Fr.* 453 (Nauck-Snell). In A. *Supp.*, the war-god Ares "lacks dance and music" (*achoron akitharin* 681).

45. Cunningham 1954, 159.

46. Medea will go to Athens "dwelling with Aegeus" (1385); the verb συνοικήσουσα can mean "living in wedlock" (Ch. 1 p. 18), so used by Medea at 242. For the various myths of Medea's life in Athens, see C. Sourvinou-Inwood, *Theseus as Son and Stepson*, BICS Supp. vol. 40 (London 1979), 18–58.

47. As Foley 1989, 79n.60 writes, "Jason begins by devaluing children for expedient reasons and ends as movingly paternal. Medea, in her movement toward masculinity, follows the reverse course." See also Pucci 1980, 162–65 and Strohm 1957, 3.

48. See Ch. 1 p. 13, and Seaford 1988, 120, 122–24 for Hera's cult titles of Τελεία ("Consummator"?) and Ζυγία ("Yoker"). Hera's ties to marriage were especially strong in Argos, exploited in Eur. *El.* (Zeitlin 1970).

49. Burkert 1977, 263–64 and 1966, 118–19 reconstructs the ritual in the temple of Hera Akraia, but the sources are late. Euripides' aetiology is surely ironic—Medea establishes a cult where Korinthians atone for a crime that they never committed.

50. Cf. the view of the *deus* in Euripides argued by Spira 1960, passim (no discussion of *Medea*), who denies irony to this most theatrical of devices. W. Schmidt, *Der Deus Ex Machina bei Euripides* (diss. Tübingen 1964), 199–200, is closer to the mark.

51. Mead 1943, 20. S. G. Daitz, "Concepts of Freedom and Slavery in Euripides' *Hecuba*," *Hermes* 99 (1971), 222, compares Medea to Hecuba—for both, "the moment of greatest physical triumph and freedom is identical with the moment of most abysmal inner defeat and enslavement." Cf. Pomeroy 1975, 109, who finds them preferable to their Sophoklean counterparts Deianeira and Antigone, for they "are successful" and "are too strong to regret their decision." Lefkowitz 1981, 5–6 and Collard 1975a, 64–66 consider the self-destructive consequences of such "successes."

52. Once Medea has secured refuge in Athens, Aegeus abruptly departs, taking no farewell of Medea (Page 1938 on *Med.* 756). It is as if the play has no more need of him; see Rehm 1985, 65–69.

53. Cf. Burnett 1973, 24: "To Athens we too escape with a sense that we are free . . . of the Jason within." Similarly, Shaw 1975, 261n.21 asserts that Athens "represents the cultural integrity missing in Corinth." For Foley 1985, 162, Euripides "consistently represents Athens as a place that can cope, ritually and artistically, with the violence represented by the terrible heroes of myth," an idea taken up by Zeitlin 1990. But far from being "free of the Jason within," Athens welcomes Medea who "entirely assumes Jason's principles and negates the position she had taken against him earlier" (Walsh 1979, 296). Put simply, Medea brings the *problems* of the play with her to Athens. How well the city "coped" is suggested in Thukydides and in many of Euripides' subsequent plays.

54. Thuk. 1.50–66. Athenian and Kerkyraian ships engaged the Korinthians in 433 B.C., "the greatest sea battle that Greeks had ever yet waged against other Greeks" (1.50.2). Athens also undertook land and sea actions against the Potidaeans who were supported by Korinth; at Olynthos, 150 Athenians were slain, including their general Kallias (1.58.3). See Meiggs 1972, 201–2 and P. Deane, *Thucydides' Dates, 465–431 B.C.* (Don Mills, Ont. 1972), 74–89.

55. This reading places *Medea* first in a series of Euripides' plays—*Hec.*, *Tro.*, *Hel.* and *IA*—that criticize the Peloponnesian War, often from the perspective of women and children who are its victims. A strong case also can be made for viewing the pan-Hellenic sentiments of *HF* and *Ion* as part of Euripides' ongoing critique of the war. Tragedies at the City Dionysia were performed in early spring, before the onset of military campaigns, and so were positioned to influence the debate about the nature and direction of Athenian policy. See G. Ley, "On the Pressure of Circumstance in Greek Tragedy," *Ramus* 15 (1986) 46, and Ch. 8 p. 118.

56. McManus 1990, 227–28.

57. MacIntyre 1981, 135.

58. As Stern and Silk 1981, 378 conclude, "The essential character of dissonance . . . is that it evokes a need for resolution which it cannot itself satisfy."

CHAPTER 8

1. *H.Cer.* 353; also 305–11, 332–33. The poem construes the agricultural cycle in terms of anthropomorphic agents operating in a narrative of withdrawal and return. See S. C. Humphreys, "Death and Time," in *Mortality and Immortality*, ed. S. C. Humphreys and H. King (London 1981), 276–77. Cf. Clay 1989, 263, who abjures an agricultural reading of the poem. She downplays (209–13) the fact that Zeus allows Hades (his brother) to abduct Persephone (his daughter) and marry her by force (but cf. *h.Cer.* 3, 30, 78–80), positing instead a thoughtful patriarch who has the entire world in his purview. However, Zeus clearly does not foresee Demeter's refusal to allow the crops to grow (*h.Cer.* 310–13), analyzed by Richardson 1974 on 312.

2. The *anodos* structure also informs Eur. *Alk.* (Ch. 6 p. 84 and Foley 1992). The same pattern operates in Ar. *Pax*, when Attic farmers hoist the goddess Peace from the underground cave where War has buried her, and Trygaios celebrates her return by marrying her handmaid Fullfruit (Ar. *Pax* 221–26, 292–317, 361–72, 426–538, 1316–57).

3. At one point the Chorus wish for a literal *katabasis*, praying that they might die with their dead sons and "descend together to Hades" (κοινὸν ἐς Ἀιδην καταβᾶσα 797).

4. Garner 1987, 118. A. N. Pippen [Burnett], "Euripides' *Helen*: A Comedy of Ideas," *CP* 55 (1960), 154, speaks of the play's "relentless playfulness."

5. On the Mysteries, see Foley 1994, 84–97; Clay 1989, 260–61; Parke 1977, 55–72; Richardson 1974, esp. 271–75, 310–14; K. Kerényi, *Eleusis: Archetypal Image of Mother and Daughter* (London 1967); and Mylonas 1961, esp. 282–85. For the Proerosia, see A. C. Brumfield, *The Attic Festivals of Demeter* (New York 1981), 54–69; Parke 1977, 73–75; Mylonas 1961, 7; and Deubner 1932, 68–69.

6. Rehm 1988, 283–88 analyzes the way that the central altar organizes the staging of the play's opening section.

7. The phrase θάψαι νεκρούς (with slight modulations) occurs at 16–17, 121, 130, 174, 385, 537, 558–59, 571, 670–71, 760, and 935. *nekroi* occurs as the last word at 121, 130, 308, 385, 471, 558, 764, 772, 940, 945, 1037, 1207, 1210, and as the first word at 25, 88, 524, 543, and 665.

8. Ch. 1 pp. 26–27. Collard 1975, 26 notes the similarity of the stage ritual to actual funerary practice in Athens. However, commenting on 857–917 (also at 1972, 47–49), he stresses the differences between the Athenian *epitaphios* and Adrastos' address (following Zuntz 1955, 13–15). Cf. Rehm 1988, 289–90 and Loraux 1986, 48, who argue that the scene follows the basic pattern of the Athenian public funeral.

9. Other funeral processions include those of Alkestis (*Alk.* 606–13, 739–46, Ch. 6 pp. 87–88), Astyanax (*Tro.* 1118–22, 1156–1255, Ch. 9 pp. 133–34), and Neoptolemus (*Andr.* 1166–1225).

10. Collard 1975, 15–16 believes that Evadne climbed a special structure painted to appear like the crags of Eleusis, which are referred to at 987, 1016, and 1045. This would weaken the surprise of Evadne's appearance, because the audience would expect such an anomalous set-piece to be used. Athena

speaks from the *theologeion*, but Collard thinks it "aesthetically unaccept-able" for the suicidal Evadne to appear there as well. Why? Staging both scenes in the same area would draw attention to the important *differences* between the young woman (dressed for her wedding) who has been vic-timized by a war that killed her husband, and the militaristic goddess (wear-ing her traditional helmet and shield) who glorifies future conflict. A more daring possibility is that Evadne used the actual theater *cavea*, perhaps leap-ing off the east *analemma* toward the area of the Odeion of Perikles. Almost all the audience could see and hear the actor without difficulty, and Evadne could be observed climbing ever higher, as the Chorus indicate (989), some-thing impossible on the *theologeion*. Such theatrical staging would bring this unprecedented scene into immediate contact with the audience.

11. Tosca plummets to her death when she discovers that Cavadarossi has been executed, but Puccini doesn't introduce her for the first time only moments before! Scholars compare Evadne's suicide to that of Laodameia in Euripides' lost *Protesilaus*; however, Laodameia was a major figure in the drama, and her death in the flames of her husband's statue probably was reported by messenger (Webster 1967, 97–98). Judging from the fragments, marriage-to-death motifs featured prominently in the play. The brief return of Protesilaus from the underworld so affects Laodameia that, when Hermes leads him back to Hades, she fashions a statue of her husband as consolation. When her father discovers her kissing the image and has it burnt, Laodameia prefers to die in the fire of her surrogate "husband" rather than to go on living. See Nauck-Snell fr. 647 and 653, and Hyginus, fab. 103–4.

12. See Collard 1975 on *Supp.* 993–94.

13. Ch. 3 pp. 43–44 and Ch. 7 p. 107.

14. See Collard 1975 on *Supp.* 93–95, 95–97, and 990–1033. The black mourning garb of the Argives strikes Theseus as inappropriate for Eleusis (93–97), but Evadne's wedding dress is doubly so. W. M. Calder, "A Recon-struction of Sophocles' *Polyxena*," *GRBS* 7 (1966), 48, thinks that Polyxena also may have dressed as a bride.

15. Earlier scholars' fascination with the Indian suttee is misleading. See Collard 1975, 354–55.

16. Theseus compared Thebes to a tyranny that "cuts down the city's brave young men/ like corn in a spring meadow" (448–49); he now turns that simile on the Thebans, swinging his mace like a scythe at harvest time. Those cut down are the "sown ones" (σπαρτὸς 578, σπαρτῶν 712), descen-dants of the original Thebans who sprang from the dragon-teeth planted in the soil. Mocking the Thebans' belief in autochthony, Theseus wonders whether these people refuse to bury the Argive heroes because they fear the enemy dead "will bear children from the recesses/ of the earth, from which will arise vengeance" (545–46). What Theseus intends as mockery proves (metaphorically) true—the funeral rites for the dead Argive Seven engender in their *sons* the desire to return to Thebes as avengers (ἀντιτείσομαι 1144).

17. See Ch. 4 p. 63; Eur. *Ph.* 77–78, 337–43, 704; and Seaford 1990a, 156–57. For political advantage through marital relations (*kēdos*), see Osborne 1985, 127–28, 131–41; J.V.A. Fine, *The Ancient Greeks* (Cambridge, Mass.

1983), 100; Humphreys 1983, 24–27; and Connor 1971, 15–18, 22. Lust for power motivates the suitors in the *Odyssey* and moves Jason to remarry in Eur. *Med.* (Ch. 7 p. 99). The *kēdos* relationship fails to bring political advantages at Eur. *Tro.* 840–59, where the marriage between the Trojan Tithonus and the goddess Eos ("Dawn") does not help save the city (Ch. 9 p. 132). In Eur. *Or.*, Pylades' loyal "caring" (*kēdeumata* 795) for his friend Orestes is contrasted with the self-serving support of Menelaus for his father-in-law Tyndareus, a formal *kēdos* relationship (*Or.* 477, 623, 752, 882–83, 1014–17); see Willink 1986 on *Or.* 795, and F. I. Zeitlin, "The Closest of Masks," *Ramus* 9 (1980), 61. At the play's end, Pylades takes Elektra as his bride and so becomes a real *kēdos* of Orestes, while Orestes himself assumes that relationship with Menelaus by marrying Menelaus' daughter Hermione—a bizarre conversion of a near-death (Orestes has a sword at her throat) into a wedding.

18. See Zeitlin 1990, 148. The Chorus do attempt to console Iphis after Evadne's suicide by invoking Oedipus' fate, a fate that Argos has come to share (*Supp.* 1078–79).

19. The word ἐραστὴς echoes Evadne's "passionate longing" (ἐρῶσα 1040) for death. For the idea of a second life, see Collard 1975 on *Supp.* 1080–81 and Bond 1981 on *HF* 655–72.

20. The Muse (mother of Rhesus) in Eur. *Rh.* 980–82 and Andromache in *Andr.* 395–96 wish they never had borne children and suffered the pain of their premature deaths. The Chorus in *Med.* (1090–1112) consider that those without children ultimately live happier lives (Ch. 7 p. 106), and Admetus wishes that he had never married Alkestis and fathered children, such is his grief over her death (*Alk.* 880–82).

21. The translation is by Carne-Ross 1979, 55.

22. Richardson 1974, 311, whose comments on lines 480–82 are very helpful. See also M. Arthur, "Politics and Pomegranates," *Arethusa* 10 (1977), 32–33 and n.59.

23. The different generational perspectives on the war reflect the public debate of the day. See Thuk. 6.12–13.

24. *Supp.* 307–13, 538–41, 558–63, 669–73. See Ch. 1 p. 21 and Ch. 4 n.9.

25. See the excellent note by Collard 1975 on *Supp.* 762.

26. Foley 1989a; Loraux 1986, 48–49, 66; and Whitehorne 1986, 67–70 think that Theseus' actions reflect the state's abrogation of female prerogatives in fifth-century Athens. For a very different view, see Ch. 1 p. 27; Gamble 1970, 391; and more generally, Dover 1974, 268–72.

27. The model here may be *Il.* 24.582–86, where Achilles has his handmaidens wash and prepare Hektor's corpse away from Priam's sight. He fears that a glimpse of the body would so move the old man that his grief would unleash Achilles' own and cause him to slay Priam. In *Supp.*, the fact that the washing of the corpses does not leave them "sanitized"—the bodies are described as blood-spattered and disfigured later at 811–12 and 944–46—underlines the validity of Theseus' position, although it provides little comfort for the women who long to hold their dead sons.

28. The event is referred to obliquely at *Supp.* 639, 860–61, 934, 1010–11 and described in detail at Eur. *Ph.* 1172–86. In the visual arts, the presence of a

ladder identifies Kapaneus iconographically (Collard 1975 on *Supp.* 497b–9), the mere mention of a proud man on his ladder probably brought Kapaneus to the audience's mind.

29. Adrastos' admission may be linked to Athens' own rejection of Spartan overtures for peace in 425 B.C. (Thuk. 4.15.2., 4.17–23).

30. That one always imagines *surviving* a war-and-disaster scenario is a continuing phenomenon: "Time passed, and now it seems/ everybody's having them dreams./ Everybody sees himself/ walking around with no one else."—Bob Dylan, "Talking World War III Blues," *Freewheelin'* (1963), Columbia JCT 08786.

31. Gamble 1970, 399 asserts that "the herald's points against democracy are not answered by Theseus, and cannot be; they are true defects to which (Athenian) democracy was prone."

32. Thersites' criticisms of the war are spurned (along with the speaker himself, *Il.* 2.225–77), but they ring truer and more problematic when repeated by Achilles (9.315–37, 369–77). D. J. Mastronarde ("The Optimistic Rationalist in Euripides," in Cropp et al. 1986, 204) notes that the Herald echoes statements made earlier in the play by Theseus when he first refuses to help Adrastos. But Mastronarde wrongly concludes that this crossover leaves "no firm ground to stand on." There is solid ground in Euripides' plays, but the audience is asked to dig through accepted truths to find it.

33. For Adrastos' selective memory, see Burian 1985, 147. Often in drama (as in life) a character comes upon a truth that is no less true even if he or she cannot act on it consistently.

34. Smith 1966, 153 calls attention to "the renewal of violence virtually in the same breath as the renunciation of it."

35. Those who validate Athena's encouragements for a new war include Zuntz 1955, 19–20, 75–78; Spira 1960, 99–101; Collard 1975, 407–8; and M. H. Shaw, "The ἦθος of Theseus in *The Suppliant Women*," *Hermes* 110 (1982), 17–18. Cf. the strongly ironic reading of Athena's call to arms, argued (with variations in temperament and style) by Grube 1941, 242; Conacher 1956, 26; Gamble 1970, 404–5; and to a lesser extent Fitton 1961, 442.

36. See Collard 1975, 8–14 (for the date and contemporary references in the play) and Thuk. 4.97–101 (for Delium).

37. Di Benedetto 1971, 158–62. The fact that he dates the play to 422 rather than a year earlier does not affect the point. See also Ch. 7n.55.

38. For the vote in the Assembly, see Thuk. 4.117.1–120.1. Gomme on Thuk. 4.118.12 suggests that delegates actually attended the theater. The City Dionysia began on the ninth of Elaphebolion, and dramatic performances ran from the eleventh through the thirteenth in the "abbreviated" season instituted during the Peloponnesian War. See Parke 1977, 125–31 and J. T. Allen, "On the Program of the City Dionysia during the Peloponnesian War," *UCPCPh* 12 (1938), 35–42. The meeting of the Athenian assembly that ratified the armistice took place on the fourteenth of Elaphebolion (Thuk. 4.118.12, 119.1–2, and Gomme's commentary). Once the armistice took effect, continuous efforts were made to extend it into a lasting peace (Thuk. 4.119.3; also 4.124.1 and 5.1), the goal of the original negotiations (4.117.1).

39. Pickard-Cambridge 1968, 59 and 67; Parke 1977, 133–34; and Goldhill 1987, 63–68 discuss the ceremony without noting its relevance to *Supp*. J. J. Winkler, "The Ephebe's Song: *Tragōidia* and *Polis*," *Representations* 11 (1985), 31–33, thinks that the play's orphans are not closely linked to the situation of fifth-century Athens. He also writes misleadingly of the Argive orphans' desire to "take their fathers' places in the city's *defensive* ranks" [my emphasis]. For a general account of Athenian support for war orphans, see R. S. Stroud, "Theozotides and the Athenian Orphans," *Hesperia* 40 (1971), 288–93.

40. Aeschin. 3.154 describes the proclamation delivered by the herald to the orphans as an "incentive to valor."

41. Collard 1975 on *Supp*. 406–8. Finley 1966, 2 observes "the elaborate political discussion of the first half of *Suppliants*." K. A. Raaflaub, "Perceptions of Democracy in Fifth-Century Athens," *C&M* 40 (1989), 49–54, notes the critique of democratic practice in tragedy, but his comments on *Supp*. are disappointing.

42. See Collard 1975 on *Supp*. 438–41. A variation of the actual formula— Τίς ἀγορεύειν βούλεται; ("Who wishes to address the people?")—also occurs at Eur. *Or*. 885; see Willink 1986 on 884–87, and V. Di Benedetto, ed., *Euripidis, Orestes* (Firenze 1965) on 885.

43. For the *patrios nomos*, see Ch. 1 pp. 26–27. For the view that Adrastos' speech to the young men of Athens included the theater audience, see Paley on *Supp*. 843, Collard 1975 on *Supp*. 842b–43, and Rehm 1988, 303–4.

44. Burian 1985, 140–43 presents an excellent analysis of this aspect of the play.

45. Euripides contrasts the effective mob-orator with the honest farmer whose position is voted down in *Or*. 902–30, 944–45. Aristophanes frequently exploits the comic possibilities of this situation, as in Ar. *Ach*. 631– 35, *Vesp*. 698–705, 719–21, and the running attack on Kleon in *Eq*. (esp. 41– 70, 486–91, 710–809, and 1111–20). See Sinclair 1988, 203–8 and Carter 1986, 82–98. Although eloquently defending direct democracy in Athens, Ober 1989, 112–18 admits the elite status of speakers in the Assembly.

46. The contrast between these two versions of Kapaneus is so striking that only special pleading can eliminate the irony (*pace* Collard 1972, 43–45, who finds "nothing surprising . . . in a Capaneus made temperate and uncompromisingly loyal for the Oration"). Conacher 1956, 23 points out "the false heroics of the funeral speech," and Fitton 1961, 438–39 notes the absurdity of Adrastos' claim that Kapaneus was affable and moderate: "Could an Athenian citizen really take seriously the advice to bring up his children to be a Kapaneus . . . ?"

47. By picking up the μάθος words used by Adrastos (who speaks of lessons and learning), Evadne seems to answer the false heroics of his funeral speech.

48. Like Iphigenia and Kassandra in *Ag*. (Ch. 3 p. 43).

49. *Helen* is dated to 412 by F. Ferrari, *Euripide, Ifigenia in Tauride e Ifigenia in Aulide* (Milan 1988), 64–65; Kannicht 1969, 21; and Dale 1967, xxiv.

50. To Steisichorus' *Palinode* Euripides adds the influence of Hera, who is

angry at losing the judgment of Paris to Aphrodite (*Hel*. 31–40, 586). See Kannicht 1969, 26–41; Dale 1967, xvii–xxiv; and J. D. Denniston, ed. *Euripides, Electra* (Oxford 1939) on 1280–83. In the second preface (1676) to his *Andromaque*, Racine writes of Euripides' boldness in *Helen*: "He openly shocks the common belief of entire Greece. He supposes that Helen has never set foot in Troy, and that after the sack of that town Menelaus finds his wife in Egypt, which she had never left." From *Jean Racine, Complete Plays*, tr. Samuel Solomon. Vol. 1 (NY 1969), 142–43.

51. Thuk. 6 and 7, esp. 6.24.1–4, 6.30–32, 7.87.5–6.

52. See Foley 1992, 134–38; Segal 1971, 569–70, 572–73, 593–600; and Lattimore 1964, 52–53.

53. For Hermes *psychopompos*, see Ch. 2 p. 35. The god leads Persephone out of Hades at *h.Cer*. 334–83. For the link between Egypt and the underworld, see Segal 1971, 559; Kannicht 1969 on *Hel*. 461–63; and F. Jesi, "L'Egitto inferno nell' *Elena* di Euripide," *Aegyptus* 45 (1965), 56–69.

54. For remarriage in the play, see Foley 1992, 148–49 and 1985, 88–89. Wolff 1973, 62–68 emphasizes the larger theme of eros and death.

55. See Wolff 1973, 64; Kannicht 1969 on *Hel*. 68–70 (Attic cults to Ploutos linked with those to the Eleusinian divinities); Rose 1959, 78, 94; and K. Holzinger, ed., *Aristophanes' "Plutos"* (Vienna 1940, rpt. New York 1979) on *Pl*. 727.

56. See D. B. Robinson, "Helen and Persephone, Sparta and Demeter," in *Arktouros: Hellenic Studies presented to Bernard M.W. Knox*, ed. G. W. Bowerstock, W. Burkert, and C. J. Putnam (Berlin 1979), 162–72; Wolff 1973, 63–64; Segal 1971, 581; and Ch. 4 p. 63. Kreusa in *Ion* also fits the Persephone/Demeter pattern (see Ch. 2 n.47 and Ch. 7 p. 102).

57. Although Ida is not specified in the second passage, Wilamowitz restores a reference to it at *Hel*. 676; see Kannicht 1969, critical apparatus on 676, and commentary on *Hel*. 676–78. Ida figures prominently in the judgment of Paris at Eur. *Andr*. 274–92.

58. An apt phrase for newlyweds on their way to establish their *oikos* (Ch. 1 p. 18).

59. For the marriage of Paris and Helen, see *Hel*. 30, 224–25, 232–37, 666–68, 690, 882, 1097, 1118–21, 1506–7, and 1672.

60. His desire for marriage at 62–63, 294–97, 314, 793–99, 833; the impending wedding at 1231, 1385–86, 1399, and 1436–40.

61. Rehm 1988, 304–6; also G. Ley, "Scenic Notes on Euripides' *Helen*," *Eranos* 89 (1991), 26, 28–29.

62. Thuk. 2.34.3; also Kannicht 1969 on *Hel*. 1261.

63. The phrase is from Zuntz 1960, 224, whose essay (along with Segal 1971) is among the best on the play.

64. Foley 1985, 225 and Whitman 1974, 48 stress the transformative aspects of Menelaus' new apparel. His bath and change of clothes also fit the wedding ceremony (Wolff 1973, 67).

65. See Ch. 5 pp. 74–75 for comparisons of a bride to a young animal, and Ch. 7 p. 102 for the mother's role in the torchlight procession. Wedding torches shine elsewhere in *Helen*—Menelaus recalls his torch-lit wedding to Helen

(638–39), and the Messenger adds his own memories as one of the torchbearers who ran after the chariot carrying the royal couple to their new home (722–25). This ritual link may account for the torches Theonoe is holding (865–72) when she comes upon the reunited couple at the tomb of Proteus. In *Tro.* 308–52, Kassandra carries her own nuptial torches as she reenacts part of the wedding ritual (Ch. 9 pp. 129–30). Torchlit wedding-processions also are referred to at *Il.* 18.492; Hes. *Sc.* 273–80; Ar. *Pax* 1316–17 and 1329–57; and they are parodied in X.Eph. *Ephesiaca* 1.8 (see Carson 1985, 80).

66. Segal 1971, 600 offers a similar reading. For the holocaust at Troy, see *Hel.* 107, 196–97, 503, 1161–62; the false beacon fires are mentioned at 767, 1126–31. Kannicht 1969 on *Hel.* 1126–31 takes up the story of Nauplius, whose beacon-fires lure the Greek ships to their ruin on the coast of Euboia.

67. As in *Alk.* (Ch. 6 p. 90), the play's "doublings" (two prologues, two "Helens," etc.) contribute to a sense of renewal.

68. Cf. Burnett 1971, 97, who thinks that "the Greek ship is filled with blood, [but] . . . only the blood of a good messenger speech." Closer to the mark is D. G. Papi, "Victors and Sufferers in Euripides' *Helen,*" *AJP* 108 (1987), 38–39.

69. Nor is Helen the only one who expresses these sentiments. Even her vanishing phantom confesses that the Trojans and Greeks died for nothing (608–11). Mistaking the real Helen for the phantom, the first Messenger chides her for claiming the war at Troy was "in vain" (620). However, when he realizes the truth, he asks in disbelief, "We endured all that suffering in vain? for a cloud?" (707). Theoklymenos, too, exclaims, "Ah Priam, and the land of Troy, ruined for nothing! (1220).

70. R. P. Winnington-Ingram, in Zuntz 1960, 238–39.

CHAPTER 9

1. As Connor 1984, 157 writes, "*logos* . . . fails to avert the violence and destruction of war and is itself narrowed, distorted, and perverted." For the moral outrage behind the dialogue, see Ahl 1984, 179–80; C. W. Macleod, "Thucydides' Platean Debate," *GRBS* 18 (1977), 243–46, and "Form and Meaning in the Melian Dialogue," *Historia* 23 (1974), 385–400 [= *Collected Essays* (Oxford 1983), 119–22, 52–67]; and Immerwahr 1973, 29–31. Regarding Melian neutrality, R. A. Bauslaugh, *The Concept of Neutrality* (Berkeley 1990), 142–46, points out that Thukydides juxtaposes "traditional, customary rules of interstate behavior, which balanced rights and obligations to the benefit of weak and powerful alike, and the newly evolved ethos of hegemonial, imperial Greek states that refused to accept any restraints on the pursuit of self-interest."

2. One of countless examples is the United States' systematic assault on Nicaragua after the 1979 revolution. A former client state during the Somoza dictatorship, Nicaragua established a nonaligned democracy under the leadership of the Sandanistas, victors in Nicaragua's first free election in 1984. Their efforts were met with an economic blockade and military interference, organized and funded by the United States. Some twenty thousand civilian

fatalities resulted, along with the destruction of the Nicaraguan economy, all under the guise of promoting "democracy." See R. Brody, *Contra Terror in Nicaragua* (Boston 1985); T. Cabestrero, *Blood of the Innocent*, tr. R. Barr (New York 1985); T. Walker, ed., *Reagan versus the Sandanistas* (Boulder 1987); Chomsky 1989, 51–73, and his *The Culture of Terrorism* (Boston 1988), 75–111.

3. Perceptive critics of the play include Murray 1946a, 127–48; Havelock 1968; Poole 1976; and G. Gellie, "Helen in the *Trojan Women*," in Betts 1986, 114–21. Among the many works using *Troades* as a prototype, see the Federal Theatre Project's *Trojan Incident* (Library of Congress Federal Theatre Project Collection, George Mason University); J. P. Sartre, *Les Troyennes* (Paris 1965); and E. Bond, *The Women: Scenes of War and Freedom* (New York 1979).

4. Speaking to the Chorus, Hecuba addresses both the widows and their "ill-wedded [δύσνυμφαι] daughters" (144). The adjective suggests the Trojan marriages that the young women have lost, and also the forced liaisons that lie ahead with their Greek conquerors. E. Craik ("Sexual Imagery and Innuendo in *Troades*," in Powell 1990, 1–15) notes the many references to rowing, and argues that the verbal play on πλάτη (oar) and πελάτης (someone who "comes close," often in a sexual way) points to the rape that the Trojan women must endure.

5. See Ch. 3nn.28 and 37; also C. Segal, "Violence and the Other," *TAPA* 120 (1990), 115–17.

6. Huddleston 1980, 46–50 and Brown 1977, 48–50 view her lyric (304–41) in terms of a traditional Greek wedding song.

7. As Evadne does in *Supp.* (Ch. 8 p. 112). See S. A. Barlow, "The Language of Euripides' Monodies," in Betts 1986, 17–18.

8. Mason 1985, 151–52 stresses the terrible incongruity of a wedding being celebrated at a moment of national disaster.

9. *Troades* is full of lamentation, cries of pain, and inarticulate expressions of grief. These provide a counter-discourse to the elaborate rhetoric of the *agōnes* (noted by Barlow 1986, 37–38). As Stanford 1983, 60–61 puts it, "To ignore the intense emotionalism as one reads Greek tragedy is like crossing the Sahara in an air-conditioned car."

10. Used of Troy at 556, 598, 1065, and 1295, the word *Pergamon* (Πέργαμος) includes the suffix γάμος ("wedded-union" or "pairing"). Euripides plays on the verbal relationship between Troy's fate and marriage when Paris destroys "the towers of Troy [πέργαμα Τροίας] by means of his hated [marriage] bed" (598).

11. Hecuba at 130–37, 498–99, 892–94; Andromache at 765–73; and the Chorus at 1114–17.

12. For the Greek view of the human body, see J-P. Vernant, "Corps obscur, corps éclatant," *Le Temps de la réflexion* 7 (1986), 19–45. As Poole 1987, 223 points out, "the physical presence of the mortal body is one of the most powerful arguments for the peculiar purchase which the theatre has on tragedy."

13. See K. Gilmartin, "Talthybius in the *Trojan Women*," *AJP* 91 (1970),

221–22. The prototype for such compassion is Achilles in *Iliad* 24, where he helps with the funeral rites of Hector (see App. C p. 146). In Eur. *Hec.* 518–20, Talthybios admits that he wept at the sacrifice of Polyxena, and he will weep again in reporting the news to Hecuba. Neither there nor in his response to Andromache's farewell to her son in *Tro.* does he manifest behavior expected of a male, much less of a soldier. See Dover 1974, 101. Cf. Menelaus in Eur. *Hel.*, who refuses to countenance tears and shows no sympathy for the city and people he has destroyed, even though he did so for a phantom (Ch. 8 p. 125).

14. As E. Fantham ("Andromache's Child," in Cropp et al. 1986, 272) notes, "The epitaph she imagines for him is a reminder to Euripides' Athenians of their own cruelty at Melos."

15. Euripides may allude to this invasion at *Tro.* 220–23, when the Chorus imagine Sicily as a possible destination.

16. Ober and Strauss 1990, 270 remind us that "Athenian political culture was created in part in the theater of Dionysos, theatrical culture on the Pnyx." See also Euben 1990, 51: "What the assembled citizenry witnessed was its past political choices, institutional forms, and cultural practices 'problematized' in the situations, themes, and characters on stage."

17. In deciding Astyanax's fate, Euripides has the Greek army follow Athenian practice by debating and voting (as they do for the sacrifice of Polyxena in *Hec.*), making the analogy between the Greeks at Troy and the Athenians at Melos even clearer.

18. When designing the great shield of Athena Parthenos, the cult statue of the city's patron goddess, Pheidias exploited the strong Athenian association between invaders torching a city and the Persians burning the Acropolis. See in particular E. B. Harrison, "Motifs of City-Siege on the Shield of Athena Parthenos," *AJA* 85 (1981), 295–301.

19. For the rape(s) of Kassandra, see Ch. 3, n.12.

20. Connor 1984, 155–57 explores the parallels between Thukydides' portrayal of the Athenians in the Melian dialogue and Herodotus' depiction of the Persians in his *Histories*.

21. Torches also played a role in the first two plays of Euripides' trilogy. See Scodel 1980, 76–79; Webster 1967, 165–76; and B. Menegazzi, "*L'Alessandro di Euripide*," *Dioniso* 14 (1951) 172–97. On Kassandra's role in *Alexandros*, see T.C.W. Stinton, *Euripides and the Judgement of Paris* (London 1965), 64–71 (= Stinton 1990, 66–70).

CONCLUSION

1. According to Foley 1982, 4, *oikos* and *polis* constituted more a "contradictory unit" than a "structural opposition." Perhaps a better image is that of interconnected circles with significant overlap.

2. What lies behind some feminist indictments of Attic tragedy is the sense that the liberated position of the critic marks the *telos* that the play in question fails to achieve, a "presentist" bias that ignores the historical context in which all but the most transcendentally liberated of us must operate.

For useful correctives, see H. Vendler, "Feminism and Literature," *NY Rev.* (May 31, 1990), 19, and M. Lefkowitz, "Feminist Myths and Greek Mythology," *TLS* (July 22–28, 1988), 808.

3. Clark 1989, 5.

4. There are traces of this "feminizing" process in epic—Homer compares Odysseus' reaction to Demodokus' song of the fall of Troy to that of a woman whose city has just been sacked and burned (*Od.* 8.523–31), and Patroclus' compassion both for his Greek comrades and for Briseis suggests that he manifests traits associated with the feminine. C. R. Beye, "Male and Female in the Homeric Poems," *Ramus* 3 (1974), 88–89, emphasizes the noncompetitive and dependent aspects of Achilles' and Patroclus' relationship, an idea developed by Halperin 1989, 84–87. Although the emotion of pity was commonly viewed as womanly (Blundell 1989, 75–76), many tragic scenes validate pity as an estimable human response for both women and men. See Dover 1974, 195–201.

5. Thuk. 1.141.3, 5; 1.142.4–1.143.2; 1.143.4–5; 2.13.2.

6. Thuk. 2.14.1–2, 12; 2.16.1–5, 15; 2.19.1 to 2.23.1.

7. Thuk. 2.55, 57, 59, 61.2, and 62.2–3. Hanson 1983, 111–27 notes that there were only six such Spartan invasions, and that they did "no widescale nor lasting damage to the agriculture of Attica." However, he acknowledges the psychic toll that these invasions took on the Athenians (1983, 143, 147–51, developed in his *The Western Way of War* [New York 1989], 4–6, 32–37). Agricultural devastation was *perceived* to be effective, making the threat of ravaging the land a potent one.

8. Hanson 1983, 33 establishes that the Spartans burnt the Attic crop of barley and wheat.

9. F. Fergusson, *The Idea of a Theater* (Princeton 1949), 72.

10. As Redfield 1982, 163 puts it, "in a wedding the happy or unhappy couple become for a moment archetypal bride and bridegroom. Their peculiarities are declared irrelevant to the archetype shining through them." For the manner in which ritual action can link past with present, see Easterling 1988, 89–91, 108–9, and Foley 1985, 62–63.

11. N. Gordimer, "The Gap Between the Writer and the Reader," *NY Rev*, Sept. 28, 1989.

APPENDIX A

1. Oakley 1982, 113–18; Redfield 1982, 192, 199n.11; and Deubner 1900, 149–50.

2. "The grammarians and lexicographers contradict each other because they draw on old sources without being able to coordinate the information based on any personal knowledge of the customs in question." P. Z. Montuoro, "Il Corredo della Sposa," *ArchCl* 12 (1960), 49; see also Sutton 1981, 156–59. The problem with the sources is acknowledged by H. S. Schibli, *Pherekydes of Syros* (Oxford 1990), 63–66, esp. nn.33–38.

3. Oakley 1982, 114 and Sutton 1989, 357–59.

4. Among numerous examples, there are several amphoras in London

(*ABV* 134.15; 141.1, *Add²* 38; 296.1, *Para* 128, *Add²* 77); a krater in Basel (see Bérard et al. 1984, pl. 135) and another in Paris (*CVA* Louvre 12, pl. 166.7, which the editor F. Villard thinks depicts gods in a chariot, but the fact that the female is veiled and holds a *stephanos* makes the nuptial identification more likely); the pyxis in Poland (*CVA* Goluchow 16.1a–c., depicting the marriage of Herakles and Hebe, in which the hero leads his bride XEK toward an interior where women are preparing the marriage bed); and numerous black-figure hydria showing mythological or mortal weddings (Florence #3799, unattributed); *ABV* 260.30, *Para* 114, *Add²* 68; 287.13, *Para* 125; 289.29, *Add²* 75; 335.5 *bis*, *Para* 148, *Add²* 91; 364.60, *Add²* 97; and *CVA* Fiesole 1, 20.4 and 23.2. Hydriai may have been used along with loutrophoroi in the marriage ritual, which might account for the popularity of wedding scenes on that vase shape; see M. Maas and J. M. Snyder, *Stringed Instruments of Ancient Greece* (Yale 1989), 55, and Ch. 2 p. 30.

5. See Roberts 1978, 180; Pemberton 1976, 116; Boardman 1958–59, 159 and n.38; P. Bocci, *CVA* Florence 5, pp. 14–15 (describing *ABV* 289.29, above n.4); E. Svatik, "A Euphronios Kylix," *ABull* 21 (1939), 266; and H. B. Walters, "Red-figured Vases Recently Acquired by the British Museum," *JHS* 41 (1921), 144 In support of this view, epic poetry makes no functional distinction between a woman's covering her head and veiling her face. See H. L. Lorimer, *Homer and the Monuments* (London 1950), 385–86, and E. B. Abrahams, *Greek Dress* (London 1908), 34–37. On the basis of late literary evidence, Carson 1990, 162–63 insists that the veil "must cover her face" and that the unveiling "signifies the official consecration of the marriage: henceforth the bride is considered to *be married*." This is simply wrong. The notion of "official consecration" is not Greek, nor was there a particular instant when a bride became a wife. As discussed in Ch. 1, a Greek wedding is best understood as a process, not the achieved "moment" of a contemporary Christian or civil ceremony.

6. Those who place the *anakaluptēria* in the couple's new house include E. Pottier and S. Reinach, *Le Nécropole de Myrina* (Paris 1887), 443; J. Toutain, "Le Rite nuptial de l'*anakalyptērion*," *REA* 42 (1940), 345–50; Huddleston 1980, 138–39n.14; Buxton 1987, 172; Sissa 1987, 116–21; and Hague 1988, 35.

APPENDIX B

1. M. D. Reeve, "Euripides' *Medea* 1021–80," *CQ* 22 (1972), 51–61; Bain 1977, 24–27; Diggle 1984, 138–39; and B. Gredley, "The Place and Time of Victory: Euripides' *Medea*," *BICS* 34 (1987), 36.

2. Bain 1977, 26–27, and his *Masters, Servants and Orders in Greek Tragedy* (Manchester 1981), 33; also Foley 1989, 83–84n.77.

3. Kovacs 1986, 343–52, followed by S. A. Barlow, "Stereotype and Reversal in Euripides' *Medea*," *G&R* 36 (1989), 166.

4. Kovacs 1986, 351.

5. Foley 1989, 85n.83, then 72. Lloyd-Jones 1980, 59.

6. M. Dyson, "Euripides' *Medea* 1056–80," *GRBS* 28 (1987), 24–26, argues

that ἐχθροῖς (1060) refers to "enemies in general," perhaps those in Athens. The argument is untenable. Elsewhere Medea insists that her ἐχθροί are Jason, Kreon, Glauke, and the Korinthians, and she uses ἐχθροὺς for Jason, Kreon, and Glauke only ten lines earlier (1050).

7. Easterling 1977, 189.

8. Lloyd-Jones 1980, 56 and 57n.13.

9. Kovacs 1986, 352n.17 and Foley 1989, 84n.79.

10. See Kovacs 1986, 347n.6. The transposition is adopted by H. D. Broadhead, *Tragica* (Christchurch 1968), 167–68.

11. As Denniston 1934, 250 (and 252.iv) puts it.

12. Michelini 1989, 116–24 distinguishes textual critics ("surgeons") from their literary counterparts ("internists"), but her defense of the speech in toto is hard going.

APPENDIX C

1. According to B.M.W. Knox, "Second Thoughts in Greek Tragedy," *GRBS* 7 (1966), 224, "What restores her resolution is not the voice of a god or his human spokesman [like Pylades in A. *Ch.*] but the thought that she will be a laughing-stock to her enemies. . . ." See also Lloyd-Jones 1980, 53 and Grube 1941, 164.

2. According to Humphreys 1983, 73, Medea's "repeated justification for killing her children is that she cannot bear Jason to laugh at her. She wants to prove that she can harm her enemies and do good to her friends (809)—a conventional definition of male *aretē* ["excellence"] which was coming under scrutiny in the late fifth century." See Garvie 1986 on *Ch.* 123; Dover 1974, 180–84; and Page 1938 on *Med.* 809–10. For other examples in Greek literature and drama, see Blundell 1989, 26–31, who provides an excellent summary of the axiom and its problems.

3. See A.W.H. Adkins, *Merit and Responsibility: A Study in Greek Values* (Oxford 1960), 153–71, esp. 154–56, and his "Values, Goals, and Emotions in the *Iliad*," *CP* 77 (1982), 292–326, esp. 322–23. See also Knox 1964, 30–31 and 1977, 196–97; Bongie 1977, 27–56; and Barlow 1986, 19. Foley 1989, 65–66 writes that the fear of being mocked "remained a dominant Greek ethical position as well as a major, even the major, principle of social organization in the archaic and classical periods. . . ." M. Dillon, "Tragic Laughter," *APA Abstracts* (1987), 108, finds little if any softening of this attitude in tragedy.

4. See K. J. Dover, "The Portrayal of Moral Evaluation in Greek Poetry," *JHS* 103 (1983), 35–48 (= *Greek and the Greeks* [Oxford 1987], 77–96); A. A. Long, "Morals and Values in Homer," *JHS* 90 (1970), 121–39; and N. Frye, *Anatomy of Criticism* (Princeton 1971), 319, who emphasizes "the importance for Western literature of the *Iliad*'s demonstration that the fall of an enemy, no less than of a friend or leader, is tragic and not comic."

5. Nagler 1974, 167–98 and M. W. Edwards, *Homer: Poet of the Iliad* (Baltimore 1987), 301–13 deal admirably with the manner in which Achilles is reconciled to the mortal, the human, and—if only briefly—the humane world at the close of the poem.

6. See Blundell 1989, 62–64, 96, 99, 101.

7. Pl. *Cri.* 49a3–d1; *Grg.* 469b12, 507d5–e6; also Xen. *Mem.* 4.8.11. For Sokrates, acting on this principle is not only less unjust, but "preferable from the standpoint of enlightened self-interest" (Dodds 1959 on *Grg.* 468e6–497c7). G. Vlastos gives an excellent account in "Socrates' Contribution to the Greek Sense of Justice," Ἀρχαιογνωσία 1 (1980), 301–24. See also Blundell 1989, 182 and D. Furley, "Euripides on the Sanity of Herakles," in Betts et al. 1986, 102–13.

8. J. H. Finley, *Thucydides* (Cambridge, Mass. 1942), 54–55; Snell 1964, 52; and W. W. Fortenbaugh, "Antecedents of Aristotle's Bipartite Psychology," *GRBS* 11 (1970), 233–50. Solmsen 1975, 133–34 views the speech as a struggle between contending passions, Medea's hatred of Jason versus her love for her children.

9. J. J. Walsh, *Aristotle's Conception of Moral Weakness* (New York 1963), 16–22. See also T. H. Irwin, "Euripides and Socrates," *CP* 78 (1983), 183–97, and C. Gill, "Did Chrysippus Understand Medea?" *Phronesis* 28 (1983), 136–49.

10. See Snell 1960, 126. For the view that Medea is unflinching in her resolve, see App. B pp. 144–45. This perception can be traced to Scholiast AB on *Med.* 1055 (E. Schwartz, *Scholia in Euripidem* II [Berlin 1891], 198), who writes that Medea kills her children not from "deliberate choice" (προαιρέσει) but from "the *necessity* of paying back her enemies" (ἀνάγκηι δὲ τοῦ τοὺς ἐχθροὺς ἀμύνασθαι). See also L. E. Lord, *Literary Criticism of Euripides in the Earlier Scholia* (Göttingen 1908), 55, 78.

11. Kovacs 1986, 346 and 350–51, a view shared by E. Christmann, *Bemerkungen zum Text der Medea des Euripides* (diss. Heidelberg 1962), 125–45; Lloyd-Jones 1980; and Foley 1989, 67–68.

12. Rickert 1987, 99, drawing on the Platonic conception of *to thumoeidēs* in Pl. *R.* 4.439e–441c3. A. Dihle, *The Theory of Will in Classical Antiquity*, Sather Vol. 48 (Berkeley 1982), 28, speaks of the "mutual interaction" of reason and emotion necessary to bring about any sort of action.

13. Rickert 1987, 111.

14. Dover 1974, 190; also Blundell 1989, 53–55, 103, 269.

15. The Nurse (*Med.* 36–37, 116–18), Chorus (811–13, 851–55, 1258–60, 1275–76, 1290–92), Medea herself (1056), and Jason (1323–28, 1389–90, 1393).

16. Exceptions include Pucci 1980, 125–26 and Snell 1964, 51. The children are specified as Medea's at 17, 116, 273, 342, 563, 780, 782, 792–93, 795, 816, 877–78, 880, 967, 1002, 1017, 1029–43, 1145, 1158, 1241, 1248, 1261–62, 1280–81, and 1325–26.

17. Descriptions of the children as Medea's *philoi* cluster around the murder, at 1247, 1250, 1262, and 1283. As Connor 1971, 43n.18 puts it, "In her intense desire to be 'a burden on my enemies and well disposed to my *philoi*' (809), she fails to recognize who her true *philoi* are." For this reason, Easterling 1977, 185 finds Medea's appropriation of the heroic code "hideously out of place. . . ." Both the Nurse and Medea herself accuse *Jason* of having done wrong (*kakos*) to his *philoi* (84, 470); however, by her own actions,

"Medea repeats Jason's offense" (Walsh 1979, 297). Recall Aristotle's formulation that "a *philos* is another [or "second"] self" (ἔστι γὰρ ὁ φίλος ἄλλος αὐτός, *EN* 1166a 32, also 1170b 6). By killing her *philoi*, Medea in effect kills herself.

18. She also hints (at 788) that Jason might die from Glauke's poisoned robes; see Elliott 1969, 118. Burnett 1973, 10 makes the point succinctly:

> The child-murder of the *Medea* is disturbing because it is child-murder; it is distressing because it follows the other murders [of Glauke and Kreon] and so appears gratuitous and unnecessary; it is infuriating because it seems to have replaced the true vengeance act, the killing of Jason.

19. My position is diametrically opposed to that of Bond 1981 on *HF* 585f.: "Euripides did not contribute much to the weakening of the traditional attitude." Cf. above n.2.

GLOSSARY

Note: When two words are paired, the second one is the plural form.

anchisteia — closely related kin.

akrasia — the state of knowing what is the right thing to do but not being able (or willing) to act on that knowledge.

amphora, amphorai — a two handled ceramic vase, often used for storing liquids.

anakaluptēria — a part of the Athenian wedding ceremony involving the unveiling of the bride in the presence of her husband.

analēmma — the side walls supporting the seats in a Greek theater, marking one side of the entrance way (*parodos*, s.v.) into the orchestra.

anodos — the "road up," used for the journey out of the Underworld and back to the land of light.

aulos — a reed instrument, akin to an oboe, used at Greek weddings and funerals, and also to accompany theatrical performances.

cavea — the seating area in a Greek theater.

chous, choes — a small wine-pitcher given to young children as part of the annual festival of the Anthesteria.

dēmos — the Athenian citizenry, conceived as a political body.

dexiōsis — a gesture frequently carved on Attic grave reliefs showing the deceased and a survivor shaking right hands.

echthros, echthroi — an enemy.

eisagōgē — the "leading-in" or introduction of a bride into her new home.

ekdosis — the "giving away" of the bride at a Greek wedding, a generic term for the process by which she leaves her natal home and enters the *oikos* (s.v.) of her new husband.

ekkuklēma — a "roll-out machine" used to expose interior scenes in the ancient Greek theater.

ekphora — the formal term for bearing a corpse to its place of burial.

enguē — an ancient "pledge" of marriage, arranged between *kurioi*, comparable to a modern betrothal.

epaulia — part of the Athenian wedding ceremony, during which gifts are given to the new bride.

epidikasia — a legal procedure that awarded an *epiklēros* (s.v.) as wife to the closest surviving male relative of her dead father.

epiklēros — literally "upon the inheritance," a term used for a brotherless daughter whose father has died, the nominal inheritor of her father's estate.

epinetron, epinetra — a curved ceramic thigh-guard (often decorated), used by women when sewing and weaving.

epitaphios [logos] — a public funeral oration delivered annually in Athens on the occasion of the state burial provided for Athenians who had died in battle that year.

exagōgē — the "leading out" of a bride from her father's home on the way to her new dwelling with her husband.

ex machina — "from the machine," used of divine appearances from on high in the Greek theater.

exodos — the final departure of the Chorus from the theater at the end of a Greek tragedy.

gamēlia — an introduction into the phratry after a wedding.

gamos — literally a "pairing," used for the Greek wedding as well as for its consummation; more generally, "sexual union."

goos, gooi — wailing cries, usually made by women over the dead.

himation — an outer garment of woven cloth.

hubris — violent overreaching, ranging from physical assault and rape to blaspheming the gods.

humenaios, humenaioi — a wedding hymn.

hydria, hydriai — a three-handled ceramic vessel for carrying and pouring water and other liquids.

katachusmata — part of the Athenian wedding ceremony where the bride is welcomed into her new home with a pouring of fruits and nuts over her.

kēdos (and cognates) — a word-group that refers both to "relations by marriage" and "funeral rites."

klinē — a couch, bed, or bier.

kōkutos, kōkutoi — a cry of grief over the dead.

kommos — in Greek tragedy, a shared lyric section between dramatic character(s) and Chorus.

krater — a large ceramic bowl for mixing wine and water.

kurios, kurioi — in Athens, a legal guardian (always male).

kylix — a wide ceramic drinking cup, frequently used for wine.

lebēs — a general term for a vessel, either ceramic or metal; occasionally used for a bathtub.

lebēs gamikos, lebētes gamikoi — a double-handled ceramic vase (usually with pedestal) associated with weddings.

lēkythos, lēkythoi — a single-handled ceramic vessel used for holding oil and perfume.

logos — speech, language; generally, the idea of [Greek] culture.

loutrophoros, loutrophoroi — a tall ceramic vase used for carrying bath water, linked closely to weddings and funerals.

makarismos — a formal greeting (from *makarios*, "blessed") both to newlyweds at their wedding and to the dead at their funeral.

numpheutria — the woman who assists a bride on her wedding day.

oikos — the Greek household, including extended family, slaves, dwelling place, and property.

oinochoe — a ceramic vessel used for pouring wine.

opisthodomos — a "back room" occasionally found at the west end of a Greek temple.

parodos, parodoi — the "side roads" into the ancient Greek theater, leading alongside the *analēmma* (s.v.) into the orchestra.

parthenos — an unmarried Greek female.

patrios nomos — the Athenian "ancestral custom," involving the state-sponsored burial of Athenians who had fallen in battle (s.v. *epitaphios logos*).

peplos — a woman's dress, usually fastened with a pin or brooch.

perideipnon — a funeral banquet.

philos, philoi — friend, loved one (applied particularly to blood relations).

polis — the Greek city, understood as a political, social, and cultural unit.

proteleia — the "preliminary sacrifice" before the *ekdosis* (s.v.) of a Greek wedding.

prothesis — the formal laying-out of a corpse before burial, during which time the body is washed, dressed, and lamented.

psychopompos — "escorter of souls," an epithet used of the god Hermes when he leads the newly deceased to Hades.

pyxis, pyxides — a small ceramic vessel with lid, used for holding jewelry or cosmetics.

skēnē — the backdrop to the playing area of a Greek theatre (formed by the back wall of the stage building), usually marked by a single entrance indicating a house, palace, cave, or other off-stage location.

stēlē, stēlai — a stone grave-marker, frequently carved with an epitaph.

stephanos — a crown or coronal worn by a bride and groom at their wedding and also by the dead as part of their funeral attire.

stratēgos, stratēgoi — an elected Athenian military leader.

sunoikein — keeping and sharing an *oikos* (s.v.), used for a married couple making their *oikos* together.

telos — "end," "goal," "fulfillment," but also a generic word for "ritual" or "rite."

thalamos — the bedchamber in a Greek house.

theologeion — the roof of stage building, above the *skēnē* (s.v.), upon which divine characters frequently appear in Greek tragedy.

thrēnos — a ritual dirge for the dead.

XEK — abbreviation for χεὶρ ἐπὶ καρπῶι, meaning "hand on the wrist," the gesture with which a groom leads his bride to their new home.

xenia — the "guest-host" relationship in ancient Greece, binding males (and their *oikoi*, s.v.) to mutual respect and assistance.

xenos — a foreigner, guest, or host; occasionally used (in the feminine form, *xenē*) for a wife in her husband's home.

xunoikein — see *sunoikein*.

BIBLIOGRAPHY

ABV, abbr. for Beazley 1956.

Add², abbr. for Carpenter 1989

Ahl, Frederick. 1984. "The Art of Safe Criticism." *AJP* 105:174–208.

Alexiou, Margaret. 1974. *The Ritual Lament in the Greek Tradition* (Cambridge).

Arrowsmith, William, tr. 1974. *Euripides: "Alcestis"* (New York).

Arthur, Marylin B. 1977. "Politics and Pomegranates: An Interpretation of the Homeric Hymn to Demeter." *Arethusa* 10:7–47.

ARV,² abbr. for Beazley 1963

Austin, C. 1968. *Nova Fragmenta Euripidea* (Berlin).

Bacon, Helen. 1982. "Aeschylus", in Luce, ed., 99–155.

Bain, David. 1977. *Actors and Audience* (Oxford).

Barlow, Shirley A., tr. and comm. 1986. *Euripides, "Trojan Women"* (Warminster).

Barrett, W. S., ed. 1964. *Euripides, "Hippolytus"* (Oxford).

Bataille, Georges. 1962. *Death and Sensuality*. Tr. M. Dalwood (New York 1977).

Bayfield, M. A., ed. 1902. *The "Antigone" of Sophokles*. Repr. (London 1960).

Beazley, John Davidson. 1932. "Battle-*Loutrophoros*." *MusJ* 23:4–22.

———. 1956. *Attic Black-Figure Vase-Painters* (Oxford).

———. 1963. *Attic Red-Figure Vase-Painters*. 2nd ed. (Oxford).

———. 1971. *Paralipomena*. 2nd ed. (Oxford).

Bérard, Claude et al., eds. 1984. *La Cité des images* (Paris).

Betts, J. H., J. T. Hooker, and J. R. Green, eds. 1986. *Studies in Honour of T.B.L. Webster* I (Bristol).

Bichl, Werner. 1989. *Euripides, "Troades"* (Heidelberg).

Bloch, Maurice. 1982. "Death, Women, and Power," in *Death and the Regeneration of Life*, ed. M. Bloch and J. Parry (Cambridge), 211–30.

Blundell, Mary Whitlock. 1989. *Helping Friends and Harming Enemies: A Study in Sophocles and Greek Ethics* (Cambridge).

Boardman, John. 1952. "Pottery from Eretria." *BSA* 47:1–48.

———. 1958–59. "Old Smyrna: The Attic Pottery." *BSA* 53–54:158–62.

———. 1988. "Sex Differentiation in Grave Vases." *AION*(arch) 10:171–79.

Boedeker, Deborah. 1991. "Euripides' *Medea* and the Vanity of ΛΟΓΟΙ." *CP* 86:95–112.

Bond, Godfrey W., ed. 1981. *Euripides, "Heracles"* (Oxford).

Bongie, Elizabeth Bryson. 1977. "Heroic Elements in *Medea* of Euripides." *TAPA* 107:27–56.

Borghini, Alberto. 1986. "Consacrazione alla Morte e Ritualità Matrimoniale." *SCO* 36:113–16.

Bowra, C. M. 1944. *Sophoclean Tragedy* (Oxford).

Bremmer, Jan N. 1983. *The Early Greek Concept of the Soul* (Princeton).

Brindesi, F. 1961. *La Famiglia Attica: Il matrimonio e l'adozione* (Florence).

Broadbent, Molly. 1968. *Studies in Greek Genealogy* (Leiden).

Broadhead, H. D., ed. 1960. *The "Persae" of Aeschylus* (Cambridge).

Brooklyn, Jerrie Pine. 1981. "Attic Black-Figure Funerary Plaques." Dissertation, University of Iowa.

Brown, Andrew, tr. and comm. 1987. *Sophocles, "Antigone"* (Warminster).

Brown, Sylvia G. 1977. "A Contextual Analysis of Tragic Meter," in *Ancient and Modern: Essays in Honor of Gerald F. Else*, ed. J. H. D'Arms and J. W. Eadie (Ann Arbor), 45–77.

Brueckner, Alfred. 1907. "Athenische Hochzeitsgeschenke." *MDAI(A)* 32:79–122.

Bruit Zaidman, Louise, and Pauline Schmitt Pantel. 1992. *Religion in the Ancient Greek City*. Tr. P. Cartledge (Cambridge; orig. *La Religion grecque*, Paris 1989).

Burian, Peter. 1985. "*Logos* and *Pathos*: The Politics of the *Suppliant Women*," in *New Directions in Euripidean Criticism*, ed. P. Burian (Durham), 129–55.

Burke, Kenneth. 1969. *A Grammar of Motives* (Berkeley).

Burkert, Walter. 1966. "Greek Tragedy and Sacrificial Ritual." *GRBS* 7:87–121.

———. 1972. *Homo Necans* (Berlin). Tr. P. Bing (Berkeley 1983).

———. 1977. *Griechische Religion der archaischen und klassischen Epoche* (Stuttgart). Tr. J. Raffan (Oxford 1985).

———. 1987. *Ancient Mystery Cults* (Cambridge, Mass.).

Burnett, Anne Pippin. 1965. "The Virtues of Admetus." *CP* 60:240–55.

———. 1971. *Catastrophe Survived* (Oxford).

———. 1973. "*Medea* and the Tragedy of Revenge." *CP* 68:1–24.

———. 1983. *Three Archaic Poets* (London).

Buxton, R.G.A. 1984. *Sophocles. G&R* New Surveys in the Classics 16 (Oxford).

———. 1987. "Le Voile et le silence dans *Alceste*." *CGita* 3:167–78.

Calder, William M., III. 1968. "Sophokles' Political Tragedy, *Antigone*." *GRBS* 9:389–407.

Cameron, Averil, and Amélie Kuhrt, ed. 1983. *Images of Women in Antiquity* (Canberra).

Campbell, David A., ed. 1982, 1988. *Greek Lyric* I and II (Cambridge, Mass.).

Cantarella, Eva. 1987. *Pandora's Daughters*. Tr. M. B. Fant (Baltimore).

Carne-Ross, D. S. 1979. *Instaurations* (Berkeley).

Carpenter, Thomas H. 1989. *Beazley Addenda*. 2nd. ed. (Oxford).

Carson, Anne. 1982. "Wedding at Noon in Pindar's *Ninth Pythian*." *GRBS* 23:121–28.

———. 1986. *Eros the Bittersweet* (Princeton).

———. 1990. "Putting Her in Her Place," in Halperin et al., 135–69.

Carter, L. B. 1986. *The Quiet Athenian* (Oxford).

Casevitz, Michel. 1985. *Le Vocabulaire de la colonisation en grec ancien* (Paris).

Cerri, Giovanni. 1982. "Ideologia funeraria nell'*Antigone* di Sofocle," in *La Mort, les morts dans les sociétés anciennes*, ed. G. Gnoli and J-P. Vernant (Cambridge), 121–31.

Chomsky, Noam. 1989. *Necessary Illusions: Thought Control in Democratic Societies* (Boston).

Clairmont, Christopher W. 1983. *Patrios Nomos*. Vol I, British Archaeological Reports 161 (Oxford).

Clark, Gillian. 1989. *Women in the Ancient World, G&R* New Surveys in the Classics 21 (Oxford).

Clay, Jenny Strauss. 1989. *The Politics of Olympus: Form and Meaning in the Major Homeric Hymns* (Princeton).

Cohen, David. 1989. "Seclusion, Separation, and the Status of Women in Classical Athens." *G&R* 36:3–15.

———. 1992. "Sex, Gender, and Sexuality in Ancient Greece." *CP* 87:145–60.

Cole, Susan Guettel. 1984. "The Social Function of Rituals of Maturation: The Koureion and the Arkteia." *ZPE* 55:233–44.

Collard, Christopher. 1972. "The Funeral Oration in Euripides' *Supplices.*" *BICS* 19:39–53.

———, ed. 1975. *Euripides*, "Supplices." 2 vols. (Groningen).

———. 1975a. "Formal Debates in Euripides' Drama." *G&R* 22:58–71.

Collignon, Max. 1904. "Matrimonium: Cérémonies du mariage," in *Dictionnaire des antiquités grecques et romaines*, III, ed. Daremberg-Saglio-Pottier (Paris), 1647–54.

Conacher, D. J. 1956. "Religious and Ethical Attitudes in Euripides' *Suppliants.*" *TAPA* 87:8–26.

———. 1967. *Euripidean Drama* (Toronto).

———, tr. and comm. 1988. *Euripides*, "Alcestis" (Warminster).

Congdon, Leonore O. Keene. 1981. *Caryatid Mirrors of Ancient Greece* (Mainz am Rhein).

Connor, W. Robert. 1971. *The New Politicians of Fifth-Century Athens* (Princeton).

———. 1984. *Thucydides* (Princeton).

Conze, Alexander C.L. 1893–1922. *Die attischen Grabreliefs*. 4 vols. (Berlin).

Cook, Arthur Bernard. 1940. *Zeus: A Study in Ancient Religion*. Vol. 3. (Cambridge).

Corpus Vasorum Antiquorum (*CVA*)—pictures and descriptions of all decorated Greek vases, indexed by museum/city.

Cox, Cheryl A.M. 1983. "The Social and Political Ramifications of Athenian Marriages." Dissertation, Duke University.

———. 1992. "On Roger Just's *Women in Athenian Law and Life*." *AHB* 6:187–96.

Craik, Elizabeth M. 1984. "Marriage in Ancient Greece," in *Marriage and Property*, ed. E. M. Craik (Aberdeen), 6–29.

Cropp, M., E. Fantham, and S. E. Scully, eds. 1986. *Greek Tragedy and Its Legacy: Essays Presented to D. J. Conacher* (Calgary).

Cunningham, Maurice. 1954. "Medea ΑΠΟ ΜΗΧΑΝΗΣ." *CP* 49:151–60.

Cunningham, M. L. 1984. "Aeschylus, *Agamemnon* 231–47." *BICS* 31:9–12.

Dale, A. M., ed. 1954. *Euripides, "Alcestis"* (Oxford).

———, ed. 1967. *Euripides, "Helen"* (Oxford).

———. 1969. *Collected Papers* (Cambridge).

Danforth, Loring M., and A. Tsiaras. 1982. *The Death Rituals of Rural Greece* (Princeton).

Davies, John K. 1971. *Athenian Propertied Families* (Oxford).

———. 1977–78. "Athenian Citizenship." *CJ* 73:105–21.

Dawe, R. D., ed. 1975 and 1979. *Sophocles Tragoediae*. 2 vols. (Leipzig).

Denniston, John Dewar. 1934. *The Greek Particles* (Oxford).

Denniston, John Dewar, and Denys Page, eds. 1957. *Aeschylus, "Agamemnon"*. Repr. (Oxford 1972).

Detienne, Marcel. 1972. *Les Jardins d'Adonis* (Paris).

Deubner, Ludwig. 1900. "ΕΠΑΥΛΙΑ." *JDAI* 15:144–54.

———. 1932. *Attische Feste* (Berlin).

De Wet, B. X. 1983. "An Evaluation of the *Trachiniae* of Sophokles." *Dioniso* 54:213–26.

Di Benedetto, Vincenzo. 1971. *Euripide: Teatro e societá* (Torino).

Diggle, J., ed. 1970. *Euripides, "Phaethon"* (Cambridge).

———, ed. 1984 and 1981. *Euripidis Fabulae* I and II. Repr. with corrections (Oxford 1989, 1986).

Dodds, E. R., ed. 1959. *Plato, "Gorgias"* (Oxford).

———. 1960. "Morals and Politics in the *Oresteia*." *PCPhS* 6:19–31.

Douglas, Mary. 1966. *Purity and Danger*. Repr. (London 1984).

Dover, K. J., ed. 1968. *Aristophanes, "Clouds"* (Oxford).

———. 1974. *Greek Popular Morality in the Time of Plato and Aristotle* (Berkeley).

———. 1987. *Greek and the Greeks: Collected Papers* (Oxford).

Dowden, Ken. 1989. *Death and the Maiden* (London).

DuBois, Page. 1979. "On Horse/Men, Amazons, and Endogamy." *Arethusa* 12:35–49.

———. 1988. *Sowing the Body* (Chicago).

Durkheim, Emile. 1925. *Les Formes élémentaires de la vie religieuse*. 2nd ed. (Paris).

Easterling, P. E. 1977. "The Infanticide in Euripides' *Medea*." *YCS* 25:177–91.

———. 1981. "The End of the *Trachiniae*." *ICS* 6:56–74.

———, ed. 1982. *Sophocles, "Trachiniae"* (Cambridge).

———. 1988. "Tragedy and Ritual." *ΜΗΤΙΣ* 3:87–109.

Ehnmark, Erland. 1948. "Some Remarks on the Idea of Immortality in Greek Religion." *Eranos* 46:1–21.

Ehrenberg, Victor. 1951. *The People of Aristophanes*. 2nd ed. (Oxford).

———. 1954. *Sophocles and Pericles* (Oxford).

Elliott, Alan, ed. 1969. *Euripides, "Medea"* (Oxford).

Else, Gerald F. 1957. *Aristotle's Poetics: The Argument* (Cambridge, Mass.)

———. 1976. *The Madness of Antigone* (Heidelberg).

Erdmann, Walter. 1934. *Die Ehe im alten Griechenland* (Munich).

Euben, J. Peter, ed. 1986. *Greek Tragedy and Political Theory* (Berkeley).

———. 1990. *The Tragedy of Political Theory* (Princeton).

Ferguson, W. S. 1948. "Demetrius Poliorcetes and the Hellenic League." *Hesperia* 17:112–36.

Finley, John H., Jr. 1966. "Politics and Early Tragedy." *HSCP* 71:1–13.

Fitton, J. W. 1961. "The *Suppliant Women* and the *Herakleidai* of Euripides." *Hermes* 89:430–61.

Flacelière, Robert. 1965. *Daily Life in Greece at the Time of Pericles.* Tr. P. Green (New York).

Foley, Helene P. 1981. "The Conception of Women in Athenian Drama," in *Reflections of Women in Antiquity,* ed. H. Foley, (New York), 127–68.

———. 1982. "The 'Female Intruder' Reconsidered." *CP* 77:1–21.

———. 1982a. "Marriage and Sacrifice in Euripides' *Iphigenia in Aulis.*" *Arethusa* 15:159–80.

———. 1985. *Ritual Irony: Poetry and Sacrifice in Euripides* (Ithaca).

———. 1989. "Medea's Divided Self." *CA* 8:61–85.

———. 1989a. "The Politics of Tragic Lamentation." *APA Abstracts* 142.

———. 1992. "*Anodos* Drama: Euripides' *Alcestis* and *Helen*," in Hexter and Selden, eds., 133–60.

———, ed. 1994. *The Homeric "Hymn to Demeter"* (Princeton).

Foxhall, Lin. 1989. "Household, Gender and Property in Classical Athens." *CQ* 39:22–44.

Fraenkel, Eduard, ed. 1950. *Aeschylus, "Agamemnon."* 3 vols. (Oxford).

Frisk, Hjalmar. 1960–72. *Griechisches etymologisches Wörterbuch* (Heidelberg).

Froning, H. 1984. "Hochzeit und Ehe," in *Griechischen Vasen,* ed. B. Korzus (Münster), 124–33.

Fuqua, Charles. 1980. "Heroism, Heracles, and the *Trachiniae.*" *Traditio* 36:1–81.

Gagarin, Michael. 1976. *Aeschylean Drama* (Berkeley).

Galinsky, G. Karl. 1972. *The Herakles Theme* (Oxford).

Gamble, R. B. 1970. "Euripides' *Suppliant Women*: Decision and Ambivalence." *Hermes* 98:385–105.

Garland, Robert. 1985. *The Greek Way of Death* (Ithaca).

———. 1990. *The Greek Way of Life* (Ithaca).

Garner, Richard. 1987. *Law and Society in Classical Athens* (London).

Garvie, A. F. 1969. *Aeschylus' "Supplices": Play and Trilogy* (Cambridge).

———, ed. 1986. *Aeschylus, "Choephori"* (Oxford).

Gay, Peter. 1988. *Freud: A Life for Our Time* (New York).

Gellie, G. H. 1972. *Sophocles: A Reading* (Melbourne).

Gentili, Bruno. 1988. *Poetry and Its Public in Ancient Greece.* Tr. A. T. Cole (Baltimore).

Gérin, Dominique. 1974. *L'Oikos dans la tragédie: "Alceste" et "Médée"* (Paris).

Gernet, Louis. 1968. *Anthropologie de la Grèce antique* (Paris).

Ginouvès, René. 1962. *Balaneutikè: Recherches sur le bain dans l'antiquité grecque* (Paris).

226 BIBLIOGRAPHY

Girard, René. 1972. *La Violence et le sacré*. Tr. P. Gregory (Baltimore 1977).

Goheen, Robert F. 1951. *The Imagery of Sophocles' "Antigone"* (Princeton).

Goldhill, Simon. 1984. *Language, Sexuality, Narrative: The "Oresteia"* (Cambridge).

———. 1986. *Reading Greek Tragedy* (Cambridge).

———. 1987. "The Great Dionysia and Civic Ideology." *JHS* 107:58–76 (repr. with changes in Winkler and Zeitlin 1990, 97–129).

———. 1992. *The Oresteia* (Cambridge).

Gomme, A. W. 1945–81. *A Historical Commentary on Thucydides*. 5 vols. (Oxford).

Gordon, R. L., ed. 1977. *Myth, Religion and Society* (Cambridge).

Gould, John. 1973. "*HIKETEIA*." *JHS* 93:74–103.

———. 1980. "Law, Custom and Myth: Aspects of the Social Position of Women in Classical Athens." *JHS* 100:38–59.

Gregory, Justina. 1991. *Euripides and the Instruction of the Athenians* (Ann Arbor).

Grieve, Lucia Catherine Graeme. 1896. *Death and Burial in Attic Tragedy* (New York).

Griffith, R. D. 1989. "In Praise of the Bride." *TAPA* 119:55–61.

Grube, G.M.A. 1941. *The Drama of Euripides*. Repr. (London 1961).

Hague, Rebecca. 1983. "Ancient Greek Wedding Songs." *Journal of Folklore Research* 20:131–43.

———. 1988. "Marriage Athenian Style." *Archaeology* (May/June): 32–36.

———. (forthcoming). *Hymenaios: The Ancient Greek Wedding and Its Songs*.

Hague, Rebecca. *See also* Huddleston; Oakley

Halleran, Michael R. 1991. "*Gamos* and Destruction in Euripides' *Hippolytus*." *TAPA* 121:109–21.

Halliburton, David. 1988. "Concealing Revealing: A Perspective on Greek Tragedy," in *Post-Structuralist Classics*, ed. A. Benjamin (London), 245–67.

Halperin, David M. 1989. *One Hundred Years of Homosexuality and Other Essays on Greek Love* (New York).

Halperin, David M., J. J. Winkler, and F. I. Zeitlin, eds. 1990. *Before Sexuality* (Princeton).

Hanson, Victor Davis. 1983. *Warfare and Agriculture in Classical Greece* (Pisa).

Harder, Annette, ed. 1985. *Euripides' "Kresphontes" and "Archelaos"* (Leiden).

Harl-Schaller, Friederike. 1972–75. "Zur Entstehung und Bedeutung des attischen *Lebes gamikos*." *JÖAI* 50:151–70.

Harrison, A.R.W. 1968. *The Law of Athens*. Vol. 1 (Oxford).

Harrison, Evelyn B. 1977. "Alkamenes' Sculptures for the Hephaisteion." *AJA* 81:411–26.

Haspels, C.H. Emilie. 1930. "Deux fragments d'une coupe d'Euphronios." *BCH* 54:422–51 and pls. XX–XXIV.

Havelock, C. M. 1981. "Mourners on Greek Vases," in *The Greek Vase*, ed. S. Hyatt (Latham, NY), 108–15.

Havelock, Eric A. 1968. "Watching the *Trojan Women*," in E. Segal 1968, 115–27.

Hayley, Henry Wadsworth, ed. 1898. *The "Alcestis" of Euripides* (Boston).

Hedrick, Charles W. 1987. "Phratry Membership and Athenian Citizenship." *APA Abstracts*, p. 136.

Henderson, Jeffrey, ed. 1987. *Aristophanes, "Lysistrata"* (Oxford).

Herman, Gabriel. 1987. *Ritualised Friendship and the Greek City* (Cambridge).

Hertz, Robert. 1907. *Death and the Right Hand*. Tr. R. and C. Needham (Glencoe, Ill. 1960).

Hexter, Ralph, and Daniel Selden, eds. 1992. *Innovations of Antiquity* (London).

Hignett, Charles. 1952. *A History of the Athenian Constitution to the End of the Fifth Century B.C.* Repr. (Oxford 1958).

Hoey, Thomas F. 1977. "Ambiguity in the Exodos of Sophocles' *Trachiniae*." *Arethusa* 10:269–94.

Huddleston, Rebecca Ann. 1980. "The Wedding Songs of Ancient Greece." Dissertation, Johns Hopkins (*see also* Hague; Oakley).

Humphreys, S. C. 1974. "The Nothoi of Kynosarges." *JHS* 94:88–95.

———. 1983. *The Family, Women and Death* (London).

———. 1986. "Kinship Patterns in the Athenian Courts." *GRBS* 27:57–91.

Hutchinson, G. O., ed. 1985. *Aeschylus "Septem contra Thebas"* (Oxford).

Immerwahr, Henry R. 1973. "Pathology of Power and the Speeches of Thucydides," in *The Speeches in Thucydides*, ed. P. A. Stadter (Chapel Hill), 16–31.

Isager, Signe. 1981. "The Marriage Pattern in Classical Athens: Men and Women in Isaios." *C&M* 33:81–96.

Jacoby, F. 1944. "*Patrios Nomos*." *JHS* 64:37–66.

Jebb, Richard C., ed. 1883–96. *Sophocles: The Plays and Fragments* 7 vols. (Cambridge, repr. Amsterdam 1962)

———, ed. 1900. *Sophocles*. Vol. 3, *The Antigone*. 3rd ed. (Cambridge).

Jenkins, Ian. 1983. "Is There Life after Marriage?" *BICS* 30:137–46.

Johansen, H. Friis, and Edward W. Whittle, eds. 1980. *Aeschylus, "The Suppliants"* (Copenhagen).

Johansen, Knud Friis. 1951. *The Attic Grave-Reliefs of the Classical Period* (Copenhagen).

———. 1967. *The "Iliad" in Early Greek Art* (Copenhagen).

Jones, D. M. 1948. "Euripides' *Alcestis*." *CR* 62:50–55.

Jones, John. 1962. *On Aristotle and Greek Tragedy* (Oxford).

Jones, John W. 1956. *The Law and Legal Theory of the Greeks* (Oxford).

Jong, Irene J.F. de. 1991. *Narrative in Drama: The Art of the Euripidean Messenger Speech* (Leiden).

Jouan, François. 1983. "Réflexions sur le rôle du protagoniste tragique," in

Théâtre et spectacles dans l'antiquité, Actes du Colloque de Strasbourg, 5–7 Nov. 1981 (Leiden), 63–80.

Just, Roger. 1989. *Women in Athenian Law and Life* (London).

Kahil, Lilly. 1983. "Mythological Repertoire of Brauron," in *Ancient Greek Art and Iconography*, ed. W. Moon (Madison), 231–44.

Kaimio, Maarit. 1988. *Physical Contact in Greek Tragedy* (Helsinki).

Kamerbeek, J. C. 1963–84. *The Plays of Sophocles*. 7 vols, 2nd ed. (Leiden), esp. Vol. 2, *The Trachiniae* (1963) and Vol. 3, *The Antigone* (1978).

Kannicht, Richard, ed. 1969. *Euripides*, "Helena." 2 vols. (Heidelberg).

Karnezis, John E. 1972. Ἡ ΕΠΙΚΛΗΡΟΣ (Athens).

Kells, J. H., ed. 1973. *Sophocles*, "Electra" (Cambridge).

Kenner, Hedwig. 1935. "Das Luterion in Kult." *JÖAI* 29:109–54.

Kirkwood, G. M. 1958. *A Study of Sophoclean Drama* (Ithaca).

Kitto, H.D.F. 1959. *Form and Meaning in Drama* (London).

———. 1961. *Greek Tragedy*. 3rd ed. (London).

———. 1966. *Poiesis*. Sather Vol. 36 (Berkeley).

Kitzinger, M. R. 1986. (Rev. of Goldhill 1984) *AJP* 107:115–18.

Knox, Bernard M.W. 1952. "The *Hippolytus* of Euripides." *YCS* 13:3–31 (= 1979, 205–30).

———. 1964. *The Heroic Temper*. Sather Vol. 35 (Berkeley).

———. 1968. [Rev. of Müller 1967] *Gnomon* 40:747–60 (= 1979, 165–82).

———. 1970. "Euripidean Comedy" in *The Rarer Action*, ed. A. Cheuse and R. Koffler (New Brunswick, N.J.), 78–96 (= 1979, 250–74).

———. 1972. "Aeschylus and the Third Actor." *AJP* 93:104–24 (= 1979, 39–55).

———. 1977. "The *Medea* of Euripides." *YCS* 25:193–225 (= 1979, 295–322).

———. 1979. *Word and Action: Essays on the Ancient Theater* (Baltimore).

———. 1983. "Sophocles and the *Polis*," in *Sophocle*. Entretiens Fondation Hardt 29 (Geneva), 1–37.

Kokula, Gerit. 1974. *Marmorlutrophoren*. Dissertation, Ludwig-Maximilians-Universität zu München (Köln). Repr. *MDAI(A)* Beiheft 10 (Berlin 1984).

Körte, A., and A. Thierfelder, eds. 1957, 1959. *Menandri quae supersunt*. Vol. 1 and 2, 3rd ed. corrected (Leipzig).

Kovacs, David. 1986. "On Medea's Great Monologue." *CQ* 36:343–52.

———. 1987. "The Way of a God with a Maid in Aeschylus' *Agamemnon*." *CP* 82:326–34.

———. 1993. "Zeus in Euripides' *Medea*." *AJP* 114:45–70.

Kraus, Christina S. 1991. "Λόγος μέν ἐστ᾿ ἀρχαῖος: Stories and Story-Telling in Sophocles' *Trachiniae*." *TAPA* 121:75–98.

Kurke, Leslie. 1991. *The Traffic in Praise: Pindar and the Poetics of Social Economy* (Ithaca).

Kurtz, Donna C. 1975. *Athenian White Lekythoi* (Oxford).

———. 1984. "Vases for the Dead," in *Ancient Greek and Related Pottery*, ed. H.A.G. Brijder. Allard Pierson Vol. 5 (Amsterdam), 314–28.

———. 1988. "Mistress and Maid." *AION*(arch) 10:141–49.

Kurtz, Donna C., and John Boardman. 1971. *Greek Burial Customs* (Ithaca).

Lacey, W. K. 1968. *The Family in Classical Greece* (Ithaca).

Lambin, Gérard. 1986. "Trois refrains nuptiaux." *AC* 55:66–85.

Lattimore, Richmond. 1962. *Themes in Greek and Latin Epitaphs* (Urbana, Ill.).

———. 1964. *Story Patterns in Greek Tragedy* (Ann Arbor).

Lawler, Lillian B. 1964. *The Dance of the Ancient Greek Theatre* (Iowa City).

Lebeck, Anne. 1971. *The Oresteia* (Cambridge, Mass.).

Leduc, Claudine. 1992. "Marriage in Ancient Greece," in Pantel, ed. 235–94.

Lee, K. H., ed. 1976. *Euripides, "Troades"* (London).

Lefkowitz, Mary R. 1981. *Heroines and Hysterics* (London).

Leinieks, Valdis. 1982. *The Plays of Sophokles* (Amsterdam).

Lesky, Albin. 1967. *Greek Tragedy.* 2nd. ed., tr. H. A. Frankfort (New York).

———. 1972. *Greek Tragic Poets.* Tr. M. Dillon (New Haven 1983).

Levin, Richard. 1979. *New Readings vs. Old Plays* (Chicago).

———. 1988. "Feminist Thematics and Shakespearean Tragedy." *PMLA* 103:125–38.

LIMC. 1981–. abbr. for *Lexicon Iconographicum Mythologiae Classicae* (Zurich and Munich).

Lissarrague, François. 1992. "Figures of Women," in Pantel, ed., 139–229.

Lloyd, G.E.R. 1990. *Demystifying Mentalities* (Cambridge).

Lloyd-Jones, H. 1971. "Addendum" in *Aeschylus.* Vol. II, tr. H. Weir Smyth and H. Lloyd-Jones (Cambridge, Mass.).

———. 1980. "Euripides, *Medea* 1056–80." *WüJbb* 6a:51–59.

Lloyd-Jones, H., and N. G. Wilson. 1990. *Sophoclea* (Oxford).

———, eds. 1990a. *Sophoclis Fabulae* (Oxford).

Lobel, Edgar, and Denys Page, eds. 1955. *Poetarum Lesbiorum Fragmenta* (Oxford).

Longo, Oddone. 1968. *Commento linguistico alle "Trachinie" di Sofocle* (Padova).

Loraux, Nicole. 1981. *Les Enfants d'Athéna* (Paris).

———. 1981a. "Le Lit, la guerre." *L'Homme* 21:37–67.

———. 1986. *The Invention of Athens.* Tr. A. Sheridan (Cambridge, Mass.).

———. 1987. *Tragic Ways of Killing a Woman.* Tr. A. Forster (Cambridge, Mass.).

Lorimer, H. L. 1931. "Two Notes on the *Agamemnon*." *CR* 45:211–12.

Luce, T. J., ed. 1983. *Ancient Writers, Greece and Rome.* Vol. I (New York).

Lullies, Reinhard, and Max Hirmer. 1960. *Greek Sculpture.* Tr. M. Bullock (London).

MacDowell, Douglas M. 1978. *The Law in Classical Athens* (London).

MacIntyre, Alisdair. 1981. *After Virtue* (Notre Dame).

Magnien, V. 1936. "Le Mariage chez les grecs anciens." *AC* 5:115–38.

Malkin, Irad. 1987. *Religion and Colonization in Ancient Greece* (Leiden).

March, Jennifer R. 1987. *The Creative Poet: Studies on the Treatment of Myths in Greek Poetry. BICS* Supp. 49 (London).

———. 1990 "Euripides the Misogynist?" in Powell 1990, 32–75.

Mason, H. A. 1985. *The Tragic Plane* (Oxford).

Mason, P. G. 1959. "Kassandra." *JHS* 79:80–93.

McCall, Marsh. 1972. "The *Trachiniae*: Structure, Focus, and Heracles." *AJP* 93:142–63.

McClees, Helen. 1941. *The Daily Life of the Greeks and the Romans as Illustrated in the Classical Collections.* 2nd ed. (Metropolitan Museum of Art, New York).

McDermott, Emily A. 1989. *Euripides' "Medea," the Incarnation of Disorder* (University Park, Pa.).

McDonald, Marianne. 1978. *Terms for Happiness in Euripides.* Hypomnemata 54 (Göttingen).

McManus, Barbara. 1990. "Multicentering: The Case of the Athenian Bride." *Helios* 17:225–35.

Mead, Louise. 1943. "A Study in the *Medea*." *G&R* 12:15–20.

Méautis, Georges. 1957. *Sophocle* (Paris).

Meiggs, Russell. 1972. *The Athenian Empire.* Repr. (Oxford 1982).

Michelini, Ann N. 1982. *Tradition and Dramatic Form in the "Persians" of Aeschylus* (Leiden).

———. 1987. *Euripides and the Tragic Tradition* (Madison).

———. 1989. "Neophron and Euripides' *Medeia* 1056–80." *TAPA* 119:115–35.

Mikalson, Jon D. 1983. *Athenian Popular Religion* (Chapel Hill).

———. 1991. *Honor Thy Gods: Popular Religion in Greek Tragedy* (Chapel Hill).

Miller, M. 1953. "Greek Kinship Terminology." *JHS* 73:46–52.

Minto, Antonio. 1919. "Corteo Nuziale in un Frammento di Tazza Attica." *Ausonia* 9:65–75.

Modrzejewski, Joseph. 1981. "La Structure juridique du mariage grec," in *Scritti in onore di Orsolina Montevecchi*, ed. di Bresciani et al. (Bologna), 231–68 (= *Epistēmonikē Epetērida*, ed. P. D. Dimakis [Athens 1981] 37–71).

Morris, Ian. 1987. *Burial and Ancient Society* (Cambridge).

———. 1989. "Attitudes Toward Death in Archaic Greece." *CA* 8:296–320.

———. 1989a. "Legislation and Lavishness in Ancient Athenian Funerals." *APA Abstracts* 139.

———. 1992. *Death-Ritual and Social Structure in Classical Antiquity* (Cambridge).

Motte, André. 1973. *Prairies et jardins de la Grèce antique* (Brussels).

Müller, Gerhard. 1967. *Sophokles, "Antigone"* (Heidelberg).

Murnaghan, Sheila. 1986. "Antigone 904–920 and the Institution of Marriage." *AJP* 107:192–207.

Murray, Gilbert. 1946. *Euripides and His Age.* 2nd ed. (London).

———. 1946a. *Greek Studies* (Oxford).

Musurillo, Herbert. 1967. *The Light and the Darkness: Studies in the Dramatic Poetry of Sophocles* (Leiden).

———. 1972. "*Alcestis*: The Pageant of Life and Death," in *Studi Classici in Onore di Quintino Cataudella.* Vol. 1 (Catania), 275–88.

Muth, Robert. 1954. " 'Hymenaios' und 'Epithalamion.' " *WS* 67:5–45.

Mylonas, George E., ed. 1951. *Studies Presented to David M. Robinson*. Vol. I (St. Louis).

———. 1961. *Eleusis and the Eleusinian Mysteries* (Princeton).

Nagler, Michael. 1974. *Spontaneity and Tradition: A Study in the Oral Art of Homer* (Berkeley).

Nagy, Gregory. 1979. *The Best of the Achaeans* (Baltimore).

Nauck, A., and B. Snell, eds. 1964. *Tragicorum Graecorum Fragmenta* (Hildesheim).

Neuberg, Matt. 1990. "How Like a Woman: Antigone's 'Inconsistency.'" *CQ* 40:54–76.

Neumann, Gebhard. 1965. *Gesten und Gebärden in der griechischen Kunst* (Berlin).

Nielson, R. M. 1976. "Alcestis: A Paradox in Dying." *Ramus* 5: 92–102.

Nilsson, Martin P. 1960. "Wedding Rites in Ancient Greece," in M. Nilsson, *Opuscula Selecta* Vol. III (Lund), 243–50.

———. 1967. *Geschichte der griechischen Religion*. Vol. I, 3rd. ed. (Munich).

Nussbaum, Martha C. 1986. *The Fragility of Goodness* (Cambridge)

Oakley, John H. 1982. "The *Anakalyptēria*." *AA* 1:113–18.

Oakley, John H., and Rebecca H. Sinos. 1993. *The Wedding in Ancient Athens* (Madison).

Ober, Josiah. 1989. *Mass and Elite in Democratic Athens* (Princeton).

———, and Barry Strauss. 1990. "Drama, Political Rhetoric, and the Discourse of Athenian Democracy," in Winkler and Zeitlin, eds., 237–70.

O'Higgins, Dolores. 1993. "Above Rubics: Admetus' Perfect Wife." *Arethusa* 26:77–97.

Osborne, Robin. 1985. *Demos: The Discovery of Classical Athens* (Cambridge).

Owen, A. S., ed. 1939. *Euripides, "Ion"* (Oxford)

Page, Denys L., ed. 1938. *Euripides, "Medea."* Repr. with corrections (Oxford 1971).

———, ed. 1950. *Greek Literary Papyri*. Vol. 3 (Cambridge, Mass.).

———. 1959. *History and the Homeric "Iliad."* Sathor Vol. 31 (Berkeley).

Paley, F. A., ed. 1857–60. *Euripides*. 3 vols. (London).

Panofsky, Erwin. 1964. *Tomb Sculpture* (New York).

Pantel, Pauline Schmitt, ed. 1992. *A History of Women in the West*. Vol. 1. Tr. A. Goldhammer (Cambridge, Mass.)

Para, abbr. for Beazley 1971.

Parke, H. W. 1977. *Festivals of the Athenians* (Ithaca).

Parker, Robert. 1983. *Miasma* (Oxford).

Parry, Hugh. 1986. "Aphrodite and the Furies in Sophocles' *Trachiniae*," in Cropp et al. 1986, 103–14.

Patterson, Cynthia. 1981. *Pericles' Citizenship Law of 451–50 B.C.* (New York).

———. 1986. "*Hai Attikai*: The Other Athenians." *Helios* 13:49–67.

———. 1990. "Those Athenian Bastards." *CA* 9:40–73.

———. 1991. "Marriage and the Married Woman in Athenian Law," in *Women's History and Ancient History*, ed. S. Pomeroy (Chapel Hill), 48–72.

Pearson, A. C., ed. 1917. *The Fragments of Sophocles*. 3 vols. Repr. (Amsterdam 1963).

Pelling, Christopher, ed. 1990. *Characterization and Individuality in Greek Literature* (Oxford).

Pemberton, E. R. 1976. "The Gods of the East Frieze of the Parthenon." *AJA* 80:113–24 and pl. 17–19.

Peretti, Aurelio. 1956. "La Teoria della Generazione Patrilinea in Eschilo." *PP* 49:241–62.

Pickard-Cambridge, Sir Arthur, rev. T.B.L. Webster. 1962. *Dithyramb, Tragedy and Comedy*. 2nd ed. (Oxford).

———, Rev. J. Gould, and D. M. Lewis. 1968. *The Dramatic Festivals of Athens*. 2nd ed. (Oxford).

Podlecki, Antony J. 1966. "Creon and Herodotus." *TAPA* 97:359–71.

———. 1966a. *The Political Background of Aeschylean Tragedy* (Ann Arbor).

———. 1989. "Another Look at Character in Sophocles," in Sutton 1989, 279–94.

———, ed. 1989a. *Aeschylus, "Eumenides"* (Warminster).

———. 1990. "Could Women Attend the Theatre in Ancient Athens?" *AncW* 21:27–43.

Pohlenz, Max. 1954. *Die Griechische Tragödie*. 2nd ed. (Göttingen).

Pomeroy, Sarah B. 1975. *Goddesses, Whores, Wives, and Slaves: Women in Classical Antiquity* (New York).

———. 1988. "Greek Marriage," in *Civilization of the Ancient Mediterranean: Greece and Rome*, Vol. 3, ed. M. Grant and R. Kitzinger (New York), 1333–42.

Poole, Adrian. 1976. "Total Disaster: Euripides' *Trojan Women*." *Arion* 3:257–87.

———. 1987. *Tragedy: Shakespeare and the Greek Example* (Oxford).

Porter, David H. 1987. *Only Connect: Three Studies in Greek Tragedy* (Lanham, MD).

Powell, Anton, ed. 1990. *Euripides, Women, and Sexuality* (London).

Pucci, Pietro. 1980. *The Violence of Pity in Euripides' "Medea"* (Ithaca).

Rabinowitz, Nancy S. 1989. "Feminism and the Re-Production of Greek Tragedy." *Theatre Studies* 34:11–23.

Raepsaet, Georges. 1971. "Les Motivations de la natalité à Athènes." *AC* 40:80–110.

Reckford, Kenneth. 1968. "Medea's First Exit." *TAPA* 99:329–59.

Redfield, James. 1982. "Notes on the Greek Wedding." *Arethusa* 15:181–201.

Rehm, Rush. 1985. "The *Agōn* and the Audience." Dissertation, Stanford University.

———. 1985a. "Aeschylus and Performance," in *Drama, Sex and Politics*. Themes in Drama 7, ed. J. Redmond (Cambridge), 229–48.

———. 1988. "The Staging of Suppliant Plays." *GRBS* 29:263–307.

———. 1989. "Medea and the Λόγος of the Heroic." *Eranos* 87:97–115.

———. 1992. *Greek Tragic Theatre* (London).

Reilly, Joan. 1989. "Many Brides: 'Mistress and Maid' on Athenian *Lekythoi*." *Hesperia* 58:411–44 and pl. 73–81.

Reinhardt, Karl. 1947. *Sophocles*. 2nd ed., tr. D. and H. Harvey (Oxford 1979).

Richardson, N. J., ed. 1974. *The Homeric Hymn to Demeter* (Oxford).

———. 1985. "Early Greek Views about Life and Death," in *Greek Religion and Society*, ed. P. E. Easterling and J. V. Muir (Cambridge), 50–66.

Richter, Giselda M.A. 1961. *The Archaic Gravestones of Attica* (London).

Rickert, GailAnn. 1987. "Akrasia and Euripides' *Medea*." *HSCP* 91:91–117.

Ridgway, Brunilde Sisimondo. 1981. *Fifth-Century Styles in Greek Sculpture* (Princeton).

Rivier, André. 1972. "En marge d'Alceste et de quelques interprétations récentes." *MH* 29:124–40.

Roberts, Sally Rutherfurd. 1978. *The Attic Pyxis* (Chicago).

Robertson, Martin. 1975. *A History of Greek Art* (Cambridge).

Robinson, David M. 1936. "A New Lebes Gamikos." *AJA* 40:507–19.

Rohde, Erwin. 1925. *Psyche*. 8th ed., tr. W. B. Hillis, repr. (London 1950).

Ronnet, Gilberte. 1969. *Sophocle, poète tragique* (Paris).

Rosaldo, Renato. 1989. *Culture and Truth* (Boston).

Rose, H. J. 1925. "The Bride of Hades." *CP* 20:238–42.

———. 1959. *A Handbook of Greek Mythology* (New York).

Saïd, Suzanne. 1981. "Concorde et civilisation dans les *Euménides*," in *Théâtre et spectacles dans l'antiquité*, Actes du Colloque de Strasbourg, 5–7 Nov. (Leipzig 1983), 97–121.

Sandbach, F. H., ed. 1972. *Menandri reliquiae selectae* (Oxford 1972).

Schaps, David M. 1979. *Economic Rights of Women in Ancient Greece* (Edinburgh).

Schefold, Karl. 1978. *Götter- und Heldensagen der Griechen in der spätarchaischen Kunst* (Munich).

———. 1981. *Die Göttersage in der klassischen und hellenistischen Kunst* (Munich).

Schlesinger, Eilhard. 1966. "Zu Euripides *Medea*." *Hermes* 94:26–53 (= "On Euripides' *Medea*," tr. W. Moskalew, in E. Segal 1968, 70–89, and 1983, 294–310)

Schnapp, A. 1988. "Why Did the Greeks Need Images?" in *Ancient Greek and Related Pottery*, 3rd Symposium, ed. J. Christiansen and T. Melander (Copenhagen), 564–71.

Scodel, Ruth. 1980. *The Trojan Trilogy of Euripides*. Hypomnemata 60 (Göttingen).

———. 1984. *Sophocles* (Boston).

Seaford, Richard. 1984. "The Last Bath of Agamemnon." *CQ* 34:247–54.

———. 1986. "Wedding Ritual and Textual Criticism in Sophocles' *Women of Trachis*." *Hermes* 114:50–59.

———. 1987. "The Tragic Wedding." *JHS* 107:106–30.

———. 1988. "The Eleventh Ode of Bacchylides." *JHS* 108:118–36.

———. 1989. "Funerary Legislation and the *Iliad*." *APA Abstracts* 140.

———. 1990a. "The Structural Problems of Marriage in Euripides," in Powell, ed., 151–76.

———. 1990b. "The Imprisonment of Women in Greek Tragedy." *JHS* 110:76–90

Seale, David. 1982. *Vision and Stagecraft in Sophocles* (London).

Sealey, Raphael. 1990. *Women and Law in Classical Greece* (Chapel Hill).

Séchan, Louis. 1927. *Le Dévouement d'Alceste*. Extrait de la *Revue des cours et conférences* 28 II 1927 (Paris).

Segal, Charles Paul. 1964. "Sophocles' Praise of Man and the Conflicts of the *Antigone*." *Arion* 3, No. 2:46–66.

———. 1971. "The Two Worlds of Euripides' *Helen*." *TAPA* 102:555–614.

———. 1975. "Mariage et sacrifice dans les *Trachiniennes* de Sophocle." *AC* 44:30–53.

———. 1977. "Sophocles' *Trachiniae*." *YCS* 25:99–158.

———. 1981. *Tragedy and Civilization: An Interpretation of Sophocles*. Martin Classical Lectures 26 (Cambridge, Mass.).

———. 1982. *Dionysiac Poetics and Euripides' "Bacchae"* (Princeton).

Segal, Erich, ed. 1968. *Euripides, A Collection of Critical Essays* (Englewood Cliffs, N.J.).

———, ed. 1983. *Oxford Readings in Greek Tragedy* (Oxford).

Seidensticker, Bernd. 1982. *Palintonos Harmonia*. Hypomnemata 72 (Göttingen).

Shapiro, H. A. 1991. "The Iconography of Mourning in Athenian Art." *AJA* 95:629–56.

Shaw, Michael H. 1975. "The Female Intruder: Women in Fifth-Century Drama." *CP* 70:255–66.

Silk, M. S. 1985. "Heracles and Greek Tragedy." *G&R* 32:1–22.

Simon, Erika. 1983. *Festivals of Attica* (Madison).

Sinclair, R. K. 1988. *Democracy and Participation in Athens* (Cambridge).

Sissa, Giulia. 1987. *Le Corps virginal: La Virginité féminine en Grèce ancienne* (Paris) (= *Greek Virginity*, tr. A. Goldhammer [Cambridge, Mass.] 1990).

Slater, Philip. 1968. *The Glory of Hera* (Boston).

Smith, Wesley D. 1960. "The Ironic Structure in *Alcestis*." *Phoenix* 14:127–45.

———. 1966. "Expressive Form in Euripides' *Suppliants*." *HSCP* 71:151–70.

Smyth, H. W. 1900. *Greek Melic Poets* (New York).

Snell, Bruno. 1931. "Sapphos Gedicht ΦΑΙΝΕΤΑΙ ΜΟΙ ΚΗΝΟΣ." *Hermes* 66:71–90.

———. 1960. *The Discovery of the Mind*. Tr. T. Rosenmeyer (New York).

———. 1964. *Scenes from Greek Drama* (Berkeley).

Snodgrass, A. M. 1982. *Narration and Allusion in Archaic Greek Art*. Eleventh J. L. Myres Memorial Lecture (London).

Solmsen, Friedrich. 1975. *Intellectual Experiments of the Greek Enlightenment* (Princeton).

Sommerstein, Alan H., ed. 1989. *Aeschylus, "Eumenides"* (Cambridge).

Sorum, Christina Elliot. 1978. "Monsters and the Family." *GRBS* 19:59–73.

———. 1981–82. "The Family in Sophocles' *Antigone* and *Electra*." *CW* 75:201–11.

Sourvinou, Christiane. 1971. "Aristophanes' *Lysistrata* 641–47." *CQ* 21:339–42.

Sourvinou-Inwood, Christiane. 1981. "To Die and Enter the House of Hades," in *Mirrors of Mortality*, ed. J. Whaley (London), 15–39.

———. 1988. *Studies in Girls' Transitions* (Athens).

———. 1988a. "Le Mythe dans la tragédie, la tragédie à travers le mythe: Sophocle, *Antigone* vv. 944–987," in *Métamorphoses du mythe en Grèce antique*, ed. C. Calame (Geneva), 167–83.

———. 1989. "Assumptions and the Creation of Meaning: Reading Sophocles' *Antigone*." *JHS* 109:134–48.

Sowa, Cora Angier. 1984. *Traditional Themes and the Homeric Hymns* (Chicago).

Spira, Andreas. 1960. *Untersuchungen zum Deus ex machina bei Sophokles und Euripides*. Dissertation, Frankfurt.

Stanford, W. B. 1983. *Greek Tragedy and the Emotions* (London).

Steiner, George. 1984. *Antigones* (Oxford).

Stern, J. P., and M. S. Silk. 1981. *Nietzsche on Tragedy* (Cambridge).

Stinton, T.C.W. 1986. "The Scope and Limits of Allusion in Greek Tragedy," in Cropp et al., 67–102 (= 1990, 454–92).

———. 1990. *Collected Papers on Greek Tragedy* (Oxford).

Strohm, Hans. 1957. *Euripides, Interpretationen zur dramatischen Form*. Zetemata H.15 (Munich).

Struck, Erdmann. 1953. "Der zweimalige Gang der Antigone zur Leiche des Polyneikes." *Gymnasium* 60:327–34.

Sutton, Dana F. 1984. *The Lost Sophocles* (Lanham, Md.).

Sutton, Robert Franklin, Jr. 1981. "The Interaction Between Men and Women Portrayed on Attic Red-Figure Pottery." Dissertation, University of North Carolina.

———. 1989. "On the Classical Athenian Wedding," in Sutton, ed. 1989, 331–59.

———, ed. 1989. *Daidalikon: Studies in Memory of Raymond V. Schoder, S.J.* (Wauconda, Ill.).

Taplin, Oliver. 1977. *The Stagecraft of Aeschylus* (Oxford).

———. 1978. *Greek Tragedy in Action* (Berkeley).

———. 1984. [Rev. of Steiner 1984] *New York Review of Books*, Dec. 6:13–16.

Thimme, Jürgen. 1964. "Die Stele der Hegeso als Zeugnis des attischen Grabkults." *AK* 7:16–29.

Thomas, Rosalind. 1989. *Oral Tradition and Written Record in Classical Athens* (Cambridge).

Thompson, Wesley E. 1967. "The Marriage of First Cousins in Athenian Society." *Phoenix* 21:273–82.

———. 1972. "Athenian Marriage Patterns." *CSCA* 5:211–25.

Thomson, George, ed. 1966. The *"Oresteia"* of Aeschylus. 2 vols. (Prague).

Trendall, Arthur Dale, and T.B.L. Webster. 1971. *Illustrations of Greek Drama* (London).

Turner, Victor. 1969. *The Ritual Process*. Repr. (Ithaca 1977).

———. 1982. *From Ritual to Theater* (New York).

————. 1982a. *Celebration: Studies in Festival and Ritual* (Washington, D.C.).

Tyrrell, Wm. Blake, and Frieda S. Brown. 1991. *Athenian Myths and Institutions* (New York).

van Gennep, Arnold. 1909. *The Rites of Passage*. Tr. M. Vizedom and G. Caffee (London 1960).

Vellacott, Philip. 1975. *Ironic Drama* (Cambridge).

Vermeule, Emily. 1979. *Aspects of Death in Early Greek Art and Poetry*. Sather Vol. 46 (Berkeley).

Vernant, Jean-Pierre. 1973. "Le Mariage en Grèce archaique." *PP* 148–149:51–74 (= *Mythe et société en Grèce ancienne* [Paris 1974], 57–81).

————. 1985. *Mythe et pensée chez les Grecs*. 2nd ed. (Paris).

Vernant, Jean-Pierre, and Pierre Vidal-Naquet. 1988. *Myth and Tragedy in Ancient Greece*. Tr. J. Lloyd (New York).

Verrall, A. W., ed. 1883. *The "Medea" of Euripides*. Repr. (London 1937).

Vickers, Brian. 1973. *Towards Greek Tragedy* (London).

Vidal-Naquet, Pierre. 1977. "Recipes for Greek Adolescence," in Gordon 1977, 163–85.

Voigt, Eva-Maria, ed. 1971. *Sappho et Alcaeus* (Amsterdam).

Von Bothmer, Dietrich. 1985. *The Amasis Painter and His World* (Malibu).

Walsh, George B. 1979. "Public and Private in Three Plays of Euripides." *CP* 74:294–309.

————. 1984. *The Varieties of Enchantment* (Chapel Hill).

Webster, T.B.L. 1967. *The Tragedies of Euripides* (London).

————. 1970. *The Greek Chorus* (London).

————. 1972. *Potter and Patron in Classical Athens* (London).

————. 1974. *An Introduction to Menander* (Manchester).

Weinsanto, Marc. 1983. "L'Evolution du mariage de l'*Iliade* à l'*Odyssée*," in *La Femme dans les sociétés antiques*, ed. E. Lévy (Strasbourg), 45–58.

Wender, Dorothea. 1974. "The Will of the Beast." *Ramus* 3:1–17.

Whitehead, David. 1977. *The Ideology of the Athenian Metic*. Cambridge Philological Society, supp. vol. 4 (Cambridge).

Whitehorne, John E.G. 1986. "The Dead as Spectacle in Euripides' *Bacchae* and *Supplices*." *Hermes* 114:59–72.

Whitman, Cedric H. 1951. *Sophocles, A Study of Heroic Humanism* (Cambridge, Mass.).

————. 1974. *Euripides and the Full Circle of Myth* (Cambridge, Mass.).

Wilamowitz-Moellendorff, Ulrich von. 1916 and 1923. *Griechische Tragödien*. Vol. 3 and 4 (Berlin).

Wilkinson, L. P. 1979. *Classical Attitudes to Modern Issues* (London).

Willink, C. W., ed. 1986. *Euripides, "Orestes"* (Oxford).

————. 1989. "Reunion Duo in Euripides' *Helen*." *CQ* 39:45–69.

Winkler, John J. 1990. *The Constraints of Desire* (New York).

————, and F. I. Zeitlin, eds. 1990. *Nothing to Do with Dionysos?* (Princeton).

Winnington-Ingram, R. P. 1980. *Sophocles: An Interpretation* (Cambridge).

————. 1983. "Clytemnestra and the Vote of Athena," in Winnington-

Ingram, *Studies in Aeschylus* (Cambridge), 101–31; modified from *JHS* 88 (1949), 130–47.

———. 1983a. "Sophocles and Women," in *Sophocle*. Entretiens Fondation Hardt 29 (Geneva), 233–57.

Wolff, Christian. 1973. "On Euripides' *Helen*." *HSCP* 77:61–84.

———. 1982. "Euripides," in Luce, ed., 1982, 233–66.

Wolff, Hans Julius. 1944. "Marriage Law and Family Organization in Ancient Athens." *Traditio* 2:43–96.

Wyse, William. 1904. *The Speeches of Isaeus*. Repr. (Hildesheim 1967).

Zeitlin, Froma I. 1965. "The Motif of the Corrupted Sacrifice in Aeschylus' *Oresteia*." *TAPA* 96:463–508.

———. 1966. "A Postscript to the Sacrificial Imagery in the *Oresteia*." *TAPA* 97:645–53.

———. 1970. "The Argive Festival of Hera and Euripides' *Electra*." *TAPA* 101:645–69.

———. 1978. "The Dynamics of Misogyny." *Arethusa* 11:149–84

———. 1985. "Playing the Other." *Representations* 11:63–94 (repr. in Winkler and Zeitlin 1990, 63–96).

———. 1990. "Thebes: Theater of Self and Society in Athenian Drama," in Winkler and Zeitlin, eds., 130–67.

———. 1992. "The Politics of Eros in the Danaid Trilogy of Aeschylus," in Hexter and Selden, eds., 203–52.

Zuntz, Günther. 1955. *The Political Plays of Euripides* (Manchester).

———. 1960. "On Euripides' *Helena*," in *Euripide*. Entretiens Fondation Hardt 6 (Geneva), 199–241.

INDEX

abduction: of Helen by Paris, 48,
169n.45, 174n.22, 195n.43; in legend,
36, 38–39, 132; linked to XEK gesture, 36; of Persephone, 36, 39, 110,
113, 170n.50, 187n.13, 203.n.1. See
also Paris; Persephone; rape
Acheron, 47, 86, 87
Acropolis (in Athens), 31, 135, 183n.25,
211n.18
actors (in tragedy): male, 8, 137; and
role-division, 72, 129, 181n.11,
185n.2, 196.48. See also dress;
performance
Admetus. See under Alkestis
Aeschylus, fragmentary plays: Nereiads,
64; Niobe, 181n.7; Toxotides,
173n.13, 176n.39. See also titles of
major plays
Agamemnon (A.). See under Oresteia
Ajax (S.), 59, 81, 146, 185n.4, 190n.36,
193n.17
Alkestis. See under Alkestis;
Persephone
Alkestis (Eur.), 40, 55, 72, 84–96, 102,
105, 136, 137–38, 165n.11, 199n.27;
Admetus, 86–93, 95–96, 205n.20; Alkestis, 8, 85–87, 93, 102, 166n.16,
168n.44, 196n.48; Apollo, 85, 90; and
cheating death, 191n.?, 192n.10; double structure of, 88, 193n.17, 209n.67;
Eumelos, 87; funeral ekphora, 87–88,
191n.9; funeral rites, 84, 85, 88,
194n.32; Herakles, 89, 90, 92–94,
195n.43; house in, 85, 89; lyric and
rhetoric, 86, 89, 191nn. 7–8; and natural death on stage, 84; and Persephone, 84, 85, 139, 191n.1, 203n.2; and
Pheres' scene, 91–92; Thanatos, 84,
85; and two-song motif, 193n.18; and
washed floors, 193n.20; wedding ritual in, 84, 88, 89, 95; wife as stranger,
55, 92–93, 136, 172n.8; xenia in, 84,
93–95
altar, 6, 17, 44; of Demeter, 110, 111,
203n.6; for Kassandra's murder, 137;
for Priam's murder, 130; for sacrifice

of Iphigenia, 35, 50; of Zeus Herkeios,
66–67, 70, 183n.25
anakaluptēria. See under weddings
anchisteia. 18, 22, 161n.48, 182n.16
Andromache. See under Andromache;
Troades
Andromache (Eur.), 192n.14, 203n.9,
205n.20, 208n.57
anodos, 36, 84, 110,113,114–115, 126,
136, 139, 168n.38, 203n.2. See also
Persephone
Antigone (S.), 26, 59–71, 76, 81, 148,
Antigone as bride of Hades, 8, 59, 63–65,
69, 137; burial rites denied, 59, 61,
181n.9; endogamy and exogamy in,
63, 114, 182n.15; eros in, 59, 62, 65;
Eurydike, 65–67, 183nn. 28–30;
Haimon, 61–63, 64–65, 137; influence of, in philosophy/drama, 69–70,
153n.19, 162n.53, 184n.39, 185n.43;
Kreon, 59–71, 81, 181n.8, 184n.35;
and transpolitical standard, 60–61,
180n.5; wedding rites denied, 61, 63–
64, 76
Aphrodite, 12, 74, 76, 106, 166n.17,
169n.50, 187n.11
Apollo, 73–74, 186n.9. See also Alkestis
(Eur.); Ion (Eur.); Oresteia (A.)
Aristophanes, 182n.22, 207n.45; Frogs,
163n.60, 186n.6; Lysistrata, 175n.34,
176n.40, 196n.1; Peace, 201n.42,
203n.2, 209n.65; Thesmophoriazusae,
172n.8, 193n.18
Aristotle, 100, 139, 153n.21, 159n.34,
216.17
Artemis, 14, 51, 74, 76, 166n.17, 176n.40,
181n.7, 186n.9. See also Brauronia
assembly (in Athens), 118, 119–20, 138,
181n.9, 206n.38, 207nn.42,45
Astyanax. See under Troades
Athena, 12, 54, 75, 146, 188n.17,
211n.18. See also Oresteia (A.); Supplices (Eur.); Troades (Eur.)
Athens. See Citizenship Law; City Dionysia; democracy; Peloponnesian War
aulos, 17, 26, 74, 186n.8